The sociology of deviance

THE SOCIOLOGY OF DEVIANCE

An obituary

Colin Sumner

CONTINUUM • NEW YORK

To Pat

The Continuum Publishing Company
370 Lexington Avenue, New York, NY 10017

Printed in Great Britain by Biddles Limited

Library of Congress Cataloging-in-Publication Data

Sumner, Colin.
 The sociology of deviance : an obituary / Colin Sumner
  p. cm.
 Includes bibliographical references and index.
 ISBN 0-8264-0693-9
 1. Deviant behavior. 2. Sociology—History. 3. Social control.
I. Title.
HM291.S884 1994
302.5′42—dc20   94-18079
                                                       CIP

Contents

Preface

I have set out to portray a history of one of the most developed forms of critical, formal, thought on the subject of moral censure, namely the sociology of deviance. The development of sociological thought about deviance provides us with a fascinating eye on the shift from the moral absolutism of the nineteenth century to the moral diaspora of the late twentieth century. In particular, its critiques of the ideology of degeneration and the theory of legalism tell us much about the present moral constitution of political hegemony. Linked to the emergence of liberalism and social democracy, and to the theory of social regulation rather than to a philosophy of punishment, its history casts an interesting light upon the very formation of modern societies.

Because this field has died, and is now being superseded by new conceptualizations, the book amounts to a respectful obituary (1895–1975). The year 1895 marks the publication of Durkheim's *Rules of Sociological Method* and 1975 marks the publication of a number of texts which effectively killed off the field.

The book very much represents materials and ideas developed in teaching the subject over the past twenty years. It attempts to find out the truth about the sociology of deviance, even if that means abandoning several hitherto axiomatic assumptions about its history. The first part of the book documents the formation of the field, from its conception in the womb of Durkheim's social theory to its coming of age in late thirties American sociology. The second part examines the heyday of the field as a popular science and critique of social control in the sixties. The third part describes its fall at the hands of the post-1968 critics. The three parts form a connected whole, and will be the basis for the subsequent construction of a new theoretical field known as the sociology of censure.

My primary interest here is to explore the theoretical matrix that held the sociology of deviance together and gave it a coherence. My concern is not with the details of empirical studies, important though they are for a comprehensive understanding of any area of social science. Through teaching, I have found that intelligent people have no problem whatsoever reading empirical studies, providing that they have studied methodology and been introduced to the theoretical assumptions, concepts and problematics which are the fundamental drive within any empirical research. Without a good understanding of the theoretical matrix of the field, the empirical studies would be nothing but a meaningless mish-mash of disparate data (or capta, or even manufacta), a long series of assorted digits which like any bits of information would be inherently valueless.

The method I have used is to construct a history of the social logic of the ideas. Concepts are set in the culture and politics of their day, and their development linked to social change. I have attended closely to the discourses of the writers, and frequently use idiomatic phrases from the time to illustrate their meaning. In many ways, this book draws on the methodology developed in my own *Reading Ideologies*. The history of a social-scientific field is not driven by a series of cumulative academic debates. Perspectives rise and fall usually because of their relation to major shifts in social relations and political debates. Therefore, the broad connections with social history are documented throughout in order to outline the character and impetus of theoretical shifts. Nevertheless, social-scientific fields are not just social effects, they are very much driven by their participants' sense of the theoretically valid approaches and the theoretical debates within the field. Such fields do have a certain inner logic, irrespective of what social scientists try to do with it at any one point in time or whether they recognize it at all. In consequence, while I clearly avoid any assumption that there is an irreversible, smooth, tide of consciousness in history and have tried to avoid drawing too tight an interconnection between successive but often coexistent perspectives, I have tried to show that there is a clear line of logical development within the field. In art, also, there are clear lines of development, within all the overlaps, regresses and vague boundaries, which are recognizable to most historians of art (e.g. from Perspectivism to Surrealism). Essentially, the field has attempted to exhaust the possibilities available to it within the theoretical matrix of its formation – there is no assumption that, just because those possibilities now appear exhausted, what will follow in the way of a new theoretical formation will automatically be markedly better. It is up to us to make it better.

Special reference is made throughout to parallel ideas and feelings in the history of modern art, in order to paint a truer picture of the ethos and ideas of the sociology of deviance. I am no art historian, but I am trying in this book to paint a picture which conveys the fullest, most accurate, message from the sociology. Such accuracy cannot be achieved without reference to the history and culture of its times – ideas that are discussed in the abstract are usually done little justice. Logic and meaning are social creatures; thus they cannot be elucidated without their sociological context. Besides, this made the book more enjoyable to write. Painting is important to me in another sense, however. As my students know, these days my lectures are attempts to paint pictures with words. I am selective in the studies and writers I discuss and make no attempt to be comprehensive, whatever that would mean. My objective is always to paint a picture which conveys the important things about the sociology of deviance. This book has that same character. I have been very selective, because I no longer believe in any concept of comprehensiveness, and have tried to talk about what I see as the important issues and writers in a way which captures the feel of the debates and changes.

The book is about a field of sociology which has died. It deals with a corpse rather than a corpus of knowledge. That may seem an odd idea to students new to academia. After all, we know professors die, but fields of enquiry? Surely there is a world out there to be investigated, and therefore the enquiry into one slice of it cannot die? And, if we say the field is dead, are we not just changing the name of the slice? In any case, why discuss a corpse? It may seem an even odder idea, and possibly even an offensive one, to those who continue to earn their living through teaching and researching in the sociology of deviance. In 1993, there are still courses on the subject, there are still journals devoted to its exotic mysteries and discoveries, and there are still textbooks under its name. Indeed, one specialist in the field wrote recently that: 'The central terrain of the sociology of deviance is no longer subject to bellicose dispute, most criminologists having become more conciliatory and catholic, engaging in a reasonably civil trade in one another's ideas' (Rock, 1988: 193). He went on to describe me as one of the two 'combative' criminologists left in the UK. Moi? Surely not? As this text shows, I am ever respectful and gentle. What Rock missed is that the lack of sustained warfare over the terrain of the sociology of deviance is actually due to the fact that the combatants over the years, in their enthusiasm for the fight, have completely demolished the terrain, rather than to any peace treaty. The terrain now resembles the Somme in 1918. It is barren, fruitless, full of empty trenches and craters, littered with unexploded mines and eerily silent. No one fights for hegemony over a dangerous graveyard. It is now time to drop arms and show respect for the dead. To change the metaphor, the only people who fought over the corpses hanging at Tyburn were the surgeons, who wished to dissect them for their new sciences, and the relatives, who wanted to revive them for obvious sentimental reasons. Perhaps, I am like one of the eighteenth-century surgeons, and perhaps Paul Rock and the other defenders of the faith are like the relatives. Perhaps I hope to dissect this particular corpse before he can revive it with his elegant prose.

Whatever the merit of the arguments in this obituary, no doubt those with an interest in reviving the corpse, along with those who still address it blissfully unaware that it can no longer respond, will continue to convey the impression that it is still alive. Indeed, ultimately, who am I to dispute reincarnation, or the value of talking in words that don't speak, or the value of talking to the dead, or the role of dead sciences in reactionary epochs in need of new justifications? Dead ideas can always be made to look like live ones, to ratify the latest fear-ridden relapse into the past. In addition, the sociology of deviance may indeed live again one day in other countries – but it would be in a space–time continuum which postmodern societies have left behind for good. In countries passing through similar stages of social development to those which gave the sociology of deviance life in the first place, it might live again. Scientific fields do not die in the same way as professors; they can have second or third lives in foreign countries. But in their homelands they do die, as living, imaginative forces for social change.

The fact is that, in social sciences, the world we study changes, partly because of the knowledge we provide about it and because of our 'scientific' interventions within its politics; and that, in turn, transforms the way we look at the world. In our case, that is certainly what has happened. We have changed the world that gave rise to the sociology of deviance and those changes have altered the way we look at that old world. The sociology of deviance no longer expresses our vision in the very new world of the 1990s. In that sense, it is dead. Its voice cannot speak.

Finally, in answer to the question 'why pick over what has already been done to death?', I want to try to present new information about the life of this sub-field of sociology, and a better perspective on that life, to give us a richer and more accurate understanding of what it was trying to achieve and why it failed – in order that we might move on with clarity and awareness. Implicitly, I feel that too many existing readings of the sociology of deviance are misleading or shallow in one way or another. Teaching this field for so long has also given me a longstanding awareness of its lack of good textbooks. I am still unhappy about the mode and level of understanding of the sociology of deviance, whether it be from left or right field. But, I do not think I realized exactly how shallow our understanding was until writing this volume. The most striking thing about writing it has been that it has demonstrated to me that we do not know our own history. So many works, re-read in the light of their history and context, actually say a lot more or a lot less than conventional knowledge of the discipline supposes. This historical re-reading of the texts has led me to talk a lot about authors who are rarely mentioned in this field, and to talk less than is conventional about some famous names. The history I have produced is not at all unrecognizable from a conventional view of the field's history, but it does, I hope, recast that history in a new light.

The book owes much to successive graduate classes in sociology at Cambridge University's Institute of Criminology from 1977 to 1991. It was started in Cambridge, England, written mostly in Victoria, Canada, and Hamburg, Germany, and finished in Barcelona, Spain. They were all extraordinarily conducive locations in terms of the sources and subject matter, and the text thus benefited considerably for being written on the move. Somehow it has emerged, showing a remarkable congruence with the circumstances of its writing, from a personal journey covering four countries, eleven major changes of residence, several domestic crises, and the constant hauling around of a Macintosh SE30 and Radius monitor. In these circumstances, my determination has had to be total but, in truth, the text has written me, not the other way round, and it is very much an obituary to a former self. If *Censure, Politics, and Criminal Justice* was a *festschrift* to a career phase, this book ends a personal cycle. It wrote itself.

I would like to give my thanks to my students in Cambridge, and elsewhere, over the years for their tremendous enthusiasm and stimulation. Support for the value of using artistic, literary and other sources not usually seen as pertinent, plus much theoretical and philosophical excitement, came particularly strongly from my 1987–8 group of friends in Cambridge, notably Rosie Gandolfi, but also Evi Krinbill, Kathleen Breed and Ruth Jamieson. The enthusiasm of these women for the value of my ideas and approach was a vital force. It is no coincidence that they were all returning to higher education in their forties – we all fed off each other's spiritual and educational revival. Evi Krinbill's knowledge and research as an artist, and student of modern European thought, made sure that my art history is not too amateurish. My conversations with Rosie Gandolfi on moral and spiritual questions were of such great value that I will be drawing on them for years to come. She did valuable background research on the historical context, and her death shortly before the completion of the manuscript was enormously saddening. Given her black sense of humour, she would have said that I have lost my one guaranteed reader. That humour is recurrent throughout the book. More than anyone else, she wanted me to begin this project and her infectious, powerful, life force and philosophical vivacity convinced me not only that this was worth doing but also that it had a personal significance to me well beyond its professional value. She taught me about the cosmic dimension of life and this book has consequently never lost sight of its congruences and co-incidences with my personal development. For example, *Les Demoiselles d'Avignon* was selected for the book cover before I even began to write, so it was extraordinary that I ended up finishing the text in Barcelona, living in the Barrio Gotíc where the picture was painted.

I also owe much to Cathi Albertyn, Dennis Davis, Katie Malleson, Richard Sparks, George Pavlich, John Lowman, Roy Light, Anita Meech, Leslie Griffiths, Rebecca Clare, Monika Leppelt, Martina Althoff, Carmen Gransee and Ulla Stammerman for their marvellous enthusiasm and support for my work. My conversations with Cathi, Dennis and Monika were particularly fruitful. Many years ago, the enthusiasm of Ian Taylor, then at Sheffield, and Mike Brogden, then at Bristol, fired my interest in the sociology of crime and deviance; working with Ian in the early 1970s was especially instructive and exciting. My very special thanks to him. It was Ian who introduced me to the work of Stuart Hall, which was seminal to my thinking in the seventies and early eighties. Stuart was my doctoral examiner in 1976 and has been a source of encouragement ever since, most recently as an adviser to the Open University Press.

The conversations I had with Hal Finestone in 1978, in Cambridge, and 1979, in Minneapolis, about symbolic interactionism have been very precious to me, especially regarding the Chicago school. Having a great sociologist and a member of that school sitting in on my Cambridge seminars was of far more use to me than it must have been to him. Although I had worked with black kids from Chicago in 1968, he gave me a feel for Chicagoan sociology that was priceless. In more recent times, I have been indebted to Maureen Maloney and John McLaren at the Law School of the University of Victoria for providing hospitality and good facilities to enable the bulk of Part One to be written; to Sebastian Scheerer and Fritz Sack at the Aufbau Kriminologie in Hamburg for their invitation to work at the Hamburg centre of criminology, their academic enthusiasm for my work, their practical support and their excellent company; and to Roberto Bergalli of the Faculdad de Derecho at the University of Barcelona for his invitation to come to Catalunya, his belief in my ability, interest in my work, practical support and warm friendship. The friendship and support of Wolfgang Deichsel, Encarna Bodelón, Amadeu Recasens, Inyaki Ribera, Gabi Löschpe, Werner Lehne, Ruth Heise and of many criminology students in Germany and Spain have also been a vital force behind the writing of this book.

My sincere thanks to the firm of McCarthy Tétrault for their Fellowship in Victoria, the Deutsche Forschungs Gemeinschaft for their grant in Germany, and the Spanish Ministry of Education for their funding in Barcelona. The University of Cambridge deserves special thanks for granting me two years' special research leave to enable this work to be done while also confronting some very modern domestic problems head-on; it was an especially progressive administrative decision, since it enabled me to follow my wife's needs to be close to her children.

Last, and of course not at all the least but actually the most fundamental of all, this book owes much to the enormous enthusiasm, love and support of my wife Pat. Our journey has taught us more than can be represented within an academic book, but some of it is reflected in these pages. Ben, as always, has been a tower of strength, giving me tremendous love and support. Jennifer, Amanda and James have all helped where they can. My mother, Marian, has kept me alive and cheerful during the times when the going got too rough, and has been a source of great wisdom. Her understanding of other people's deviance is priceless. She has been a bedrock of certainty during an awesome personal journey. This book would never have emerged at all without her.

Finally, John Skelton at the Open University Press deserves a medal for his patience and many thanks for his consistent support for and belief in my work.

PART ONE

A new deal for degenerates?
The sociology of social deviation
1895–1940

1 Durkheim, modernity and doubt: the birth

Deviance is a feature of modernity. We are only just beginning to realize the full meaning of this, as modernity is challenged by the fragmentations and reconstructions of the *fin de siècle*. The proposition does not simply affirm that modern life produces some very bizarre events and practices. It also means that the concept of deviance is an intrinsic part of the ways of thinking and seeing characteristic of the modern phase of social history. Indeed, in its fullest meaning, it captures the fact that modernity itself is deviant in certain respects:

> On the one hand there have started into life industrial and scientific forces which no epoch of human history had ever suspected. On the other hand, there exist symptoms of decay, far surpassing the horrors of the latter times of the Roman Empire. In our days everything seems pregnant with its contrary . . . The victories of art seem bought by the loss of character.
>
> (Marx, 1856; quoted in Berman, 1983: 19–20)

Furthermore, it follows that as the modern phase of capitalism ends, or is in process of being superseded by its next phase, we will see signs that deviance is no longer an appropriate way of seeing. Its sense, its referents and its social context are already changing greatly, with the consequence that we begin to cast our vision in other terms. Already its vitality as a concept seems to have expired.

In this way, deviance is totally bound up with modernity. We can see, therefore, that a respectful appreciation of the sociology of deviance must recognize (a) the necessity of reading it within this historical context of modernity and (b) the value of the dimension of critique as the recovery of a culture as well as an attack on its failings. To capture some sense of this culturally specific character of the sociology of deviance, we will juxtapose it with other ideas and representations of its day, notably those of art. Perhaps, to play with Marx's aphorism, insofar as the sociology of deviance betrays the loss of a sense of character in modern times we can restore some balance by reference to the 'victories of art'.

Modernization refers to a whole collection of social processes involved in the rise of industrial or monopoly capitalism and the formation of the welfare state (see Berman, 1983: 16). The process that concerns us particularly in this study has often been described, in sociology, as 'the breakdown of traditional social control', or, in criminology, as 'the growth of crime'. In *The Communist Manifesto*, itself one of the great icons of the crisis in 'traditional' authority, the social processes underpinning the emergence of the sociology of deviance are well described:

> All fixed, fast-frozen relations, with their train of ancient and venerable prejudices and opinions, are swept away, all new-formed ones become antiquated before they can ossify. All that is solid melts into air, all that is holy is profaned, and man is at last compelled to face with sober senses, his real conditions of life and his relations with his kind.
>
> (Marx and Engels 1848; trans., 1968: 38)

This passage points to several dimensions of deviance as a feature of modernity which twentieth-century sociology tried to grapple with. Industrial capitalism may have melted much of the old normative order, but what was constructed in its place has always been profoundly transient and elusive. The attempts to restore 'law and order' or to bring back 'traditional values', so frequent a feature of modern politics, succeed only briefly, and then only in erecting fragile rhetorical images which collapse like castles of sand against an unrelenting tide of deviance, disobedience and dissidence. Even during their snatched moments of glory, their meaning is invariably unclear, ambiguous or morally eroded by their supporting sectional economic and political interests. The meaning of deviance thus, like so many features of modernity, has a 'now-you-see-it-now-you-don't' character. It is also, almost always, 'pregnant with its contrary' – normality. The supposed universality of morality has melted into air. Definitions of the normal abound and change rapidly. What is seen as deviant is so often redolent with normality and what is seen as normal is so often redolent with deviance; and both are constantly changing. It was within this highly nebulous space that the sociology of deviance was born.

Seen in this light, the sociology of deviance has not been as immature, ambiguous or vague as some of its positivist critics have claimed. It was born in a nebulous world, and the vista before its eyes was vast, mobile and infinite; it had few fixed landmarks; and the violent combustion of its own inner elements (the contradictory social forces demanding its formation and delivery) meant that its own slight substance was constantly in danger of being torn asunder. It is little wonder that it took a long time to reach even an uncertain maturity and that, when it did, it promptly blew itself into little pieces. This is indeed the biography of a thoroughly modern star.

Émile Durkheim, the French sociologist, brought the child into the world, in the confusing swirl of a modernizing France in the 1890s, through his general writings on sociology. His work created a conceptual space for the embryo to form, grow and later emerge. Durkheim's maleness should therefore not stop us from seeing him as the mother of the sociology of deviance. Durkheim died in 1917, while the child was still young and while Durkheim himself seemed largely unaware of the child's existence. At this point, the child still had no name; Durkheim had been too busy founding the discipline of sociology in general. Fortunately for the child, Durkheim's ideas became increasingly important in American sociology. So the child was quietly adopted and spent an exciting, if somewhat anomic, adolescence in the tough American cities of the Depression and the New Deal. It was finally given a name by various, suspicious but paternalistic, American sociologists in the late 1930s, although it was only after 1951 that everyone agreed to call it the sociology of deviance.

In prosperous post-war America, the new field flourished and a lot was written in its name. It became rich and famous, at least in sociological circles, and had a pretty wild time during the heady days of the 1960s before taking a brief, ill-fated trip back to its European homeland in 1968 to escape some unpleasant criticisms about its involvement in class inequality, state oppression and corporate crime. That trip was to bring it face-to-face with the realities of its indulgent obsession with drugs, homosexuality, prostitution, petty delinquency and a whole host of victimless crimes. Befriended by an enthusiastic but suspicious cadre of European sociologists who tried to convert it into a justification for some very alien politics, our rich, but fatherless and very confused, orphan lost all coherence and eventually died somewhere in mid-Atlantic ravaged by the full range of its own internal contradictions.

No one knows quite when or where the death occurred exactly, and to this day no sociologist has ever admitted paternity. What is clear, however, is that by 1975 European sociologists and historians were writing about crime, law and social regulation as if the sociology of deviance was no longer alive. This sad tale of an insecure immigrant child, with no name, a neglectful, male mother and a conflictful teenage, was perhaps bound to be one of hedonistic excess in adulthood and a violent come-uppance. In any case, let us begin at the beginning and turn to the role of Durkheim in initiating the whole saga.

The formation of the concept of deviance

Quételet or Durkheim?

Piers Beirne has temptingly suggested that the concept of deviance was actually formed in the writings of Adolphe Quételet, a Belgian astronomer and mathematician (Beirne, 1987). Quételet's 'social mechanics' attempted to apply statistical methods from the natural sciences to 'social facts'. Through the collection of statistical data on human and social character-istics, Quételet believed he could establish the nature of 'the average man' and his moral behaviour. The more extensive the empirical data, the more accurate the picture of 'the average man'; an idea that is by no means dead even today. Following Aristotle's *Nichomachean Ethics*, Quételet was convinced that 'the average man was one who regularly chose the mean course between the extremes of deficiency and excess' (Beirne, 1987: 1159):

> The virtues of the average man thus comprised 'rational and temper-ate habits, more regulated passions, [and] foresight, as manifested by investment in savings banks, assurance societies and the different institutions which encourage foresight' (Quételet 1842: 78). With the noncriminality of the average man, Quételet frequently juxtaposed the criminality of vagabonds, vagrants, primitives, gypsies, the 'in-ferior classes', certain races with 'inferior moral stock', and 'persons of low moral character'. With the virtues of the average man, he juxtaposed the vices of those deviants who engaged in crime . . . The practical outcome of Quételet's criminology was the application of his binary opposition of normality and deviance to the domain of penality.
>
> (Beirne, 1987: 1159–60)

From here, of course, it was a short step for Quételet to claim that if governments could identify the causes of crime among the 'morally inferior classes', while at the same time encouraging the virtuous qualities of Mr Average with his nice little savings account, they could reduce the amount of crime in the society and maximize the degree of moral virtue. For the poor this was to mean fair but effective criminalization, and for the 'sav-ings banks' and 'assurance societies' it was boom time.

In my view, Quételet certainly used a concept of deviation, but this was not the concept of deviance which founded the sociology of deviance. It is a conception of deviation from the average or mean, coupled with an old Greek notion of moderation as virtuous. This is deviation as statistical abnormality and immoderate behaviour. The concept which founds the sociology of deviance, on the other hand, is that of deviation from the social norm or collective sentiment, whatever its virtues or faults. Such a deviation is deviant whether or not it is statistically normal or psychologi-cally moderate. In this sense, deviance is determined by social norms whatever their moral content. Ironically, such a concept of deviance is po-tentially separable from a sense of moral equity; the norm is all-powerful and can come to be divorced from morality or justice. If this is correct, the concept of social deviance was first formed as a conceptual space with any sort of theoretical coherence in the work of Émile Durkheim, and is only fully developed in the sociology of the twentieth century.

Durkheim and modern ways of seeing

Deviance is a concept within sociology; its roots cannot be retraced except through the history of its sociological conceptualization. The meaning and value of the concept cannot be recovered from a popular culture of the past, because only in the 1970s did the term begin to enter popular discourse in any noticeable way. As Rock acidly and usefully observes:

> It is not even evident that people do talk about deviance with any great frequency. Instead they allude to specific forms of conduct without appearing to claim that there is any single, over-arching category that embraces them all. They may talk of punks, addicts, glue-sniffers, extremists, thieves, traitors, liars and eccentrics, but they rarely mention *deviants*. It may only be the sociologist who finds it interesting and instructive to clump these groups together under a solitary title.
>
> (Rock, 1985: 200)

Nor can the meaning and value of the concept be simplistically derived from some economic analysis of the logic of capitalism, for the simple reason that there are many mediations between a modern concept, its generative theoretical discourse, the practical foundations of that discourse and the logic of capital. Deviance is fundamentally a concept constructed within sociological theory, albeit within the context of twentieth-century welfare capitalism and its concomitant cultural formations. The recovery of its intellectual value and meaning must therefore begin with one of the founders of sociological theory, Émile Durkheim (1858–1917), since it was he who first developed the network of concepts in a theoretical discourse which defined the conceptual space that later sociologists entitled deviance. Durkheim may not have used the term deviant much, but within his theoretical discourse the embryo formed which later grew into the sociology of deviance.

Durkheim was writing at a time of profound and rapid social change in France. The Third Republic was established in 1877 and 55 ministries followed in the period up to 1914 (Hawthorn, 1976: 114). The crucial stages of industrialization were over by 1870 and 1882–1900 was a period of commercial and industrial depression. France was establishing itself as the second colonial power through gaining administrative control over important parts of North Africa, Indo-China and West Africa. Culturally, it was increasing in self-confidence and optimism as it gradually asserted itself against the influence of German culture. Wagner gave way to Debussy; the naturalism of Flaubert and Zola was contested by the transcendental symbolism of Baudelaire and Rimbaud; and generally a gloomy realism was increasingly confronted by a flamboyant mysticism. In penal policy, the use of the guillotine was giving way to the birth of parole and the suspended sentence, and the internal prison population was supposedly halved in the last quarter of the century, although that was partly owing to the increased use of penal colonies in places like New Caledonia and Guiana. As in other spheres, the old sat uneasily next to the new. Times were changing and consequently so were ways of seeing. These changes in vision are important for understanding the ambiguity of, and sense of ambiguity in, Durkheim's work.

By changes in ways of seeing during this period we are not just referring to the invention of the filament light bulb, although that undoubtedly enabled us to see more. Nor are we just referring to the invention of the box camera and the cinematograph or the discovery of the X-ray, important though they are to the modern revision of ways of seeing. Certainly, in a physicalist sense, we could see deeper and represent our vision in more creative ways. But, more importantly, the relation of the viewer to the observed was changing, and becoming decidedly more ambivalent.

Modernity in France offered its now customary paradoxes in the ways that vision changed and comprehended itself. On the one hand, the Paris exhibition of 1889 revealed the Eiffel Tower, that great symbol of modern industrial enterprise and engineering power. A work of art designed by an engineer, it gave a vision of all Paris from on high, enabling snapshots of all around, yet its monumental reach for the sky was also visible from all quarters. The power of modern technology – enabling surveillance from an elevated, distanced position and displaying itself to a mass audience, yet immune to and protected from dialogue – sustained the positivist vision which had been developed in the previous century (see Hughes, 1981: 9–11):

> in its height, its structural daring, its then-radical use of industrial materials for the commemorative purposes of the State, it summed up what the ruling classes of Europe conceived the promise of technology to be: Faust's contract, the promise of unlimited power over the world and its wealth.
>
> (*ibid.*: 11)

In stark contrast, within the art of the artist such a vision was in grave doubt. The convention of perspective, dominating painting since the Renaissance, had enabled pictures of reality to be mapped in correct proportions on flat sheets of paper, but was now challenged as a misleading representation of the relation between eye, brain and object. 'It is an ideal view, imagined as being seen by a one-eyed, motionless person who is clearly detached from what he sees. It makes a God of the spectator' (*ibid.*: 17).

The work of Cézanne from 1890 onwards, on the other hand, showed a fascination with the relativity of vision, the intensity and complexity of nature, and the practical process of constructing images on canvas. As Hughes puts it, the declaratory 'this is what I see' becomes replaced by the doubtful 'is this what I see?' Doubt becomes central, relativity is all. Doubt becomes a touchstone of modernity itself; 'fundamental doubt is the father of all knowledge' (Weber, 1949: 7). Doubt perhaps was the father of the concept of social deviation. In 1905, Einstein's theory of relativity anchored the power of this new view of vision in proving that all vision was relative to the time, space, location and speed of both spectator and object. Picasso and the Cubists took this one step further and took apperceptual doubt to the extreme of our comprehension. Picasso's early work, such as *Les Demoiselles d'Avignon* (1907, on our front cover), is classical: 'no painting ever looked more convulsive. None signalled a faster change in the history of art' (Hughes, 1981: 21). Deeply ironic, the picture questions what is solid and what is void, and 'whatever else these five women may be, they are not victims or clowns' (*ibid.*). Picasso himself called it the *Brothel of Avignon*, after the brothel in his old neighbourhood of Barcelona (Cole and Gealt, 1989: 267). The women were prostitutes. Inspiration for their faces came from ancient Iberian stone heads and the collections of African masks in Paris.[1] But, in truth, 'Solid apprehensible reality has vanished'. Such paintings were 'metaphors of relativity and connection; in them, the world is imagined as a network of fleeting events, a twitching skin of nuances' (Hughes, 1981: 29).

Like other Picasso paintings from around this time that parody black African art, there is a strong suggestion of the power of women, the return of the repressed, and a fear of that part of the moral–political universe of the European imperialist patriarchy which was still largely captive, suppressed, marginalized, censured and unconscious. Prostitutes had been painted by Van Gogh and Gauguin's pictures of Tahitian maidens are well-known. Picasso's own *Olympia* of 1901 depicted 'a sexualized black . . . [an] image of the primitive female as sexual object' (Gilman, 1985: 102). An earlier version of *Les Demoiselles* contained a figure of a man holding a skull – the artist as victim, suggests Gilman. The imagery and substance of what was later to be called deviance were beginning to surface through the filters of white, liberal, middle-class, Eurocentric, masculinist thought. As Freud said of adult female sexuality, it represented a 'dark continent' of psychology (Gilman, 1985: 107). Yet, like madness and crime, it held secrets for the insightful observer such as Picasso or Freud; maybe, if Foucault (1967) was right about madness, the secrets of life itself, secrets not amenable to the cold rationalism of the scientific Enlightenment.

During this period, of course, Freud developed the theory of the unconscious and the concept of the normality of repressing painful experiences and desires. Like vision, discourse was being seen as relative, transient and interactive. Even the ramblings of the disturbed could be made intelligible through dialogue and the analyst's awareness of the psychic world beneath the veneer. In art, the recognition emerged that the viewer and the viewed were part of the same field and that the image projected on to canvas represented a result of their respective movements and interactions. The viewer affected the view. The sovereignty and patriarchy of the I were now compelled to interact with the hitherto suppressed and static It (see Foucault, 1967: 253, 272–4; 1980b: 78–9; Hughes, 1981: 17; Sumner, 1990b). Thus released from cultural servitude, the various objects of condescension and censure began to roam around the imagination, creating fear and fascination. They haunted the unconscious of art for many years to come. Framed within the general culture of the epoch, as fascinating, revelatory, exotic and frightening, in a vision riddled with doubt, relativity and ambiguity, the legions of the repressed also became the object of the emerging sociology and social anthropology. Later, some were to become the main focus, and some probably the unconscious, of the sociology of deviance.

In other social-scientific disciplines, similar reverberations of the crisis in the *ancien régime* of Victorian vision were being felt. Of course, in economics and politics, the question of socialism loomed like a threatening spectre over old Europe. Marx's legacy was challenging the viability of individualistic capitalism through workers' movements everywhere, and archaic structures of political domination were being reorganized. In jurisprudence, Dicey was openly recognizing that welfare legislation had to pre-empt the demands of the growing collectivism, and that the rule of law must involve social provisions, not just individual rights. In psychology and philosophy, questions were being raised about the certainty of perception, and its flat, linguistic description. Whether perception was detached from emotion and culture, and above the exigencies of interaction, was increasingly doubted. A phenomenological perspective was emerging which challenged the crude empiricism of the positivist vision, and offered new images of the thoroughly social character of vision. It made it altogether quite difficult to separate the phenomenon allegedly observed from the emotional, political, linguistic and cultural conditions of observation.

Deviance, crime and ambiguity in Durkheim's sociology

The tension and ambiguity within modernity's self-understanding, and within its emergent ways of seeing, are evident throughout Durkheim's writing about crime, law and deviance. On the one hand, he expressed a nineteenth-century positivism which

- saw criminal statistics as the true indices of the moral state of society;
- assumed a distanced, elevated, scientific posture towards crime, allegedly free of political commitments;
- saw law as an accurate index of the collective sentiment rather than sectional interest;
- was still inclined to judge many individual 'criminals' as morally or psychologically pathological.

On the other hand, he also expressed an early twentieth-century vision of doubt, irony, relativity and depth, which

- saw crime as a social category defined by the collective sentiment of the day rather than any universal values;

- doubted the ability of societies to exist without crime or moral censure;
- appreciated that social deviants can be visionaries or critics pointing the way toward social reform;
- recognized the modern contradiction between the relentless search for profit and the need for moral regulation throughout society.

Both dimensions of the modern vision in Durkheim are united in the themes of social constructionism, namely that society is a structure or organized entity which is only constructed by a complex historical morass of interactions between human beings in a variety of social roles and institutions, and that these human actions are themselves only constructed through interaction with the constraints of the social structure. But it is an ironic, modernist vision of social structure. It is ironic in observing that the modern social structure promotes the rise of individuation and individualism at the same time that it demands new forms of collectivism and social integration. The freedom at last offered to people by modernity is thus only fleetingly grasped as they continually lose themselves in the wash of rapid social change and collective angst. Everything is pregnant with its contrary, and all that is solid melts into air.

Durkheim's view of modernity was based on some very different beliefs from those of Marx and Engels. Marx saw religion as the 'spiritual aroma' of the 'vale of tears', and Engels had said that 'Money is the god of this world; the bourgeois takes the proletarian's money and so makes a practical atheist of him' (quoted in Cain and Hunt, 1979: 178). But, for Durkheim, writing in critique of Labriola's historical materialism, 'religion is the most primitive of all social phenomena. It was the source, through successive transformations, of all other manifestations of collective activity: law, morality, art, science, political forms, etc.' (quoted in Lukes, 1973: 232). Durkheim did not deny that collective representations came from something outside of themselves and that they are therefore connected with the rest of the social world, but for him the economic was 'secondary and derivative' to the collective sentiment. Overall it seems that Durkheim's sociology was that of a collective psychologist who regarded the collective soul and ideals as the driving force of a society while admitting that such a force was, in turn, connected to and influenced by the forms of social organization (see Lukes, 1973: 230–6). Consequently, Durkheim's sense of the crisis of modernity is based on a perception of the decline of religion with the rise of industrial societies, and with a concomitant decline in the self-conscious attachment of the individual to society, in favour of the 'cult of the individual' (*ibid.*: 153–8). The *conscience collective* was becoming more secular, rational and individualistic. It thus required active adherence to values of individual dignity, equality of opportunity, social justice and the work ethic, if modern society was to achieve any stability. The problem is, of course, that such values are constantly undermined by the logic of industrial capitalism and the partiality of the patriarchal, class states of twentieth-century imperialism.

This social structural contradiction creates a problem of discipline, which Durkheim clearly recognized, despite his beliefs about religion:

> Until very recently, it was the function of a whole system of moral forces to exert this discipline . . . the influence of religion was felt alike by workers and masters, the poor and the rich. It consoled the former and taught them contentment with their lot by informing them of the providential nature of the social order, that the share of each class was assigned by God himself, and by holding out the hope for just compensation in a world to come in return for the inequalities of this world. It governed the latter, recalling that worldly interests are not man's entire lot, that they must be subordinate to other and higher interests, and that they should not be pursued without rule or measure . . . Actually, religion has lost most of its power. And government, instead of regulating economic life, has become its tool and servant . . . industry, instead of being still regarded as a means to an end transcending itself, has become the supreme end of individuals and societies alike. Thereupon the appetites thus excited have become freed of any limiting authority . . . Ultimately, this liberation of desires has been made worse by the very development of industry and the almost infinite extension of the market.
>
> (Durkheim, 1970: 254–5)

How resonant these words are today in the age of a resurgent and 'almost infinite' theology of the market! This infinity of desire, moral deregulation, or anomie, is, for Durkheim, an intrinsic, structural tendency of industrial capitalist societies (Giddens, 1971a: 84–5). However, he clearly believed that it can be disciplined and reduced by government initiatives towards higher, social goals. In his view, the state should act energetically to develop and sustain civic ethics and individual rights in order to integrate individual wealth production with social stability through the liberation of individual personalities in a disciplined manner (see Lukes, 1973: 268–74). By arguing that the urgent duty and task of the state was to bring the anomic condition of society to an end, Durkheim's position is rounded off and he can clearly be seen as an early theorist of what we would now call social democracy.

This vision of modern industrial capitalism specifies that 'the state of crisis and anomy is constant and, so to speak, normal' within industry (Durkheim, 1970: 256), and that this condition has spread throughout society. Durkheim's description of the impact of anomie on individuals within industry gives us a sharp insight into why exactly he thought crime and deviance were normal within capitalist societies:

> From top to bottom of the ladder, greed is aroused without knowing where to find ultimate foothold. Nothing can calm it, since its goal is far beyond all it can attain. Reality seems valueless by comparison with the dreams of fevered imaginations . . . A thirst arises for novelties,

unfamiliar pleasures, nameless sensations, all of which lose their savour once known. Hence one has no strength to endure the least reverse . . . all these new sensations in their infinite quantity cannot form a solid foundation of happiness to support one during days of trial.

(Durkheim, 1970: 256)

Suicide was therefore disproportionately manifest among those classes where the infinity of desire offered no moral protection against economic hard times and disappointments, and this has subsequently become a famous argument on that particular subject. But, clearly, the thesis runs beyond suicide, and its spirit has been recaptured in many forms in later literature and films, for example in the film *Carnal Knowledge*, where the endless search for sexual novelty is revealed as an intrinsically unfulfilling quest. The 'thirst for novelties, unfamiliar pleasures' and 'nameless sensations', grounded in a social state of moral de-regulation, is one of the deepest existential conditions of modernity, and one important cultural basis of modern sexual crime and deviance; just as a morally de-regulated common greed is one of the cultural preconditions of extensive unlawful property acquisition. Durkheim's argument does not merely predicate the normality of extensive theft and fraud: the infinite, de-regulated dreams of fevered imaginations permeate all kinds of social activity.

Our frequent use of the word de-regulation consciously reminds us that Durkheim's arguments still have a precise purchase. Like the 1920s in the USA, which we will discuss in the next chapter, the 1980s in the UK were years when financial services' de-regulation was one of many major forms in which the market economy of raw enterprise was politically celebrated and re-instituted at the expense of a variety of social considerations. Privatization produced many a private hell, and the official suicide figures rose along with unemployment. No doubt also, the subsequent partial de-regulation of the television industry will, as in North America, reduce the standard of its average output, and enable it to join the press in the production of an 'idiot culture' (Bernstein, 1992). Durkheim's arguments about the deterioration of the social fabric brought about by unregulated capitalism clearly cannot be dismissed as antiquated. The phenomena he was trying to explain are recurrent.

Durkheim's explanation of suicide has, of course, many other facets, which have been widely discussed elsewhere (e.g. Giddens, 1966; S. Taylor, 1982). However, to illustrate Durkheim's insights, we will dwell on them for a moment longer. The anomic suicide was only one of four types he described. There were also egoistic suicides, which spring from 'excessive individualism' (Durkheim, 1970: 209), and where 'the bond attaching man to life relaxes because that attaching him to society is itself slack' (*ibid.*: 214–15). 'He effects communion through sadness when he no longer has anything else with which to achieve it' (*ibid.*: 214). In this instance, social disintegration brought about by events, for example the death of a spouse,

reduces the comforting protection of social ties against acute disappointments or depressions and the individual is more likely to lose his reason
to live. I use 'his' because Durkheim thought women were closer to nature,
having a 'rudimentary' sensibility (*ibid.*: 215), and therefore less imbued
with 'sociability' and reason; a classic example of how even liberal European thought could not theorize the world of the suppressed in a fully
sociological way at the turn of the century. On the other hand, sounding
suspiciously like a contemporary socialist or feminist for a brief moment,
Durkheim in another passage explains his key assumption about the dangers of 'excessive individualism':

> There is, in short, in a cohesive and animated society a constant
> interchange of ideas and feelings from all to each and each to all,
> something like a mutual moral support, which instead of throwing
> the individual on his own resources, leads him to share in the collec-
> tive energy and supports his own when exhausted.
>
> (Durkheim, 1970: 210)

He thus theorized one of the major values of true socialism or feminism.

There was also a third type of suicide described by Durkheim: the altruistic. Here, society holds the individual 'in too strict tutelage' (*ibid.*: 221),
as, for example, in India (within Hinduism) or Japan ('The readiness of the
Japanese to disembowel themselves for the slightest reason is well known'
(*ibid.*: 222) – Eurocentric, as well as patriarchal, condescension is a frequent feature of Durkheim's theoretical bequest to the sociology of deviance). Durkheim also talks of the high suicide rate among soldiers, with
their 'aptitude for renunciation . . . taste for impersonality [and] habit of
passive submission' as a result of 'prolonged discipline' (*ibid.*: 234). Had
he written *Suicide* a little later, he might have included the suicidal infantry
charges of the 1914–18 war so well documented in *All Quiet on the Western
Front*. Like excessive individualism, excessive discipline disturbs the moral
balance protecting the individual from self-destruction.

Finally, there are fatalistic suicides, a type often neglected by commentators[2] and only discussed by Durkheim in a footnote (*ibid.*: 276n.). This
is the suicide of individuals who feel hopelessly trapped by 'excessive
regulation . . . futures pitilessly blocked and passions violently choked by
oppressive discipline' (*ibid.*). Durkheim mentions the suicides of the 'very
young' husband and the childless married woman, but also those of slaves
and others suffering the effects of despotism or multiple oppression. He
could have legitimately added the suicides of young prisoners and of rural
women in underdeveloped societies (see Haynes, 1984, 1987). The increase in suicides by young prisoners in the UK over the past ten years
could easily be given a Durkheimian explanation.

What should be drawn from Durkheim's analysis of suicide? Students of
the sociology of deviance often mistakenly summarize Durkheim as arguing that the rate of suicide increases in situations of social disintegration and
that greater social integration reduces the suicide risk. It is a pardonable

error since Durkheim himself clearly regards the two types of suicide based on excessive or oppressive discipline (altruistic and fatalistic suicides) as the effects of a more 'primitive morality' or 'lower' form of social bonding (e.g. Durkheim, 1970: 238). This matches his well-known arguments about the mechanical solidarity of 'primitive' societies, which supposedly involves minimum independence of thought and action. It also corresponds with his, much criticized, view that legal regulation in 'primitive' societies, with their very strongly collective sentiments, tended to repression rather than the restitutive measures of modern, highly differentiated societies. Durkheim thus tended to talk of the suicides of modern societies as being mainly those involving excessive individualism and moral de-regulation. However, as the account above suggests, it is much more accurate to say that the logic of Durkheim's overall thesis is that suicides increase when there is an imbalance in the system of social discipline; especially since it is arguable that he massively underestimates the number of altruistic and fatalistic suicides in modern times.[3] The need for balance in social regulation or discipline is very important in Durkheimian thought, and is indeed central to his construction of the theoretical space for the modern sociological concept of deviance, as we shall now see.

Durkheim regarded certain facts of life as social facts. These are matters, such as speaking our native language, which we are not directly obliged to accept but whose performance or recognition are indirectly necessary if we wish to take part in our society's practices. They are aspects of collective bonding which exercise a certain constraint upon us and which as individuals we are not free to ignore. The criminal law is another important example for Durkheim. In the form we know it, criminal law is a normal fact of life in modern industrial societies, as is a recurrent, stable, rate of suicide. Social facts are 'normal' for Durkheim when they are generally distributed across a particular type of society at a given stage of its evolution (1966: 55). A social fact is normal 'when it is present in the average society of that species' (*ibid.*: 64). Like criminal law, crime was, in this sense, normal in all societies, as were specific crime rates, so far as Durkheim was concerned. Crime may appear 'pathological', but it is normal: 'There is no society that is not confronted with the problem of criminality' (*ibid.*: 65).

Even a society of saints will criminalize certain actions or attitudes. In that society, 'faults which appear venial to the layman will create there the same scandal that the ordinary offence does in ordinary consciousnesses' (*ibid.*: 69). So, for example, bad taste, which is merely lightly censured in 'ordinary' societies, would be punished in such a holy order. In other words, if what we now censure as crime was to disappear, we would find something else to criminalize. Essentially, the reason Durkheim gives for this bleak state of affairs is that crime, as a social fact,[4] 'is a factor in public health, an integral part of all healthy societies' (*ibid.*: 67).

Durkheim's justification for this controversial, and ironic, position is pivotal for any understanding of his role in the sociology of deviance, and for the subsequent development of this whole sub-field of sociology. He argued that individuals are always, ultimately, sufficiently different from one another that many will differ from the collective norm, and of these divergences 'there are some with a criminal character' (*ibid.*: 70). The criminal character of some divergences is not a result of the criminogenic personality traits of certain individuals, even though some of these individuals may actually be completely mad or bad, but an inevitable social consequence of the range of individual deviations from the collective norm: 'What confers this character upon them [these divergences from the collective norm] is not the intrinsic quality of a given act but that definition which the collective conscience lends them' (Durkheim, 1966: 70). Durkheim, in 1895, sixty-eight years before Becker published *Outsiders*, was clearly arguing that deviance or crime was a definition given by the collective moral consciousness, and not a particular type of behaviour.[5] He was outlining the view that, in any society, there would always be a range of individual divergences or deviations from the authoritative norms of behaviour, speech and action, and that some of these divergences or deviations would always be censured as criminal. Other divergences would remain as mere deviations – collectively, therefore, as deviance. By the same token, deviance cannot be removed by excess repression or discipline, as all parents know as a matter of common sense. Even a dictatorship which disciplined crime severely, a society far removed from the holy order of saints, would thereby generate a heightened condemnation of lesser deviations, and would eventually criminalize those too, in a never-ending spiral of repression and judgemental interference into private life. This perhaps remains the best explanation so far of the bizarrely extreme censure of incorrect bed-making in concentration camps such as Auschwitz (see Levi, 1988: 93).

> If the collective conscience is stronger, if it has enough authority practically to suppress these divergences, it will also be more sensitive, more exacting; and, reacting against the slightest deviations with the energy it otherwise displays only against more considerable infractions, it will attribute to them the same gravity as formerly to crimes. In other words, it will designate them as criminal.
>
> (Durkheim, 1966: 70)

What Durkheim was effectively doing in these passages was creating a new theoretical discourse based on the register: crime, deviation, divergence, difference, collective sentiment/norm. He was making a trichotomous distinction between crime, deviation and difference, as three degrees of individual divergence from the social norms of behaviour, practice, demeanour, speech, etc. *In all societies, he was saying, a degree of individual differentiation is inevitable, whatever the social norms or sentiments; some of those differences will be lightly censured as deviations, others will be strongly censured as crime. It was this theoretical position which effectively founded the sociology of deviance.* It is perhaps this key insight which ultimately also explains why the sociology of deviance would later come to a fruition in the USA, a society where individual difference was not only massive because of the enormous immigrations but also celebrated as a major icon of its distinctive national culture and history. Such a society needed a space between crime and difference if it was to remain democratic and stable.

The crucial break Durkheim made from Quételet's notion of Mr Average as statistically normal and morally moderate was twofold: (a) the collective norm in any area of being was no longer to be equated with moderation or health – the breach of that norm could be healthy and the norm could be quite immoderate; (b) what was normal and what was degenerate were not solely distinguished by the statistical normality of the former and the statistical deviation of the latter – the degenerate could be the statistically more frequent or, even worse, it could be in power. Moderation could be pregnant with its contrary. Durkheim must have had a sense of what was coming. No longer was it simply a question of crime-as-degeneracy versus law-as-virtue, and no longer was it a question of statistics telling us what was normal or pathological. Broadly drawn, over-repressive, criminal laws could turn the whole citizenry or a whole group into a criminal class.[6]

It is true that Durkheim, *à la* Quételet, used the term normal to refer to 'social conditions that are the most generally distributed' (*ibid.*: 55), and also thought that it would be 'incomprehensible if the most widespread forms' were not at the same time 'the most advantageous' (*ibid.*: 58). But, quite unlike Quételet, Durkheim strongly argued that health or morbidity could not be defined in the abstract and could only be defined in relation to a given species or type at a given phase of its development: 'One should abandon the still too widespread habit of judging an institution, a practice or a moral standard as if it were good or bad in and by itself, for all social types indiscriminately' (*ibid.*: 56). The divorce from the *Nicomachean Ethics* was complete. Moreover, Durkheim was clearly prepared to defy convention by recognizing the normality of crime and refusing to deny the social healthiness of crime simply to avoid offending the legislators and moralists who were busy condemning it. Quételet had allowed a moral judgement to interfere with the logic of his professed method, whereas Durkheim even went on to outline a variety of useful functions which crime, as an aggregate, served for society.

To recap, crime and deviance were, for Durkheim, an inevitable feature of all societies because of the range of individual differences from collective/authoritative social norms and sentiments. What exactly was criminal, or deviant, or merely difference, was defined by the collective consciousness. Moreover, law and morality varied from society to society, and even within a society as social conditions changed. The censure of crime and deviance was therefore a thoroughly social fact, and a normal, healthy, aspect of all societies. It was not determined by transcendental values or the pathology of individuals. It was fundamentally a sociological matter. Modernism had triumphed over absolutism; who now knew right from wrong?

For each kind of society, a given level of the censure of crime and deviance was normal. Therefore, if, in any one society, the level of discipline was either excessive or too lenient for the structure of that society, that excess or leniency was pathological, in Durkheim's terms, and would cause social damage. Durkheim's immersion in the developing science of anthropology, and his consequent awareness of other cultures, was evident. A new respect for the integrity of each and every culture was emerging. For Durkheim, too much repression was the usual problem, not too little, and the damage it caused is bound up with what Durkheim saw as the social functions of the censure of crime and deviance and of crime and deviance as social practices. The excessive censure of crime and deviance would restrict individual freedom so much that the society would not be flexible enough to permit or encourage criticism, difference or idiosyncrasy, and, therefore, to change and develop healthily. As Durkheim wrote in his debate with Tarde, crime could only cease to exist 'if the *conscience collective* dominated individual *consciences* with such an ineluctable authority that all moral change would be rendered impossible' (quoted in Lukes, 1973: 309). There was, in short, a trade-off between the censure of crime and social dynamism.

The benefits of crime, for Durkheim, were that (a) its 'originality' often encouraged progress in improving the organization of the social structure because it indicated the need for changes in that structure or in the collective morality, and (b) it sometimes, as in the case of the creative deviance of original thinkers like Socrates, even anticipated the collective morality of the future (Durkheim, 1966: 71). Crime, therefore, can indicate that social change is necessary and that there is a sufficient degree of openness, free play or tolerance within the social system to enable progressive change. Clearly, both the creativity of the criminalized action or speech and the degree of severity of the censure of crime were relevant for Durkheim in assessing the social functionality of censuring certain matters as crimes. It was not solely the social censure of crime which determined crime's social functions. However, it is equally clear that, for Durkheim, the degree of severity of the social censure of crime is a crucial index of a society's capacity for progressive change, and that *a society needs a degree of tolerance of the area between crime and mere difference to sustain its flexibility and capacity for change, i.e. it needs a substantial space for deviance.*

According to Athenian law, Socrates was a criminal, and his condemnation was no more than just. However, his crime, namely, the independence of his thought, rendered a service not only to humanity but to his country. It served to prepare a new morality and faith which the Athenians needed, since the traditions by which they had lived until then were no longer in harmony with the current conditions of life. Nor is the case of Socrates unique; it is reproduced periodically in history. It would never have been possible to establish the freedom of thought we now enjoy if the regulations prohibiting it had not been violated before being solemnly abrogated . . . Contrary to current ideas, the criminal no longer seems a totally unsociable being, a sort of parasitic element, a strange and unassimilable body, introduced into the midst of society. On the contrary, he plays a definite role in social life.

(Durkheim, 1966: 71–2)

It should be clear by now that Durkheim strenuously refuted any suggestion that he is an apologist of crime. He likened crime to pain. There is nothing desirable about pain, but it is normal and useful (*ibid*.: 72n.).

Durkheim's foundations and their effects in later sociology

The theoretical space Durkheim created for the sociological concept of deviance should now be clear. In brief summary, and in some kind of logical order, the overall foundations he laid down are as follows:

1 The importance of a scientific method of analysis and research, as against mere speculation or moral outrage (see his attacks on Tarde, quoted in Lukes, 1973: 302 *et seq*.). He was not content with a merely partisan social policy, nor with derogatory moral descriptions of criminals.
2 The development of the view that criminality was defined by social morality, which was connected to the social structure, and not given in any absolute moral code or in the intrinsic wickedness or personal deficiency of any individual censured as criminal.
3 The establishment of the idea of the social normality of crime, and of the inevitability of an increased amount of crime in highly differentiated societies with a high degree of individualism. Closely associated with this premise is the conception of the healthiness of a certain degree of crime in any society and the unhealthiness of an excessive, authoritarian disciplining of crime.
4 The insight into the value to a society of some crimes and deviations in pointing up the need for amelioration of inequities, rigidities or antiquities.
5 The belief in the need for a flexible moral order and social structure in order to enable social progress and legitimate the social order, and thus to prevent that society collapsing into a heap of separate fragments. Flexibility meant, in practice, creating a space between crime and difference, a space in which censure was light and which he called deviation. Given Durkheim's distinction between degrees of censure, between those of crime and those of mere difference, and his belief in flexibility or moral tolerance in highly individuated modern societies, a sociological concept of deviation, although barely and infrequently named by Durkheim, was born as the concept of the moral space somewhere between crime and difference.
6 This space which Durkheim created in his theoretical discourse for the concept of deviations, or deviance, was one that was also demanded

politically by his denial of the fundamentality of the class question. Durkheim's anti-Marxism does not need to be described here (see Giddens, 1971a: 95–100). One key statement will suffice for our purposes:

> The malaise from which we suffer is not located in a particular class; it is general throughout the whole society . . . it is not simply a question of diminishing the share of some so as to increase that of others, but rather of remaking the moral constitution of society. This way of putting the problem is not only truer to the facts: it should have the advantage of divesting socialism of its aggressive and malevolent character with which it has often, and rightly, been reproached.
>
> (Quoted in Hawthorn, 1976: 125)

This 'remaking' of the 'moral constitution' required a greater flexibility, which in turn would create a neutral space somewhere between good and evil. Accommodative in character, and susceptible to a detached science, Durkheim's social-democratic political leanings sustained his invention of that theoretical space; although who today would deny the recurrent relevance of remaking society's moral constitution? When Durkheim died, that space was ready to be filled by the inherently neutral-sounding, almost clinical conception of deviance. Out had gone the old contestation of class moralities and in came the art of social control. Not too much, not too little – society was now a big melting pot which had to be prevented from bubbling over by the correct degree of social regulation. Out goes the class state and in comes the desire for a state which could make conflicting social interests 'converge toward one dominant aim' (Durkheim, 1970: 255). Another new term entered the sociological vocabulary as 'social control' took over from class pacification as the regulatory strategy of modernism. One euphemism was to follow another as the modern utopia of social regulation was gradually formulated within the sociologies of law and deviance. The wise state of social democracy, in theory at least, would aim for progress, mediation and equality as well as freedom, and therefore not mindlessly suppress the realm of deviation, and would sanction the thriving of difference, while subjecting its suppression of crime to scientific advice, public opinion and open-minded debate. Marxism, like moral absolutism, would thus give way to liberal pragmatism. The sociology of deviance never completely left these foundational political parameters from the cradle to the grave. When it did make some alliance with Marxism in the early 1970s, it paid a fatal price.

They were foundations which were to give rise to and structure the sociology of deviance for the next seventy years. Such was the enormity of Durkheim's role as the mother of this embryonic field. A hierarchy of morality, crime/deviance/difference, had been created. Without even properly naming that embryonic middle space, that locus of moral conflict, ambiguity and innovation, Durkheim had left a conceptual offspring available for sociological analysis for years to come, one that was in tune with the tide of modern history.

Some of the subject's most fundamental characteristics were formed within the womb of Durkheim's theory of modern societies; so much so that one distinguished sociologist, Robert Nisbet, even claimed that 'There is little doubt that Durkheim has been for three-quarters of a century, and remains today, the preeminent theorist in sociological treatments of deviant behavior' (Nisbet, 1975: 209). His claim that without the 'uniquely Durkheimian content' social problems textbooks would have little left 'above the level of simple description and enumeration' (*ibid.*) is, however, an overstatement for several reasons:

1 Durkheim rarely talks of deviance explicitly and usually refers to crime.
2 Durkheim did not elaborate in any detail a theory of deviant behaviour or of the social conditions precipitating the censure of deviance, merely the general outlines of such a theory.
3 Post-1945 sociology developed the substance of the sociology of deviance well beyond the limited content sketched in by Durkheim, and in some ways which offend Durkheim's democratic beliefs.

However, Nisbet is correct in perceiving that Durkheim's 'analyses of deviant behaviour' were but 'special instances of his general theory of social structure' (*ibid.*: 209–10), and that, therefore, Durkheim created a general theoretical framework for the subsequent sociological analysis of deviance. As Taylor *et al.* (1973: 67) rightly argue, Durkheim made the crucial break with 'analytic individualism' and therefore, I would argue, lodged a conception of deviance, albeit almost entirely embryonic, within a distinctively sociological theory of social development.

Durkheim's contribution to the modern sociology of deviance, and indeed modern sociology in general, is not at all a remote one, lest anyone think that laying down foundations is a distant activity (cf. Lukes and Scull, 1983: 20). Like Durkheim, Talcott Parsons, in the 1950s, also integrated a concept of deviance into his theory of social systems and regarded the 'dimension of conformity–deviance' as 'inherent in and central to the whole conception of social action and hence of social systems' (Parsons, 1951: 249). Like Durkheim, later sociologists such as Park, Becker and Matza fostered the approach of appreciative naturalism which suspended any preconception of individual 'deviants' as necessarily pathological (cf. Lukes and Scull, 1983). In short, contrary to the assessment by Lukes and Scull, Durkheim stood against moral absolutism in principle and generally hoped for a social-democratic state structure moving towards increasing moral flexibility. Indeed, Durkheim's hopes could be said to have anticipated directly what later symbolic interactionist sociologists portrayed as actual moral and political structure within liberal democracies, and Park's work can be seen as the direct key empirical link between the two. We will discuss that later, but for the moment let us remember that the two American sociologists who first, consciously, developed a sociology of deviance as part of a general sociological theory, Parsons and Lemert, both acknowledged Durkheim's influence. Parsons (1951: xi) said it was 'immense'.

Edwin Lemert, in his early writings on deviance, began to use the Durkheimian concepts of 'social differentiation and individuation', which, he commented, he had 'rescued from the limbo of older textbooks on sociology, dusted off and given scientific airing' (*ibid*.: 21).

At the time he was writing, Durkheim was not so warmly appreciated. His great critic, Gabriel Tarde, was not noticeably impressed. Tarde (1912: 8) observed that there was an 'infatuation . . . for questions relating to delinquents, to offences, and penalties' and that this 'fever' was itself one result of the 'crisis of morality'. He devoted a long passage of sarcastic wit to pouring cold water over the concern of what he saw as the bored, affluent, intellects of the day who studied 'that which has always been repulsed with disgust; the shameful miseries, the hideous wounds, the heart of the scoundrel or of the prostitute fallen into the depths of the gulf; pederasty, sapphism, every variety of mental alienism or of moral aberration' (*ibid*.: 9). Tarde bemoaned what he perceived as the new confusion about right and wrong, observing that 'the modernization of morality' involved an assault on traditional morality, 'the only kind which is alive or survives in our hearts', by circumstance and by 'the leagues against it' who 'have thus far only served to befog it without succeeding in replacing it with anything durable' (*ibid*.: 11). Such comments bear close resemblance to Hitler's later attack on the degeneracy of avant-garde culture (see pp. 65–6). Tarde's classically conservative discourse did go on, in traditional style, to put socialists in the company of 'criminals' in their mindless assault on tradition, but, like Durkheim, he recognized the tide of moral change and saw it 'spreading at a pace unknown to our ancestors' (*ibid*.). Even he admitted that the criminal law needed reform, advised by scientific criminology, if it was to shape some harmony out of the maelstrom of change.

Tarde's comments point up the political and moral context within which the new scientific sociology of deviance emerged, and thus the limits of its subsequent impact. It was born during a period of economic depression in France after the major phase of industrialization, and thus proletarianization, was complete. It was a time of political confusion in need of a new moral constitution to ground a new social stability. Capitalism was entering its monopoly phase and rapidly expanding its international operations. The legions of the oppressed, the working class, women and the colonized throughout the globe were decreasingly content to remain as dark spectres haunting the unconscious of the white, male, bourgeois patriarchy. Their stirrings were demanding a more democratic recognition, both in terms of greater participation in the political processes whereby they were systematically misrepresented, and in terms of the moral censures whereby their claims and resistances were denounced as degenerate, insane or subversive. Their structural subordination need not change very much, but the terms in which it was justified needed modernizing in order to become more generally acceptable. Bourgeois hegemony had to be recast to survive the onslaught of the new century. A militaristic pacification of the 'natives' was no longer sustainable.

The new moral constitution demanded by post-Durkheimian sociology in the twentieth century set itself two political tasks. First, it had to absorb the continual volcanic eruption of all-too-public conflicts stemming from the fundamental social contradictions of class, gender, nation and empire, and to represent them in an intellectual, clinical and scientific rhetoric as private deviations stemming from mere surface fractures. The sociology of deviance was born within a progressive, liberal optimism about the possibility of mitigating the worst evils of industrial capitalism, and a conservative reluctance to accept oppositional forms of life as anything other than 'moral aberration' (Tarde). Second, it had to publicize the moral weaknesses of the current regulatory structure of society, of which excessive crime was the symptom and the condemnation. The adjustment of the moral-regulatory structure was as important as the adjustment of the faulty behaviour of deviants and criminals. Moral reconstruction demanded the perfection of the newly coined art of social control to prevent excessive discipline and reduce chronic anomie. Ideological cement had to be poured down the volcanic fissures in the social structure, and state intervention should curb the remaining excesses of both capital and labour. The state had to become the state of society and not just the capitalists' state, thus avoiding it becoming the socialists' state.

Crime had to be punished and difference appreciated. The deviance in between was to be the debating site for the new moral flexibility so close to Durkheim's heart. Thus it was that the sociology of deviance became the new science of moral ambiguity. This careful but caring observation and assessment of moral worth would then, without any bias other than the commitment to moral tolerance, advise the new technicians of social regulation in the profession of social control. Deviance would be sieved and sifted to filter out excessive discipline and real crime, the twin enemies of the emergent social democracy. The new sociologists of deviance had their mandate in Durkheim's legacy. They were to become the conceptive ideologists of repressive tolerance and moral ambiguity. From the very beginning their role was scripted within the modernizing vision of the corporate welfare state in advanced monopoly capitalism, and thus restricted by the basic contradictions of modern liberalism. That is why their role did not emerge in practice until a New Deal had been struck. Their political platform had to be established first. It was to be created within the United States during yet another depression.

Notes

1 African masks were also the subject of a painting by Nolde in 1911. Nolde believed in cultural renewal through 'primitivism' and like Gauguin went to the South Seas.

2 See, however, the discussions in S. Taylor (1982) and Pearce (1989).

3 Foucault's work on discipline, for all the sophistication of his notion of disciplinary power, and for all his stress on 'mildness-production-profit' (1977a: 219), lacks any real theorization of the question of balance.

4 Not as an individual action, it must be emphasized. Durkheim (1966: 66n.) rightly insisted that just because the social fact of crime is normal we must not infer that each individual person labelled criminal is psychologically normal.

5 Becker was also certainly no more specific than Durkheim in explaining why collective norms had a particular moral-political substance at any particular historical conjuncture.

6 The case of Tanzania's Economic Sabotage (Special Provisions) Act of 1983, which prohibited the possession of unaccountable cash and thus criminalized the whole population for a perfectly normal occurrence, is the most extreme one I personally have experienced. Some of the legislation of Stalin, Hitler and, later, South Africa would provide other examples; not to mention the criminalization of whole tribes in India under colonial rule.

2 Immigration and the urban jungle: social realism and the godfather

The imagination is certainly a faculty which we must develop, one which alone can lead us to the creation of a more exalting and consoling nature than the single brief glance at reality – which in our sight is ever changing, passing like a flash of lightning – can let us perceive.

(Vincent Van Gogh)

The Great War of 1914–18, or the Great European Civil War as some Africans call it, severely battered the optimism of the early modernists. The chaos and destruction accentuated the already towering waves of emigration to North America as Europeans sought a new world free from the restrictive chains and painful political conflicts of the old. A war which saw the senseless slaughter of millions could hardly have done otherwise. The European imperial patriarchy had exposed its stark and corrupt inhumanity, and the flimsiness of its claims to eternal power and moral superiority. Lenin had taken power in crisis-stricken Russia. By 1919, Europe was on the edge of socialist revolution. Prime Minister Lloyd George told the Triple Alliance that the people were ready for rewards after their sacrifice in the Great War, so that if there were a strike the government would be defeated and a constitutional crisis precipitated; and that the Alliance must be ready to take over the functions of state or withdraw (Rosenberg, 1987: 74). His bluff worked and the unions withdrew. Ireland demanded home rule and the Dublin uprising was brutally crushed. If Germany had fallen to the communists, all of Europe might have followed. The League of Nations was formed to prevent another catastrophe, while severe reparations for the war were being charged against Germany, thus ensuring further strife. And most British women had finally got their vote by 1928, without so much as a murmur, after all the censure and opprobrium dumped on the suffragettes. The legions of the oppressed were beginning to make their political presence felt.

In art, the Cubist and Futurist imaginations of doubt and relativity now shared life with the more certain but scarred and violent memories or visions of Beckmann, Dix, Marc, Grosz and Soutine, and the mysterious abstractions of Kandinsky and Mondrian. Direct, unemotional, represen-tation of physical reality was now neither necessary nor desirable. The exploration of painful emotions was both; as was a little lightness and levity occasionally. Images of psychic torture and fearful pain abounded. As Beckmann wrote in 1920, we 'must participate in the great misery to come, we have to lay our hearts and nerves bare to the deceived cries of people who have been lied to . . . the sole justification for our existence as artists . . . is to confront people with the image of their destiny' (quoted in Hughes, 1981: 290). Indeed, many of the works of this period painted the human being in a condition of terror which pre-dated the strikingly similar photographs later to emerge from the concentration camps by around twenty years. Existential angst in paintings had been a common subject since the works of Munch and Schiele, but the lunacy and mechanical horror of the war demanded even harsher images or even less 'realistic' abstractions. Some, revolted by the idiocy and carnage, began the Dadaist movement. Their manifesto was announced in Berlin. In German, 'dada' is 'simply idiotic babble' (Cole and Gealt, 1989: 284). Dadaist art meant nothing and often just threw together the images or sounds of everyday urban life. Surrealism, however, launched in 1924, began to delve deep into the unconscious (see Chapter 3). Modern art in search of meaning and soul was producing some brilliant concoctions, even if it was also clearly very disturbed. It wanted to explore the subjective, the variability of meaning, and the relation between the new mechanical world of Henry Ford, who began his mass production in 1913, and a disturbed human condition. Its objects, rhythms and styles were to be reproduced in the sociology of the period, whose unifying theme was to be the relation between the all-too-human individual and the all-too-mechanical economic system.

For a brief moment, until Lenin's death in 1924, Soviet art displayed all the hope and imagination glimpsed in Futurism before the war. Tatlin's tower, inspired by Picasso, would have captured many of the themes of European modernism, and have become the Soviet Eiffel, but there was never enough steel to build it. Social utility was setting in and abstract forms emerged as a mechanical prelude to the geometric architecture of the Bauhaus and the functionalist town planning of Le Corbusier. Under Stalin, art became propaganda and socialist realism was inaugurated. In the USA, pictorial documentation of urban reality took the form of social realism and, a little later in the UK, it took the form of the photography and films of the Mass Observation group. Machines and mechanization had entered art, and art had returned to flat perspective, but this time not to document the beauties of rural Arcadia or the joys of the virgin birth. This time it documented the sufferings of the inner-city poor and the calamity of the urban jungle, albeit via the now openly admitted perception and feeling of the artist. Edward Hopper's paintings stood out in the USA of the twenties and early thirties. His aim was to produce 'the most exact description possible of my most intimate impressions of nature' (Hopper, 1945: 1). The results were an evocative photo-call of some of the classic scenes of urban America: the gas station, the road lined with telegraph poles, the pharmacy, street corners with unemployed, downtown Manhattan, attractive-looking women in fitting fashions, the quiet Sunday morning scene and the corner bar. For example, his *Early Sunday Morning* (1930) expressed his feeling about the monotony, drabness and anonymity of the typical small-town street. These were bleak and hard times. There were other forms of painting too, mostly about rural life, but none achieved any great excellence until after the immigration of European artists following Hitler's rise to power in 1933 and Roosevelt's mass-commissioning of artistic work in the late thirties. This was the time for American artists such as Sheeler, whose work turned the material world 'into abstraction, allowing the viewer to forget his own situation', or Demuth, who saw utility in the current scene and thus a basis for optimism (Taylor, 1979: 176). It was a time of artistic obsession with hard work and with the application of machines and science (Hughes, 1981: 330).

Lang's *Metropolis* was a powerful indictment. This was very much a time for photography. In the hands of someone like Sheeler, attention could be directed to the precise form of things, not just their narrative context: common, concrete, reality could be seen as 'a complete and changeless formal structure in its own right' (Taylor, 1979: 178). Social realism was 'poor art for poor people', as Rothko called it later. A propagandist form which rejected modernism, it had grown partly out of the social realist art from Mexico, then under a socialist government, and partly because American poverty provided fertile soil for any form which focused on the misery of the unemployed. The victories of Cubism, Futurism, Expressionism and Surrealism now coexisted with the loss of character exhibited and documented by social realism. It was within the documentary form that American sociology of the 1920s was to express its acceptance of life's 'changeless' patterns or to criticize mildly some of the social costs of the everyday urban maelstrom.

Capone, Prohibition and *laissez-faire*

The thirty years before Al Capone's arrest in 1931 had seen great fortunes made in the USA, by the few who had appropriated the land and industry. It also saw the rise of a progressive reform movement, a liberal élite, committed to regulating corporate activities, conserving natural resources, providing humane treatment for the poor, cleaning up the machinery of government and improving social conditions on every front (see Gibbons, 1979: 20–1). It was a period which had seen the emergence, amongst some progressives, of the view that government if 'staffed with professional experts and responsive to a properly enlightened people' could not only increase its efficiency but also enable better social adjustment to economic development (Hawley, 1979: 10). However, the 'people's capitalism' of the twenties sought to heal social divisions through a raw expansion of production. GNP in the USA rose by 40 per cent and unemployment virtually disappeared for a short time as Fordist mass production and Taylorist scientific management established a more social organization of the market economy (*ibid.*: 80–5). New schemes to increase welfare, participation and education in the factory accompanied a newly discovered, war-affected, sense of social trusteeship within the management ranks of productive private property (articulated best in Berle and Means's *The Modern Corporation and Private Property*, 1932). They sat uneasily next to a new wave of 'corporate plunderers' who milked the 'free market system' for all they could. In both cases, corporate bureaucracy flourished as merger followed merger. Without accepting Hawley's implicit evolutionism, we can see the relevance of his conclusion:

> In many respects the central story of the American experience from 1917 to 1933 is the story of a search that failed. It is the story of men deeply influenced by the organizational experience of a democracy at war and seeking, against various obstacles, to draw from that experience a set of ordering mechanisms capable of coordinating an expanding organizational economy and fostering peaceful progress in the social and international spheres . . . the building and testing of these mechanisms was an important link in the chain of events leading to the New Deal programs and the mechanisms they brought into being.
>
> (Hawley, 1979: 227)

This rapid and spectacular phase of industrialization and urbanization left millions of Americans remaining in poverty (Gibbons, 1979), and in a state of effective civil disenfranchisement, as in the case of the blacks and women, or largely relegated to arid reservations, as in the case of the surviving aboriginal culture. Realism was the mood by the end of the twenties; the optimism of the Progressive era in the USA was beginning to wilt. People realized that the violence and lawlessness of the frontier had settled down not to disappear but to become the 'American way of life' (see Bell, 1962; also Brogan, 1985: 392). Brogan (1985: 392) comments that from 1865 to 1929

> laws and legal processes were altered, re-interpreted, perverted or ignored; the interests of working men and women were trampled upon; the appeal to the greed, foresight or gambler's instinct of the wealthy led to innumerable shady operations; the principles of political economy were re-invented, and the interests of the consumer, the ultimate consumer, were for long ignored.

Moreover, on top of the fundamental divisions of class, gender and race, this new 'land of opportunity' was riven with cultural hostilities and tensions. The massive immigrations of the early part of the century had mostly brought in people from eastern and southern Europe. Their desperation to rise above poverty, their ingrained resentment towards state power, their Catholic or Jewish religious attitudes and their tight, almost feudal, rural kinship ties did not easily gel with the lifestyles of the small-town, rural or metropolitan established Protestant élites of older America.

This polyglot cultural formation created by the new immigrations was resented by the traditionalists as a recipe for social chaos and the collapse of order. Even the progressives were somewhat alarmed. Bigotry, intolerance, discrimination and racism abounded. As McLaren (1990: 17) observes, interest in eugenics had grown. The traditionalist, conservative, element wanted to bar the incoming cultures and protect 'real America'; the liberal progressives sought to 'Americanize' them through education, training and social work. In fact, during the twenties, the concepts of our fledgling immigrant branch of sociology were to grow and grow, quietly, within an American, liberal-progressive thought concerned at a time of rampant mass production to assimilate alien cultures which it never really valued (at its most radical, it was only occasionally prepared to accept a limited version of cultural pluralism[1]).

Despite rigorous screening by the immigration officers of Ellis Island, the expansion of American capital had sucked in a huge reserve army of European labour which the USA was not yet sufficiently organized as a society to deal with, either efficiently or humanely. Until the Great War in Europe, the policy of virtually free entry had been defended and maintained. Between 1886 and 1916, some 19 million immigrants had entered the USA (Hawley, 1979: 11). However, during the Great War, industrialists had managed without immigrant labour from Europe, calling up the emancipated reserve army of black labour from its own deep South. Consequently, still disturbed by the horror of the war, and in a mood of isolationist suspicion of the foreign-born and of the evils of a violent, archaic, rural Europe, President Harding's new and very conservative government passed the Johnson–Reid Act of 1924 (the Natural Origins Act), drastically restricting immigration from anywhere other than Northern Europe. Paralleled by the now-regular lynching of blacks in the South,[2] and by sporadic red scares such as the one which led to the much-protested execution of Sacco and Vanzetti,[3] this closing of its doors was a reflection of America's economic buoyancy and political self-satisfaction in the twenties, as well as of the depth of its ethnic divisions. An already loose society structured as much by ethnicity as by class, the United States closed in on itself and entered a period of sustained moral de-regulation, otherwise known as the roaring twenties.

The growing new cities of the pre-war era had already spawned an assault on traditional values and lifestyles; an assault which Hawley (1979: 14) has justly termed 'cultural modernism'. In Greenwich Village, a cultural vanguard had proclaimed the need for a new art and a new morality. By the time of the twenties, spontaneity, flexibility and hedonism had emerged as modernist themes to such an extent that the threat of cultural disintegration was further heightened. Combined with liberal progressivism, as in Durkheim's France, cultural modernism was all set to challenge and reconstruct the moral concepts, attitudes and practices of the conservative establishment. As the Ku Klux Klan reacted in rage towards the 'uppity negro', the 'arrogant intellectual', the 'slick urbanite', the 'subversive socialist' and many more (Miller, 1968: 216), F. Scott Fitzgerald celebrated a world of wealth where 'Charm, notoriety, mere good manners, weighed more than money as a social asset' (quoted in Hoffman, 1968: 310).

In popular culture, flapper skirts shortened, the limits of petting were debated, and Freud's writings shattered sexual taboos. 'Nice girls' were smoking cigarettes and drinking, 'openly and defiantly, if often rather awkwardly and self-consciously' (Allen, 1969: 254). They got the vote in 1920. 'The new psychology, with its high sexual content, paralleled the sex education movement and the change in moral standards traditionally associated with the new freedom of women and World War I' (Burnham, 1968: 385). Psychoanalysis flourished, and the mental hygiene movement boomed while popularizing the cult of the self. Public interest in private experiences became a central feature of now astonishingly successful, mass-market magazines like *True Story* and *True Confessions*.[4] Americans read Freud to say that sex was the pervasive, driving force of human history. For many, it became a truth that 'The first requirement of mental health was to have an uninhibited sex life' (Allen, 1969: 259). There was a fascination with the irrational, abnormal, bestial and perverse. The notion of the personality deviation became ubiquitous. There was, indeed, 'a revolution in manners and morals' (*ibid.*: 256). Women exposed to the obscenities and macabre hedonism of the war in Europe had returned, their 'torn nerves' craving 'the anodynes of speed, excitement and passion':

> They found themselves expected to settle down into the humdrum routine of American life as if nothing had happened, to accept the moral dicta of elders who seemed to them to be living in a Pollyanna land of rosy ideals which the war had killed for them. They couldn't do it, and they very disrespectfully said so.
>
> (Allen, 1969: 257)

Social deviation was being democratized in the USA in its first age of popular culture. Abnormality was no longer to remain a privilege of the few. Everyone now had a right to claim his or her own neurosis in this curiously American revolution:

> The simultaneous interest in self and interest in the abnormal reflected the common concern of the time about 'normality'. The public in general had become vividly aware of the idea of normality when intelligence tests became standardized and widely publicized. *The idea of deviation in the form of feeble-mindedness was refined to include personality traits. Not surprisingly, therefore, in the 1920s a number of personality tests appeared, designed to detect personality deviations. So great was the concern about normality that a discipline*

known as industrial psychiatry grew up to try to eliminate misfits from industry just as they had been screened out of the Army. The mental hygiene movement similarly popularized this concern about abnormalities of every kind: eccentricities could in a rather romantic way take on the quality of portending sinister events in the hidden self. *The possibility that abnormality might include most people –* which fascinated the self-centered – grew not only out of the discovery of abnormality in garden-variety aspects of life but out of the publicity about shell shock, which *underlined the well-established idea in popularized psychiatry that it is difficult to draw a line between normal and abnormal.*

(Burnham, 1968: 383–4, emphasis added)

Morality was being urbanized as the twenties roared on (Ostrander, 1968: 349). The old idea of social control as effective informal regulation by shared folkways (W. G. Sumner, 1959; Ross, 1969) was becoming meaningless, and a demand for a new form of social control would soon manifest itself, calling for the systematic, bureaucratic management of the social world and its new pluralism of desires; a management based upon industrial psychiatry, mental hygiene, the new psychology and the growing science of sociology. The groundwork was laid for Roosevelt, the social democrat, to challenge Hoover, the pillar of free enterprise; for sociology to join with socially aware psychology and psychiatry; and for the concept of social deviation to challenge the concept of individual pathology.

As in the France of Durkheim's day, in the 1920s capitalism in the USA reached for the sky, to use a loaded phrase that Hollywood westerns were later to make famous. The Empire State Building overtook the Eiffel, and its symbolism of the cigar proclaimed America's self-satisfaction as the home of free enterprise, albeit with new, record, trade tariffs. The cigar took no different a meaning in the mouth of Al Capone, and expansion through the protection racket was to become a familiar theme of urban America. Lindbergh flew solo across the Atlantic to Paris, the intellectual and artistic capital of the old world, and the motor car became a mass-market commodity. The world was suddenly becoming a smaller place. Harding's administration of millionaires and 'rogues' (see Brogan, 1985: 507) launched a decade of self-indulgence and leisure, a decade characterized by the Charleston, low taxes, anti-unionism, rackets, drinking, gambling, black jazz and the growth of Hollywood. Only by the end of the decade did realism set in, demanding a serious social adjustment to the new 'freedoms' (Allen, 1969: 266).

The massive contradiction between this ethos of 'freedom' and the unpopular diktat of Prohibition became a fertile breeding-ground for bootlegging and gangsterism, organized as scientifically and systematically as 'legitimate' industry. Two billion dollars' worth of business shifted from the old established brewers and the bar-owners to the bootleggers and the 'hoods'; money which they continually reinvested in gambling, prostitution, labour unions, regular business[5] and extortion. Was this what Quételet meant by saving for the future?

Syndicated crime developed on a massive scale in Chicago and New York, and the mob bought itself a posse of politicians and police officers to match its increasingly large holdings in conventional business. An unofficial society grew within the body politic of the official one: everything was pregnant with its contrary. The lunacy of Prohibition in a country long committed to serious drinking had the effect of generating a state within a state. Between 1927 and 1931, Capone appeared to run Chicago. It had always been a city with plenty of crime, but now Capone was to combine the terroristic power tactics of the Sicilian feudal baron with a Taylorist systematization of the processes of production, sale and distribution. Backed up by his private army of stormtroopers, and in a manner akin to that of Mussolini, Hitler and Stalin, Al Capone, following Johnny Torrio, effectively modernized Chicago's crime industry.

President Harding's appointees had not set a great example of moral probity in the early twenties. Following his death, they were soaked by a wave of graft scandals. Swindling and embezzlement seemed to be an integral part of the fabric of banking and the stock market. But no one seemed to mind too much as long as they got their piece of the action, whether it was a laid-back slice of the Gatsby cake or a double-figure percentage of the Capone extractions. America was on the make and on the move.

As the new motor industry created thousands of jobs in Detroit and Chicago, the labour force migrated. At the heart of America's railroad system, Chicago had always been a key point for immigrant labour and it now saw much of the newly migrant labourers from the East and South. Not surprisingly, its well-established 'mob', under Capone's domination, grew fat and famous, its city hall became a model of corruption and ethnic politics, and its university developed fast in the new sciences of sociology, psychology and economics. A bloated microcosm of the so-called melting pot, Chicago became America's centre of gravity, and with gravity is the best way of seeing it.

Capone's empire, along with those of Torrio before him and O'Banion alongside him, was protected by ruthless violence. Gang murders became routine events and official figures record 703 of them in Chicago during the Prohibition period from 1920 to 1934. At times during this period, the city witnessed so many bombings and assassinations that many concluded that there was a civil war in process. Huge profits were made from the production and supply of illegal liquor, the speakeasies, the brothels and the casinos. The Internal Revenue reckoned Capone amassed around $20 million. Yet during his period of total control between 1927 and 1931, none of the 227 gang murders resulted in any court convictions (Allsop, 1968: 277). During the whole Prohibition period, and after, murder could be committed with impunity, even against policemen, because 'the mob' had bought off virtually everyone who mattered in city hall and the police force. 'Big Bill' Thompson, for so long the mayor during these violent times, died in 1944 leaving a hoard of $1.75 million in his home (*ibid*.: 359). Indeed, it was the Republican politicians who, in 1923, invited Capone into Cicero, later his headquarters, to secure the 'right' election result during a time of dangerous enthusiasm for Democratic Party reformism. Similarly, in the early twenties it was the big brewers and senior politicians who encouraged, enabled and advised Capone's boss, Johnny Torrio, in the setting up of the illegal supply of beer and spirits. Very little of the expansion and modernization of crime would have been possible without the initiative, support and corruption of large sectors of the local ruling classes. Capone's role in this whole process, however, earns him the title of the godfather of the sociology of deviance. His criminal corporatism so thoroughly confused images of normality with the spectres of abnormality that it was the major, practical, home-grown, basis for the softening of the terminology of degeneracy.

For the mob to become an effective part of government, it also had to have some assent from the general public, and Capone's popularity at the time, not to mention the coy and ambivalent admiration of the American public ever since, suggests that the mob, however scary, were not at all unpopular. Perhaps Capone's entrepreneurial achievements represented a triumph for the enterprise of the poor immigrant over the more established, legitimated, rackets of the hypocritical, New England, puritan élite – for, after all, the federal political leaders were closely connected to an earlier class of robber barons. On the other hand, such a view seems overly symbolic and romantic compared to the hard structural reality of the gradual triumph, during the twenties, of the new forms of business organ-ization (Taylorism, corporatism and military-style bureaucracy) in both legal and illegal capitalist enterprise (see also Hawley, 1979). None the less, Capone's appeal was real. The core of it is well described by one anonymous sociologist who mixed with Capone's men while doing research:

I couldn't look upon the gangs of the Prohibition period as criminals. The people of Chicago wanted booze, gambling and women, and the Capone organization was a public utility supplying the customers with what they wanted. It couldn't have operated for one hour without the public's consent. It was the 'good' people who kept the gangsters flourishing. The big civic leaders and industrial moghuls would get up at a meeting and denounce corruption – and then go on to a cocktail party, or back to the office, to argue with their bootleggers about the quality of the last delivery of liquor ... Capone and the others really believed that they were running the city, but I don't believe they were. They were the executives and the techni-cians. The city was being run by the politicians and City Hall, and the big bosses weren't interested if the gangsters killed each other, providing they kept delivering the money. I had respect for Capone. In the Depression he did wonderful work. Before the New Deal got going they set up block restaurants for the unemployed, free food with the compliments of the Organization – and you didn't have to listen to any sermons or get up and confess.

(Quoted in Allsop, 1968: 241)

Allsop (1968: 245) observed that rogue financiers, like Insull and Yerkes, stole more than the hoods ever did, and hurt more innocent people in doing it. The blur or merger between legal and illegal capitalism was too obvious to permit many popular illusions about conventional government. So the gangsters did not get a bad press from the writers they frequently met in the new jazz clubs or at the opera:

> The gangsters did not appal the writers and journalists the way they did most men; they knew them personally; Chicago was a jungle anyway, and Prohibition was decidedly unpopular. Most of the journalists considered the dangerous beasts not the prowlers of the underworld but the dinosaurs who holed up in their La Salle Street skyscrapers and sallied forth to hi-jack streetcar franchises and utilities stock.

(Allsop, 1968: 245)

Whatever the relative merits of one set of extortionists over another, it is worth noting the preponderance of Irish, Sicilians and Jews amidst the gangland community. As Allsop observes, these groups had a profound distrust of established bourgeois élites, and of the machinery of justice, since they had suffered at their hands far too often. Crime, class and ethnicity appeared inseparably linked and, as the thirties arrived, it became harder for sociologists to ignore those connections. But, more than that, empirical reality in Chicago during the 1920s had profoundly compromised any conception of crime as a prerogative of individual pathology, or, indeed, as a category that made sense outside of political judgement. The widespread corruption manifest in all parts of its urban jungle, and the distinct lack of ethical state direction of the whole society, effectively devastated 'wicked individual' theories of crime. At a time of high crime and manifest social pathology, any purely individualist explanation of the criminal act was doomed to ridicule; and perhaps for ever. However, logic and history remind us that reactionary thought still had the option of moving in the direction of 'collective biologism', as McLaren (1990: 27) calls it, or the belief that whole cultures or races could be pathological. It took it. The Sicilians, for example, were often on the receiving end of this type of moral thinking during the twenties; not to mention the later Nazi genocide of the Jews.

Meanwhile, in 'legitimate' business, in the late twenties, New York financiers tried to buy back the control they were losing to Chicago and the other new boom cities (e.g. San Francisco). Share prices inflated ludicrously, and ballooned out of sight once the swindlers and incompetents got into the act. The bubble burst famously in 1929. A generation's savings were wiped out within a week as the nation's financial system collapsed. Quételet turned over in his grave and share values dropped several times the amount of currency then in circulation. Trust in the banks and in credit disappeared. Industrial expansion came to a halt and people sold anything to produce cash. Unemployment rose as trade contracted, and by 1932 it had grown to thirteen million (Brogan, 1985: 531). Charity, bread lines and garbage-picking were the new social features of urban America. But the society was still not organized to deal with social problems on any, let alone this, scale. Even charities ran out of money, the unemployed were left to their own devices and communist organizations had a rare flourish. The ageing President Hoover could not give up on the dogma of individualism and make the state responsible for food, work and shelter. Roosevelt was elected to fulfil his promise of a 'new deal' and inaugurated in 1933.

Immigration into the USA and Canada, eugenics and social control

There was a huge emigration to the new world up to 1914. Did Durkheimian ideas emigrate too? Were they allowed in and what was the ideological context of reception? A key indicator of the moral categories used in the 'new world' at this time is the list of exclusion categories used by the immigration authorities to screen prospective immigrants. What better place has there ever been to judge a country's moral priorities than its assessment of immigrants?

As we noted earlier, by 1918 the optimism of the progressive era was fading, and 'The growing success of eugenics in popularizing fears of degeneracy was a symptom of a decline of faith in nineteenth-century liberalism' (McLaren, 1990: 17). In the USA, Canada and the UK, McLaren argues,

> the rise of eugenics symptomized a shift from an individualist to a collectivist biologism by those who sought to turn to their own purposes the fears raised by the threat of 'degeneration'. Individualism, materialism, feminism, and socialism were said to be rampant. The purported surges in venereal disease, tuberculosis, alcoholism, divorce, and labour unrest were pointed to by the nervous as evidence of the erosion of traditional values. Early Victorian science had reassured the middle class of the harmony of religious and scientific truths and the possibility of social peace and industrial harmony. This vision had been momentarily lost.
>
> (McLaren, 1990: 27)

This is not even to mention Germany, where this movement was later to produce events of unprecedented horror.

The eugenicists of the early twentieth century, wherever they were found, tended to reject the *laissez-faire* politics of earlier social Darwinists and Malthusians. Blaming degeneracy upon the environment, they believed

that state intervention and social programmes were necessary for the reproduction of healthy populations. A new bio-politics was required, to use
Foucault's phrase (see Foucault, 1980a: 166–82; 1980b: 25–7), for it was
clearly insufficient to rely on the ruling classes' innate ability to reproduce
themselves healthily.[6] It is perhaps a commonplace to observe the sexism,
racism and class snobbery built into the eugenicists' assessment of what
was degeneracy and health (see the examples in McLaren, 1990: 13–27),
but it is still essential, as is the potent observation of the similarities
between eugenics and the scientific socialism of that period.[7] The sciences
of the social, during the early twentieth century, seemed tied to a parochial
moral–political vision limited by patriotism, familialism and philanthropy.

Anti-egalitarian, in locating hereditary degeneracy solely among the lower
classes, and anti-feminist, in blaming feminism for women's alleged desertion
of their 'eternal obligation to society' to get healthily and regularly pregnant,
the eugenics movement gained much ground in North America, occasionally,
and bizarrely, supported by socialists and feminists. These neo-Darwinists,
such as McBride of McGill University in 1924, now called for the sterilization of prostitutes, criminals and drunkards (McLaren, 1990: 24), or
for the creation of a 'human stud book' (quoted in *ibid.*: 25) to ensure that
only fit persons were encouraged to reproduce the species. Archbishop
Cody of Toronto was to write in 1916 that the state had a duty to 'prevent
the propagation of the feeble-minded' (quoted in *ibid.*: 26), and one Alice
Ravenhill, an English émigré to British Columbia, claimed in 1915 that

> The next enemies of the Empire will need to be better prepared than
> the Germans, for the women are leaving nothing undone. Their soldiers
> are to be well-born, for they are making a study of eugenics. They
> are to be well-bred, for they have their domestic science and they are
> solving moral problems.
>
> (Quoted in McLaren, 1990: 26)

Professors, such as Jackson, whose positions in zoology departments and
knowledge of relevant topics like rat-ranching in Manitoba gave them a
supreme confidence in their ability to manipulate the evolution of the
human species, mimicked the earlier outpourings of Galton and Pearson,
and provided us with a rich reminder of the role of zoology in the formation of criminology. As Foucault (1977a: 253) said, criminology formed
around 'a zoology of social sub-species'.

Eventually, thirty-one American states, from 1897 onwards, would pass
legislation enabling and encouraging sterilization of the 'feeble-minded', and
Canada's two most western, and least Catholic, provinces passed Sexual
Sterilization Acts in 1928 and 1933, providing that 'mental defectives'
could be sterilized if consent was given. Alberta, like California, later
abolished the consent proviso, taking it very close to the Nazi legislation.
All these governments were concerned with high immigration rates into their
territory, with the allegedly high involvement of immigrants and 'defectives'
in crime, and with the high cost of maintaining mental institutions, which

often seemed to be disproportionately full of foreigners (see McLaren, 1990: 95). The desire to preserve 'native' purity, the need for healthy soldiers in the army, the new power of the medical profession after the Great War, a siege mentality and a resistance to footing the bill for social welfare costs were conditions which often combined to produce a powerful wave of eugenicism, which has only recently,[8] and never wholly, subsided. The movement was also strongly sustained by the desire to ameliorate high infant mortality rates. In Canada, Helen MacMurchy's important work downplayed the importance of economic causes and lack of government provision in favour of stressing failure of maternal care and ignorance. Again, the lower orders were held responsible and the state increased its intervention in, and medicalization of, the whole process of childbirth. Clearly, welfare statism was on its way, but fired by some very mixed motives and many dubious ideas.

The question of immigration was central to the North American consciousness of this period. The dominant perspective and concern was well articulated in the Canadian National Committee for Mental Hygiene report of 1920 on Manitoba:

> the feeble-minded, insane and psychopathic of that province were recruited out of all reasonable proportions from the immigrant class, and it was found that these individuals were playing a major role in such conditions as crime, juvenile delinquency, prostitution, pauperism, certain phases of industrial unrest, and primary school inefficiency.
>
> (Quoted in McLaren, 1990: 60)

Canada was only rejecting one 'mental defective' out of every 10,127 immigrants, while the figure for the more restrictive USA was one to 1,590 (*ibid.*). IQ tests were developed during the period around the Great War and were now being deployed to support claims that 40 per cent of American immigrants coming through Ellis Island were feeble-minded. These tests, now quite visibly monuments to cultural blindness and discrimination, feigned to justify restrictions against Southern and Eastern European immigrants. In any case, American immigration was further restricted in the early twenties. Canadian immigration legislation of 1910 already barred the mentally defective (including the 'feeble-minded'), the diseased and the physically handicapped. Pressure from the United States in the early twenties led to measures which barred illiterates, reduced the numbers of Southern and Eastern Europeans, and effectively stopped (for the moment) the entry of Asians and blacks (*ibid.*: 58).

As in the USA, the great immigration fear in Canada centred on crime. It was believed that foreigners committed the bulk of crime and that this was primarily because so many of them, within certain select, ethnic groups of course, were 'feeble-minded'. *Social and racial degeneration were mutually overlapping fears.* North America perceived that it had become the 'dumping-ground' for the 'riff-raff' of the world. So, in 1929, the Canadian Council on Child Welfare claimed that immigrant feeble-mindedness, spreading with 'cancerous tenacity', was responsible for 'filth, disease, criminality, immorality and vice'; not that this prevented Canada hypocritically allowing in 165,000 Central and Eastern Europeans to farm its great prairies to profitable effect (*ibid.*: 64–5). Immigration policy and practice has never ceased to be a wonderful site to observe the eternal struggle between rhetoric and pragmatism. Ultimately, it was the Depression which finally closed Canada's doors to massive immigrations, but the discourses of eugenics had, ironically, at least taken the progressives into the Establishment.

Durkheim's ideas were received in North America within this social context, and it is within the discourses linking crime, urbanization, ethnicity, degeneration and national self-preservation that their reception is best understood. The 1920s justification of state intervention into the creation, reproduction and cultivation of the population lay in both 'nativism', or the defence of traditional, 'settler', values, and liberal welfarism, both of which were fond of using the new social sciences to validate their moralizations. Sometimes, conservatives, feminists and socialists could speak as if with one voice on what should be done about the evils of the day. Durkheim's utopia of a social state developing flexible policies aware of the needs and limits of each individual and group may, on the surface, have looked close to its realization. However, our analysis has indicated that this was more of a mirage, condensed out of the fears and aspirations of the established white élites, than a reality. Nevertheless, both the traditionalist-sexist-racists and the liberal-socialist-feminists did deploy a discourse which centred upon the needs of the social whole, and relied upon the reputation of the new scientific management. It was decreasingly acceptable to put down the poor or the immigrants because they challenged one's economic interests; it could now be done acceptably by reference to the needs of the whole social system, backed up by social-scientific evidence and justified as social control (see also Mayer, 1983). Such reference required a new vocabulary to distinguish it from the old paternalistic, class-specific rejections of the undesirable. It began to emerge in the 1920s, and the sociology of deviance would soon acquire its name, as part of this new science of social control.

Changing the language of social censure and rejection

The debate in the USA about what to call undesirable and rejected individuals and conditions is revealed well in an article of 1921 by Harry Laughlin in the then relatively new *American Journal of Sociology*. Laughlin's essay suggests that policy-makers and intellectuals, at least, were beginning to reconceptualize and rename the derogatory categories used to organize social regulation in a variety of state concerns. Durkheim's ideas were received within this political–intellectual context.

From the essay, it appears that Laughlin worked for the Eugenics Record Office, who in turn were serving the Bureau of Census. He authored a study of state institutions which covered 'all types of individuals who require social care or attention of one sort or another' (Laughlin, 1921: 55). That report called its list of such agencies 'State Institutions for the Socially Inadequate'; a title which is rich and resonant with its time. The 'Socially Inadequate' referred to the following people:

(1) Feeble-minded, (2) Insane, (3) Criminalistic (including the delinquent and wayward), (4) Epileptic, (5) Inebriate (including drug habitués), (6) Diseased (including the tuberculous, the syphilitic, the leprous, and others with chronic infectious segregated diseases), (7) Blind (including those with greatly impaired vision), (8) Deaf (including those with greatly impaired hearing), (9) Deformed (including the crippled), and (10) Dependent (including children and old folks in 'homes', ne'er-do-wells, tramps, and paupers).

(*ibid.*: 56)

Laughlin comments that, in devising these new categories and the new general category of the socially inadequate, he and the Census Bureau were aiming to 'serve the social sciences well in their efforts to classify social handicap' (*ibid.*: 57). However, it seems that his new category and list of 'descriptive subheadings' caused a bit of 'a tempest in a teapot', mainly among sociology professors.

Much to his obvious chagrin, the leading authorities of the day could not agree to his new categorical system to replace 'our old friend' the 'three Ds' (the defective, dependent and delinquent), although they did agree that the old term was unsatisfactory. Laughlin clearly had not calculated for the eternal and transhistorical difficulty in getting sociologists to agree on what to call things. Cynics may say that some things do not change, but of course, as any self-respecting sociologist would argue, the point is that constructing an agreement between sociologists on terminology is as difficult as constructing social unity itself, precisely because agreeing terms is a central part of creating social unity – schools of sociological thought are merely representative of general social divisions. So the time was not yet right for Laughlin's proposed change of categories to gain general assent, although it was right enough to have it aired in discussion. In the end, the Bureau of Census decided to continue to use the old, 'conservative' term, the 'defective, dependent and delinquent classes', because it gained more general approval than any other term, although not without expressing some resentment at the resistance of the professors. Apparently, letters using the new categories were sent out to 576 state institutions, and only three of these objected to the new classification system. Laughlin, somewhat sarcastically, concluded in resignation at the obstinacy of the academics that 'What is needed is a term hoary with age, but still venerable on account of its great current service' and that to establish the proof of its serviceability one should just perhaps, as Jack London advised, use it continuously until it falls into the common language.

What was this amusing and arcane debate really about? What was the problem Laughlin was trying to resolve? What caused the horrible 'tempest in a teapot'? He defined it himself with unmatchable candour and inimitable language, in a passage which should be regarded as classical:

> all students of social structure agree that a general non-enumerative title is needed to designate all of those classes in modern society which need special care, restraint, or direction, who as a group do not contribute in net to the general welfare (nor at all except as they may awaken altruistic conduct in their more fortunate fellows), but who on the contrary in net entail a drag upon those members of the community who have sufficient insight, initiative, competency, physical strength, and social instincts to enable them to live effective lives without particular social custody.
>
> (*ibid.*: 68)

The three Ds won't do any longer, nor will the Seven Devils, Professor Giddings's awesomely witty list of 1919 (the depraved, deficient, deranged, deformed, disorderly, dirty and devitalized). What is needed, argued Laughlin, is a general category to specify those who are a 'drag upon' the 'effective' community and who need some kind of 'social custody', those people whom the strong and insightful must do something about. Another D, this time for deviance, was to emerge two decades later, but it was to elude Laughlin. He remained convinced that 'the socially inadequate' was the best candidate for the job, despite the fact that most serious candidates to replace the devil seem to begin with D. Apart from the three Ds and the Seven Devils, in our own time we have witnessed the popularity of Degenerate, Deviant, Dissident, Daft, Debauched, Diseased, Diabolical, Defiant, Disobedient, Destructive, Disruptive, Dysfunctional, Disorganized, Demagogic and Demonic. The Ds are clearly becoming more political; no doubt connected to the debate about Democracy and Dictatorship.

For Laughlin, a socially inadequate person was defined as one who 'by his own purpose, initiative, and efforts, chronically is unable to maintain himself as a self-supporting and useful member of the organized society in which he finds himself' (*ibid.*: 69). Whether women were, in principle, capable of being 'socially inadequate' is therefore unclear.[9] He saw social inadequacy as 'generally the result of personal, mental, physical, or temperamental handicap, either inherited or acquired' (*ibid.*), and he regarded it as a 'degenerate' quality that could be inherited by the offspring. He had no doubt that most social inadequates were of this type (i.e. 'cacogenic'), and that only a few were of the 'eugenic' type (i.e. carriers of 'valuable' traits). Laughlin's views illustrate the attitude of the period. The concept of individual pathology still predominated (see also Gibbons, 1979: 19–35), and Durkheim's theoretical offspring was ahead of its time. Indeed, Oberschall (1972: 187–8) suggested later that the sociologists of early twentieth-century America were often economists who had broken away to study the three Ds. Until the emergence of the Chicago school of sociology, their analyses clearly regarded crime as pathological behaviour resulting from individual deficiency, despite their frequent remarks about the criminogenic effects of poverty and bad social influences (see Gibbons's (1979: 28–35) comments on the texts by Parmelee, Gillin and Parsons). Nowhere was there to be found the kind of break from the determinism of individual pathology which is so distinctive of the Durkheimian legacy in Chicago. Laughlin's renaming exercise merely tried to tidy up the contemporary terminology of the time; its conceptual character is typical. Its significance lies in its uniquely open expression of the desire to move away from the pejorative categories of degeneracy and pathology into something more neutral-sounding.

The responses of the sociology professors, including some now famous names, are themselves indicative. E. A. Ross and several others thought that 'socially inadequate' would suffice, but Willcox preferred 'public charges', Kelsey used 'social debtors', Fetter liked 'abnormal' (the test of abnormality being the lack of economic support) and Albion Small, the founder of the Chicago school, would have retained the three Ds or used synonyms such as 'the sub-social classes; the incompletely socialized classes; the defectively socialized classes' (Laughlin, 1921: 57–9). Clearly, in the 1920s, what was emerging within the earlier moralistic condescension was a recognition of the *de facto* existence of an organized state response to the social problems of capitalist political economy, of the necessary expansion of that state response and of the need for a realistic as well as comprehensive language within which to administer the state's 'social debtors' and 'public charges'. The principles of capitalist political economy were now being reformulated during this explosive but *laissez-faire* period in American history. During this time of expansion, the cost of its industrial reserve army was important to the state, but, since this was no longer the initial stage of capital accumulation, the reserve army could seriously be expected to have *learned* not to be delinquent, unemployed, blind or crippled and could therefore be seen as inadequately socialized rather than merely wicked. To develop a line incompletely forged by Foucault (1967: 259–60), if unreason had been part of nature in the middle ages, it had been subdivided during the birth of capitalism and turned into individual deficiency, and now, in the roaring twenties, that deficiency was being transformed into a failure of the social. Economic inability through faulty learning was becoming a social inadequacy rather than an individual pathology. The administrative-scientific language of social censure was changing. The impetus behind this change was felt strongly within American sociology, and it was within the work of the Chicago school that it was most clearly expressed.

Park, Durkheim and the Chicago school

The Chicago school of sociology was at the forefront of sociology in the USA from around 1920 for two decades. Its substantial contribution to the field of criminology has been well described (see Faris, 1967; Matza, 1969; Bulmer, 1984; Pfohl, 1985; Beirne and Messerschmidt, 1991) and therefore needs no detailed repetition here. During the period which we are dealing with in this chapter, 1920–33, the concept of social deviation remained unadopted. However, the research of the Chicago school did effectively develop and focus Durkheim's ideas about crime, providing graphic illustrations of the value of seeing the formation of crime and crime rates as thoroughly social or collective products, and amplifying Durkheim's sense of the level of crime as an index of the level of social integration. Moreover, in applying and advancing a whole range of qualitative fieldwork techniques and in espousing the symbolic interactionist social psychology of G. H. Mead, these sociologists established a theorized method, or methodology, for studying social action as a reflexive, purposive and creative response to objective social conditions. As such their work constituted a decisive break from Positivist statistical analysis and behaviourist psychology. From now on, the importance of a person's cultural viewpoint and learned choices in determining their practical responses to the social environment was firmly established as essential to all kinds of sociological thought. These developments were crucially important preconditions of the later formation of the sociology of deviance, as a field of social science with a distinctive methodology and focus.

Strongly directed by Robert Park, a crime reporter and drama critic before graduating from Harvard, Berlin and Heidelberg, to 'tell it like it is' through fieldwork 'out there' on the streets, and well organized and supervised by Ernest Burgess, the researchers of the Chicago school produced detailed, fine-textured accounts of the urban world around them (see Smith, 1988). Based on both quantitative and qualitative data, their studies frequently focused on small-time crime and delinquency, although very rarely upon the more ambitious activities of the mob.[10] They portrayed petty crime as no great long-term threat to the state of society and thus further developed the Durkheimian space within which later American sociologists could begin to think and talk about that area between crime and difference as social deviance.

Their perspective has often been described subsequently as 'appreciative' (see, especially, Matza, 1969: 24–40) because they attended closely to the subjective perceptions of the people they studied. This appreciation of the humanity and dignity of people who, in the past, had been treated with such scornful condescension can be seen in the following brief excerpt from Anderson's *The Hobo*:

> The part played by the jungles [places where hobos congregate] cannot be overestimated. Here hobo tradition and law are formulated and transmitted. It is the nursery of tramp lore. Here the fledgling learns to behave like an old-timer. In the jungles the slang of the road and the cant of the tramp class is coined and circulated. It may originate elsewhere but here it gets recognition. The stories and songs

current among the men of the road, the sentiments, the attitudes, and the philosophy of the migratory laborer are all given due airing. In short, every idea and ideal that finds lodgment in the tramp's fancy may be expressed here in the wayside forum where anyone who thinks may speak, whether he be a jester or a sage.

Suspicion and hostility are the universal attitudes of the town or small city to the hobo and the tramp. Accordingly, the so-called 'floater' custom of passing vagrants on to other communities is widespread. The net effect of this policy is to intensify the anti-social attitude of the homeless man and to release and accentuate criminal tendencies.

(Anderson, 1923, reprinted in 1975: 25–6)[11]

The Chicago school also translated the new social Darwinism, so prevalent within American intellectual culture of that time, and the specific ideas of Simmel, Durkheim and Dewey, into a series of empirical researches which essentially portrayed petty criminals and delinquents as normal people caught up in difficult and competitive social environments.

- Neo-Darwinism, or 'collective biologism', had the impact on the culture of the time of lending readiness to any view that suggested that the weaker cultures or societies would go to the wall in the surging tides of social competition. In the work of the Chicago school this cultural theme took the form of an emphasis on the 'natural history' of the city. Delinquency and crime were seen 'as part of the natural history of the settlement process experienced by newly settled groups in the urban community' (Gibbons, 1979: 43). Like Durkheim, and subsequent 'modernization' theorists of crime (e.g. Shelley, 1981), the Chicago school saw high crime rates, optimistically, as a temporary imbalance in the process of evolution of modern societies. Like societies, once ethnic groups settled down and established themselves on a suitable territory their crime rates were supposed to diminish naturally.
- Simmel's sociology emphasized that knowledge was fragile and based on experience. Life was grounded in forms of association, and always in flux, constantly producing new meanings. As Rock (1979: 38) puts it, in the Simmelian view, 'analytically and ontologically, the petty materials of sociation are prior to the grand structures of sociological theory' and society is thus 'a pulsating web of relations whose interplay produces order and change'.
- Dewey's philosophy, a pragmatic translation of Hegel, focused on the unity of subjective and objective in social action or praxis. Practical reason was thus the current manifestation of the evolution of the collective consciousness – no recourse to transcendental reasoning would get us any further. The social psychology of the act was the crux of what we could know, and even the meaning of events was always subject to continuous redefinition and debate. Knowledge must be indeterminate and processual (see Rock, 1979).

In sum, it can readily be seen how all these intellectual elements in Chicagoan thinking very much reflected and related to the real world of 1920s Chicago all around them. This was a world of change, action, rapid development, de-regulation, competition, conflict and adaptation. Chicagoan knowledge reflected that, and emphasized perception, action, adaptation, innovation, group formation and group conflict.

Many commentators have ignored the immigration of Durkheim's theoretical offspring into this setting, and some have even blatantly denied it. For example, Bulmer (1984: 222) states that Durkheim's work was only 'slightly known by American sociologists before the late 1930s and 1940s' and that Park virtually ignored Durkheim. Textbooks are often written as if the Chicago school of sociology were unaware of Durkheim's writings. This is palpably invalid. One of the earliest essays by the man usually considered to be its intellectual driving force, Robert Park, was very much an explicit translation of Durkheim's ideas for the American scene (Park, 1921). Indeed, the 'green bible', the introduction to sociology which Park produced with Burgess (1924), openly displayed the enormous impact of Durkheimian thought (pp. 27–43, for example). In short, it seems to me that specialists in empirical method, or proponents of empiricism, have often completely misrepresented the relation between European social theory and American empirical sociology, when in fact so many American sociologists did their graduate work in Europe (or were born there) during the first third of the century.

In his *American Journal of Sociology* essay of 1921, Park raised the question which so troubled Durkheim: 'How does a mere collection of individuals succeed in acting in a corporate and consistent way?' (Park, 1921: 5). This he explicitly defined to be the problem of 'social control'. The Durkheimian drive to develop social regulation in a morally de-regulated society is reproduced in Park's thought, with the effect of emphasizing the new concept of social control developing in American sociology, against that of W. G. Sumner and E. A. Ross. Park discussed and quoted Durkheim's ideas at length, before concluding that for an epistemological 'realist' like Durkheim the two distinctively social facts were social processes (or relations) and public opinion (or collective representations), and that the dispute with the nominalists, such as Tarde and Giddings, reduced to the question of whether these social facts were real in the sense of objective or material (*ibid.*: 17). For Park, their objectivity was inconsequential for all practical purposes, and the Chicago school were content to follow W. I. Thomas's dictum that 'if men define situations as real, they are real in their consequences' (Thomas, 1932: 572). What mattered to Park was that, following Durkheim's view of modernity, the touchstone of a society over a collection of individuals was 'corporate action' (Park, 1921: 19), not like-mindedness. Social unity in modernity could not be based on imitation or 'herd consciousness', but had to be rooted in the unified and unifying practices of different individuals from a plurality of cultures: the classical problematic of twentieth-century liberal pluralism, with all its merits and deficiencies. It is this problematic that logically and politically generates the modern(ist) concept and problem of social control. As Park himself concluded, 'From this point of view social control is the central fact and the central problem of society' (*ibid.*: 20). No more, no less.

Indeed, Park then defined sociology itself as merely a 'method for investigating the processes by which individuals are inducted into and induced to co-operate in some sort of corporate existence which we call society' (*ibid.*). That is the exact significance of the whole field of the sociology of deviance and social control. It has been logically and politically at the heart of the philosophy of liberal pluralism, the project of corporatism and the theory of social democracy for the whole of the twentieth century. Seen from the standpoint of the roaring twenties in Chicago, it is obvious why. 'Social control' seemed so important. Without some degree of regulation rooted in some genuine collective unity its inhabitants were faced with an unlimited civil war; and, at the international level, without cooperation and regulation a further world conflagration could arise.

Mead, the social-psychological inspiration of the Chicago school, drew very similar conclusions about law and social control to those of Durkheim (Mead, 1918). He observed that the strength of the law lay in our respect for its symbolic values, not in its deterrent value. Punishment, he flatly declared, 'preserves a criminal class' (*ibid.*: 583). Law, however, did unite a population around some common ideals and interests, even though punitiveness itself did nothing towards rehabilitating the offender or eradicating crime. 'Seemingly, without the criminal the cohesiveness of society would disappear and the universal goods of the community would crumble into mutually repellent individual particles' (*ibid.*: 591). But, unlike later writers such as Tannenbaum (see Chapter 5), Mead could not see how crime control by law could be combined with crime regulation through 'comprehension of social and psychological conditions' (*ibid.*: 592). The two approaches seemed to him to be totally contradictory. In the end, Mead felt that the maturer approach was the latter, a 'social control' guided by the positive objectives of social reconstruction, the nurturance of a healthy self within the offender and a move beyond war (both civil and international). His philosophy was clear: only when we can regulate our societies without attempting to annihilate offending individuals will we know that we have conquered the roots of our civil and existential insecurity.

Given the character of their intellectual preferences, and given the practical restrictions of the mob on the limits of fieldwork, it is perhaps unsurprising that the Chicago sociologists who studied crime are famous for the view that crime and delinquency were disproportionately committed by people trying creatively to survive in the inner-city, 'transitional', zone of rooming houses and employment exchanges, a zone which had the least resources in the competitive struggle for existence (see Shaw and McKay, 1931). This area of social deprivation, according to the criminal statistics analysed by Shaw and McKay, was a criminogenic one, whichever ethnic group occupied it at any one time. The 'zone of transition', as they called it, was the run-down area next to the central business district which housed one wave of immigrants after another, before, according to the theory, they got work, established themselves and moved out to the suburbs. It was a zone of the city, they claimed, which tended to develop a 'cultural tradition' of delinquency.

In fact, although the Chicago school became famous for the thesis that 'socially disorganized' areas were criminogenic, their work was more diverse and complex than that, and, overall, is best examined chronologically in the light of the social history of the day. During the period up to Roosevelt's election in 1932, their studies tended to explain high crime and delinquency rates by reference to a neo-Darwinist ecology of the city, stressing competition and succession, combined with a Meadian learning theory which emphasized the learning of delinquent values in peer groups following clashes between immigrant and official cultures.[12] Culture was an important concept prior to 1933 as well as afterwards (see Park's essays of the 1918–37 period published in Park, 1950: Chapters 1–4, 21, 27 and 28; Shaw, 1929). The school began to thematize culture conflict as the major source of individual mental conflict (see Shaw and McKay, 1931; Finestone, 1976: 97–9; Burgess's comment in Shaw, 1930: 186; Wirth, 1964: 229), whereas towards the late thirties, the direction was towards a stronger sense of the economic and political dimensions of social *structure*.

One might expect that, given the social history of this expansionist, corrupt, free-market period, the overall argument would have been that the delinquent had, in fact, learned well the values of the dominant culture of the day and applied them creatively to acquire the property, status, pleasure, leisure and mobility so prized by that culture, despite his or her parents' attachments to older, rural, mid-European values (see also Matza and Sykes, 1961). However, the argument typically was that the delinquent had actually *failed* to learn the dominant cultural values and had learned delinquent values instead (see Burgess's statement in Shaw, 1930: 197).[13] In 1939, Edwin Sutherland was to articulate a sophisticated statement of this position in his now-famous theory of differential association (Sutherland, 1939, 1947). But it was a view that had been frequently stated in the 1920s (e.g. Thrasher, 1927; see also Finestone, 1976: 68–75). Thrasher's extensive study of Chicago gangs documented the fact that gangs had well-developed moral codes of their own, and Park had argued that, while the impersonal world of the city was dependent upon law as the major means of social control, there was a discrepancy between the legal culture and the culture of the primary (usually ethnic) group which gave rise to delinquency. Therefore, since the world of the primary group contained the only effective social control (i.e. parents), it was necessary to create agencies to try to bring the two cultures into synchrony – i.e. you get the kids to learn well the norms of the legal culture (Park, 1925b: 99–112).

Quite simply, there was always a view underpinning the research of the Chicago school which saw the growth of criminal and delinquent values as more likely when society itself was in a state of economic, political and moral de-regulation. As such, their work was implicitly and subtly critical of Hoover's *laissez-faire* policies, although in their writings they often rested content with criticisms of existing correctional policies (see Finestone, 1976: 116–49; also Smith, 1988: 218).

Wirth and culture conflict

Probably the most sophisticated theoretical essay of this period came from Louis Wirth in 1931 (reprinted in Wirth, 1964); although Frank (1925) had already recognized that social problems were an index of lifestyle- or value-conflicts between individual habits and social needs. Wirth stressed the importance of culture conflict, and, in a foretaste of things to come, indicated the implications of that recognition (see also Sutherland, 1934). Signalling the growing impatience with criminology, Wirth (1964: 229) began by declaring that 'The history of criminology as a science is a record of the successive fumbling with anthropological, psychological and sociological hypotheses which have not brought us appreciably nearer to an understanding of the problems of misconduct.' He rejected the tendency to look for a single, universal theory of criminality, and saw culture conflict as only one, albeit major, causal condition. He also critically noted the medical-psychiatric bias in scientific and professional accounts of human behaviour, arguing that cultural traditions were at least as important as personal characteristics in explaining problematic individual behaviour:

> Whatever may be the physical, the psychological and the temperamental differences between various races and societies, one thing is certain, namely that their cultures are different. Their traditions, their modes of living and making a living, the values that they place upon various types of conduct are often so strikingly different that what is punished as a crime in one group is celebrated as heroic conduct in another. The obvious fact about the relativity of social values is so strikingly expressed in some of our earliest sociological literature, such as Sumner's *Folkways*, that one may indeed wonder why it has not furnished the starting-point for the sociologists' research into delinquency and crime.
>
> (Wirth, 1964: 230–1)

Indeed; and, in so saying, Wirth signalled the launching of a tendency away from moral and cultural absolutism in American sociological theory. However, like many of his day, Wirth also bemoaned the passing of homogeneous cultures where 'class differences were negligible', where societies without crime were possible, and where formal punishment was 'unknown and unnecessary' (*ibid.*: 231). In his utopian view of such cultures (or was it a utopian projection of the world he desired in America?), Wirth supposed that

The control of the group over the individuals is complete and informal, and hence spontaneous. The community secures the allegiance, participation, and conformity of the members not through edicts of law, through written ordinances, through police, courts and jails, but through the overwhelming force of community opinion, through the immediate, voluntary, and habitual approval of the social code by all . . . Even in such a community personal rivalry and friction and the impulsive violation of the mores may perhaps never be ruled out entirely, but such a community can at least be relatively free from external and internal cultural schisms which are the source of so much of our own social strife and personal and social disorganization.

(Wirth, 1964: 231)

The mutation away from such communities and societies was prompted by trade, migration and the transfer of tradition from one generation to the next. It created problems of adjustment which could only be understood by reference to the cultural matrix involved.

From there, Wirth moved to a statement which to my knowledge was *the very first outline of the new concept of social deviation* emerging in American sociology. He began by claiming that all sociologists would have agreed at that time (1931) that *'human conduct presents a problem only when it involves a deviation from the dominant code or the generally prevailing definition in a culture, i.e., when a given society regards it as a problem'* (Wirth, 1964: 232; emphasis added). In saying this, he was at one and the same time reiterating Durkheim's position, extending Park's analysis, registering the impact of the new anthropological work on other cultures, and borrowing the term deviation from psychiatry (see *ibid.*: 233). It was also perpetuating the illusion that delinquents were actually deviating from dominant cultural codes. Wirth's synthesis was a seminal one. It led him to draw on the idea from sociological psychiatry that 'every major category of behavior deviation may be considered as an index of a social disturbance' (Frank, quoted in *ibid.*). Wirth went on to condemn 'traditional legal conceptions of crime' as very much responsible for our 'arbitrary' evaluations of 'social behavior, moral conduct, delinquency, and crime', and to welcome the increasingly 'elastic' features of the legal system (e.g. the juvenile court) and 'our determination to break away from iron-clad legalistic restrictions'. The 'official conception of crime' had fostered our refusal to 'see misconduct in the relative perspective of the cultural setting in which it occurs and which makes it into the peculiar problem which it is' *(ibid.*: 232):

Not until we appreciate that the law itself – even if in extremely arbitrary form – is an expression of the wishes of a social group, and that it is not infallibly and permanently in accord with the cultural needs and definitions of all the social groups whom it seeks to restrain, can we begin to understand why there should be crime at all.

(Wirth, 1964: 232–3)

When we bear in mind that Wirth was focusing his attention upon immigrant families, we can see the full import of what he had said. Immigration had inspired the drive to a corporate society and now that drive had to recognize the severe, social limits of legalism for the successful completion of its project.[14] *Control had to become not just social but also democratic, and deviation had to be seen as social not personal; otherwise punishment would be discriminatory and counter-productive.* In addition, personality had to be linked to culture, otherwise practical intervention was pointless, or target-less, in the face of unassailable difference. We will return to this aspect of Wirth's essay in the next chapter, for his work was very much a bridge between two eras.

Community development and immigrant culture

As Wirth's essay reminds us, the optimism and reformism of the early Chicago school work was very pronounced. There was a clear feeling that if communities could be reintegrated through 'community development' schemes then delinquency must fall. Sadly this thesis has proved wrong more than once in the twentieth century, and, as Finestone's detailed analysis confirmed (1976: 136–45), the more integrated (i.e. more middle-class) communities in Chicago were the ones which attracted the greater funding and stronger organizations, while those with the higher crime rates were much harder to support.[15] Cultural assimilation of ethnic groups through 'community development' schemes, and bridging the generation-gap through youth work, amounted to an approach which 'was almost trivial in the face of the realities of Chicago politics and economics' (Snodgrass, 1976: 16). It did little to combat the serious crime of the day. On my reading, it simply missed the point. Immigrant kids were not the main problem; nor really was cultural diversity. The root problem in Chicago was the social destructiveness of raw, free-market, individualism and, of course, the contradictory logic of capitalism itself. Entrepreneurialism was the dominant culture and youth had learned it well, whether immigrants or not. As our earlier analysis of the social history of the period indicates, to focus on cultural conflicts, value conflicts, inter-generational conflicts or community disintegration in practice amounts to little more than an extension of the general tendency in the hegemonic culture to blame juvenile immigrants for the crime problem, and a complete failure to analyse the role of the political economy of the mob and big business in creating so much serious crime in Chicago.

Yet times were to change very quickly and very soon, so that one could not make the same criticism of the post-1933 work produced by the school. That work was to become increasingly sensitive to the recalcitrance of the class structure, and therefore it was increasingly a critique of social structure (see Finestone, 1976: 93). In any case, it would be wrong to suppose that the Chicago school consciously blamed immigrants for the crime problem, or that they blamed them on racial grounds. Indeed, paradoxically, their general emphasis on the criminogenic character of run-down urban areas generally amounted to a substantial rebuttal of superficial racist assumptions which supposed that particular ethnic cultures were weak and therefore criminogenic. They showed that inner-city slum areas generated high crime rates whichever ethnic group populated them, and therefore that ethnicity was irrelevant. Moreover, for its time, Park's work on race and race relations was progressive (Park, 1950). However, the culturalist tone of their account left the Chicago school open to the more subtle charge that, in the 1920s, they were focusing upon immigrant culture rather than the market economy. In addition, a more profound, but equally effective, racial bias lay within their theoretical adoption, up to the early thirties, of neo-Darwinism, in this context subsequently to be known as the 'ecological' approach to delinquency. Weak social environments were said to produce a weak commitment to conventional values through poor cultural transmission processes (or inter-generational conflict). Weak culture (notably involving 'disintegrated' families), however much it was seen as transient and disconnected with ethnicity, was thus said to compound weak environment. But does not socially extensive crime suggest that this so-called weak commitment to conventional values was true of most of America in the roaring twenties? Extensive and open 'delinquency' across the classes looks more like a product of socially unorganized capitalism and a corresponding culture of individualistic acquisitiveness than of immigrant cultures in socially deprived ghettoes. Far from being weak, the commitment to 'conventional values' may have been all too strong in the roaring twenties: a lesson that may have to be re-learned in Fortress Europe of the 1990s, as immigrants who are sometimes all-too-committed to capitalist values are yet again targeted as responsible for inner-city crime by established populations often all-too-committed to preserving the capital they hold.

Notes

1   It is worth remembering that 'many urban progressives had been born on farms in the Mid-West and shared rural intolerance and provincialisms: when they discovered that the working classes in the cities were untrustworthy, frequently wanting more than the middle classes were prepared to concede, they too fell back on proposals which might restore order . . . Similar tensions lurked behind the rising tide of anti-immigrant feeling. Nativism had a long history behind it' (Brogan, 1985: 478–9).

2   Four hundred and sixteen black people are recorded as having been lynched between 1918 and 1927.

3   America's equivalent to the Dreyfus affair which so concerned Durkheim. Sacco and Vanzetti were two radical Italian-Americans convicted of murder on

dubious evidence. They seem to have been the internal scapegoats of the conservative and xenophobic retrenchment which ended the progressive era of
Woodrow Wilson, and which also stimulated the Prohibition legislation of
1920 (the Volstead Act). This latter law fed off the perception that most
brewers were German.

4 Perhaps for censures to become truly and fully social, a public interest in
private troubles had to be mass-marketed and legitimated. *True Confessions*
may thus be more important in the history of morality than we thought.

5 The gangleader Dion O'Banion, for example, was often to be found hard at
work in his florist's shop, arranging flowers, when he was taking time out from
his illegal rotgut racket (see Allsop, 1968: 82). Capone himself 'ran an organization which owned or had stakes in breweries, distilleries, warehouses, truck-
companies, garages, bars, nightclubs, dance-halls, restaurants, brothels, racetracks
and casinos, and which was beginning at the time of his retirement to infiltrate
its extortion racket into unions, film production and dozens of trades and
industries' (*ibid.*: 276).

6 Nietzsche anticipated all this, of course, in what ought to be a textbook for all
criminologists, *The Genealogy of Morals* (1967).

7 It is a fascinating fact that, in his youth, Canada's most famous socialist, and
first leader of the New Democratic Party, Tommy Douglas, published an MA
thesis in 1933 which was a typical eugenic study, arguing that the physically
and mentally subnormal caused much of the distress of the Depression. These
misfits were seen as likely to be the progeny of immoral women, and thus
caught up in a vicious cycle of 'immorality, promiscuity and improvidence'
(McLaren, 1990: 8). Douglas concluded that marriage should be restricted to
those holding certificates of health, that the unfit should be segregated on state
farms, and that the defective should be sterilized. His views were abandoned
after a visit to Germany in 1936, when he saw the arguments taken to their
logical conclusion (e.g. compulsory sterilization of the feeble-minded and the
beginnings of the genocide of the Jews).

8 It was only in 1972 that the sterilization legislation was repealed in Alberta and
British Columbia.

9 Possibly, since the male sociologists of this period saw the maintenance of
women and girls as the responsibility of the male breadwinner (see Thomas,
1928), they were excluded conceptually as well as linguistically.

10 As Harold Finestone, a doctoral student there in the 1930s, once told me in
conversation, in response to my query about the lack of studies on the mob
itself: the mob was the government at that time, and you don't do fieldwork
on the government, do you? The only major study of organized crime was by
Landesco (1968).

11 Anderson's book remains a classic text. It is a perfect introduction to all the
strengths and weaknesses of the sociology of the Chicago school (see the commentary by Matza, 1969).

12 I am indebted to Hal Finestone's work (1976), and to several rich conversations with him in and out of class, for sensitizing my thoughts to the stages of
development of Chicago sociology.

13 Shaw and Burgess, for example, 'chose to maximize the cultural elements in
delinquency. Indeed, they moved increasingly towards a cultural determinist
approach, that is one in which cultural elements have primacy in the definition

of specific situations in which delinquent behavior is the outcome' (Finestone, 1976: 99). Finestone, correctly in my view, sees such cultural determinism as contradicting the premises of symbolic interactionism.

14 Sociology of law really developed a great deal during the 1930s and it seems to me that this conflictful relation between legal procedure and the social was at the root of this wave of growth.

15 Perhaps the apotheosis of this idea came during the War on Poverty in the 1960s, when the well-established organizations for delinquents were more than able to use the federal funds which came their way, but not perhaps to the ends favoured by the donors (see Tom Wolfe's amusing account of this process in his *Radical Chic and Mau-Mauing the Flak-Catchers*, 1970).

3 Degeneration, cultural diversity and the New Deal

Dumb yearnings, hidden appetites are ours,
And they must have their food.

(Wordsworth, *The Prelude*)

During the 1920s, Chicago sociology did not develop the concept of crime very far, although its humanistic methodology, its awareness of immigrants' problems and its sense of the objective character of social changes had led it to see only a short gap between serious crime and minor difference. 'There but for the grace of God go I' was not its motto but, as the twenties ended and the Depression began, it increasingly looked like it.[1] Nevertheless, crime and delinquency were still partly seen as effects of the weakness of individuals, as well as outcomes of social contradictions affecting their primary associations or groups. The inner-city poor and unemployed, whatever their nationality, were still seen as a weak and defective species in the neo-Darwinist struggle for survival. A degeneracy model was still quietly active, even if the Chicagoans had turned it into an effect of social ecology.

Nevertheless, at least in principle, the Chicagoans had detached degeneracy from any one nationality. As Matza so lucidly put it:

> How describe the fact of diversity in urban America yet maintain the idea of pathology? That was the Chicago dilemma. The Chicagoans never resolved it, though they came closer than their critics imagine ... Pathology remained secure; it was merely moved on a bit from its personal lodging and relocated at the social level ... The shortcoming of the Chicago school was that it never coherently organized these experiences [of loneliness, anonymity and ennui] into humane conceptions. Instead it tried to fit them into prevalent ideas of pathology

or social disorganization . . . By describing loneliness, despair and misery, the Chicagoans had laid a groundwork on which subsequent sociologists could develop a conception of diversity that appreciated the *variable quality* and the *variable tenability* of different styles of life.

(Matza, 1969: 45, 50)

In any case, towards the end of the 1930s the analytic line of Chicagoan sociology was to change, along with the whole language of pathology.

Degeneration was to give way to social deviation. Sociological psychiatry was to meld with psychoanalytic sociology and, indeed, the whole centre of gravity of American sociology was to shift towards Washington and New York. A stronger sense of social structure was in the making; across the Atlantic, but not disconnected from a European realization that modern society was degenerating into a profoundly sick state. This new perspective on social structure and degeneration was to be developed or influenced in the 1930s by men who had often studied in Germany, just emigrated from Germany or had German parentage. Even today, being in Germany induces a stronger sense of social structure, and the fear of degeneration seems ever alive as waves of new immigrants beg entry, but in Hitler's Germany that sense of structure must have been overwhelming, its most terrifying feature being the state's targeting of degeneracy for complete annihilation. Ultimately, it began to look like degeneration was an idea for things people truly did not understand, thoroughly disapproved of and wanted to eradicate; it thus explained nothing, is violently dangerous and extremely enduring. Perhaps, then, it is not surprising that the concept of the degenerate individual is transcended in American sociology at the very same moment that the concept (and the reality) of the degenerate society appeared.

In this chapter, we will explore the intellectual conditions and features of this transformation. It is a story of a sharp deepening of the analysis of the relations between culture, personality and social structure. It will be hard to be precise about this process. What I want to do is to paint a picture of the overlapping and interrelating concepts and feelings, and their oppositions, which finally condensed in the concept of social deviation via a radically revised way of seeing human behaviour. Again, my primary concern is less with the neat delineation of all the elements of the constitution of deviation and their precise interrelations, probably an impossible task in any case, than with an insight into the changed *way of seeing* which overdetermined the emergence of the concept of social deviation. Lewis Mumford once commented, 'a thousand years separate 1940 from 1930', and so it seems sometimes.

The New Deal

The Wall Street crash of 1929 had shattered the mood of optimism, and poverty emerged on a greater scale than ever seen before. Or perhaps it was the ineradicable face it now presented. Either way the private protection racket was becoming unfashionable, and the cry for social security and honest hard work now made itself heard. In 1931, Capone was finally sentenced on tax evasion charges, although his many murderous deeds remained completely unpenalized. The party was over. It was now less than obvious that *laissez-faire*, free-market, economics plus better communications between the social divides would naturally evolve into corporate society. Leaving the development of society to the 'natural' evolution of local forces had proved a massive and disastrous failure. The stage was now taken over by the 'Feds'. They had learned much from the last few wild years of city-hall corruption and gang warfare. It was the Internal Revenue not the Chicago police who nailed Capone, and it was to be federal reforms of the social structure not local gestures at philanthropy which rescued American capitalism in the thirties.

Roosevelt (FDR) was inaugurated in 1933 with a mandate to provide a new deal and 'discipline and direction under leadership' (inaugural speech, quoted in Brogan, 1985: 536). Immediately, he set to work on the fundamental economic problems: the reform of the banking system (see Hutton, 1991b) and getting people back to work. Federal finance was made available to bail out the reliable banks, industry, farmers and homeowners. Secure credit was back. The federal government increased its powers over the whole banking system and weak banks were not allowed to reopen. To the horror of 'the city', the Securities and Exchange Commission was set up in 1934 to regulate the activities of Wall Street. Gradually, confidence in the financial side of the economy was reconstructed through the establishment of a federally regulated system of corporate financing, which was to serve America well, until Eisenhower restored the jungle of market self-regulation in the 1950s. People were also put back to work in a variety of public work schemes, 'under quasi-military discipline' (Brogan, 1985: 540), including the USA's first publicly owned electricity supplier, the Tennessee Valley Authority. The 'moral and spiritual values of work' were more important for Roosevelt than giving mere dole money. As he also said, 'honest work is the saving barrier between them [the Americans] and moral disintegration' (quoted in Bremner, 1985: 75). As in seventeenth-century France, 'labour did not seem linked to the problems it was to provoke; it was regarded, on the contrary, as a general solution, an infallible panacea, a remedy to all forms of poverty' (Foucault, 1967: 55). It was held to have the magical power to abolish poverty 'by a certain force of moral enchantment' (*ibid.*). Brogan (1985: 540), however, comments that 'it was rank socialism, but no one seemed to care' and certainly it seems that FDR's policy was regarded as socialistic. FDR had a more accurate judgement of himself. He saw himself as a 'Christian and a democrat', a unifying force who spoke for the average American. He wanted a 'cooperative commonwealth' to produce the 'age of the common man'. The working class was being federally reintegrated into a more corporate USA (in the USSR, Stalin abolished class by decree in 1936).

Prohibition was repealed, and competition from illegal capital was thus undercut overnight. Legal capitalism had been rescued and protected through what for America was undoubtedly a flood of federal legislation. In return for the suspension of the anti-trust laws, free trade unionism was permitted again. Trade union membership tripled by 1938. Faced with the higher taxes needed to fund Roosevelt's reforms, and resentful of losing control over the economy, the tycoons and magnates of big business were increasingly unhappy. Roosevelt was the people's champion and the battle-lines were sharply drawn for the 1936 election. His policies had created six million jobs and won over large sections of the electorate. He won by a landslide and the Republicans were on the verge of political extinction. His position was now very secure internally. Externally it was weaker because of continuing high trade tariffs. FDR changed nothing there. The world had sought help from its strongest economy in the early thirties yet none had been forthcoming, so it turned its back. Economic nationalism was rife, and major wars were brewing in Europe and South-east Asia as Germany and Japan expanded.

Roosevelt's success inspired progressives to believe that a new social harmony was on the agenda. The opening section of the National Industrial Recovery Act of 1934 set the tone when it talked of 'general welfare', the unity of capital and labour under federal supervision, and the conservation of natural resources (quoted in Brogan, 1985: 545). Soon, industrialists in various places agreed, in theory at least, to the abolition of child labour in the cotton-mills and the mines, minimum wage schemes and reduced working weeks.[2] Whatever its failures, its frequent abuse of administrative and constitutional power, and its red tape, the New Deal contained a clear vision of social unity and democratic capitalism which altered the tone of American culture. Hearst, the newspaper tycoon, told his editors that the 'President's program is essentially communism' (Piven and Cloward, 1971: 91). Symbolically, and perhaps more significantly than even the huge unemployment relief programme because of its lack of obvious utility for American capital, the Indian Reorganization Act of 1934 was passed and it effectively enabled the subsequent self-recovery of aboriginal societies. Land was given to them and the Act 'recognized tribal authority, encouraged the adoption of modern forms of tribal government, and did something for Indian education' (*ibid.*: 557). All sections of American society were now to be part of the American dream. By the same token, of course, new expectations of success, status, upward mobility and property acquisition were created and they required their satisfaction.

Such a dream thus created its own antithesis. Apart from big business, Roosevelt never fully captured the support of the conservative wing of his own party. Much worse, and more embarrassing politically, he received continual obstructiveness from a very conservative Supreme Court. Some key parts of his New Deal programme were ruled unconstitutional by the Court, despite the presence of support for it from Justices Brandeis, Stone and Cardozo (now legendary figures in American jurisprudence). Roosevelt's clumsy, and dictatorial, attempts to alter the political balance of the Court ended in defeat and energized his enemies all the more. At this stage, the forces for social reconstruction and social control were, ironically, but perhaps not surprisingly, being most rigorously resisted by the supreme agency of the law. The law, its splendid isolation and conservatism shored up by the sacred constitutional doctrine of the separation of powers, stood firm as the supreme political and ideological articulation of the old *laissez-faire* economy, declaring the whole National Recovery Administration unconstitutional in 1934, and in 1936 striking down the Agricultural Act (passed to rescue farming) and two other Acts which tried to establish better working conditions in mining and minimum wages for women workers in New York (Brogan, 1985: 551–64).

Roosevelt's clashes with the Supreme Court teach us an important lesson. In contemporary sociology, it is so common to see 'law and social control' spoken in the same breath, yet they are not the same, even now, and certainly in Roosevelt's time they were frequently in opposition. Social control is a concept with a very specific meaning and history – it should not be used interchangeably with law. It is a conceptual and historical error of major proportions to assume that the mechanisms of social control have always comfortably subsumed the juridical institutions, or even subsumed them at all. If such subsumption now exists it had to be fought for and constructed politically. Indeed, social democracy has also had to learn the historic value of legal procedure and administrative openness. These processes have yet to be thoroughly analysed theoretically and historically.[3]

In short, while the political and ideological climate of the New Deal emphasized the watchwords of cooperation, reconciliation and unity, there was strong opposition from the forces of individualism and *laissez-faire*. Societal needs and individual profits were still very much at odds. More-over, the Depression continued. Roosevelt may have created six million new jobs, but that still left another six million or so out of work and poverty was a long way from being eradicated. Massive discrepancies of wealth still existed between rich and poor. To make matters worse, fearing infla-tion Roosevelt himself temporarily reduced the public spending programmes during 1936–7 and showed much hesitancy. Momentum was lost and some important proposed new legislation was never passed. Appetites had been whetted and many had been frustrated – a social fact of some rel-evance to Merton's anomie theory (see pp. 120–21). Rhetoric had con-demned social uselessness and economic recklessness, yet reality spoke volumes about unemployment, the power of big business, and the con-servatism of the courts. Federal bureaucracy had grown powerful and Washington was established as the saviour of the nation, yet millions remained effectively powerless. Roosevelt had laid the foundations of the American welfare state, but no social contract had yet been concluded and many had not yet reached the bargaining table. Park's fully 'corporate' society was only half-formed. Or, on a more cynical analysis, Roosevelt had quelled popular unrest with his earlier measures and, after the 1936 landslide, he cut back and retrenched, leaving many of the poor back where they were: welfarism as a temporary strategic tactic to reintegrate disaffected groups (Piven and Cloward, 1971: 41, 111–17).

It is against the backcloth of these changes in American political economy and society that we can more fully understand what happened within the sociological analysis of crime and social control. Without such a historical understanding the profound shifts and new statements of position which were now to occur, and to create the ideational platform for the eventual full emergence of the sociology of deviance after 1945, are merely abstractions without any root, theories without a reference or points within a meaningless list. What happened in American sociology after 1933 was intimately tied to the Depression and the political responses to it within American society. Roosevelt created the political-ideological platform for these ideas to be thought. He unleashed the ideological forces of progressivism within American sociology. Or as some have argued, by the end of 1937 the demands of the labour movement and the interests of the unemployed gave the New Deal a social-democratic tinge never before present in US reform politics. But, by the late thirties, the platform was only half-formed and the Depression still under way. The forces of classical capitalism were still well established. Reform was partial. A dream of open-ended social ascent was mobilized. Uncondensed in a completely new reality, it festered as an open sore within the collective psyche impatiently awaiting its remedy.

Art, degeneration and national-social reconstruction

Gramsci died in 1937. Always aware of the important role of ideology and culture in the construction of political hegemonies, and a sometime theatre critic, he had articulated the most sophisticated socialist understanding yet of the operations of power within modernity. Like Hitler and Roosevelt, he had understood that political hegemony is an active project that must engage the national imagination and the moral constitution of the people. Even the King of England could not marry a divorcée, and especially an American. Edward's abdication in 1936 was an eloquent testimony to the importance of morality and emotion in the construction of systems of power. In the same way, Speer's architecture and the 1936 Berlin Olympics spoke to the specific cultural symbolism embedded in any political order. We can all dream, and many did in the thirties, but the contents of the dreams vary enormously. In this section, we will see what the art of the period offers us about the contents of those dreams.

The New Deal in art

The New Deal was not just a series of events in political economy. It had an affinity with 'all that is denoted by the term "culture"' and sustained a substantial 'cultural synthesis' (Lawson, 1985: 155, 173). It was part of a general cultural transformation, part of the search for a cultural democracy. Berle and Means had argued that the US economy had matured. It was moving beyond the frontier and the dream of endless resources and opportunities. Americans now had to pool resources, plan, equalize, and thus enable a cultural shift from a world of materialism to the spheres of the intellect, the spirit and art. John Dewey, in a number of texts between 1929 and 1935, had argued that individuality is best realized in association and that the local community was the best vehicle for such growth-producing association. His *Art and Experience* of 1934 saw art as the highest expression of individuality and art as most beautifully derived from social experience. His work generally displayed an abiding concern with ethics, something some New Dealers were not too anxious about. FDR himself, for example, could be 'careless of civil liberties' (Badger, 1989: 8): the Japanese-American concentration camps, the investigation of political opponents by the FBI and the toleration of the segregation of and discrimination against the blacks were all telling examples.

After the crash of 1929, 'the technological promise of the expanding urban culture seemed less reassuring as a substitute for personal accomplishment' (Taylor, 1979: 192). Artists wanted to find their place in the culture. Some (for example, Wood and Curry) tried to rediscover rural values, memorializing in painting the homely practices and folk heroes that survived the onslaught of dehumanizing cities; others focused on effects on the individual and what might be done about it (for example, Gropper's cartoon picture of a sweatshop, and Shahn's unemployed at the railroad or his *Passion of Sacco and Vanzetti*). Rural regionalism in art had strong nationalist, conservative, implications in the way that it extolled the virtues of small-town, Mid-West, all-American life. Its values mirrored so much of the sociological writing on social pathology in the USA since the turn of the century.

Since 1900, cultural relativists and social democrats, such as the social psychologist G. H. Mead, had opposed discrimination against immigrants and blacks by arguing for the distinctness of primary cultural groups and the notion of a 'culturally unified nation of distinctive local groups' (Lawson, 1985: 160; Melossi, 1990: 118). Some of this feeling was later to be captured poignantly by Bob Dylan's song 'Pity the poor immigrant' and the whole *John Wesley Harding* album. Such yearnings, expressed clearly in the Chicago sociology of the twenties, were to receive their food under Roosevelt. The 1935 Federal Art project gave artists a lot of work to do, and art became a live element in many local communities. Art reached out, became a unique feature of FDR's national reconstruction, and became more integrated into society, although by 1938 'un-American art' (i.e. art with 'communist' leanings) was under severe scrutiny (Taylor, 1979: 199). The period became a nationalistic one of appreciation of things American, the vernacular, culture and anti-élitist populism. It is a fact which gives new meaning to the description of symbolic interactionist sociology's faithful accounts of local community culture as 'appreciative' (Matza, 1969).

The Federal Art project rescued American art and stimulated a journey from mediocrity to excellence. The New York Museum of Modern Art had been founded in 1929 and many European artists came to the USA in the late thirties. They were welcomed, and the 1938 Van Gogh exhibition 'took the country by storm' (Taylor, 1979: 201). The American art world was beginning its rise to pre-eminence within the post-war art world, New York taking over from Paris, at the very same time that the victories of modernist art were being so abusively denounced in Munich; when Europe was fighting to preserve the kind of world that could sustain art at all.

During the thirties, in the USA, there was a great surge of artistic interest in the deep reaches of the psyche, nature, culture and religion. Freud was making his mark, and so was anthropology. The violent sexual imagery of Surrealism was one notable manifestation of this interest in the unconscious, as well as a sign of the growing violence of the period. The European Surrealists were the precursors of the American Abstract Expressionism of the forties. Their work became immensely popular in the USA, from the thirties onward, especially since New York became a Surrealist refuge around 1940 (for Breton, Masson, Tanguy and Dalí). Ernst's *Europe after the Rain* (1940–2) portrayed the sense of foreboding – a scenario which looks like an aftermath of a nuclear attack.

Pictures like Magritte's *Rape* (1934), Bellmer's *Doll* (1935), Giacometti's *Woman with Her Throat Cut* (1932) and Picasso's *Seated Bather* (1930) reveal the full power of the silent movie that was running in the back of the European unconsciousness at this time. *The Seated Bather* described the fear of women's sexual power which Dalí openly admitted. Fear of women, frustration and the growing sense of the violence in all things were an integral part of the thirties exploration of the psyche. The philosopher Bataille, so revered later by Foucault, supposed that 'copulation is the parody of crime' (quoted in Hughes, 1981: 255). The sense of apocalypse was growing, and not just in Surrealist form. Grosz's savage indictments of humanity, and particularly the German version, were revived from the 1920s to acquire a new popularity in America, to which he eventually emigrated. Giacometti's *Woman with Her Throat Cut* was part scorpion and part sacrificial victim: Germany, in astrology the nation of the scorpion, was stirring.

Surrealism is more important to our tale than even this, however. Its important connection with the sociology of deviance is through the mediation of Freud and the discovery of the unconscious. As we will see later in this chapter, and in Chapter 4, the American appropriation of Freud and the growth of a 'pop psychology' were crucial preconditions of the formation of the concept of social deviation and of the whole perspective of the sociology of deviance. André Breton, the leader of the Surrealist group, had worked at a psychiatric centre during the First World War and his helping of patients to recall their dreams was, he said, to constitute 'almost all the groundwork of Surrealism . . . interpretation, yes, always, but above all liberation from constraints – logic, morality and the rest – with the aim of recovering their original powers of spirit' (quoted in Hughes, 1981: 212). The first Surrealist manifesto was in 1924 and many of its great works were painted around that time (for example, by Miró and Dalí), so, not surprisingly, many of the Surrealists had not read Freud's work and their purpose was, usually, somewhat differently framed. They were heirs to an older tradition of romanticism whose key idea was that the study and liberation of mental disorder gave access to the 'dark side' of the human mind, what Foucault was to call the realm of unreason (see Chapter 11). Their art thus celebrated, exhibited and emancipated the bestial, the infantile, the insane, the naive, the violent, the raw, the sexual, the feminine, the fantasy, the poetic, the excretion and the imaginative interchangeability of objects and meanings. All the suppressed human materials which constituted the diabolic root of degeneracy and later the emotional-moral substratum of social deviance were let out from their cages in an orgy of passionate self-cleansing. Deviance was emerging from its enforced hibernation in the unconscious to become a fully social form.

The most famous of their group, Salvador Dalí, illustrated the significance of Surrealism perfectly for our purposes, especially since he was eventually expelled from the Surrealist group and declared himself a 'deviant surrealist' (quoted in Maddox, 1990: 87). He always said he was the true Surrealist. Dalí revelled in his genius, deviance and madness, always maintaining that the only thing that distinguished him from the madman was that he was not mad: 'I was to become the prototype *par excellence* of the phenomenally retarded "polymorphous pervert" having kept intact all the reminiscences of the nursling's erogenous paradises' (quoted in Maddox, 1990: 9). Dalí read Freud and Nietzsche in the early 1920s and put himself through agonizing tortures of self-analysis, assessing his dreams in minute detail and acquiring an acute graphic familiarity with his own childhood obsessions, fears and desires. His memories of his early experiences and the icons of his obsessions and traumas were to be externalized consistently in his paintings from the mid-1920s onwards. Indeed, without any knowledge of Dalí's autobiography it would be virtually impossible to make an intelligent reading of his paintings.[4] A confirmed oppositionist and exhibitionist, Dalí committed himself to a sustained exposition of the non-rational, his dreams, his fixations and his philosophies: 'My whole ambition in painting is to manifest the images of concrete irrationality in terms of authoritative precision . . . images which for the moment can neither be explained nor reduced by logical systems or rational approaches' (Dalí, quoted in Descharnes and Néret, 1992: 126). He described his method as 'paranoiac-critical activity', whose 'infinite possibilities . . . can only originate in obsession' (*ibid.*). Like other Surrealists, Dalí was committed to preventing reason from preventing him expressing his feelings on canvas. The unconscious was given free rein, and consciously so, with precision. Free association ruled in this calculated assault on all known relations between signifier and signified. Consciously, Dalí sought to liberate himself from the rule of his father, and all other authority (including Breton and

Picasso). As with other Surrealists, this liberation of the unconscious was often to reveal disfigured images of women and of women as archetypally unreal mannequins, but also images of cannibalism, rural bliss (Northern Catalunya), masturbation, masks, narcissism, individual and social dependency, life and death, human reproduction and supersession – all interspersed with icons of childhood obsessions.

Exhibited in New York in 1931, Dalí became very popular in the USA and eventually took refuge in California from 1940 to 1948. He later became a close friend of Jack Warner and worked with Disney and Hitchcock. He had become identified with the sublime but precise fantasy, a master of the magical and the absurd. Gradually, he became one of the household names of the twentieth century. A master of public relations, he became known popularly as a comic of the absurd, alongside Harpo Marx whose sketch he once did, rather than the Catalan ascetic and explorer of the unconscious he more often was. 'Reality' was subverted, and the hidden reality of the mind sublimated. Life, and death, were demonstrably ambiguous as catachresis was legitimized. He was a provocative illusionist, and his works are too diverse to summarize here. For my purposes, *The Persistence of Memory* (1931), where watches are made to melt like Camembert around the dismembered head of the painter against a background of rocky beach typical of Northern Catalunya, and *Metamorphosis of Narcissus* (1937), where a hand holding an egg sprouting a narcissus flower mimics the figure of Narcissus contemplating his navel, are perhaps the most significant of his paintings. All sense of normality was flouted: time melted, memory and reflection provided little certainty and things changed places with their opposites. Dalí's achievement was to make the inner deviance of reality tangible, perceptible and recognizable. A true modernist, he had a total disgust with the cannibalism of the mechanical, consumer, world and our subservience to its rationality. Things were truly pregnant with their contrary. Deviance, after Dalí, could not help but be recognized as part of the normal. It was becoming the truth of the superficially conventional. But, we should not forget, Dalí always saw himself as a traditionalist in his acceptance of the depth of existing spiritual reality, and his love of his native geography was no different from that of the American folk artists of the early thirties.

Of course, Catalan nationalism was soon to be assaulted violently by Franco's fascism. Like most other Surrealists, Dalí got out, rightly supposing that the fascists would not see his art as anything other than degenerate. The German bombing of a Basque town during the Spanish Civil War was not only a taste of things to come, it inspired Picasso to paint *Guernica* in 1937, a year that is recurrent throughout this chapter. In its tortured forms, *Guernica* brilliantly expressed the pain and agony of the pre-modern world being obliterated by the excrescences of modernism. It is 'the most powerful invective against violence in modern art' (Hughes, 1981: 110). After the war, with full national reconstructions well under way, the drift to a disengaged abstractionism with little clear direction and a strong sense of meaninglessness overtook many an artist. It was difficult for many to sustain belief in any of the grand systems of political ideology of the twentieth century. Both the mechanical world of the free market and nationalistic socialism had taken a battering. Hughes's observation is that *Guernica* was 'the last modern painting of major importance that took its subject from politics with the intention of changing the way large numbers of people thought and felt about power' (*ibid.*).

'Entartete Kunst': *art and degeneracy*

George Grosz, one of the Berlin Dadaists, arguably a founder, is particularly important for our tale. Like other members of this socialistic movement, one of his most frequent images is that of the war-cripple, but his portrayals of the Weimar republic were equally savage. In *Daum Marries* (1920) the husband is a dummy, 'a zero whom society has programmed with certain desires to turn him into an efficient consumer. Grosz makes this clear through the disembodied hands manipulating the information in his head. They rhyme neatly with the other hand, seen tickling Daum's nipple to keep her interest up. The only possible bride for such a bachelor is a whore, whose passions are as mechanical as his actions' (Hughes, 1981: 75). The prostitute was frequently attacked in Grosz's paintings, with no less violence than capitalism itself. She was the bringer of syphilis and ruin, and the economy was evil itself. In Grosz's Germany, apart from the workers' movement, all human relations were sick and poisonous, irrevocably tainted by evil. His vision is of an epoch which 'is sailing down to its destruction' (quoted in Cole and Gealt, 1989: 284). For Grosz, like other Dadaists, the Weimar republic, Germany's weak social democracy of the twenties, was itself 'a political mutant, a war casualty, displaying the surface marks of democracy while leaving the real power in the hands of capitalist, cop, and Prussian officer' (Hughes, 1981: 73). Like Dix and others, Grosz had served at the front and had been irrevocably crippled mentally by the experience. His emigration to America in the thirties did not leave behind his hatred of Nazism, which inspired 'increasingly violent and brutal imagery' (Cole and Gealt, 1989: 285). He ended up in an asylum.

The significance of Grosz for us is that the emigration of European art to America did not and could not sever its roots in angst. In sociology, after the war, the émigrés continued to wrestle with new explanations of the dis-ease, and the locals lapsed into the fantasy of a non-ideological cybernetic social system immune from all major disease. American art after the war may have tried to transcend the violence and suffering of social reality through its imagery of the eternal and the healing power of nature, but it was a method destined to failure; just as any sociology, such as post-war American sociology of deviance, which glossed the violent roots and paranoid-critical character of social deviation as both practice and category, had also to fail. Those roots have a long history, relating well beyond capitalism to some well-established archetypes of human consciousness, and their character at times is intransigently evil. They are not unchangeable, and they are not always bad, but they are not discoverable at the surface. The events of the thirties stimulated American art to explore the unconscious to a greater extent than ever before, and later American sociology became more psychoanalytic; but the sociology, like the art, can be seen to have papered over the problematic of degeneration. For, while it was 'cool' to spoof away the idea of degenerate individuals or groups, it was also all too easy for Americans to ignore or forget the European memories of degenerating societies. Memory was indeed persistent. It was to take the Vietnam war before America was truly shaken out of its postwar fantasyland. Suffice it to say here that degeneration may have been a totally problematic concept within the social sciences, with roots in a now-discredited eugenics and a historically obsolete vein of psychiatry, but its reference points in social reality, history and the psyche were still all too real during the 1950s.

What Grosz had painted in the twenties was, in 1937, to vent its spleen on art itself. *Entartete Kunst* was the name of the most popular art exhibition of all time.[5] It took place in Munich, significantly in the anthropological museum, before touring Germany and Austria for the next four years. It attracted over four million people. Its name in English is degenerate art. Its business was to display, insult and discredit many famous works of modernism, notably works of Expressionism, Dadaism, Cubism and Constructivism. The exhibition contained several great works by German painters such as Beckmann, Nolde and Dix, apart from classics by Kandinsky, the Bauhaus group and Chagall. It derided avant-garde art, what it portrayed as Jewish art (misleadingly, for few of the artists were Jewish), favourable representations of black people, black music (jazz in particular) and the whole culture of individualism. The abuse took the form of graffiti, commentary and extracts from speeches by Hitler or Goebbels next to the art works. It was a concerted and conscious attack on modernist art and the whole culture of individualism as an anthropological deformation. An alternative showing of similar art in London soon afterwards, as a direct response to the Munich exhibition, was supported by, among others, Picasso.

Entartete in German 'suggests biology, natural growth, a natural species gone so far off its genetic course as to be virtually unrecognisable – a perverse mutation. For the Nazis this was an exact characterisation of modern art. It was not simply odd or avant-garde, or a bit decadent, but actually diseased' (Collings, 1992). Modern art was specifically represented as insane. The captions and speeches in the exhibition included 'Insanity at any price', 'The negro becomes the racial ideal of a degenerate art', 'The Jewish longing for the wilderness reveals itself', 'Insult to German womanhood', 'Revelations of the Jewish racial soul', 'Cretin' and 'Whore' (the last two by pictures of nudes). There was a systematic slandering of the vision of modern artists as similar to the vision of the mentally ill. Modernist artists were censured as being like the insane, the deformed, the homosexual, the black, the communist, the criminal – sick, socially useless, mutants, suffering from racial inferiority, who might have to be destroyed. Some of the exhibited paintings were condemned simply because they displayed too much sensitivity; others (for example, by Nolde) were by members of the Nazi party baffled to find that their imaginative vision was held to outweigh their loyalty to the party; and a few were there by mistake. Approved Nazi art was of the neo-classical, imperial, type which stressed power, obedience and healthy bodies. What they called degenerate art starkly revealed their own mentality, that of the archaic, little man with big fears about modernity.

The mentality displayed in the censure was a sparse, crude, simple, ignorant and fearful one which seemed to want to reduce the wonders of German culture to the lowest common denominator. It could be seen, ironically, as a degenerate version of German culture; a version where the culture had shrunk to its lowest and simplest form but in a dis-eased state. Hitler had plainly stated that he would not tolerate any art which was not 'immediately comprehensible to the average German'. Indeed, Goering said that the word culture made him want to reach for his revolver. Following the extensive Nazi book-burning of the thirties, one can only conclude that the philosophy of degeneracy is one that fears and forbids the exercise of the imagination, in case it should lead to the exercise of choice and independence. Obedience to the Führer was central to Nazi ideology, and it is striking how fiercely *Entartete Kunst* denounced imagination, sensitivity, individualism and modernism. Collings argues that the exhibition was directly related to the pogroms and the death camps, for it used modern art to prove that degeneration existed and to legitimate its destruction. Gilman (1985: 235–7) suggests that its linking of Jewishness with insanity prepared the way for the exterminations to move from the mentally ill to the Jews. While they are no doubt both correct, it is also worth observing that to prove the existence of degeneration the Nazis had to draw successfully upon something, namely the extensive fears in Germany of a social-democratic, multicultural, weakening of the national heritage. The little man and the lowest common denominator appealed to many. The positive values of social-democratic multiculturalism were at the root of Roosevelt's success in an opposite direction. In general, it was a time for the common man, comprehensible art, cultural nationalism, statism and the return to simple values. It was a time to stem the tide of conflict seen as coming from cultural difference. In Germany, it was a time for the voices of raw, conservative, reaction to modernity to display their anger, fear and philistinism. However, after Hitler, the term degeneration was never to have any credibility again within the human sciences, and its field of operation was annexed by the concept of social deviation. So let us not forget Hitler's chilling words:

> Even before the turn of the century an element began to intrude into our art which up to that time could be regarded as entirely foreign

and unknown. To be sure, even in earlier times there were occasional aberrations of taste, but such cases were rather artistic derailments, to which posterity could attribute at least a certain historical value, than products no longer of an artistic degeneration, but of a spiritual degeneration that had reached the point of destroying the spirit . . . it is the business of the state, in other words, of its leaders, to prevent a people being driven into the arms of spiritual madness.

(Hitler, quoted in Gilman, 1985: 233–4)

The social and psychological character of action

The connections between individual existence and social structure were never more blatantly obvious in the USA than in the thirties. Unemployment on so vast a scale could hardly be put down to individual fecklessness. The collapse of the whole banking system could not be attributed to individual speculators. Nor could any of it be blamed on uniquely American characteristics, since the Depression was worldwide. The scenario demanded a more general and more profound sociological analysis than that provided by the Chicago school hitherto, and whole populations screamed for their saviour, their *Übermensch* (Nietzsche, 1967).

Reich argued in 1942 that six thousand years of authoritarian patriarchy all over the globe had produced a deeply rooted 'character-structure'[6] whose subservient psyche was 'incapable of freedom',[7] dependent upon authority and not about to be revised overnight by a short burst of social reformism (or, as we have seen, by communism):

In the form of fascism, mechanistic, authoritarian civilization reaps from the suppressed little man only what it has sown in the masses of subjugated human beings in the way of mysticism, militarism, automatism, over the centuries. This little man has studied the big man's behaviour all too well, and he reproduces it in a distorted and grotesque fashion. The fascist is the drill sergeant in the colossal army of our deeply sick, highly industrialized civilization . . . It follows from all this that the social measures of the past three hundred years can no more cope with the mass pestilence of fascism than an elephant (six thousand years) can be forced into a foxhole (three hundred years).

(Reich, 1970: 17, 31)

Would-be saviours arose and were duly mythologized and worshipped. America's was Roosevelt, Germany's was Hitler, and the two were frequently, if somewhat mistakenly, compared. The cartoon character Superman was born and the welfare of the whole was to be preserved by individual magic. Yet, of course, for many decades to come, the concept of magic was to remain neglected within the sociological analysis of Western societies, and reserved mainly for the burgeoning anthropology of what were still called primitive cultures.

The previous period had delivered a comprehensive and comprehensible message about the inherent social costs of free-market individualism, but its recipients in the thirties could only read it through the clouded ideological blinkers of their national cultures. In a funny sort of way, this fact was directly reflected in a new vision whose propositions gradually became axiomatic within American sociology during the 1930s, and which focused upon the prism of culture. The action of the Other (the criminal, the working class, the communist or fascist, the female, the primitive, the mad, the child and the eccentric) was now increasingly seen as social, as physical movement given meaning and coherence by the individual actor's cultural attitudes, perceptions and obligations, yet also as still distinctively 'psychological', as behaviour driven by strange, autonomous psychic forces to some degree unconscious to the individual. It was as if the new conception of a multiplicity of social actions of equal moral weight in a complex, multicultural, society could not yet be adopted without the retention of older notions of individual pathology, or of deep-rooted fears of social degeneration being caused by intercourse with defective individuals or groups. The actions of the powerful, the normal, the scientist, the male, the Westerner, indeed the 'self' that authored so much of the dominant discourse, remained, of course, 'rational', not 'psychological', needing no other justification or understanding outside of its own supposed transcendental logic. Difference was being embraced, but without a 'letting-go' of ancient prejudices. It must have been like sex with the devil: exciting and exotic, but terrifying and self-destructive. Nothing would be the same ever again; a large part of a long psychic past would have to be released. This is not exactly the period of *Sammy and Rosie Get Laid*, but rather a time of Margaret Mead's 'shocking' revelations about the sex lives of the Samoans. Miscegenation, of course, had long been feared. The British colonists, and the American South, had been at their most punitive and irrational in dealing with the black accused of raping a white woman. Hitler took the fears of miscegenation to a new, apocalyptic, level. In the social sciences, the concept of culture was the field within which the West wrestled with its demons, its psycho-sexual roots and its conscience.

Degeneration, psychoanalysis and sociology

The European critical consciousness of the day was, in my view, mirrored uncannily, and extremely creatively, in the new teachings of what might be called psychoanalytically influenced sociology.[8] This new formation within sociology was at this stage somewhat amorphous and nebulous; the battle-lines between left and right had yet to be firmly drawn (indeed this sociology's critique of orthodox Marxism was as important as its critique of behaviourism: Jacoby, 1977). But the problems it was trying to explore, and its undoubted insights (which remain very influential today), can be clearly seen in Fromm's precocious but elementary essay of 1929, entitled

'Psychoanalysis and sociology' (Fromm, 1989). A more developed statement in a later text is a better indication of his position:

> This . . . is directed not only against sociological theories which
> explicitly wish to eliminate psychological problems from sociology
> (like those of Durkheim and his school), but also against those theories
> that are more or less tinged with behaviouristic psychology. Common
> to all these theories is the assumption that human nature has no
> dynamism of its own and that psychological changes are to be under-
> stood in terms of the development of new 'habits' as an adaptation
> to new cultural patterns. These theories, though speaking of the
> psychological factor, at the same time reduce it to a shadow of
> cultural patterns . . . Though there is no fixed human nature, we cannot
> regard human nature as infinitely malleable and able to adapt itself
> to any kind of conditions without developing a psychological dynam-
> ism of its own. Human nature, though being the product of historical
> evolution, has certain inherent mechanisms and laws, to discover
> which is the task of psychology.
>
> (Fromm, 1941: 29)

Durkheim's legacy was clearly being challenged for its inadequate theory
of human psychic processes, and so was that of the Chicago school. Fromm's
work was seminal and launched a wholly new problematic which to this
day remains a challenge to Western psychology. For Fromm, it was not
enough to theorize collective representations as the mere outcome of
mundane social interactions. The dead hand of the psychic past always
hung over our responses to the immediate. Experience was not just temporal, but also archetypal. Interaction was very rarely a fluid exchange by
fully functioning, open, reflexive and responsive individuals; that was a
goal to be aimed at through extensive therapy. First, we had to recognize
that the reality was one of empty, superficial, often oppressive, interactions
by individuals committed primarily to themselves, to the retention of their
property and social standing, and to the retention of six thousand years'
worth of repressive psychological baggage.

Clearly, a merger between sociology and psychoanalysis was beginning
to take place. Fromm had, in fact, moved to Chicago in 1933, to its
Psychoanalytic Institute, and, as we shall see in Chapter 4, that may have
had an indirect impact on the emergence of the concept of social deviation
in 1937. Later, after the war, the leftist version of this new formation in
sociology was usually known as critical theory,[9] while the conservative
version was to be most clearly articulated in the work of Talcott Parsons.[10]

However, Meadian social psychology, following Dewey's praxis-oriented
line of thought and still producing a descriptive and superficial account
(dream?) of individuals' reflexive interactions with social conditions, was
very popular within American sociology in the thirties. This approach,
embodied in much of the symbolic interactionist sociology of the Chicago
school, remained clearly at the forefront of American sociology until around

the time of Roosevelt's re-election in 1936 when it began to be challenged. It too emphasized the ideational-social component of human action, but not so much in terms of an external, historically loaded, 'culture' as in the shape of the immediate 'significant other', the concept of the people we choose daily as significant in assessing the meaning of our own actions. When we add up all our present significant others in the form of an assumed social audience, we get what Mead called the generalized other. Mead's conception of the generalized other pointed up the way that our actions are always structured by our definition of self as well as of the immediate, local, situation we are in, and that these definitions always involved our abstracted expectations and perceptions of the reactions of our significant others. It is a concept which was to have monumental significance within the sociology of deviance in its heyday during the 1960s, and which was undoubtedly of central importance to many in the formation of the sociological conception of deviation at the end of the thirties. The following, unfortunately turgid, passage, put together from one of his student's notes, captures the exact sense in which G. H. Mead's concept of the generalized other was *the* concept which the sociology of deviance used later to link the individual to the social structure, the micro-world of everyday life to the society as a whole:

> The organized community or social group which gives to the individual his unity of self may be called the 'generalized other'. *The attitude of the generalized other is the attitude of the whole community* . . . only in so far as he takes the attitudes of the organized social group to which he belongs toward the organized, co-operative activity or set of such activities in which that group as such is engaged, does he develop a complete self or possess the sort of complete self he has developed. And on the other hand, the complex co-operative processes and activities and institutional functionings of organized human society are also possible only in so far as every individual involved in them or belonging to that society can take the general attitudes of all other such individuals with reference to these processes and activities and institutional functionings, and to the organized social whole of experiential relations and interactions thereby constituted – and can direct his behaviour accordingly.
>
> *It is in the form of the generalized other that the social process influences the behaviour of the individuals involved in it and carrying it on, i.e., that the community exercises control over the conduct of its individual members*; for it is in this form that the social process or community enters as a determining factor into the individual's thinking.
>
> (Mead, 1962: 154–5; emphasis added)

In Chicago sociology up to the mid-thirties, this notion had involved a focus on communities and upon parent–child relations, rather than upon the significance of others involved in state institutions, the media or the mob. Perhaps this was because the logical emphasis of the theory was upon those whom we *chose* to recognize as significant others, rather than those whose significance has been more or less *forced* upon us. It thus had said little about the macro-structure, the history or the structuring effects, on our symbolic interactions, of the nation's political economy and its institutional forces. Inevitably then, until the mid-thirties, it had nothing powerful to say about the ideological effects of fundamental divisions in the social structure, or the 'dark stirrings of the unconscious' (Jung). Nevertheless, the passage from Mead above shows clearly how enormously important any social deviation had now become to the realization of the corporate society envisaged by Park. Social control had been conceptualized as the central task in establishing a corporate society in America, and it was to be achieved through persuading a diverse population to internalize a single generalized other, that of the community. Sharing the community's attitudes was pivotal to the whole project of a social-democratic America in the early work of the Chicago school.

The other, significantly different, view of the matter, owing much to the increasing influence of the thought of Freud, was developing in the 1930s, and not just in Europe. This was the view that the expression of powerful and evil social forces, or of pathological tendencies in modern societies, could best be explained by a historically informed social theory which had a psychoanalytic dimension built into it. Against Marxism, but in support of an historical perspective, Freud had written earlier in the century:

> a child's super-ego is in fact constructed on the model not of its parents but of its parents' super-ego; the contents which fill it are the same and it becomes the vehicle of tradition and of all the time-resisting judgments of value which have propagated themselves in this manner from generation to generation. You may easily guess what important assistance taking the super-ego into account will give us in the understanding of the social behaviour of mankind – in the problem of delinquency, for instance . . . It seems likely that what are known as materialistic views of history sin in under-estimating this factor. They brush it aside with the remark that human 'ideologies' are nothing other than the product and superstructure of their contemporary economic conditions. That is true, but very probably not the whole truth. Mankind never lives entirely in the present. The past, the tradition of the race and of the people, lives on in the ideologies of the super-ego, and yields only slowly to the influences of the present and to new changes.
>
> (Freud, 1973: 99)

To some, psychoanalysis also seemed to offer more to sociological theory than behaviourism or symbolic interactionism. American sociology was developed in this direction by a variety of scholars, such as Parsons, who were well read in European social-scientific literature without ever becoming committed Freudians, and by the escape to freedom (i.e. New York or

Chicago) in the 1930s of many critical German intellectuals steeped in the literature and debates of psychoanalysis such as Fromm, Reich, Marcuse, Adorno and Horkheimer.[11] No doubt also, the very enthusiastic general reception in the USA given to psychoanalytic concepts from the 1920s onwards must have encouraged sociologists to consider their value. The distinctively American and quite parochial character of a Chicago sociology focused on community was now to be challenged by a more cosmopolitan, more federal and more theoretical social analysis focused on society as a whole. The centre of gravity of American sociology was shifting back to the East Coast. Freud was beginning to impact upon the analysis of social structure, just around the time that Washington was beginning to create a social structure worthy of analysis. To understand fully this new psychoanalytically influenced sociology, an area of great importance to our overall argument, a little detour through psychoanalysis is necessary.

Freud's *Civilization and Its Discontents* was published in 1925, Wilhelm Reich published *The Mass Psychology of Fascism* in 1933 and Erich Fromm *Escape from Freedom* in 1941. The titles alone tell the story. A growing crisis was looming on the horizon of the whole globe. There were ample grounds for suspecting the truth of Freud's belief that the repressed unconscious contained some horrific things which would cause great pain if they were unleashed. With much experience of being outsiders, Jewish intellectuals, in particular, had good grounds for being concerned with mental illness. As Gilman (1985: 153–4) observes, illness, and psychopathology especially, had long been linked with Jews, as a sign of their cosmopolitanism and their close links with urbanism and modern life. By 1880, Gilman writes, the Jews were firmly linked, in anthropological and psychiatric circles, with psychopathology as exemplified in the views of Charcot and Kraeplin. Indeed, Cesare Lombroso, the founder of criminal anthropology who is often mistakenly cited as the founder of criminology, wrote *Anti-Semitism and the Jews in the Light of Modern Science* (1893) in order to counter this biologistic view of alleged Jewish pathology. Lombroso later became famous, of course, for his studies portraying criminals and prostitutes as constitutionally degenerate. Well, ideology and self-interest have always had an intimate relationship, as we see when we realize that Lombroso was Jewish. His book argued that the Jews were indeed suffering excessively from degenerative tendencies but that this was the result of their continuous persecution throughout European history (see Gilman, 1985). It is a pity he could not have extended his social awareness of the impact of persecution to the working class, women and blacks (not to mention Southern Italians), instead of reserving it for his own significant others. In any case, by the twentieth century, leading eugenicists, such as Nordau, had openly asserted the degeneracy of the Jews, and his book *Degeneration* had been dedicated to Lombroso. Thus, as Gilman argues, the decadence of the city and modern civilization is linked to psychopathology and sexual deviation through the figure of the Jew, and therein lies a major part of the significance of Freud for urban American thought and culture in the 1920s and 1930s.

The fear of the degeneration of the species was strong in Europe as well as in North America in the 1920s, and the figure of the Jew even more relevant. As we saw in the previous chapter, from the point of view of collective biologism, negative historical moments were being explained by a concept of degeneration, in the same way as biological retrogressions. When the Depression precipitated its projection on to a scapegoat in the Germany of the 1930s, the dominant ideology had long prepared its racial target. It is therefore unsurprising that degeneration is a theme echoed and much revised in the writings of Freud.

Freud had worked under Charcot and his early work was constantly involved with the concept of degeneration and its applicability to psychological development. He himself used the concept in his earlier writings. Indeed, as so often seems to be the case, deviant sexuality was the sign of degeneracy which attracted the analyst's interest (see Foucault, 1980b, for an account of the history of psychiatry in relation to deviant sexuality; Szasz, 1972, 1973; Gilman, 1985: 215–16). However, Freud gradually became strongly disinclined to attribute many psychopathologies to any kind of pre-natal degeneracy and shifted the focus of his explanations to the first few years of the child's life, i.e. he moved towards a purely psychological account (Gilman, 1985: 204–16). In 1905, talking specifically about sexual deviations,[12] he makes some remarks on the concept of degeneracy which are as good as any made later by commentators on the problems of the concepts of crime and deviance:

> The attribution of degeneracy in this connection is open to the objection which can be raised against the indiscriminate use of the word in general. It has become the fashion to regard any symptom which is not obviously due to trauma or infection as a sign of degeneracy. Magnan's classification of degeneracy is indeed of such a kind as not to exclude the possibility of the concept of degeneracy being applied to a nervous system whose general functioning is excellent. This being so, it may well be asked whether an attribution of 'degeneracy' is of any value or adds anything to our knowledge. It seems wiser only to speak of it where several serious deviations from the normal are found together, and the capacity for efficient functioning and survival seem severely impaired.
>
> (Freud, 1977: 48–9)

Later in this essay, in rejecting the view of 'inverts' as degenerate, Freud pointedly adds that inversion (e.g. homosexuality) is also found 'in people whose efficiency is unimpaired, and who are distinguished by specially high intellectual development and ethical culture' (*ibid.*: 49). By 1917, Freud was openly rejecting concepts of degeneracy, hereditary origin and constitutional inferiority as effective explanatory concepts,[13] and stating that psychiatry made careful investigations to be able to say to the ego that

'Nothing has entered into you from without; a part of the activity of your own mind has been withdrawn from your knowledge and from the command of your own will' (quoted in Gilman, 1985: 208). In another powerful passage from that year, on obsessional neurosis, he also wrote that

> Psychiatry gives names to the different obsessions but says nothing further about them. On the other hand it insists that those who suffer from these symptoms are 'degenerates'. This gives small satisfaction; in fact it is a judgment of value – a condemnation rather than an explanation. We are supposed to think that every possible sort of eccentricity may arise in degenerates. Well, it is true that we must regard those who develop such symptoms as somewhat different in their nature from other people. But we may ask: are they more 'degenerate' than other neurotics – than hysterical patients, for instance, or those who fall ill of psychoses? Once again, the characterization is too general. Indeed, we may doubt whether there is any justification for it at all, when we learn that such symptoms occur too in distinguished people of particularly high capacities, capacities important for the world at large.
>
> (Freud, quoted in Gilman, 1985: 209)

Evidently, while still using the statistical concept of deviation, Freud by this time thought in terms of a trichotomy of the different, the substantially deviant and the degenerate. But it was not a theorized distinction and lay undeveloped.

Overall, we can agree with Gilman that Freud undermined the view that sexuality leads to degeneracy, and in fact tended to see degeneracy as truly an illness of civilizations rather than individuals. Freud's work ran opposite to much of that in medicine, which, as Gilman (1985: 214) puts it, tended to understand 'the normal' as 'that which was not degenerate, and the sexually normal was defined by the most powerful of contrastive models, that of deviant human sexuality'. Medicine was becoming increasingly and rapidly important in Western societies during the early twentieth century, and the war of 1914–18 brought doctors to the forefront of social administration. Yet their view of deviation, and of health, was stunningly normative. Freud's work contained within its voluminous covers an approach to individual health and social illness which could only support a high degree of neutrality towards the very different or the socially deviant. He felt a profound ambivalence and scepticism about the alleged healthiness of statistical normality. His life's work proved conclusively that the socially normal, respectable and successful could be psychologically deviant, and that the psychologically normal could be socially very deviant.[14] So, statistical normality could no longer automatically be equated with health, nor could the status and lifestyle of a decaying upper class. The lunacy of that class, in creating and sustaining the horrors of the 1914–18 war, became obvious to the working classes, the cannon fodder, all over Europe. Overlaid with the communist overthrow and denunciation of the evils of the *ancien régime* in Russia in 1917, this perception of the unhealthiness of the old order of normality grew and workers' unrest was prevalent throughout Europe from 1918 to 1921. Freud's conclusions were being massively reinforced, and the moral tables were being turned over.

Freud wrote in 1915 that 'In the confusion of wartime in which we are caught up . . . we ourselves are at a loss as to the significance of the impressions which press in upon us and as to the value of the judgements which we form' (quoted in Gilman, 1985: 212). Moreover, once the war of 1914–18 had wreaked its havoc, it was obvious too that the statistical normality of violence could not possibly mean that violence should be automatically privileged as one of the ideals of good moral judgement. Normality and healthiness were now divorced. The moral world needed reconstruction. The criteria of moral judgement were in disarray, and modern man was in search of a soul, to paraphrase Jung. The world of the Absolute had died in the trenches of the Somme. Yet the world of the Dissolute crashed in 1929 on the floors of Wall Street. There were no easy answers, especially since the revolutionary, communist, escape route had soon proved itself stillborn, unready for the real world, through the rise of Stalin and the ruthless political machine of the 'new class'.

In 1933, Jung commented prophetically:

> [Modern man] has seen how beneficent are science, technology and organization, but also how catastrophic they can be. He has likewise seen that well-meaning governments have so thoroughly paved the way for peace on the principle 'in time of peace prepare for war', that Europe has nearly gone to rack and ruin. And as for ideals, the Christian church, the brotherhood of man, international social democracy and the 'solidarity' of economic interests have all failed to stand the baptism of fire – the test of reality. Today, fifteen years after the war, we observe once more the same optimism, the same organization, the same political aspirations, the same phrases and catch-words at work. How can we but fear that they will inevitably lead to further catastrophes? Agreements to outlaw war leave us sceptical, even while we wish them all possible success. At bottom, behind every such palliative measure, there is a gnawing doubt. On the whole, I believe I am not exaggerating when I say that modern man has suffered an almost fatal shock, psychologically speaking, and as a result has fallen into profound uncertainty.
>
> (Jung, 1933: 230–1)

That uncertainty was so profound that like a boil it had to be lanced. It just had to be removed one way or another. Modern people were living with insufficient inner spiritual life to give them direction and ethical judgement, older moral codes were discredited, religion was disavowed, old standards were mocked and there was nothing solid to grab hold of except the whirlwind of manic, direct experience. Mead's psychology was the superficial existentialism of the modern being in search of a soul – all it gave us to hold on to were our transient definitions of the situation and our fleeting experience of significant others in the local community. It was part of the problem, not the solution. Its latent, yet blatant, existentialism could not explain the holocaust that was to follow. Jung explains the problem, in a brilliant passage of such value to us, and so neglected, that it is worth quoting in full:

> we of today have a psychology founded on experience, and not upon articles of faith or the postulates of any philosophical system. The very fact that we have such a psychology is to me symptomatic of a profound convulsion of spiritual life. Disruption in the spiritual life of an age shows the same pattern as radical change in an individual. As long as all goes well and psychic energy finds its application in adequate and well-regulated ways, we are disturbed by nothing from within. No uncertainty or doubt besets us, and we *cannot* be divided against ourselves. But no sooner are one or two of the channels of psychic activity blocked, than we are reminded of a stream that is dammed up. The current flows backwards to its source; the inner man wants something which the visible man does not want, and we are at war with ourselves. *Only then, in this distress, do we discover the psyche* [emphasis added] . . . Freud's psychoanalytic labours show this process in the clearest way. The very first thing he discovered was the existence of sexually perverse and criminal fantasies which at their face value are wholly incompatible with the conscious out-look of a civilized man . . . no culture or civilization before our own was ever forced to take these psychic undercurrents in deadly earnest . . . This distinguishes our time from all others. *We can no longer deny that the dark stirrings of the unconscious are effective powers* [emphasis added] – that psychic forces exist which cannot, for the present at least, be fitted in with our rational world-order.
>
> (Jung, 1933: 233–4)

Uncertainty's fires needed quenching, and maybe the life-current did search deep into the recesses of the modern unconsciousness for the extinguisher – only to find the archetype of the superman-god. Certainly, reflective intellectuals in social science had now discovered the psyche. But, to qualify Jung, the form of the political solution was not automatic from thereon out. The required social reconstructions of the middle 1930s demanded their legitimations. But, in each country, national culture or history was to shape the form of the solution. Culture was crucial and was about to be theorized as such, as we shall see later.

Both the USA and Germany yearned to defeat the forces of degeneracy. A thoroughly modern America was to find its solution in a social nation-alism and took the route of scientific social management; Germany, on the other hand, with its unresolved archaism and anger, found its solution in its 'national socialism' and targeted degeneracy in its traditional-mythic individual embodiment, the Jews. Elsewhere, the Soviet Union, under the banner of communism, and through a violent assault upon the peasantry, launched the collectivization of agriculture and a rapid industrialization to bring it into the twentieth century and to create the foundations for a bureaucratic class state. Diverse solutions, but they were all aimed at producing *social systems* to replace the old collections of communities which passed for societies. The abstract concept of the social system slowly began to emerge within American sociology, as the theoretical alternative to a sociology based upon Meadian symbolic interactionism, and came to maturity in the 1950s as we shall see in Chapter 7.

Parsons's theory of social action and Merton's concept of unintended consequences

Sociology could hardly have continued to be satisfied with existential models of human interaction. To move with the flow of history, it somehow had to encompass the 'dark stirrings of the unconscious' within its new theoretical schemes of *social action*. Moreover, sociology had to allow for modern societies' and modern individuals' lack of control over their destinies by reference to some notion of the *unintended consequences of action*, and thus of the effective if unintended *functions* of social systems of action. Even further, because of the discoveries of anthropology, it had to account for the unique forms of social action in different societies or subgroups by using a non-evaluative concept of *culture*, and we shall look at that concept in the next section. We cannot even leave the matter here, however, because there are two more ingredients to be discussed before we can see how the final deviance cake was baked. They were the conception of *language* as a social entity and the new sense of importance of political *ideology* in the construction of social forms, both of which emerged in the more critical sociologies at the end of the thirties. We will turn to each of these developments in turn. Their net effect, logically, was to register the beginnings of a profound critique of the simple observability of human behaviour and motive. Sociology in general was now losing its innocence. It was realizing that things were not what they seemed. The moral, cultural and epistemological innocence of the boys from the small farms of Idaho was confronted by the complex, decadent world of a decaying Europe; the perspective shift required was enormous. To their credit, their standpoint did shift, and rapidly, although never enough.

The new psychoanalytically influenced sociology which emerged in the late 1930s contained each of the innovations mentioned above – they were to combine around 1937, as we shall see in Chapter 4, in an unholy, unstable and often contradictory alliance with Meadian sociology and the residues of the concept of degeneracy, to form the theoretical foundations of the sociology of deviance.

Social action, as goal-oriented, reflexive action aware of the views of others, was by 1937 a well-established concept within Meadian sociology. While arriving from a different route, Talcott Parsons's elaboration of a theory of social action in his book of that year anchored the centrality of that very general concept within American sociological theory. Mead had drawn upon Dewey, but Parsons gathered much from Weber and Durkheim (on the significance of the rise of Parsonian theory in sociology, see Gouldner, 1970: 138–48). Mead's conception had stressed the choice of means and ends within action, and the overall normative orientation of the 'actor'. Reflecting the increasing influence of European phenomenology, Parsons (1937: 46) also argued that, while the external world does influence perception, the frame of reference for his theory of action is subjective in that the crucial thing about action is that it expresses the world of the actor as it appears through the perception of that actor. What directed Parsons away from the tendency towards methodological individualism in Meadian sociology, however, was his strong insistence on distinguishing the structure of an individual's action from the structure of a whole system of social actions, and the relative weighting different normative elements might have in the analysis depending upon whether the initial standpoint was the individual action or the whole social system of actions.

Only the seeds of a theory of the role of the normative in binding social systems of action were present at this stage, but they emerged clearly in *The Social System* (1951), a book strongly influenced by a reading of Freud and the latter's concept of the introjection of norms. In 1937, Parsons only briefly mentioned Freud and Freudian categories, and, significantly, he sidestepped yet recognized the concept of the unconscious by treating the *conscience collective* in Durkheim's work as the collective conscience rather than the ostensible consciousness of an aggregate of real individuals (see Parsons, 1937: 309 and 359). Even at this stage, he was clearly articulating the important, modernist, idea that the normative binding of a society may not appear straightforwardly as itself within the consciousness of a given individual (*ibid.*: 50–1, 360–1). Commenting critically on a mistaken route Durkheim took, Parsons stated perceptively that 'It is not a subjective community of belief and sentiment which is the source of solidarity, but rational orientation to the same set of phenomena in the environment of action, an "objective" source of uniformities' (*ibid.*: 360). In short, in contrast to Mead, Parsons recognized that the normative binding effected by a *conscience collective* is not only not necessarily effective through shared, conscious beliefs and norms, but it is not necessarily the prime cause of unified systems of social action at all (that remains an empirical question in each specific case).

Parallel with, and conscious of, Parsons's writing, Robert Merton, also at Harvard for a time (Crothers, 1987), elaborated the notion of the 'unanticipated consequences of purposive social action' (Merton, 1934, 1936). Combining themes from Parsons, and Thomas and Znaniecki, Merton reviewed a new translation of Durkheim's *Division of Labour* and concluded that, while there was insufficient precision in Durkheim's recognition of the causal role of the subjective element in social action, the French sociologist had confirmed that through the organs of 'social control', such as law, 'the accord of individual wills is constrained for the consonance of diffuse social functions' (Merton, 1934: 322). This 'incisive analysis', commented Merton, 'refutes one of the basic doctrines of an atomistic sociology', and recognizes the 'role of social ends' and 'the doctrine of emergence' (*ibid.*: 323). In this way, Merton attempted to bring some concordance between sociological and political accounts, emphasizing the properties of social systems as wholes alongside the modern American celebration of the subjectivity and processual character of social action. Reflecting the powerful, even earth-shaking, societal movements apparent at that time, while holding on to the role of the individual in social construction, Merton skilfully Americanized Durkheim. By stressing the purposive character of social-order construction while also recognizing the systemic patterning of social action, Merton delivered two clear counter-conceptions: (a) the concept of the unanticipated consequences of social action, and (b) the concept of the idiosyncratic, deviant or 'innovative' (to use his later term) response to systemic contradictions. These two notions were to play a major role in post-1945 sociology of deviance, and were combined to great effect in Merton's famous essay of 1938 on 'Social structure and anomie', which we will discuss in Chapter 5. It can be noted here that, while the two concepts in the 1934 essay were little more than a systematic elaboration of Dewey's conception of the open-ended and indeterminate character of praxis, they do represent a clear-headed way of linking the analysis of social systems with the analysis of individual action without returning to a closed, positivistic determinism or lapsing into an ahistorical voluntarism. Their formulation by Merton certainly provided two key tools for so much sociology of deviance to come.

By the 1960s, sociologists of a whole variety of theoretical persuasions were fond of opening their accounts by observing the unintended consequences of deviance or social control, or by asserting the social innovation involved. Subsequently, David Matza has succinctly demonstrated the weaknesses of Merton's work, and that of structural functionalism generally, but, as he himself agrees, Merton's ideas sponsored a new 'moral innocence' (Merton's phrase) which encouraged the study of the '*actual workings* of deviant phenomena' (Matza, 1969: 62), rather than taking their cause, motive or effect for granted as scripted moments in the historic defeat of Evil by the forces of Good.

Culture, language and ideology: the meaning of deviance

Culture was a concept that came into common currency in the social sciences in the USA during the twenties and thirties (see, for example, Shaw, 1929; Blumenthal, 1936; Gillin, 1936; Horney, 1936; Thurnwald, 1936a; Sellin, 1938; Frank, 1948; Park, 1950; Benedict, 1961). It became an especially obsessive issue in the mid-thirties. But it was a very specific conception of culture that was emerging. Bauman (1973: 17) calls it 'the differential concept of culture', and he defines it, very significantly for our purposes, in this manner:

> [it] is employed to account for the apparent differences between communities of people (temporally, ecologically, or socially discriminated). This usage locates the differential concept of culture among numerous 'residue concepts', contrived frequently in the social sciences *to explain away the sediment of deviant idiosyncrasies unaccountable for by otherwise universal and omnipotent regularities* (where it shares the ascribed function with ideas, tradition, life experience, etc.).
>
> (Bauman, 1973: 17; emphasis added)

Once it had been recognized, the purposive character of human action meant that the social sciences began in earnest to observe that people did not just invent technology or mate with partners but also selected meanings, icons, images, concepts, ideologies, myths, rituals and other symbolic items. The movement against behaviourist psychology and crude biologism, whose discursive myth of objectivity effectively constructed people as objects, thus stressed a selective, arbitrary, capricious, sometimes wayward subjectivity and its artefacts. The symbolic creations, rituals and traditions of subjectivity, which seem to be so important in determining our actions, could not easily be accounted for by Western rationality and were often put down to culture or custom. This is culture as a residual explanation when all else fails. To some extent, therefore, culture in the 1930s was the same as social deviance.

One of the earlier meanings of the word deviant is 'wayward'. This meaning seems to have been unexceptional up to the eighteenth century. It is interesting and quite significant that wayward carries a gentle, more tolerant connotation than criminal or perverted, just as folly does in relation to madness. Bauman's definition is therefore doubly potent, because the differential concept of culture does not just seem designed to 'explain away deviant idiosyncrasies', as he perceived, it also seems to be part of a discourse which could work either to effect the creation of a concept of difference as healthy diversity or to affirm the deviance of Other worlds. Its very theoretical formation seems to be premised on some notion of totally inexplicable and strangely different social action, with the norm, of course, being Western culture. In this way, it is clear that, in the 1930s, the period of 'the common man' and the democratization of art in America, difference, deviance and culture were virtually synonymous. Their interrelation was a very vague one indeed. It seems to me that the conception of difference was deployed inside the concept of culture prevalent at that time in order to disentangle human divergence, a positive thing, from the negative stigma of pathology and the condescension of censure. Thus disentangled as a mere difference, it could be documented by the sympathetic or appreciative ethnographic sciences and rendered accessible to ordinary human understanding. However, when they were thousands of miles away on remote islands in the South Pacific they tended to fascinate as differences, whereas when they were found within the USA, with its heavily institutionalized racism against blacks, they often produced fear, disapproval and stigma, and were seen as deviance. In this sense, deviance was linguistically locked up within the differential concept of culture, and as that concept was developed and analysed the concept of deviance was able to unfold.

In 1926, Malinowski published *Crime and Custom in Savage Society* and its tone and arguments illustrate Bauman's point well. Malinowski was one of the first to declare the goal of the ethnographer to be to understand the 'native's point of view, his relation to life' and 'his vision of the world' (Malinowski, 1926: 25). Anthropology was beginning to explore and document the 'less developed' societies, and the white Western world was fascinated with the strange patterns of behaviour it perceived in the exotic world of 'the primitive'.[15] The repression of a very significant Other was being undermined and confused. Dark continents of the Western unconscious were being opened up:

> Miscegenation is a word from the late nineteenth-century vocabulary of sexuality. It embodies the fear not merely of interracial sexuality, but of its supposed result, the decline of the population...
>
> The Other's pathology is revealed in her anatomy, and the black and the prostitute are both bearers of the stigmata of sexual difference and thus pathology... The 'white *man's* burden', his sexuality and its control, is displaced into the need to control the sexuality of the Other, the Other as sexualized female.
>
> (Gilman, 1985: 107)[16]

The flashing pioneers of the imperial science of anthropology were exposing publicly something which had been denied and stuffed away in the back of the mind, namely the humanity of those people killed, raped, infected, exploited, interfered with and subjugated in the colonies. The offending but recognizably human 'idiosyncrasies' of the colonized had now to be neutralized if guilt was to be smoothed. Seeing them as features of a 'different' culture probably succeeded in this objective, and was much more acceptable to the conscience than the old, hierarchical concept of culture which legitimated their colonization as 'savages'. This was probably doubly true when Freudian psychodynamic theory was additionally imported in order to explain personality by culture via the concept of the unconscious (see Brown, 1964: 118–24; Bauman, 1973: 28–9). Different mating rituals, child-rearing habits or toilet-training techniques proved that They 'must be very different from us really'. The sex–race matrix of so much subsequent anthropology is ample testimony to the enduring fascination with that which can not be thought, that which was suppressed in the concept of the primitive and the idiosyncrasy of Other cultures. Reich, of course, was one of many who would soon recognize the important sexual-racial fears of fascism; the unlocking of the demons in the

Western psyche during the Depression was to have terrifying and bizarre consequences during the Second World War. That war paradoxically also gave experiences to soldiers from Africa and Asia which were to be pivotal in the nationalist political unlocking of the colonies from the yoke of empire a decade or so later (Worsley, 1967).

However, Europeans such as Malinowski or Reich were no more influential than American sociologists and anthropologists in uncovering the patterns of 'primitive' (or delinquent) culture. Thomas had already done much in this direction before he published his essay 'The comparative study of cultures' in 1937. His earlier book with Znaniecki (Thomas and Znaniecki, 1927) was to become a classic. It had shown in many ways how American society had still not developed much of a general culture (or as Thomas and Znaniecki put it, 'it is still very far from a thorough-going teleological systematization of values and a rational control of attitudes'; see Smith, 1988: 98), and had criticized the idea of introducing culture 'from the outside' via social work agencies. Janowitz, of the post-war Chicago school, was later to describe one of Thomas's other books, *The Unadjusted Girl* (1928), as 'a landmark in the emergence of a sociology of deviant behavior' (Janowitz, in Thomas, 1966: xxvii), but he gives no reason for this claim. The book may have been one of the few specific texts on girls within the criminology of this period, but it is mostly empiricist description of the worst kind, in my view, because its few interpretive comments merely reinforce the male–colonial view that the woman's place is in the home. Female delinquency is viewed as a result of inadequate 'investment' in the girl as a valuable asset to the family and society as a future wife and mother. There is very little cultural sensitivity or appreciativeness in the following passage, for example:

> The girl as a child does not know she has any particular value until she learns it from others (in the family), but if she is regarded with adoration she correspondingly respects herself and tends to become what is expected of her. And so she has in fact a greater value. She makes a better marriage and reflects recognition on her family. But we must understand that this sublimation of life is an investment ... And there are families and whole strata of society where life affords no investments ... In cases of great neglect, the girl cannot be said to fall, because she has never risen. She is not immoral ... but amoral – never having had a moral code.
>
> (Thomas, 1928: 98)

He clearly saw girls, and maybe everyone, as culture-free until socialized – empty vessels who must learn.

Thomas's essay of 1937 flatly opposed the neo-Darwinist cultural evolutionism of the early anthropologists which supposed (a) that culture evolved in a unilinear, invariant sequence, (b) that the 'higher' cultures were a result of superior mental endowment and (c) that different levels of culture resulted from more or less favourable geographic and economic conditions. Hence, in his view, no urban anthropology of crime could legitimately blame particular ethnic groups for currently high crime rates. On the contrary, Thomas argued, 'diversities in behaviour and culture are the result of different interpretations of experience' and, therefore, there could be no uniform cultural evolution but merely a history, geography and sociology of differences (Thomas, 1937: 184–5). Culture as such, therefore, amounted to no more than a habitual and institutionalized set of 'definitions of the situation' peculiar to a particular social group. No basis for an understanding of culture as social forms based on higher intelligence or more fortunate economic conditions has been sustained, he said. This is the differential concept of culture enunciated boldly, with more than a small sideswipe at Park's approach to cultural construction which saw culture as conditioned by the 'biotic substructure' of 'human ecology' (Park's concept of which is, in my view, merely a limited version of the concept of economy; see Park, 1937: 12–15).

Thomas's articulation of the differential concept of culture may seem extremely relativistic, but it was merely one of several such formulations during that period. One of the most well known was that of Ruth Benedict, the anthropologist:

> The cultural pattern of any civilization makes use of a certain seg-
> ment of the great arc of potential human purposes and motivations
> ... The great arc along which all the possible human behaviours are
> distributed is far too immense and too full of contradiction for any
> one culture to utilize even any considerable portion of it. Selection is
> the first requirement.
>
> (Benedict, 1961: 171)

As Bauman (1973: 21) comments, this voluntarism is indeed extreme and assigns 'well-nigh unlimited freedom to purely cultural choices'. But, as he is well aware, the differential concept of culture celebrated difference and shunned all overt attributions of pathology. It thus registered a great doubt about Western civilization, the full critique of which only began after decolonization. Like language and difference, culture was seen to constitute communities, and, in an America seeking community and social integra-tion, it became a major and positive value, in defiance of the old 'universal categories of the human mind'. In the liberal American sociology of the 1930s then, culture came to signify difference, diversity and the arbitrari-ness of language and symbols (or ideology). *In this strict sense, difference and deviance were thus installed in progressive American thought of the 1930s as a fundamental presupposition of the policy of normative integra-tion.* Whatever the content of the consensus was to be, it had to reflect the diversity now elevated to the centre of American culture, and, indeed, it had to reflect the concept of culture then rising within the heart of Amer-ican diversity.

There was, in the middle thirties, a striking convergence between anthro-pology and sociology in the way that they both strove to conceptualize the psychically repressed, but now exposed as very human and social, worlds of oppressed populations as *cultures*, or subcultures, of deviation or major difference. It is little wonder that the interpretations of crime and deviance in the 1930s and 1940s took a distinctly culturalist tone: crime and deviance in America were to be seen as the learned responses of strange urban cultures, or *subcultures*.

The cultural character of deviation, and the voluntarism inherent within the differential concept of culture, was strikingly illustrated by Lindesmith (1938) in his classic essay on drug addiction. The essay is interesting as an attack on the moralism of extant scientific theories of addiction and on the weakness of psychiatric analysis, but remains an ideal exemplar of early symbolic interactionist sociology. Essentially, its thesis was that opiates do not in themselves cause addiction, as evidenced by their unknowing and non-addictive consumption in hospitals, but that addiction is determined primarily by the individual's belief, supplied by, or learned in, a cultural milieu, that the drug alleviates his or her distress. Addiction to opiates, Lindesmith argued, is generated in the process of using the drug consciously to alleviate withdrawal distress, as evidenced by his case data and addicts' argot. Psychiatrists labelled addicts as psychopaths, yet the percentage of 'high-grade morons' among addicts was low. Besides, he observed, insanity generally confers an immunity to addiction because it reduces the ability to manipulate the cultural symbols systematically so as to render the regular use of the drug meaningful to the individual. Our societies, he said, were too busy trying to establish moral fault in the drug user instead of scientifically identifying the mechanisms which produce a commitment to systematic drug use. Following Mead and Durkheim, Lindesmith claimed that the physical effects of the drug do not become effective in influencing the social and psychological life of the individual until that individual has interpreted drug use favourably in terms of the significant symbols and collective representations of the pertinent cultural milieu. Addiction, then, was a symbolic process. The culture of the user's group supplied its rationalization by defining the situation as effective in alleviating distress and by introducing the motives and ideas which enable the user to define the experience as pleasurable (see also Becker, 1963: Chapter 3). The essay remains a good example of the extremes of culturalism and of the failings of conventional psychiatry. It revealed the moralism and the insult involved in psychiatry's attribution of psychopathy, but it also demonstrated the thinness of the new culturalists' conception of culture. The degree to which group evaluations and the phenomenon of the addictive tendency are invested with wider economy and power remained a concept for the future. Cultural symbols and their learning were all, and they were deployed to de-stigmatize certain crimes.

Wirth's essay of 1931, 'Culture conflict and misconduct' (Wirth, 1964), discussed in Chapter 2, was a forerunner of much of the later subcultural analysis. He had argued that human behaviours only became social problems when they were defined as being in breach of the dominant cultural codes, and that cultural conflicts were, therefore, central to an accurate understanding of crime and delinquency. Noting the coherence and import- ance of the cultural and moral codes of delinquent gangs, he had been struck by their frequent condemnation of official culture as hypocritical. As he acutely pointed out, our conduct can appear genuinely moral to us when we can get our significant others to accept and approve of it (*ibid.*: 236). Therefore, it is important, he argued, that we study crime and delinquency in *cultural areas*, not just 'natural areas' *à la* Park and Burgess. Just as importantly, for our purposes, Wirth went on to argue that we also had to study the personal meanings which individuals give to cultural values, since a 'culture has no psychological significance until it is referred to a personality' (*ibid.*: 239). Similarly, cultures are only built up and passed on through the habits and choices of individuals. Culture and personality were, for Wirth, thus indissolubly and dialectically linked. Consequently, it is not enough merely to interview delinquents; social scientists had to talk to their relatives and peers too. Their whole cultural milieu required observation and analysis, in order that we might document the 'reflected judgments and conceptions of others' (*ibid.*: 240) which make up so much of their attitudes. In particular, Wirth argued, the sociologist should attend to the frequent sense the delinquent has of being an outcast. Immigrant youth often feels alienated from its parents' generation as well as from the host society, and therefore this sense of exclusion is a powerful force in the construction or expression of its delinquency.

In another essay that year, Wirth observed that sociologists had a positive role to play in child guidance clinics if they brought their awareness of the cultural and situated character of action to the diagnosis of behavioural problems. The extent of sociologists' interest and participation in such clinics at that time was such that Wirth thought it might even be worth coining a new division of sociology called 'clinical sociology'. Such a so- ciology, guided by its culturalist tenets, could combine with psychiatry to provide a more complete analysis of the individual's problems. For example, sociology could point out to the psychiatrists that 'behavior is recognized as a problem only because it takes place in a culture which has given to the action of the individuals the imprint of its definitions of conduct' (Wirth, 1931: 60).

This culture–personality couplet was crucial to the emergent sociology of deviance. Wirth's analysis laid down many theoretical and methodological foundations, which both he and others were to build upon at the end of the thirties. For example, Sutherland's much-discussed theory of differen- tial association was consciously indebted to Wirth's ideas (Gibbons, 1979: 47). Sutherland's earlier work (1934) had emphasized culture conflict, and his exposition of differential association theory in 1939 stressed that systematic criminal behaviour was based upon learned norms within a delinquent or criminal subculture. In the light of the discussion in this chapter, Sutherland's famous theory now seems highly derivative and relatively lacking in insight as a sociological excursion, although Gibbons is probably right to acclaim Sutherland's huge overall contribution to criminology.

We should also record Wirth's further suggestion that psychotherapy and 'social treatment' sometimes needed to do more than reconnect troubled individuals with their childhood loyalties and experiences and to link them with their class context, thus enabling them to give their everyday life a new social significance other than that related to their cultural heritage (Wirth, 1964: 243; see also Wirth, 1931). Changed social milieus and experiences can make a dishonest child behave as an honest one – the crucial determinant being the identification with a cultural ideal. For Wirth, like the rest of the Chicago school in the early thirties, the reconstruction of cultural milieux was vital to the solution of the problem of delinquency; but, unlike his colleagues, he had a sense of the growing importance of class, and the resolution of class inequalities, to the construction of a coherent American culture – more of this in Chapter 5.

Interestingly, this period, which saw the emergence of 'cultural anthropology', also fostered an interest in black culture within a young graduate student who was a jazz musician and later to become perhaps the most well-known sociologist of deviance of all, namely Howard Becker[17] (see Debro, 1970). As a progressive sociologist influenced by critical black anthropology, and as a musician interested in black jazz, Becker's own character formed at the centre of this curious matrix of anthropology and social democracy and made him eminently suitable to express the spirit of the sociology of deviance ... and the book containing his famous exposition of the theory of deviance begins with a commentary on a story from Malinowski's *Crime and Custom in Savage Society* (Becker, 1963).

Language, multiculturalism and propaganda

The changes in American sociology did not rest with the focus on culture. An expanded recognition of the cultural character of language soon followed. In recognizing the rhetorical and value-laden character of the concept of degeneracy, Freud had already observed the power of words in naming things. In developing the therapeutic practice of psychoanalysis, he had established the importance of language and linguistic associations as a means of revealing the deepest, least conscious, contents of the psyche. During the period Freud was writing, Saussure had laid down the methodological foundations of modern linguistics, and, by the end of the 1930s, Wittgenstein had elaborated upon the binding of the meaning of words to the social context of their use. Like Durkheim and Freud, Saussure's standpoint was that individual experience could only be understood in its interrelation to collective restraints or social norms. Words, like ideas and feelings, were seen as meaningful only because of the collective norms governing their significance.

Taking an example from sport, the expansion and popularity of the game of cricket in the West Indies during the early twentieth century would be meaningless without any knowledge of the social norms built into the game, the technical way in which they are built into the game and the insiders' language in which they are expressed. A theory of imperialism would be insufficient. As the great Trinidadian writer C. L. R. James observed, in nineteenth-century English public schools, ' "A straight bat" and "It isn't cricket" became the watchwords of manners and virtue and the guardians of freedom and power. All sneering at these as cant or hypocrisy is ignorance or stupidity' (James, 1969: 163). Indeed, to an outsider, the physical movements of cricket itself are totally incomprehensible without reference to the rules of the game and their interrelation with its vitally important code of ethics, or without the use of special linguistic terms to describe the activity in a meaningful way. Or as Culler (1974: xiii) says about soccer, 'Wherever there are two posts one can kick a ball between them, but one can only score a goal within a particular institutional framework.' Social actions are only meaningful with respect to instituted social rules, the established codes of ethical conduct and the language necessary to describe and constitute the action as meaningful.

Saussure argued that language was an abstract social system independent of the will of individuals and composed of a series of interrelated signifiers. These interrelations were in themselves arbitrary, 'unmotivated', unique to each language and governed by no law of nature. It was only the inter-relation between the signifiers in a language which gave each of them a distinct meaning (see Sumner, 1979: 104–30). Like Durkheim and Freud, Saussure stressed the importance of recognizing the social, and thereby restrictive, character of interpersonal norms. The notion of linguistic codes used in speech described a dimension of the social character of our being. Even the language we use implicates us within a culture or subculture. Our words convey distinct pictures, colour-toned by the linguistic nuances of cultural prejudice or taste. For Wittgenstein, when we talk we utter words and only later get a picture of their life (see Winch, 1963: 150), whereas for Berger (1972: 7), seeing came before words and words never quite bridged the gap between impression and meaning. Whichever position is preferred, the twentieth century had brought the recognition of the relations between language and culture, and how ambiguous yet powerful they are. American sociology after 1920 began to share this vision and subsequently developed a strong sense of the power of language, especially as expressed in the modern mass media of communication.

Robert Park's experience as a journalist had been translated into an abiding concern within Chicago sociology with the power of newspapers (see Park, 1925a). Indeed, the classic manual of sociology produced by Park and Burgess (1924) seemed to follow that line of thinking which sees modern society itself as a creation of 'the artificial means of communication', such as the printing press (*ibid*.: 422). Its authors take the view that every social grouping has its own language, which can involve a distinct dialect or argot. Subsequent field studies in Chicago were full of illustrations of the language of their subjects (for example, Thrasher, 1927). Indeed, the sociological study of argot was a major theme within the Chicago school. Language was taken to signify and express the (sub)culture of the group, and, as Park and Burgess (1924: 423) comment, in language ahead of its time, the fact of different 'universes of discourse indicates how communication separates as well as unites persons and groups'. They went on to observe that any unity that exists in public opinion is rooted in the shared information supplied by newspapers (*ibid.*: 316):

> A public is, in fact, organized on the basis of a universe of discourse, and within the limits of this universe of discourse, language, statements of fact, news will have, for all practical purposes, the same meanings. It is this circle of mutual influence within which there is a universe of discourse that defines the limit of the public.
>
> (Park and Burgess, 1924: 791)

Openly following Hobhouse and W. G. Sumner, this public opinion was said to be a sublimation of the custom and folkways of the people. Law is therefore close to public opinion in that it is also based upon custom in its attempt to frame workable rules of conduct which will keep pace with the times (*ibid.*: 799). The 'green bible' of American sociology had thus developed a clear view of the important place of language in a dialectic between custom, interaction, language, universes of discourse, newspapers (later the mass media), public opinion and law. It thus accelerated the movement away from the theory of language as a direct expression of a set of universal mental categories. Language was now clearly seen as thoroughly social and cultural.

Language, logic and culture

For our purposes, the most articulate commentary in this period on the character and location of language within the dialectics of the social was written in 1939 by C. Wright Mills, who was then an MA student in Texas before going on to become probably the most globally popular of all American sociologists. Mills's essay, entitled 'Language, logic and culture', showed an awareness of the European writings on the concept of ideology, which had recently been brought to focus by the New York publication in 1936 of Mannheim's *Ideology and Utopia*[18] (preface by Louis Wirth of the Chicago school).

Mills argued that theories of ideology, and theories of mentality and knowledge generally, lack a developed theory of the mind which would give a more precise rendering of the knowledge–society relationship. The Marxian concept of reflection, and conceptions of the collective unconsciousness, were much too vague for his taste, and the Meadian concept of the generalized other mistakenly incorporated the whole society instead of mere 'selected segments' (Mills, 1967: 427n.). Mills felt, however, that while Mead's statements on this point are 'functions of an inadequate theory of society and of certain democratic persuasions' they were not logically necessary to his general social theory of the mind, and therefore did not detract from it substantially (*ibid.*). Drawing consciously upon Mead and Peirce, Mills argued that logic and reason were derived from 'the standpoint of the generalized other' (*ibid.*: 427). Pre-empting Foucault by thirty years, and apparently unaware of the clash between Peirce's pragmatism and Saussure's structuralism, he concluded that the principles of logic and the rules of proof used to establish knowledges were 'conventional without being arbitrary' (Nagel's phrase), being shaped and selected by the 'instrumental character' of specific universes of discourse. That is, they expressed value preferences. In one highly significant phrase, he captured the importance of his essay for our purposes: 'What we call illogicality is similar to immorality in that both are deviations from norms' (*ibid.*: 428). Mills thus joined the group of American sociologists who first used the Durkheimian conception of deviation as a breach of social norms irrespective of its health or pathology from any absolutist standpoint. But, clearly, he was probably the first to connect it openly to a need for a revision of empiricist epistemology.

From this standpoint, Mills could then deny the prevailing orthodoxy in American sociology and argue that the breakdown in a system of social control, as for example in the form of a high crime rate, was only a 'social problem' from the standpoint of a specific universe of discourse, and thus not an objective problem. As he said, 'Dominant activities . . . determine and sustain modes of satisfaction, mark definitions of value preference; embodied in language, they make perception discriminatory' (*ibid.*: 429). Language was indeed social, but it embodied the discriminatory perceptions and value preferences of a generalized other which was far from being a unitary collective consciousness. The generalized other for Mills was 'constituted by the organized attitudinal implicates of cultural forms, by institutional ethos, and by the behaviour of economic classes' (*ibid.*: 431). It was, in short, distinctly sectional, and therefore language was morally and culturally loaded.

Words, argued Mills, mediated social behaviour; language actively contributed to social organization. Language is thus deeply implicated in the formations of class, culture and power. Mills then arrived at the great, and too frequently forgotten, insight that words and their meanings are often the focus, or surrogates, of 'cultural conflicts'; also later seen as sites of political contestation over censure (see Albertyn and Davis, 1990; Sumner, 1990a). As 'the ubiquitous string in the web of human behaviour', language, he argued, was a 'system of social control' in that it organized patterns of collective interaction through its immanent exhortations and evaluations: 'Along with language, we acquire a set of social norms and values. A vocabulary is not merely a string of words; immanent within it are societal textures – institutional and political coordinates. Back of a vocabulary lie sets of collective action' (Mills, 1967: 433).[19] Mills had thereby done more than reinforce the new awareness of the social character of language and its significance for systems of social control. He had signposted the direction of the sociology of deviance of the future. Our adolescent field was now soon to acquire an acute sense of the importance of the linguistic labels social groups attached to behaviours they disapproved of. Labels, it was increasingly observed, are intimately tied to culture and politics (see, for example, Tannenbaum's work, discussed in Chapter 5). While Mills articulated this view better than anyone in the late thirties, others were aware of the discriminatory and evaluative character of language, as is amply evidenced in the American sociological literature of the time. It is little wonder then that the period was to witness a major change in the very language of pathology, a language that had not altered its fundamental character in over a hundred years.

Language and motive

Mills's account of the sectional yet cultural character of language, embodying the value preferences and instrumental needs of specific groups and institutional orders, was a clear extension of Meadism. It ran directly counter to Freudianism and more structural perspectives on language and social action. It naturally led him, in a famous essay of 1940, to argue, well in advance of 1960s ethnomethodology, that motivation itself was an artificially constructed, socially acceptable, story which satisfied the expectations of the generalized other. For if language expressed a specific universe of discourse, and if interaction was always 'situated' in terms of an awareness of the definitions of significant others, how could individual motives be justifiably ascertained outside of the individual's situated and socially acceptable account of motivation with its own context-specific vocabulary? Logically, for Mills, the situated social account of motive must therefore be the only ascertainable motive for the action. As we shall see later, this eloquent piece of sophistry, an open attack on Freudian accounts of the unconscious motive and an implicit critique of the Weberian concept of rational action, became very important within the sociology of deviance in giving people censured as deviant a voice. Deviance, at last, could now speak its own name.

Motives were not the wellsprings of action but 'typical vocabularies having ascertainable functions in delimited societal situations' (Mills, 1967: 439). They pre-empted and answered awkward questions to account for oneself. 'Motives are words' (*ibid.*: 441). 'They do not denote any elements "in" individuals. They stand for anticipated situational consequences of questioned conduct. Intention or purpose . . . *is* awareness of anticipated consequence' (*ibid.*). '"Business or Pleasure?" Institutionally different situations had different *vocabularies of motive* appropriate to their respective behaviours' (*ibid.*: 442). Even war is sustained, although, significantly, not caused, by the 'motives accompanying institutions of war'. Motives are thus 'relatively stable lingual phases of delimited situations' (*ibid.*). So a satisfactory motive answered the questioners of a social act, an unsatisfactory one was recognizably inappropriate to the situation.

Motive thus understood was a socially acceptable reason for action and therefore a cause of that action (here Mills does owe a debt to Weber). The internalization of socially appropriate motives was a key mechanism in the integration of societies, Mills went on to argue, and it helped 'line up conduct with norms' (*ibid.*: 445). Thus, Freud made the error of taking subculturally normal accounts of motive as real motives. Mills commented that in much of urban America 'Individualistic, sexual, hedonistic, and pecuniary vocabularies of motives are apparently now dominant' (*ibid.*: 447). If 'alternative conduct' was justified in these terms, it was least likely to be challenged 'among dominant groups'.

On this view, labelled deviation in the USA was not so much breach of certain collective norms of behaviour as the proffering of socially inappropriate justifications for any kind of conduct; and confessed deviation might well amount to the mere proffering of a motivated and socially acceptable account of nothing. A list of what Americans see as deviance offered two decades later by Simmons (1969) suggests that Mills may well have been empirically correct. That list clearly implies that damage done to an individual or to the society will not necessarily arouse the greatest moral indignation. Even in the sixties, America was still obsessed with its collective norms, in this case with maintaining the integrative social norms it had taken so long to construct.

David Matza (1969: 58–9) later argued that functionalist sociology eliminated pathology with a 'cavalier spirit' and 'spoofed it out of existence', adding that the post-1945 neo-Chicagoans were little better. He was right, but our description of Mills's important essay, lodged in a conflict-theory tradition, shows that Matza understated the argument. Pathology was being spoofed out of existence by the whole of American sociology during the late 1930s. Mills's argument suggests that a deep cynicism, or moral nihilism, had set in. After all, if intentions are merely situationally appropriate motives sanctioned by a popular morality which sociologists of the time readily recognized as malleable by the mass media and the propaganda machine of the war, then pathology was merely a discursive moment in a highly constructed and totally political conversation between consenting adults in public.

American sociology by 1940 was only involved in the global war in a very distant way. Pearl Harbor (1941) was yet to evoke a rather more abusive, less tolerant, conception of motive and character, prompting the USA to annihilate over 150,000 Japanese people at Hiroshima and Nagasaki. The mood of the society and its sociology in the late thirties looks, with the benefit of hindsight and the analysis of its art, distant, introspective, abstracted, cynical and somewhat numb. It was as if Chicagoan and culturalist sociology until the mid-thirties[20] had been self-consciously and quietly engaged in the process of redefining pathology as mere cultural difference from noticeably absent, but much desired, collective norms, when it was interrupted by an immigration of horrified German intellectuals, and discovered that the rest of the world was in the process of mercilessly liquidating its enemies with the most psychotic instruments and psychopathic methods at its disposal in an orgy of unparalleled violence. Ooops! It was as if American sociology, like a naughty boy caught red-handed, started muttering to itself, looking at its feet and gazing blankly into distant space. It was hard to deny that the onset of the 1939–45 war made the world look a very sick place. This was not, on the face of it, a good time to be abandoning the concept of pathology.

American sociology of the late 1930s often, perhaps like the protestations of the boy caught in the act, manifested much cynicism and several embarrassed disavowals which denied everything, including not just pathology but also good and evil, right and wrong, truth and lies, and even logic itself. It had been caught out in a very fertile period of isolationist, self-protective, reflection, and it then became hard to pursue its own indigenous line of thought without considering a plurality of bewildering alternatives. It did not quite know which way to go. No wonder that, for a while, all became a babble of competing universes of discourse! It was virtually inevitable, at this point, that somewhat foreign concepts of ideology and propaganda would take the sociological stage as temporary palliatives while America pursued a search for the truth of its own soul – or at least a profitable alternative. The Millsian script was beautifully played, again and again, by Humphrey Bogart. His films, from 1935 through to 1956, revealed an essentially decent soul, within the trappings of some shady occupations and some cynical attitudes to political ideologies and universal truths, who always found the right thing to do in the end. Truth and morality in Mills may have been clouded by the fears of an almost universal evil, but they remained alive and self-protective.

Ideology, propaganda and social deviation: Wirth and artificiality of consensus

Circumstances and theory demanded the use of the concept of ideology. Louis Wirth did more than most in American sociology to establish its significance for the emergent sociology of deviation. Wirth had moved beyond the theory of the city (see *The Ghetto*, 1928) and had written the introduction to the translation of Mannheim's *Ideology and Utopia* in 1936. That introduction is a classic of its time, and indeed exemplary of modernist ideas. He was then to produce an essay in 1940, significantly entitled 'Ideological aspects of social disorganization', which encapsulated many of the various themes and tendencies we have discussed so far. It marked a point of no return. At a minimum, the essay articulately registered the significant shift in Chicagoan sociology towards a more structural analysis, and towards an open fusion with some of the classic ideas in European sociology deriving from the work of Marx and Weber. With Bretton Woods in 1944, the emergence of the Marshall Plan, the IMF and NATO, American isolationism was receding on all fronts, and its successor, American imperialism, came forward to try to save the world. Wirth's fusion of ideas in 1940 registered in the sociology of deviation a fusion that was about to register politically on a world scale. America was in the process of reconstructing itself and now the American attempt at reconstructing the world was to begin.

A German Jew who had settled in the USA in 1924, Wirth was, by 1936, in the process of Americanizing some distinctively European ideas (see Smith, 1988: 154). Believing that America 'belongs to the future' and was socially 'unfinished', and observing the crisis and pessimism among German intellectuals, Wirth saw a convergence arriving between European and American social theory. Echoing my inferences about the significance of Mills's essay on language and culture, Wirth had complained in 1936 of 'our vanishing sense of a common reality' and the 'disintegration in culture and group solidarity' (Wirth, in Mannheim, 1936: xxiii). What he goes on to say about modernity (*ibid.*: xxiii–xxvi) should be compulsory reading for all sociology students. It can only be condensed here.

Wirth extended, and moved beyond, his earlier analysis of culture-conflict (discussed in Chapter 2) by drawing upon the Durkheimian con-cept of anomie to argue that 'much of life's activity loses its meaning' in the modern world. He perceived a lack of 'common faith', 'community of interest', 'common norms, modes of thought, and conceptions of the world': 'even public opinion has turned out to be a set of "phantom" publics' (*ibid.*: xxiii). Consequently, he argued, there was a general lack of social stability and integration: 'The world has been splintered into countless fragments of atomized individuals and groups.' Correspondingly, individual experience is itself fragmented and partial. Therefore, the intellectual world too is fragmented – into a 'battlefield of warring parties and conflicting doctrines', where there is no trust, no shared cosmos and no shared language of facts, interpretations, methods or criteria of truth and relevance. It is a world full of misunderstanding and people talking past each other, held together only by *words* which have different meanings in different interest groups. All this is compounded by the struggles for personal power, status and money which block any residual wish for shared understanding and the furtherance of common knowledge. Sounds familiar, doesn't it? Academia in modernity. No matter; Wirth firmly registered the view that both morality and pathology were merely words with sectional or partisan meanings. The accentuated individualism of American modernity had annihilated the folkways which were for W. G. Sumner, and other early sociologists, the very basis of popular morality – by implication, the tra-ditional cultures of the waves of immigrants were now massively frag-mented or, at least, in flux. In short, moral nihilism in American society was well founded and new social bonds had to be forged urgently.

Subsequently, in his essay of 1940, Wirth took the Park–Mead–Mills line on universes of discourse and social interests a couple of steps further forward by arguing that ideologies are 'an elusive but significant part of our contemporary landscape' which cannot be ignored as factors in the definition of 'social problems' (Wirth, 1964: 44–5). Durkheim's line of thought is thus continued but significantly modified by Wirth. Indeed, his own earlier emphasis on culture was now being replaced by a focus on ideology. Problems of social maladjustment or social disorganization, he argued, do not just arise out of 'the nature of men or things' (*ibid*.: 45), they arise out of our ideological perception. Ideologies, however, are not 'irrelevant epiphenomena' but crucial guides to identity, clarity, action and allegiance. Then, in a classic but rarely discussed statement, he observes that

> our contemporary social problems cannot be adequately treated and ... the situations to which they refer cannot be understood unless one takes due account of ideological involvements ... *Despite the work of a long line of social scientists who have indicated that the situations we call social problems are problematical only because they represent deviations from socially accepted norms and expectations, there is substantial evidence to indicate that even some contemporary sociologists continue to deal with social problems as if they did not involve evaluational elements.*
>
> (Wirth, 1964: 45; emphasis added)

This is an astonishing remark in an astonishing essay, partly because it depicts the role of ideology in the sociology of deviance many years before its critics 'discovered' it (e.g. Liazos, 1972; Taylor *et al.*, 1973; Thio, 1973; Sumner, 1976; Fine, 1977), but mainly because *it formulated in the clearest way, and also criticized, a definition of the object of the new field of sociology of social deviation before anyone else committed to a concept of social deviation had really elaborated one.* It was highly indicative, in my view, that at the very moment of its adoption in American sociology, a leading sociologist was noting the ideological character of the conceptions of deviance. A concept of ideology was later to play an important role in the mainstream understanding of deviance (see Becker, 1963: 7, 38, 172–6; Lemert, 1972: 68). Wirth's comments, and the emerging *Lebenswelt* expressed within them, ensured that it could not have been otherwise. Wirth had played an important role in making sure that the ideological character of definitions of deviance was understood right from the beginning.

This ideological character was an issue which eventually was to divide sharply the two major tendencies within the sociology of deviance, structural functionalism and symbolic interactionism. The functionalists, following the line developed out of Durkheim by Merton, never accepted that the function of an act or institution was not an objective, unproblematic given but something defined in the course of history by ideology and politics. Their whole conception of system-function supposes the existence of a value-free rationality able to identify such a thing, whereas for the symbolic interactionists, following the Chicagoan line of development, the function of deviance or social control is 'decided in political conflict, not given in the nature of the organization' (Becker, 1963: 7). As Becker added, referring to the claim that there were social rules everyone might agree upon, 'I doubt whether there are many such areas of consensus' (*ibid.*: 8). From the fusion, or confusion, of ideas around 1936–40, there emerged two distinct divisions of the sociology of deviance and on no point did they diverge more clearly than on the issue of the ideological definition of deviance and its functions. In this sense, Wirth's essay was a watershed. It was a halfway point between the Chicago school and 1950s normative functionalism, and a clear precursor of the latter.

There is something else in the comment by Wirth which is worth picking out. It is something that seems distinctly North American, and something that I have never seen commented upon. He said that ideological factors help to constitute what is problematic about a social problem but that otherwise it is deviation from a social norm which is constitutive. From my own experience of living in North America, it seems that deviation from norms is a much censured thing in itself, however trivial the norm or non-damaging the breach. Conformity to norms is highly valued as a thing in itself. What Durkheim had said was that deviation is defined by the collective sentiments, and he clearly believed that divergence could be responded to as crime, deviation or mere difference. Divergence *per se* has, in European cultures, rarely been seen as a problem; paradoxically, given the violent historic conflicts in Europe over wealth, religion and politics. Indeed, in England, for example, eccentricity has always been the source of much humour and amusement, but not censure. In France, too, the passions of personal expression and enjoyment have always been highly valued. But my feeling is that, in North America today, non-conformity is not tolerated very much in principle, and conformity is celebrated; paradoxically, given the tremendous emphasis on the freedom of the individual to do his or her own thing. This does not mean that all divergence is treated as deviation, nor that all deviation is treated as criminal, but there is a tendency in that direction. Paradoxically again, this is probably because, as we have seen, North America has opened its doors to so many diverse and divergent cultures that conformity to social norms became prized and privileged for its value for the possibility of societal organization. Social control could not do without it. This process seems to have accelerated apace in the late 1930s and reached its apogee in the 1950s, although it is still a striking feature of North American life.[21] This conception of social deviation, I would thus contend, is a distinctly American one, and is not identical to that of Durkheim, despite its partial roots in his ideas. Deviation in the USA not only refers to the breach of a particular social norm, it refers to the breach of social norms in general, as an act of non-conformity, as a form of *deviance*. It has a double meaning. *Deviance in North America is not just an aggregate of deviations, but a generic term for non-conformity*. Non-conformity is not willingly equated with mere difference. From the late thirties onward, paradoxically again, at the time of fusion with the whole range of European sociology, the sociology of deviance emerged as a distinctively American field of study. It has distinctively

American cultural overtones: the words do not mean the same as in Europe! Like the sons and daughters of the immigrants, Durkheim's offspring developed a distinctively American identity, and Wirth's essay signalled the beginning of a lively entry into American adulthood.

Wirth's argument in the essay of 1940 was grounded in the perception that ideologies have infiltrated 'the sphere of popular discourse'. They offered positive guidelines which helped make sense out of chaos. 'They aid us in reducing excessive individuation and indifference in respect to social problems by furnishing us with goals by which more or less articulate groups become integrated' (Wirth, 1964: 44–5). On the other hand, they compounded the confusion because there were so many competing ideologies on offer. Like Parsons (1951), Wirth saw the importance of a system of shared norms and understandings as a precondition for the emergence of an organized society. No doubt, both writers thought that the USA needed a shared normative system as much as anything else at that time, both to create some lasting social integration and to avoid the European terrors of fascism and communism (see Wirth, 1964: 52). Wirth's discourse is inexplicable (after his 1936 essay, in Mannheim's book, which suggested no basis at all for a coherent future society) without understanding the immigrant's desire for peace and conformity above all else. The normative basis for consensus was unclear, but the emotional drive demanding it was powerful.

Implicitly bringing out the full logic of the positions of Park and the Chicago school, and following de Tocqueville explicitly, Wirth argued that 'functional interdependence' in communities was not enough to found societies, and only societies were capable of collective action. Community integration was insufficient, a true (national) society had to be created. To achieve that, Wirth claimed, amidst deafening echoes of the politics of his day, it was necessary for people to rediscover some 'common understandings'. In what ought to have been recognized by subsequent sociologists as a classic statement of the *raison d'être* for the creation of the sociology of deviance, and as *the* classic restatement of what I have argued to be the embryonic Durkheimian conception of social deviation, he then declared that

> The degree to which there is agreement as to the values and norms of a society expressed in its explicit rules and in the preferences its members manifest with reference to these rules furnishes us with criteria of the degree to which a society may be said to be disorganized.
>
> But not all deviations from norms are to be regarded as *prima facie* evidence of social disorganization. It is possible to have a wide range of individual differentiation and deviation from norms in a society without approaching a state of social disorganization. Not all conduct we call crime is to be interpreted as social disorganization; nor is the incidence of divorce to be taken at face value as a measure of family disorganization.
>
> (Wirth, 1964: 46)

Three comments are required on this pioneering statement. Firstly, Wirth's repeated use of the term deviation without any commentary on the significance of that usage suggests that the concept of social deviation had become firmly established in American sociology by 1940. Secondly, Wirth was clearly following Thomas and Znaniecki's *The Polish Peasant in Europe and America* (1927), and Durkheim, in refusing to conflate individual immorality, pathology or deviation with social disorganization; the latter is seen as a historic and political property of the distinct realm of the social. America's entry into the world of social democracy was thus firmly intellectually anchored within its sociology. The question of how to organize the social structure was now on the agenda, something that is well reflected by the number of articles on planning, the use of science and the nature of democracy in the 1937 issues of the *American Journal of Sociology* (see, particularly, Allin, 1937; Hankins, 1937; Ross, 1937; Speier, 1937; also Chapin, 1936, in the first ever article in the *American Sociological Review*). Thirdly, as I suggested earlier, Wirth's remarks highlighted the importance of shared value preferences and normative conformity to the political formation of an integrated American social order, despite the pluralism and tolerance apparently implied in his refusal to take all deviations as major signs of social trouble. What deeply concerned him, along with other intellectuals and politicians in Roosevelt's America, were those deviations from social norms which involve 'substantial disbelief in the validity of the violated norms' (Wirth, 1964: 47n.). The cultural and political matrix for the McCarthyism of the early 1950s, and for other campaigns against disbelief in the newly sacred, yet unclear, normative consensus, was now being founded. Roosevelt's treatment of conservative judgements by the Supreme Court in 1937, his proposal, before consulting anybody of significance, to appoint up to six extra Justices if those over 70 did not 'voluntarily' retire, was a monumental signpost to the shape of things to come (see Brogan, 1985: 563). The American, avuncular, imperial role as policeman ('Uncle Sam') of the world's ideological health was formed internally on a national-ideological basis before being imposed on the globe.

What Wirth had consistently argued was that its history had brought America to the point where it was suffering much social disorganization because of 'conflicts between norms'. The contradictions of capitalism were exonerated. Indeed, in the cities, he observed, it was more a case of an 'unorganized society' than a disorganized one: 'The interpenetration of diverse ethnic and cultural groups in the urban world has resulted in the enormous multiplication of value systems, each one of which is binding only upon a segment of the population and upon individuals in specific segments of their round of life' (Wirth, 1964: 48). The centrality of immigration, and the mistaken culturalist ideology of social disorganization, to the formation and history of American sociology was never indicated more succinctly. From here, it was clear that it was of little use to rely on 'custom and a common form of life' (*ibid*.: 49) as a basis for consensus or law. The ideas of W. G. Sumner were thus diplomatically consigned to the dustbin of history. Because 'more formal and rational bases' for achieving social unity were required, Wirth concluded that 'formal education and propaganda' are the techniques typically and necessarily invoked in contemporary practice.

When norms are not believed to have any 'intrinsic validity', 'supporting ideologies come into play with reference to the institutions and values that are threatened' (*ibid.*). These ideologies are of primary importance to sociologists, because they are as much accurate statements of causes of social action as they are rationalizations for it. They are of primary importance to societies because, in so far as they are principled, they are more effective sources of social solidarity in complex, secular societies than the fear of sanctions. Their importance to the emerging sociology of deviance was well stated by Wirth:

> Before we can discover why and in what ways individuals deviate from the norms most of which those who adhere to them take for granted, we must discover what norms people are expected to meet, what same meaning they have for the various participants and spectators in the society or social world in question. *A cursory survey reveals that such consensus as does exist in modern Western society when it is not at war is extremely limited, in the sense that those who participate in the consensus constitute only a small portion of the total society.*
>
> (Wirth, 1964: 53; emphasis added)

Any realistic sociology of deviance must therefore attend to the fundamental question of the distribution and effect of the plurality of social norms and political ideologies. Consensus cannot be assumed in complex, secular modern societies, it has to be constructed. Indeed, Wirth argued, in highly individuated, culturally pluralistic societies such as the USA, there is even difficulty in forming segmental ideologies (as the labour movement has found). Moral pluralism was clearly the starting assumption for the construction of normative consensus, and so it became for the sociology of deviance.

In the USA of 1940, Wirth felt, ideologies were mainly experienced as relatively sectional, precise, doctrines disseminated through propaganda by specific interest groups, and therefore they commanded little unqualified loyalty. Departing from Park's view that ideologies are like customs in directing and unifying group or societal activities (Park, 1939a), Wirth took the more critical line that, in the competitive struggle between interest groups, ideologies can become tactical weapons deployed against both inner and outer enemies. As such, they may be used to conceal true interests and to provide self-interested justifications. Again expressing the whole ideology of the New Deal, Wirth contended that *laissez-faire* was no longer a workable policy and, to establish consensus, propaganda had become necessary, using the full weight of the modern mass media. Given the rise of democracy and the democratization of the means of communication and education, the dissemination of 'interested' ideas had become 'an art and a big business' (Wirth, 1964: 56).

Propaganda thus became an art-form at the time that art was being savaged by propaganda. The victories of art had now truly been bought by the loss of character. 'Propaganda has become the price we pay for our literacy and our suffrage' (*ibid.*). Simplified views of the world, superficial arguments and inflexible manifestos thus replaced the more flexible, but élite, activity of the search for truth:

> We have become the victims of the mouthpieces and loudspeakers of those who have acquired the power to make decisions and those who seek to wrest it from them. *Propaganda has become the chief means for enlarging the scope of the consensus and the number of persons sharing it, and the consensus we get as a result is often an unstable and spurious one* ... Particularly in an urban world, where a wide variety of schemes of conduct representing divergent social worlds meet, clash, and interpenetrate, the chances of any one set of norms surviving or emerging as sacred for all are slender. Here, if anywhere, we should find doctrines and principles losing force and faith decaying as sophistication progresses. The disillusionment of their respective sympathizers that has followed in the wake of the tactical twists and turns of Communist and Nazi policies toward one another's program has been a startling event.
>
> (Wirth, 1964: 56–7; emphasis added)

The acute anomie and sheer anxiety of the period are well revealed in this passage. Again, the sense surfaced that, in a world of normative pluralism, all political thought is ideological or sectional, yet the dissemination of ideology through propaganda only heightened the feeling of normlessness and lack of truth. All absolutes were thus relative, and the meaningless had become the new absolute.

The exhortation to morality was thus betrayed by the sectionality of the world which it purported to unite. Cynicism prevailed:

> Every faith is suspect, no prophet is regarded as infallible, no leader sincere, no mission inspired, and no conviction unshakable ... When the symbols representing the values of a society fall into such a state of decay, we approach the condition of *anomie* which Durkheim describes as a state of social void or normlessness in which certain types of suicide, crime, family and community disorganization, and social disorder flourish.
>
> (Wirth, 1964: 58).

Durkheim was thus appropriated into American sociology of deviance, mistakenly, as the creator of a concept of normlessness rather than a critic of moral de-regulation. Merton's more accurate representation in his earlier essay of 1938 was superseded gradually by this very 'new-American' version, and Durkheim became conscripted into the social movement towards consensus- and norm-creation through propaganda, rather than being recognized as the advocate of structural and political development through moral flexibility.

Thirty or more years before Habermas articulated the same kind of scepticism about technocratic rationality and the stability of its political legitimacy (see Habermas, 1971, 1974, 1976, 1979), Wirth had perceived that, when the spontaneous acceptance of norms can no longer be relied upon, all efforts 'to discover a deliberate and consciously contrived basis for conformity' reveal the ambiguity and division of value-systems, with the result that none is universally acceptable and conduct becomes 'increasingly privatized' (Wirth, 1964: 58). Wirth concluded that, without the specification of social norms and their meaning, the study of personal and social disorganization must be doomed to inadequacy (*ibid.*: 58–9). It was an observation that was only to gain real force in American sociology after the war. Habermas, much later, put the point about the privatization of conduct this way:

> The personalization of what is public is thus the cement in the cracks of a relatively well-integrated society, which forces suspended conflicts into areas of social psychology. There they are absorbed in categories of deviant behaviour: as private conflicts, illness and crime. These containers now appear to be overflowing.
>
> (Habermas, 1971: 42–3).

These private, individual, containers of deviance thus have the illusory appearance of an objective existence disconnected from the lack of spontaneous acceptance of shared cultural norms:

> Once divorced from the normative and political conjuncture that give it meaning, 'deviant behaviour' was ready as an apparently neutral object of knowledge to serve in the power-laden practices of policing, tutelage and discipline, as an agency in the processes of domination and social regulation . . . The deviant was now identifiable directly, as an 'inadequate', 'undersocialized', or 'inappropriately' socialized cultural rebel: as a rebel without a cause. Properly fitted up, after an identification parade where only the police and a carefully cultivated public opinion were present, the Deviant, and subsequently a whole rogues' gallery of Deviance, was constructed in a way that took some knocking down. The fact that the concept of deviant behaviour was still used by radicals in the seventies is testimony to its significance for the age of the welfare state and for social-democratic reformism at any time.
>
> (Sumner, 1990a: 18–19)

Wirth had a sense of what was coming.

In the 1930s, the new psycho-social technicians of the welfare state, who would treat the individual containers of deviance, were largely figments of the social architects' imagination.[22] They were later to become the proud possessors of a concept of social deviation which would enable them to proclaim their professional neutrality while walking the traditional beat of class/gender/ethnic policing. Perceived normlessness was to be healed by the sticking plaster (or Band-Aid as the Americans so appropriately call it) of democratic communication. Listening to the plurality of voices, hearing their difference through understanding their culture and language, and recognizing the need for a more general ideology which would genuinely enlarge the scope for moral consensus was to be the neo-Durkheimian, post-Freudian, social-democratic recipe for social reconstruction after the holocaust of war and the demise of political extremism. Propaganda would not work in the long run. Society could not survive on a permanent war footing. But the society was in dis-ease. It was in need of treatment (see Frank, 1948, discussed in Chapter 4). So the psychoanalytic couch was to be installed in every niche of the peacetime social system so that the patient could be heard and understood. Communication was vital. Society was to speak through its disturbed members. Despite different universes of discourse, different languages and different subcultures, the strategy had to work: to generate the new shared norms and agreements, a new social contract, which would seal off any more horrendous explosions from the depths of the untamed collective unconscious.

The sociology of deviance was therefore literally to become equivalent to sociology itself, as a monitor of the progress of social control, of social integration, of the mechanism for establishing a fully corporate society. Its rise to adulthood saw it propelled out of the inner city slums into a prestigious career with the federal government, as we shall see in Chapter 7. For now, we must turn to the more specific shape of these uneasily converging new sociological conceptions, in the form of the union between sociological psychiatry and psychoanalytic sociology. The late 1930s was a formative period for the sociology of deviance and, like a plutonium bomb detonation, its radiation waves were still passing through the sociology of social control right up to the late 1960s.

Notes

1 It was finally mentioned with approval by Tannenbaum in his book of 1938.
2 The New Deal worked less well for the mass of small farmers in the USA. Its policies benefited the big commercial farmers and many of the small fish gave up and moved to the cities (see Brogan, 1985: 551–5). This urban migration during the thirties brought much new labour to California, one of the preconditions of the post-1945 power of the 'sunshine' state.
3 At the time of writing, thought is still mistakenly divided into two camps. There are those who talk about law as though it is almost completely separate

from the processes of politics and the principles of social policy, and there are those who talk as though law has been almost completely subsumed under the rubrics of party politics and policy imperatives. In fact, neither position is correct as even a static description, because the position of law within the matrix of social regulation is strong but uneasy. The conflicts faced by Roosevelt reappear at regular intervals. In any case, the relation between law and social regulation should always be analysed dynamically or historically in order to reflect the constantly changing position of law within the overall forces of domination.

4 This discussion was also aided by a visit to the Museu Dalí in his home town of Figueres in Catalunya. This, as Dalí said, is not so much a museum as a permanent monument to his memories. He designed it himself, even down to the smallest detail.

5 The exhibition was recently reconstructed by Stephanie Barron, curator of the Los Angeles County Museum of Art, and toured the USA extensively in 1991 before I saw it in Berlin in May 1992. I am indebted to the organizers for some of the information discussed in this section.

6 This phrase, interestingly, was also used by Gerth and Mills (1954) a few years later.

7 See also *Escape from Freedom* (1941) by Erich Fromm.

8 Having resisted the temptation to call this psychoanalytic sociology, I then discovered a book with that very name (Weinstein and Platt, 1973): yet another example of the old adage 'look and ye shall find'. However, I prefer the more cautious term, to anchor the relative autonomy and strength of the sociological core within this new mixture emerging during the 1930s. Certainly, during this same time, there was a style of sociology growing within psychoanalysis which may merit the term psychoanalytic sociology (see Weinstein and Platt, 1973: 18).

9 On the early writings of this left wing of psychoanalytically influenced sociology, see Jacoby (1977: 73–100).

10 Fromm published *Escape from Freedom* in 1941, and Parsons published his first major book, *The Structure of Social Action*, in 1937. Both books turned out to be manifestos for two very different political stances within sociology, yet they shared the same cultural–ideological matrix (see also Fromm, 1929, in Bronner and Kellner, 1989; Parsons and Bales, 1956; Parsons, 1963). The two divergent lines can be seen to re-converge in the 1970s in the work of Habermas and Luhmann. Habermas's *Legitimation Crisis* (1976) is a classic in this respect, but see also Luhmann (1985). The significance of German social theory throughout this whole line of thought is obvious and can hardly be overstated.

11 Freud himself left Vienna for London in 1938. Mannheim also moved to London in the thirties.

12 Freud used the term deviation in the old nineteenth-century sense of statistical deviation (for example, Freud, 1977: 46). The normative judgement contained in such an attribution remained buried in Freud's work, just as much as in that of Quételet. However, Freud, being the rigorous scholar that he was, did explicitly comment that 'The relation between these [sexual] deviations and what is assumed to be normal requires thorough investigation' (*ibid.*). Moreover, by frequently refusing to generalize from a single instance, he effectively began to disentangle the various deviations and to take each one on its merits, rather than lumping them all together as (equal) signs of degeneracy.

For example, in the text quoted above, on sexual 'inversion', he states that the facts show that sexual inversion does not necessarily impair efficiency, ethics or intellect (*ibid*.: 49). He even goes on to doubt whether there is 'such a thing as innate inversion', on the grounds that if such alleged cases were 'more closely examined, some experience of their early childhood would probably come to light which had a determining effect upon the direction taken by their libido' (*ibid*.: 51).

13 However, it is clear that he saw constitutional factors as at least some part of the new explanation of neuroses and psychoses (see Freud, 1973: 189).

14 'What is most interesting about Freud's struggle with the concept of degeneracy is that he was never able to abandon it completely even when he saw its implications . . . The dark center of human history, like the mirage of degeneracy, is explicable in terms of the projection of fears onto the world. Freud's necessary grappling with the model of degeneracy gave him a deeper understanding of the implications of the rhetoric of science and sent him to the power of language as a means of understanding not only the individual but society . . . But they [Freud and Kraus] also sensed the potentially destructive power of such projections linked to the political power of an explanatory model such as biological degeneracy. Central to the model and to the understanding of the Other is the definition of the Other in sexual terms, for no factor in nineteenth-century self-definition was more powerful than the sense of sexual pathology' (Gilman, 1985: 215–16).

15 The connections between anthropology and the sociology of deviance suggested in this chapter are resonant with Gouldner's (1975: 37–8) criticism of Becker's school of deviance as 'zookeepers of deviance' (see also Chapter 9).

16 The painting on our front cover has significance in this regard.

17 Becker is on record as getting into sociology after being 'turned on' by Cayton and Drake's *Black Metropolis* (1946), the importance of ethnographic detail and the 'vision of a comparative science of communities' inspired by Lloyd Warner and anthropology (see Debro, 1970: 159).

18 Mannheim was another German émigré, but to the LSE in London. His book attempted to move beyond Marx's theory of ideology to produce a general account of the social determination of all knowledges. Contrary to Marx, its arguments tend to relativize the epistemological value of all ideologies (see Larrain, 1979: 100–22).

19 Mills in this manner provides the earliest set of sketches of a thesis which has more recently been developed, in my own work, as a theory of social censures as contested linguistic-ideological sites of moral-political disapproval (Sumner, 1990a). I have to confess my ignorance of the contents of Mills's paper before I elaborated the concept of social censure. Awareness of it does not, however, alter any of my formulations. Mills's work is a mere sketch of a possible foundation for the later argument – nowhere, to my knowledge, does he actually develop a censure-style argument. Ultimately, his sociology lacked a sufficiently developed sense of social structuration, and remained too wedded to a kind of radical Meadism to ground a sophisticated theory of ideology.

20 Not of course the critical sociology of the émigré Frankfurt school, but the distinctively American sociology rooted in good old isolationist America.

21 The authoritarian, self-righteous, symbolist, evangelical, intolerant, sometimes hysterical tone and character of current campaigns for 'political correctness' in North America, focusing on the offensiveness of language which might

indicate racist, sexist, imperialist or other such anti-social attitudes, suggests that the form of North American moral consciousness has not changed at all since the 1950s (see Fennell *et al.*, 1991; Mallet, 1992; and Chapter 11). To a European, one of the most peculiar features of this form of moral consciousness is the way it focuses on signs of 'substantial disbelief in the validity of the violated norms' to use Wirth's phrase. It seems to be the disbelief that is crucial, not so much the deviation as such. The effects in the national culture are lack of perceived social freedom, private oppression by pervasive and invasive social norms, and nationalistic xenophobia – the same effects noted by 'a European' in 1920 (probably Znaniecki; see Smith, 1988: 109). As Albion Small, one of the founders of American sociology, commented, 'the corporation-dominated property system' recalls 'the extemporized dictatorship of Lenin' (*ibid.*). The importance of social control and ideological conformity to the project of a corporate American society seems as vital as in Park's day. It is as if Americans have to sit down together and form a consensus (however artificial) before they can act politically, which may seem absurd to the European accustomed to moral, political and cultural conflict as a way of life but, of course, is actually a statement of fact in the American polity. The truth may be that there is so much cultural divergence in North America that this is the only way any authentic political reality can be constructed.

22 Thomas and Znaniecki (1927) had outlined a theory of the role of 'social technicians' which involved mutual learning between institutional America and the immigrant communities so that the immigrants could participate fully in the emergent culture and then social control would flow organically from a corporate society. Immigrant assimilation and democracy were thus to be achieved.

4 The potent union of psychiatry and sociology

Around 1937, the broad shifts in sociological theory and American society discussed in Chapter 3 precipitated a radical shift in criminological thought through a unique convergence between psychoanalytically aware sociology and sociologically aware psychiatry. A clear rejection of the residues of Lombrosian criminal anthropology, this convergence produced a clear focus on social deviation, a concept with deeply psychiatric overtones yet lodged firmly in a sociological perspective. It was a moment of formation which left an enduring mark on the character of the new field.

In this chapter, we will look at the details of this apparently strange union of sociology and psychiatry to see how it mediated the shifts in general sociological theory and the specific formation of the sociology of social deviation. The union had of course other more practical roots than the intellectual ones discussed in Chapter 3. As noted in Chapter 2, the combination of techniques of mass production, concepts of scientific management and popular psychology had already engendered the emergence of industrial psychiatry. This, in turn, had probably drawn much from military psychiatry.

In 1937, an extraordinary development occurred. The *American Journal of Sociology* (AJS) devoted a whole issue to ways in which psychiatric and sociological ideas could be fruitfully merged. Already the very first volume of the new *American Sociological Review* (ASR) had carried two articles on the relations between sociology/anthropology and psychoanalysis (Bain, 1936; Horney, 1936). Indeed, that this journal had begun at all, that it was now the official journal of the American Sociological Society, that it expressed a conscious revolt against the dominance of the Chicago school (Smith, 1988: 134–6) and that it was based in New York suggested that significant changes in American sociology were afoot. It was historically appropriate that the ASR was based on the East Coast, the centre of federal operations; it signalled the emergence of a sociology concerned with social structure, social functions, universal laws of the psyche and operational social planning.

Society as the patient

In an essay of 1936, Lawrence Frank had already dramatically challenged the old view that individual sickness caused social problems. Cashing in many of the conceptual themes emerging in the thirties, using the term deviant and the phrase 'deviation from social norms' comfortably, and drawing on a growing union of psychiatry and sociology, he openly stated that there was a new realization that 'our culture is sick, mentally disordered, and in need of treatment' (Frank, 1936, reprinted in 1948: 1). The focus was now upon society as the patient. Both Tawney and Rank, he said, had shown that it was society, not merely the individual, which was sick:

> Anyone who reflects upon the present situation in which our Western European culture finds itself cannot fail to see that we have passed from the condition in which deviations from a social norm could be regarded as abnormal. Today we have so many deviations and maladjustments that the term 'normal' has lost almost all significance. Indeed, we see efforts being made to erect many of the previously considered abnormalities into cultural patterns for general social adoption.
>
> The disintegration of our traditional culture, with the decay of those ideas, conceptions, and beliefs upon which our social and individual lives were organized, brings us face to face with the problem of treating society, since individual therapy or punishment no longer has any value beyond mere alleviation of our symptoms.
>
> (Frank, 1948: 1)

Dalí and Grosz stood vindicated.

The sense of social de-moralization and cultural disintegration was a strong one. Again, we see a sense of culture defining 'our' difference, or the specificity of the societal form. And, again, we see a sense of moral crisis. Social problems, argued Frank, were all symptoms of the same disease. From crime, through prostitution and family disorganization, to gastric ulcers, all social deviations were in fact 'human reactions to cultural disintegration' (*ibid*.: 2). They were socially censured as the bad behaviours of bad individuals and this gave us the comfortable feeling that society itself was healthy. Then, if the individuals could be 'corrected', our hope was that the 'natural', social, forces would flow unhindered and solve our social problems in the due course of things. This, Frank argued, is a 'social mythology' of normality and order which has dominated both lay and professional thinking for many years. The way forward, he suggested, was through the culture–personality couplet, which taught that individual behaviour of all kinds was very much a response to cultural 'demands and opportunities'. Yet again, culture was rendered as the prism through which normality was constructed, and he made a strong hint that therefore we should not be so intolerant of the individual 'deviant'. It was the society that was sick; the symptoms, for Frank, were lack of moral homogeneity and disintegrating culture. As with Wirth, the perception was of cultural conflict as the root of social degeneration, but Frank went deeper and saw the difference between the symptoms and the cause – the acquisitive society.

> so-called social problems and the seeming perversity of individuals become intelligible. They are to be viewed as arising from the frantic efforts of individuals, lacking any sure direction and sanctions or guiding conception of life, to find some way of protecting themselves or of merely existing on any terms they can manage in a society being remade by scientific research and technology. Having no strong loyalties and no consistent values or realizable ideals to cherish, the individual's conduct is naturally conflicting, confused, neurotic, and antisocial, if that term has any meaning in the absence of an established purpose and ideal.
>
> (Frank, 1948: 5)

No profession, Frank claimed, had been able to avoid succumbing to the practice of racketeering, so individuals should not be heavily censured for being unable to maintain old standards. The focus of attention should be the problematic cultural patterns. Like Wirth (1931), he argued that the old legal doctrine of individual responsibility and guilt was a complete block to understanding. Seeing society as the patient absolved the individual from guilt and took social problems as symptoms of 'progressive cultural change'. The only viable answer to such problems was cultural reorganization. The culture of individualism had brought about complete cultural disintegration, so a new culture or normative order had to be put in its place. However, enforced conformity created its own problems: 'the current practices of repression and enforced conformity may be regarded as reactions of neurotic, if not psychotic, individuals against the present cultural disorder that has produced their own distortions' (Frank, 1948: 8). Without collective cultural reconstruction, human values would not be conserved – but they could not be abandoned in the course of reconstruction. Normative unity had to be chosen, not forced or manipulated into being.

The Durkheimian character of this argument is more than evident, and this was amplified even louder in another essay, when Frank (1948: 16) spoke of social problems as signposts towards something better. However, Frank went into a lot more detail than Durkheim on the techniques of social construction, and perhaps had we been more mindful of his much neglected book we might have been readier for the reintroduction of Hayek's thought in the 1980s with the rise of the 'New Right'. Frank denounced Hayek's critique of state planning for ignoring cultural traditions of freedom and individualism in the West, thus underestimating our capacity to prevent social planning becoming statism. In making his point, Frank (1948: 87) demonstrated that proposals for a welfare state in the UK and USA were merely expressions of 'the ethical-moral traditions' of their people. The case for the creation of a *social* system, as opposed to a jungle of egoism or a machine of collectivism, was a renewal and development of the moral principles of human growth and health. The creation of an egalitarian-but-human normative order and its accompanying welfare apparatuses, to replace the acquisitive society ethic, was itself an act of moral renewal to be carried out in an ethical manner.

In the 1970s, had we read Frank and drawn the lessons, we would have anticipated that the return of the ethic of raw acquisitiveness in the Western 'enterprise culture' would necessarily entail the abandonment of any commitment to having a 'social' system and the consequent deconstruction of the welfare state. We would, therefore, have expected the resurgence of older categories of individual pathology and total personal responsibility to replace the more social-democratic conceptions of social deviance, social structure and ethical social reconstruction. The abandonment of the social dimension of political economy, and the return of the meaning of society as the court and leisure networks of the rich, inevitably meant the undercutting of the social relations which sustained the concepts of social deviance and social control. The demise of these concepts in the 1970s was therefore overdetermined.[1]

1937 and the sciences of degeneracy

Criminology

Earlier in 1937, the AJS had published a devastating and definitive assault on the 'Lombrosian myth in criminology' by Lindesmith and Levin. Lindesmith did his doctorate under Edwin Sutherland, one of the early PhDs from the Chicago school of sociology, whose first textbook of 1924 had contained a strong critique of 'such arguments as those of Lombroso' (Gibbons, 1979: 36).

Lindesmith and Levin demonstrated that the idea that Lombroso's constitutionalist theories and studies of 'the born criminal' made him the founder of scientific criminology was a complete myth, and, even worse, a myth which was mainly American. Citing the earlier social-statistical work of Guerry and Quételet, the early nineteenth-century English debates about juvenile delinquency and the ethnographic/historical work of Mayhew and Avé-Lallemant, Lindesmith and Levin showed that the 'militant biological determinism' of Lombroso and his colleagues in the last quarter of that century was a mere 'interruption' in the history of a very sociological criminology. They noted the extensive criticism of Lombroso's work in Europe, and claimed that his theories were rejected before they were even translated. Their thesis was that Lombrosianism, an importation of biology and eugenics into criminology, was seized upon arbitrarily by twentieth-century American criminologists attracted to Darwinism. Restating the view that crime was essentially a product of social organization, what they took to be the classical axiom of criminology, Lindesmith and Levin denounced the criminal anthropology of Lombrosianism as an ill-informed, American criminological fad.

This fascinating outburst ends with a healthy dose of typical late thirties' scepticism about the neutrality of science:

> The progress of science is often portrayed as a majestic and inevitable evolution of ideas in a logical sequence of successively closer approx-imations to the truth. We have shown that this conception does not apply to criminology wherein myth and fashion and social conditions have often exercised an influence quite unrelated to the soundness of the theories or to the implications of accumulated evidence. One of the sources of protection against invasion by fads, and against these extra theoretical influences, of which criminology of today has not availed itself, is a sound appreciation of its own past.
>
> (Lindesmith and Levin, 1937: 671)

This is a sentiment that the present text more than reinforces. In this same year, Sellin (1938: 3) observed that criminology is a 'bastard science grown out of public preoccupation with a social plague'.[2] These condemnations should not blind us to the fact that 'scientific' criminology in the USA was still enthusiastically pursuing constitutionalist accounts (see Beirne and Messerschmidt, 1991: 474–89), as evidenced by the studies of Hooton (1939) and Sheldon (1949) and the psychiatrically oriented work of the Gluecks (1950). But sociological criminology was growing in confidence and stature, and its relations with any criminology which owed much to biologism and behaviourist psychology were increasingly hostile. Of course, sociology was also critical of any 'a-social' psychiatry (e.g. Wirth, 1931).

The sociology of deviations

In the next issue of the AJS in that same year, we find to our astonishment[3] that every article concerns the relations between sociology and psychiatry. While astonishing for its intensity, and because accounts of the sociology of deviance have completely ignored its significance (except Pitch, 1980), the issue picked up an undercurrent that had grown to a torrent with the impact of shell-shock, Freud, the publicization of private issues and the rise of industrial psychiatry. As we saw in Chapter 3, sociologists had been showing so much interest in child guidance clinics that, in 1931, Wirth coined the term clinical sociology and discussed the relations between sociological and psychiatric accounts of behavioural problems. Most sociologists, argued Wirth (1931: 50), were more 'content with armchair speculation' than first-hand contact with the people they wrote about. This seems wide of the mark, and self-justificatory, in the classical age of 'hands-on', pragmatic, investigative, fieldwork-oriented sociology, but it did illustrate the intensity of the common sociological belief that suggested changes in the child's social environment, combined with medical/psychiatric counselling from social workers and psychiatrists, could reconstruct and control the child's behaviour (*ibid.*: 64).

Each article in this special issue of the 1937 AJS is of significance and interest, but we will focus on three in particular.[4] The first, by the psychoanalyst Alfred Adler, talked of the 'deviations' of criminals, sexual 'perverts', neurotics, suicides, etc. becoming manifest when they are blocked by a life-problem 'which demands more social interest for its solution than they have acquired' (Adler, 1937: 774). The 'antisocial solution' was thus a result of the blocking of the drive to success embedded in the life-force. Normal, right and successful resolutions came from people who feel part of the collective and thus feel a real social interest. This thesis is, of course, very similar indeed to the famous argument of Merton published a year later (yet who refers to Adler's essay?). Like Merton, Adler saw one way of reducing individual failure as the reduction of the expectations put upon individuals. Whether the failure is an active striving to crime or a passive retreat into unsocial behaviour, the current generation, he felt, were 'lacking in the right degree of social interest'. The other way to reduce their likelihood of failure was to increase their degree of social commitment or interest. Sociology and psychiatry converged on this point, he observed, perfectly capturing the momentum of the sentiments and concepts of the day. He then proposed that work to increase social interest should begin at an early age, in the schools, and should be done by specially trained teachers, with the aim of getting the children to look always towards the 'welfare of mankind'.

The second article was also by a Chicagoan psychoanalyst, the criminologist Franz Alexander. His essay supported the contemporary drive to integrate psychiatry and sociology. He claimed that sociologists recognized fundamental human drives and instincts, and that psychoanalysis assumed the existence of 'certain historically determined cultural ideals' incorporated in the super-ego (Alexander, 1937: 782). Sociology, he argued, needed to develop its implicit theories of human psychology, while psychology needed to recognize the historical and cultural character of certain mental processes. For example, if individuals with unresolved hostilities against members of their family also suffered from social handicaps, such as economic deprivation, they were more likely to convert their hostilities into 'aggressive antisocial behaviour'. Psychology, culture and class were thus combined to explain criminal behaviour in a radical move away from constitutionalist and behaviourist theories in criminology, and away from theories within sociology which merely stressed lack of urban community integration.

In this sophisticated way, Alexander foreshadowed so much of what was to come in criminology and the sociology of deviance in the following thirty years. Durkheim had never synthesized the individual's pathology with the anomie of the society, nor did he have a developed sociological account of individual psychological states. His offspring was growing up and developing an identity of its own.

Alexander (1937: 785) went on to castigate theories of class consciousness which suppose that people only develop motivations based upon rational insight. Foreshadowing criticisms of the 'new' criminology made in the 1970s, and in direct opposition to the positions of Marxists such as Lukács (1971), he dismissed the view that economic factors alone explain 'current ideologies and political attitudes' and drew attention to psychic/emotional factors such as those analysed by Freud; for example, the attachment of group members to a leader, reflecting the passive dependent love of the son for the father. Social theory, he argued, all too often ignored the irrational or non-rational response, and understated the variety of emotional reaction; thus anticipating Parsons's later theorization of deviance as non-rational behaviour (Parsons, 1951). Psychoanalysis, in turn, Alexander argued, was too prone to reducing complex group events and practices to the effects of individual psychology, to the neglect of the multiplicity of social determinants. War, therefore, cannot be seen as an effect of a single psychological process, such as the unleashing of a collective unconscious, when it is constructed by the ruling classes and fought by the working classes. A notion of repressed sadism does not explain either the outbreak or the social organization of war. In this vein, psychoanalysis had been reproached in the thirties (by, *inter alios*, Dollard, 1935) for neglecting the environmental causes of mental illness (see also Davis, 1937, discussed in Chapter 5). However, Alexander declared, following Fromm's doctrine, that cultural patterns did not explain individual life-histories, they merely pointed to psychological tendencies shared by that particular cultural group:

> What psychoanalysis offers to sociology is the knowledge of a great variety of psychological mechanisms, but what it cannot offer is the etiological explanation as to precisely which psychological mechanism and which emotional attitudes, of all possible ones, will develop at a certain historical moment in a certain group. Such an etiological explanation must be a historical and sociological one.
>
> (Alexander, 1937: 799)

In this formative intellectual moment, the nature and limit of sociology itself was being redefined.

The contemporary problem for psychoanalysis according to Alexander was that American society had a 'lack of generally accepted group evaluations and ideals' (*ibid.*: 801). Ideals were changing rapidly and there were many conflicting standards. Consequently, the individual was offered no clear guide, status or purpose in life and much neurosis, crime and corruption resulted. Therefore, it was more appropriate to change the environment than the individual, and treat society as the patient (citing Frank). These remarkable arguments have rarely been commented upon, yet they marked a watershed within aetiological criminology and a major shift in the analysis of human pathology.

Alexander's positions, again foreshadowing Merton (1938), pointed to the need to adjust society's infinite cultural ideals and to reach some shared normative understandings, rather than to address the iniquities of the class structure. The problems of crime and mental illness were now being seen, in principle, as thoroughly *social* problems and, indeed, the term social problems now comes into very frequent usage.[5] But what ideology should American society adhere to? Here again, Alexander raised an idea which was to gain much attention over the next few years (see Chapter 7), in contending that the pioneer ideology of frontier society was no longer applicable in 'a highly organized and standardized industrial civilization which has passed the phase of economic expansion'. Most people of his day could not 'live up to the ideals of personal initiative and success won by courage and enterprising spirit' (Alexander, 1937: 801). Crime was the only way they could seriously do that within a social structure which 'requires an extreme subordination to powerful industrial units in which the place of the individual is rigidly prescribed and to a high degree restricted' (*ibid.*). Alexander concluded that 'the increasing spread of crime and neurosis' went hand in hand with 'rapid changes in social structure' and 'the incongruence between new subjective needs and antiquated group ideals' (*ibid.*: 802). Individualism was no longer an appropriate dominant ideology: 'The relatively rapid transition from economic expansion to economic overorganization did not leave time for the development of a new appropriate ideology. Tradition lags behind the hard facts of social development' (*ibid.*: 801). In a nutshell, Alexander thus captured the sociological problematic of his age; a year before Merton's famous paper. Indeed, reading Alexander's essay is a prerequisite to understanding what Merton was saying, and puts Merton's explanation of crime into its exact historical context.

Crime, as Durkheim had declared, was seen as a sign of the need for social change. That change was to be located in the dominant ideology, not in the class structure itself. But, to his credit, Alexander did see that the formation of new, more appropriate group standards could not just be foisted on the people through propaganda, because standards corresponded with 'the fundamental social structure'. On that basis, he made the prophetic suggestion that a combination of sociology and psychoanalysis could scientifically supply the knowledge of psychological mechanisms and social-structural features which would facilitate the required adjustment of 'group attitudes and standards to the changes in the social structure'. Clearly, the politico-cultural solution of the age was to deploy science in the reconstruction of a new normative unity, rather than to reduce discrepancies of class. Faith in science had clearly not been lost, and we witnessed another round of social engineering to follow that in the UK and

France. So similar to the policies advocated by Durkheim, this political line again illustrates the close relation between the growth of social democracy and the growth of the sociology of deviance. A political ideology which perceived 'antisocial' action as partly rooted in social-structural mal-adjustment, and partly in individual character, would naturally want to describe that action in terms, such as social deviation and antisocial behavi-our, which portrayed it partly as a social matter and partly as individual weakness.

Like Adler, Alexander took children as the target of his recommenda-tions for the development of better social control. In his case, a loving family which enabled the voluntary and integrated emergence of a super-ego was seen as more effective than education based on intimidation or punishment. Indeed, any kind of education would fail without the back-up of a secure existence in the world. Democracies, he argued, must provide a minimum standard of security if they were to sustain the confidence in authority necessary for voluntary conformity. Unfortunately, paranoia, fear and mistrust, which Alexander saw as universal in his day, were a major block to the emergence of a coherent normative order. That paranoia could only be effectively muted by better child-rearing practices; the role of psychoanalysis being to formulate the principles of proper child-rearing.[6] Another key theme of post-war criminology and social policy was thus articulated (see, for example, the later work by Bowlby, 1952, and Fried-lander, 1947). The rhetoric of the welfare state, like that of Alexander's essay, had developed from the 'new deal' to include the provision of a minimum psycho-social security and scientific child-rearing.

The third essay from this symposium on psychiatry and the social sciences which warrants our attention was by Herbert Blumer, a leading Chicagoan sociologist in the symbolic interactionist tradition.[7] Blumer questioned what he saw as the psychoanalytic view that social disorgan-ization might flow, in an unconsciously motivated way, from individual disorganization stemming from difficult childhood experiences, and in so doing he laid some vital foundations for the heyday of interactionist so-ciology of deviance in the 1960s. His essay is yet another large eye on the formation of the sociology of deviance, and yet again much neglected. Arguing that it was more likely that individual disorganization flowed from social disorganization, and that, therefore, better child-rearing would not solve the problem, Blumer made the profound and quite Durkheimian observation that individual neurosis or peculiarity did not necessarily lead to social disorganization. Discounting extreme forms,[8] such as psychotic outbreaks which lead to incarceration, Blumer took a consequential and precocious step forward:

> I refer merely to those expressions which lead one's fellows to regard him [the neurotic individual] as queer, unnatural, unreliable, or un-social. If such conduct is not defined by the group in such a way as to elevate the individual into a special social position, the tendency

is, I think, to encyst him and to this extent remove him from the web of social relations.

(Blumer, 1937: 875)

So under what conditions do neurotics contribute to social disorganization, if at all? Blumer's highly Durkheimian answer was that it depended upon 'the factor of social discipline'. Blumer suggested that, where discipline was lax, neurosis could accentuate disorder, so that social disorganization bred antisocial action and consequently further social disorganization. However, he pointed out that, at that stage, the process whereby social disorganization, for example in the family, affected the individual personality was not well documented or understood. He clearly felt that socially disorganized situations created distressing experiences and thereby might bring neurotic 'dispositions' to a head, although they did not 'implant such dispositions' (see also Horney, 1936). Nevertheless, he also suggested that perfectly well-adjusted people could become quite disorganized and confused in socially disorganized situations which placed conflicting demands on the individual. When that occurred, individuals could suffer 'acute and disturbing self-consciousness' because of the sharp disjunction between self-conception and actual social status occupied. Moreover, individual motivation to arrive in this situation may have been perfectly conscious, thus intensifying the distress, and if there were no escape options the individual might lose personal orientation and abandon his or her existing life-project. 'We need to know the effect on self-conception and personal organization as the individual begins to respond to the disturbances in this psychological milieu. The desired knowledge requires collaborative efforts of psychiatrists and sociologists' (Blumer, 1937: 877).

This provisional but pioneering statement by Blumer marks an overall position on the social process of becoming deviant that was to become axiomatic and central in the sociology of deviance after the war:

1 Individual disturbances did not necessitate social-structural malaise.
2 Social-structural malaise did not necessitate individual disturbance, although it made it likely.
3 It was not necessary to have prior personality problems to be disturbed by a diseased social structure.
4 Whatever the cause of the individual disturbance, its severity could produce an exit from social status, either voluntarily or by use of external force.

It is certainly doubtful that there was a more precise or sophisticated statement of the symbolic interactionist position on the relation between individual pathology and social structure before Blumer's formulation. Acclaimed or not, it was the precursor of the detailed analysis of the collective processes involved in individual deviant identity-adoption most notably exemplified later in the writing of his neo-Chicagoan colleague, Erving Goffman.

The new disciplinary matrix

The sociology of social deviation was forged in the heat of this alchemy between sociology and psychiatry in 1937, although obviously, as I have shown earlier, the elements for the formulae had been produced in the three decades before.

The 1937 issue of the AJS, and especially the essays we have considered here, represented a major clarification of the relations between sociology and psychiatry, and between individual and social pathology. Cross-disciplinary borrowings, theoretical errors, methodological differences and political implications were all recognized, and much conceptual sharpness was achieved. Ground-rules for a happy coexistence were formulated, before, no doubt, all parties continued along the paths they were already well along. I have no knowledge of the exact impact of the special issue upon sociological opinion at that time, although the subsequent ignoring of the issue by later sociologists is nothing short of remarkable. Logically, it seems clear that after this symposium not only was there no scientific deadwood in the way of sociology beginning to study social deviation, but much conceptual groundwork was established leading very much in that direction. It was clear that, despite all that the psychoanalysts had said, there was a distinct field of social processes to be examined, a field which focused upon the interactions between the perpetrators of milder social deviations, their immediate social context and the people who responded to those deviations, with an eye to the negative changes on both the deviant and the social setting produced by those interactions.

It should be equally clear that, despite the influence of the sociologists, a field remained which focused upon serious deviation and major crime and which had not been significantly rethought in sociological terms. Lombrosianism was dead, but not buried. Psychosis and serious crime remained primarily the province of the psychoanalysts and the penal reformers. Degeneracy lived on in the guise of psychopathology; a shrunken form but a live one. After this symposium, serious crime as well as childhood would become the main focus of psychiatric studies of psychopathology, and, by the same token, the analysis of societal anomie was logically insufficient to establish firmly a sociology of serious deviance or major crime.

Academic territory had been defined, divided and allocated, the ground-rules for a new disciplinary matrix established. For sociology, the negotiation, imposition and adoption of normative status through social interaction was central. The question of the response to socially significant differences, so important to the culture–personality framework of perception, had to be studied in all its sociological ramifications. The term 'socially significant differences' is mine. The term that sociology used to map this phenomenon in the late 1930s was social deviations. A little later, in the 1950s, it would call its field of study the sociology of deviant behaviour.

Notes

1 As was the demise of social-ism, social-ist parties and social democracy.
2 It may be of interest to observe that Sellin (1937: 898), in a comment on the Lindesmith and Levin article, describes their criticisms of Lombroso as 'censures'. It is curious how a term can, for many years, live a subterranean life, being frequently mentioned without its merit being recognized.
3 It was astonishing, because my theoretical enquiries led me to suppose *a priori* that there must have been some kind of conjunction between sociology and psychiatry around the late thirties in order to precipitate the adoption of the term deviation with its psychiatric connotations – and there it was. I was quite unaware of this issue of the AJS before reaching this conclusion. I had not read Pitch (1980). This seems yet again to teach us that we do not really know our own intellectual history, and that, as Foucault so amply demonstrated, we often ignore the blindingly obvious in favour of something more grandiose. This 1937 issue has not been given the significance it deserves in criminology or the sociology of deviance. In my view, this is because its own self-understanding is all too often ahistorical and focused on individual thinkers or the abstract relations between ideas rather than on the *social logic* of discourse or the dialectical relations between knowledge and politics.
4 I will ignore the biologistic essay by Burrows (1937) which seems to regard violent behaviours as organismic deviations, but it is worth noting that he retained the nineteenth-century usage of deviation. The essay by Elton Mayo (1937) welcomed collaboration with psychiatrists, and the increasing sociologization of psychiatry, but saw it as of only limited use, in studying psychoneuroses. H. S. Sullivan's contribution (1937) argued the case for the use of psychological and psychoanalytic training for social scientists concerned to document with sensitivity 'the private history of great events' (W. I. Thomas). The comment from anthropology to this symposium on psychiatry and the social sciences came from Sapir (1937), with wit and sophistication. However, it largely supports Alexander's positions and warnings on the sociologists' use of psychiatric metaphors to talk about cultures, emphasizing that, while culture may be the coin of the realm, psychiatry must not cease its invaluable search for the invariant features of human personality, and that there is a large gap between collective culture and individual personality.
5 Despite his sociological inclinations, Alexander still retains a view of humans as animals with 'aggressive destructive influences' which need controlling socially. The super-ego and the formal systems of social control are needed to restrict 'original nonsocial tendencies' (Alexander, 1937: 803).
6 The essays by Schilder (1937) and Slight (1937) in this special issue both contribute to this theme. Schilder was concerned with the impact of social disorganization on children's emotional development and open learning abilities. He too emphasizes that the attitudes of the parents are crucial for the child's future social adaptation. Slight argued that education should ensure individual flexibility and willingness to compromise, as otherwise frustrated idealism will continue to produce social disorganization. This is a very Durkheimian theme and one not commonly discussed in the sociology of deviance. Slight felt that neurosis, delinquency and crime were likely products of lack of flexibility. Hence, individual ability to adjust to change was as important as structural flexibility.

The latter, of course, was vital in this period because popular gullibility to reactionary propaganda had to be counteracted by rapid, reformative change and sensitive government.

7 Blumer, along with Wirth, was also an associate editor of the journal at that time. Ernest Burgess was the editor.

8 This was something the symbolic interactionists were to do repeatedly over the following thirty years, and their sociology of deviance thus became very much a sociology of minor crimes, victimless crimes and morally ambiguous deviations. Blumer's distinction, therefore, is somewhat indicative. It suggests that symbolic interactionist sociology initially saw itself as a complement to psychoanalysis and penal policy, which were to deal with the serious neuroses and crimes. Certainly, its attitude at the moment of the formation of the sociology of deviance around 1937 did not imply any attempt to theorize the whole question of crime.

5 The coming of age of the sociology of deviation: persistent class and cultural conflict

The formation of an analytical matrix for a sociology of social deviation, with its academic territory, base assumptions, competing theoretical lines, key concepts, preferred research methods and connections with the social-democratic programme of cultural reconstruction, had thus more or less taken place by the end of 1937. It combined themes from Chicagoan sociology with concepts from the developing, East Coast, structural-functionalist approach, in an uneasy and often contradictory mixture. Such combination did not always occur in the same texts of course, but in several of the major texts that emerged around this time it was very evident, as we shall now see.

By the late thirties, it was clear that the Depression had only been partially defeated by the New Deal. The persistence of the class structure, despite the welfare reforms and controls over big business, was unmistakable. A sense of the recalcitrance of a dis-eased social structure was pervasive, an analysis of local processes of community disorganization and individual responses to malintegration no longer sufficient. There was more awareness now of the general pattern, the macro-picture, the whole social structure, the total cultural environment and the role of the federal.

A series of texts then appeared evidencing the coming of age of the sociology of deviation. This chapter is devoted to a brief review or parade of their contents and key features. The texts are important as moments of formation of the new field. A close perusal is valuable, for discourse has no inner secret other than its manifest contents, if only we would see them rather than searching for an authoring ulterior motive. Our earlier discussion of more general intellectual movements should make their connections with the earlier pioneering statements of Wirth and Frank very clear.

In 1937 and 1938, several major sociological publications emerged using with some frequency the terms deviate, deviant and deviation. Eventually, a book called *Social Deviation* was published (Ford, 1939), the first with such a phrase in its title. The terminology of deviance now gradually began to replace the existing concepts of individual pathology in sociology, and the conceptual matrix around social deviation began to replace that of the degeneration matrix. They did so along the lines of Durkheim's analysis but with a distinctively American flavour. They expressed a new understanding of social conflict, rooted firmly in the American experience of extensive immigration, cultural diversity, the Depression, extensive organized crime and popular psychology.

The paternity of the Durkheimian concept of deviation was never openly declared; as I suggested in Chapter 1, it was probably, literally, in doubt. Nevertheless, the concept's adoption in its teenage years did firmly register the recognition in sociology that the social censure of certain social manifestations was not so much caused by individual pathologies within 'offenders' as produced by social-structural tensions, conflicting cultural norms, individual refusal or inability to conform and a punitive dominant mentality.

Mental hygiene and class

Even the least progressive of these texts, 'Mental hygiene and the class structure' by Kingsley Davis (1938), is valuable in that it reconnects us with the earlier liberal thought discussed in Chapter 2. Davis reminded his audience that the mental hygiene movement was then nearly thirty years old, and that, as both social movement and social science, it was always in danger of becoming discriminatory. By 1938, that movement had renounced the prevention of specific mental diseases and was more concerned to 'treat' the customs and institutions which fostered 'bad mental hygiene' (spokesman quoted in Davis, 1938: 55). 'Bad mental hygiene' was now being used to understand and define industrial unrest and 'social parasitism', and the dangers of class moralizing were obvious to Davis. Defining class, remarkably, in purely moral terms as 'relative inferiority and superiority of persons in one another's eyes' (*ibid.*), Davis proceeded to argue

- that the mental hygiene movement was driven by the middle-class, New England establishment, purveying the Protestant ethic of an 'open-class' society with mobility there for the enterprising to take;
- that this moral philosophy defined the movement's conception of mental health and resulted in a 'psychologistic' view of it;
- that this moral individualism concealed the social character of mental hygiene; and
- that it hid its moral biases behind a façade of science.

Mills's essay of 1943 was to say similar things, but Davis, being a structural functionalist and not a radical, concluded that mental hygienists were not enforcing 'alien class standards' upon the lower orders, but merely enforcing the 'standards of the entire society' (*ibid.*: 64). How instructive discourse can be in a 'science' during the moment of its final formation!

How Davis reached this conclusion after his initial arguments about class is of great interest to us. Having examined the concepts of mental health in the mental hygienists' work, Davis concluded that the 'only consistent criterion' of every definition is 'normal behavior' (*ibid.*: 59). 'Normal' in the hygienists' work, he stated, referred to a confusion of the statistical average of actual behaviour and an ideal standard of behaviour, but 'ultimately the normative sense prevails'. Thus, the definition of mental health is a 'value-judgement', reflecting the authors' subscription to the central value system of their culture, an evaluation system which is not critical of the society's basic institutions. Moreover, he observed, the hygienists did not counsel a conformity with statistically average behaviour but a conformity with ideal standards, notably the individualistic standards of the Protestant ethic: 'they inculcate the dominant morality of a mobile society' (*ibid.*: 61). His study of seventy hospitalized cases then supported the conclusion that most admissions involve a high element of class evaluation: 'Sanity lies in the observance of the normative system of the group' (*ibid.*: 62). The normative system defined sanity and crime. Deviance could no longer be defined in an asocial way. However, Davis resisted the inference from this that sanity and crime are class constructs. He claimed that, in any culture, 'class ideologies are merely specialized parts of the central ideology, which is not identified simply with the outlook of the dominant class, but with that of all classes' (*ibid.*: 63). No reason was given for this extraordinary assertion except that it was supported by studies on schizophrenia, as if such studies could possibly justify such a broad claim. Therefore, he contended, poor mental hygiene was not a divergence from class morality but a divergence from the 'ultimate norms which unify the whole society' (*ibid.*). These norms are unspecified, but he claimed that they provided for and incorporated the 'ideological peculiarities' of any particular class. So, therefore, the key question for Davis was not whether there was a class system but whether the system was 'unified by a nucleus of common values'.[1] When central values were incompatible or conflicting then mental hygiene problems emerged: 'Mental conflict is engendered, then, not so much by the vertical structure itself as by inconsistency within the structure' (*ibid.*).

What is also interesting here is the way in which Davis expressed the social-democratic utopia of his day. The social contract of the New Deal was elevated to a fact rather than a project. Davis exhibited the new awareness of class in late thirties sociology only to subsume it under the utopia of a consensual normative order. Normality, however, is at least recognized as a social or cultural construct.

The persistence of class, anomie and the need for moral regulation

This same theoretical recognition and then incorporation of class occurred in Merton's famous essay of 1938. So much has been written on this article that I will restrict myself to a few points, partly also because I have already shown that Merton's essay is but one part of a much bigger ideological/historical current, and that much of what he said had been said before in a number of places. His essay is important because it openly defined the new field, expressed many of the theoretical themes of the time and unified them in a very coherent form.

The crucial point about Merton (1938) is that he did not see poverty as the major criminogenic force but the disjunction between 'culturally defined goals' and the 'institutional norms' regulating 'the acceptable modes of achieving these goals'. Like Davis, he saw the problem as one of 'cultural malintegration' (*ibid.*: 673). Unlike Davis, he specifically and consciously designed his conceptual scheme 'to provide a coherent, systematic approach to the study of socio-cultural sources of deviate behaviour' (*ibid.*: 672). The sociology of deviation had now emerged as a mature field aware of its own identity. Merton was the first, to my knowledge, to define his field specifically and publicly as the study of 'deviate behaviour'.

Drawing heavily from Durkheim and, like Durkheim, not denying 'the relevance of biological and personality differences' to 'the *incidence* of deviate conduct' (*ibid.*: 672, n. 2), Merton argued that the 'distribution of statuses and roles through competition must be so organized that positive incentives for conformity to roles and adherence to status obligations are provided *for every position* within the distributive order' and that 'Aberrant conduct' can be seen as a 'symptom of dissociation between culturally defined aspirations and socially structured means' (*ibid.*: 674). This represented a version of Durkheim's theory of anomie. But whereas Durkheim had talked of moral de-regulation, Merton's essay focuses upon 'demoralization' of the means to property acquisition. As he put it, echoing Frank, 'The extreme emphasis upon the accumulation of wealth as a symbol of success', divorced from a 'coordinated institutional emphasis', made 'Fraud, corruption, vice, crime, in short, the entire catalogue of proscribed behavior' increasingly common (*ibid.*: 675–6). On this analysis, citing Davis and Parsons, the break from biologism was achieved through the view that basic values or goals were cultural products not biological drives. Culture is a crucial concept in Merton's analysis of 'deviate behavior'. However, in historical context, it is the persistence and acceptance of class, within criminological theory, which Merton registered above all. As he himself observed, the current evidence suggested that 'our class structure is becoming rigidified and that vertical mobility is declining' (*ibid.*: 679n.).

Merton took the example of organized vice in Chicago. Given the low status of manual labour and the limited availability of unskilled manual work, organized vice was a very attractive option 'in terms of conventional standards of achievement' (*ibid.*: 678–9). He concluded that this 'anti-social behavior is in a sense *called forth*' by cultural conventions *and* (his emphasis) 'the class structure'. Those 'handicapped by little formal education and few economic resources' are culturally encouraged to accumulate wealth but culturally denied acceptable ways of doing that. Like Davis, he defined this as a situation of incompatible cultural demands. Still speaking the language of handicap, he saw the results as being 'psychopathological personality, and/or antisocial conduct, and/or revolutionary activities' (*ibid.*: 679). Deviant behaviour was thus defined by Merton, and, like Blumer, he saw social-structural disjunctions as its producers, not individual deficiencies. Individual handicap had now become social handicap. Psychopathology was retained as an operative concept, but it now became an effect of cultural contradictions, not a cause of cultural division. Moreover, Capone's significance was finally recognized as the 'triumph of amoral intelligence over morally prescribed "failure"' (*ibid.*). New Deal sociology had completed its historic recognition and adoption of the concept of social deviation.

We might note that, in Merton's formulation, it was unclear exactly where deviance stood in relation to crime and difference. What was clear was that deviance was unified by its infraction of dominant moral codes. It was *social* deviance – its coherence was linked to social norms, not any logical place between crime and difference.

Where next? Change the class structure, provide more jobs? No, this was 1938 and the New Deal had clearly not worked miracles. Now was the time to batten down the hatches, to limit the sociological damage stemming from the raising of popular expectations. What Merton advanced was the idea that the 'open-class ideology' was now merely a 'sop' to 'the masses' to legitimate the status quo, and, like Davis, his solution, implicitly, was to change the culture rather than the class structure. Welfare capitalism in the USA had reached its economic limits for Merton (only four years after its inception!) and therefore the culture should be adjusted to those limits because it was not poverty that caused crime but the cultural significance attributed to it. The concept of deviant behaviour, alongside the sociology of deviance, was in this way to become part of the mature ideology of the welfare state, as a recognition of the cultural character of 'psychopathological personality, and/or antisocial conduct, and/or revolutionary activities'. Its efforts subsequently were therefore to focus upon the adjustment of culture and ideology to the recalcitrance of economic and other practical facts, with an intent to reduce cultural discrimination and to remove counter-productive censures and regulations. Cultural consistency and normative integration were to be the goals, and sociological science had an important place in the tactics.

Culture conflict, conduct norms and scientific criminology

Sellin's book *Culture Conflict and Crime* applied the new knowledge that was forming within American sociology to criminological theory in general. Like Lindesmith and Levin, he launched an attack on the positivistic conception of science and, drawing on Poincaré's work, he argued that scientific knowledge was necessarily temporary and incomplete. Like many modernists, he emphasized the indeterminacy of knowledge. So, in criminology, given the social or cultural variability of definitions of crime ('which is too familiar to the social scientist to require any demonstration'; Sellin, 1938: 23), there were no grounds for taking legal definitions of crime as valid sociological definitions of types of behaviour, nor for limiting criminology to the study of officially defined crimes:

> The unqualified acceptance of the legal definitions of the basic units or elements of criminological enquiry violates a fundamental criterion of science. The scientist must have freedom to define his own terms, based on the intrinsic character of his material and designating properties in that material which are assumed to be universal . . . if a science of human conduct is to develop, the investigator in this field of research must rid himself of the shackles which have been forged by the criminal law . . . The legislator and the administrator on the one hand, the scientist on the other, speak different languages, fundamentally irreconcilable. This is as it should be, for they are pursuing essentially different ends . . . Confinement to the study of crime and criminals and the acceptance of the categories of specific forms of 'crime' and 'criminal' as laid down in law renders criminological research theoretically invalid from the point of view of science.
> (Sellin, 1938: 23–4)

What a revolutionary statement for criminology, and what a silence has surrounded it since!

The language Sellin found for the social scientist of crime began with the idea that we are all born into a culture and that this culture becomes embodied in the mind as personality. So, yet again, the culture–personality dynamic was the theoretical matrix of the analysis.

Sellin's version of the sociological problematic of his day led him to a further formulation that established the birth of the sociology of deviation, and again, despite being twenty-five years before that of Becker, it has been much neglected. Sellin anchored something Mead had already said, but in much crisper, simpler terms, which was that individuals oriented their action to groups, groups had norms regarding the appropriate conduct of action in given circumstances, and these norms, which Sellin called conduct norms, defined normality and deviation (Sellin, 1938: 28). Abnormality, therefore, was merely that which involved 'deviating from a conduct norm'. Conduct norms are 'products of social life' and therefore, Sellin could have gone on to argue, deviation is social. Although not voiced, the concept of social deviation was clearly adopted. In fact, what Sellin did go on to say was that, in complex cultures, conduct norms emanated from all social groups and therefore often clashed. They were thus not the creation of any one group, nor were they limited to the political sphere, nor were they necessarily embodied in law. Their breach was to be called abnormal conduct, and the term crime reserved for offences under the criminal law. It is interesting to consider here that Sellin could logically have used the phrase cultural deviation, as could many other sociologists given their analysis – the reason he and they did not, I believe, is that, as explained in Chapter 3, the differential concept of culture already had the concept of social deviation from dominant norms more or less built into it.

Sellin concluded that these 'facts lead to the inescapable conclusion that the study of conduct norms would afford a sounder basis for the development of scientific categories than a study of crimes as defined in the criminal law' (*ibid.*: 30). The sociology of deviation was now at war with mainstream criminology: a conflict that was to recur frequently in the 1960s and 1970s. Sellin urged sociologists to study the development of conduct norms, their interrelation, their relation to other cultural elements, and their violation and its patterns. A version of the subsequent sociology of deviance had been outlined. It is a forerunner of the central thesis of Garfinkel's ethnomethodology developed in the 1950s (Garfinkel, 1967; Cicourel, 1976), because it was distinctive in Sellin's conception that what was really important was not the formal rhetorics of morality or the general principles of moral conduct, but rather the specific norms people apply to the appropriateness of specific action in specific circumstances. The concept of conduct norm has the undisputed merit of going beyond the principles of morality to include implicitly the more informal, less voiced, nuanced, practical, 'hands-on', 'little' rules which connect general principles to specific situations at specific times in specific places and contexts.

Sellin's 'frame of reference' and research programme for the sociology of 'abnormal conduct' contained themes such as culture conflict, social anonymity, impersonal social control and normative confusion, which we have already observed in the writings of Park and Wirth. A distinctive point he made, which took the thesis further and which was later developed by Lemert, was that some life situations are governed by such conflicting norms that no matter what the individual's response it will violate the norms of at least one social group. Such cultural conflicts were seen as an inevitable feature of 'social differentiation' (a term also used by Lemert in his classic text of 1951). Abnormal conduct, or social deviation, was thus now openly theorized as part of everyday life in the modern, pluralistic world of the USA and, again, the extent of twentieth-century immigration was explicitly seen as a central condition for this. Despite this position, Sellin was sceptical about claims of high immigrant crime rates and of culture conflict as a cause of crime. Like many at the end of the 1930s, he thought that low economic position was actually more likely to be the cause of high official crime rates, a key indicator of social degeneration (see, for example, Ross, 1937). Slums, he said, 'exist in more or less all cities, even where there are no immigrants, and their degenerative influence has been noted in the literature of the last hundred years at least. These areas then create delinquency among the children raised there, no matter who lives in them' (Sellin, 1938: 96).

The community production of crime and the limits of frontier culture

Tannenbaum's book *Crime and the Community*, published in 1938, contained probably the strongest statement of the intellectual themes discussed in Chapter 3. In the most forthright manner, it drew out the obvious but radical implications of 1930s American sociology, and outlined the first ever version of what later became famous as the deviance amplification theory. From the outset, deviance amplification was but one facet of a general sociological perspective on social deviation. It was a logical corollary of the whole problematization.

In no uncertain terms, Tannenbaum laid the blame for crime fully at the door of the community, its methods of social control and its values. The text amounts to an indictment of frontier society; and, unlike so many who had talked in general of culture-conflict and problematic cultural norms, Tannenbaum made some very specific criticisms of the American way of life. America was being clearly told it had to grow up. A labour historian and authority on Latin America, Tannenbaum called for stability, equity, justice, peace and a healthy dose of critical self-examination.

Tannenbaum's basic standpoint was that modern societies shared the same Manichean vision of good and evil as archaic ones and that they too needed their devils or scapegoats: people who could be portrayed as qualitatively different from the rest of the community, then blamed and punished for their difference. Mocking the Lombrosian and psychological positivism which attribute physical or psychological abnormality to 'the criminal', Tannenbaum declared that 'the deviate' is simply one who challenged the values, habits and lifestyle of the community. The underlying cause, then, of the attribution of evil in older times, or abnormality in modern times, may 'lie in the inability to accept deviation from the "normal"' (Tannenbaum, 1938: 7). Using terms like deviate and deviation freely, Tannenbaum saw the censure, stigmatization and exclusion of the deviant as a means of reinforcing collective identity and holding on to a social order without having to question the institutional set-up: 'we seem driven to defame and annihilate those activities and individuals whose behavior challenges and repudiates all we live by' (*ibid.*: 8). In fact, he continued, criminals were usually well-adjusted to their own social groups and not necessarily any of the things usually attributed to them. It was crime which was the 'maladjustment', and it arose out of the conflict between a group and the community at large (*ibid.*). The better question, therefore, was not what individual deficiency caused the crime but what drew the individual to the criminal group and why the criminal group was in conflict with society. Noting the 'natural' steps from exhibiting behavioural problems, to truancy, to delinquency, and then to crime,

Tannenbaum focused on the criminal career, a notion developed by Thrasher (1927) and Shaw (see Finestone, 1976) that was to become central to the sociology of deviance of the 1960s.

Again foreshadowing much of what was to come on the role affiliation (Matza's term) played in the development of a criminal career and on the significance of group affiliation for any analysis of the efficacy of social control, Tannenbaum drew out the full importance of the gang for the sociology of crime and deviance. Referring only to boys, as was usual with the sociology of this period, he portrayed the gang as the boy's main social world, his source of identity and the primary source of his value-system.[2] For the first time in the developing sociology of crime and deviance, it was clearly observed that if society declared war on a gang it merely strengthened the group and enhanced its resistance.

The reactions of others, argued Tannenbaum, were central to us. Conduct was very much a response to situations created by others. Once formed as coherent, conscious entities in an urban world of conflicting values and interests, such social groups as gangs would not be battered into submission by punitive criminal justice policies. Such an external, coercive and alien form of repression could never function as a system of social control, given that the latter phrase implied voluntary commitment and integration. As he put it, if 'the deviation could be compensated by having its need met', then the conflict with authority might not be serious (Tannenbaum, 1938: 13). But the problem was that children's needs were not being met; other systems of social control were failing. Deviation was, therefore, very much a problem located in authority and control, not in the individual deviant. The family, schools, police and community organizations had to rethink their approach, the implicit assumption being that once the welfare state was properly organized there would be no major outstanding needs to be met by delinquent gangs, and therefore much less delinquency. Like much subsequent work from the labelling perspective, Tannenbaum came close to the essence of the matter but stopped short: what if authority could never, by definition, provide what the kids need? What if teenage kids *need* to be rid of controlling authority? He never posed the question: under what conditions can authority accept adolescent rebellion without repressing it? Nor did he ask: can 'social control' ever resolve problems so intimately tied up with lack of economic equity or democracy? Moreover, in the final analysis, what are the moral and political values which could unite warring generations, classes and races in a world of unresolved economic and political contradictions?

Nevertheless, Tannenbaum's analysis was acute. His account of the way deviation arose out of simple, everyday conflicts of interest, compounded by authority's repression of the underdog's version of events, is a classic (*ibid.*: 16–19). It represents an almost complete statement of the amplification thesis developed in the sociology of deviance in the 1960s. It shows how differentiations are created where none need exist if everyone's needs and interests were valued equally. In so doing, it reiterated that the problem was a normative one, a question of values, but it turned the tables and demonstrated how it was the values of the powerful that had to change. Tannenbaum argued that the community definitions of the acts in question as evil, and then of the perpetrators as evil, worked to create a sense of grievance and injustice which was compounded by subsequent formal stigmatization and punishment: 'The young delinquent becomes bad because he is defined as bad and because he is not believed if he is good' (*ibid.*: 17–18). As the delinquent career turned into a criminal one through repeated suppression, attitudes hardened on both sides and the following punishments became a raw 'clash of wills'. Both sides' attitudes were intelligible, and both were self-defeating. The 'dramatization of evil' involved, however, changed the situation completely. It labelled the delinquent a criminal and put him or her into a new social world:

> The verbalization of the conflict in terms of evil, delinquency, incorrigibility, badness, arrest, force, punishment, stupidity, lack of intelligence, truancy, criminality, gives the innocent divergence of the child from the straight road a meaning that it did not have in the beginning and makes its continuance in these same terms so much the more inevitable . . .
>
> The process of making the criminal, therefore, is a process of tagging, defining, identifying, segregating, describing, emphasizing, making conscious and self-conscious; it becomes a way of stimulating, suggesting, emphasizing, and evoking the very traits that are complained of. If the theory of relation of response to stimulus has any meaning, the entire process of dealing with the young delinquent is mischievous in so far as it identifies him to himself or to the environment as a delinquent person.
>
> The person becomes the thing he is described as being . . . the emphasis is upon the conduct that is disapproved of . . . The harder they work to reform the evil, the greater the evil grows under their hands . . . The way out is through a refusal to dramatize the evil.
>
> (Tannenbaum, 1938: 18–20)

Re-reading this classic statement, one wonders why Becker, Lemert, Matza and others in the 1960s did not devote more time, or give more acknowledgment, to Tannenbaum's work. They later said very little that he had not outlined here. Moreover, close attention to Tannenbaum's text reveals such a Durkheimian position that one wonders why Tannenbaum did not acknowledge Durkheim. On the interpretation of Durkheim in Chapter 1, Tannenbaum's formulations must be regarded as a full and precise maturation of the Durkheimian embryo. Again, we see the collective sentiment and its enforcement agencies as the forces which constantly create and re-work the distinctions between innocent difference, irritating deviance and deplorable crime. What Tannenbaum did, based upon an intellectual heritage which he barely acknowledged, was to flesh out the implications of this thesis in human and practical terms. Clearly, the dramatization of evil had to have these consequences: society, or the community, produced the folk devils it feared; moral panics were endemic; and punishment was a mere ritual to shore up the virtue of the condemners. Deviation was merely 'an innocent maladjustment'; it was society that needed treatment. Poor IQ was as useless for a career in crime as it was in criminology:[3] the pathology belonged to society now. Indeed so did the criminal.

Tannenbaum went on to elaborate the exact ways in which the criminal was produced by the community. Acidly, he pointed out that it was the community which gave the criminal his ideas and his purpose, and which gave 'him his methods too, whether these be graft, political pull, or the use of the machine gun' (*ibid.*: 25). At last, the exact correspondence between the criminal and legitimate worlds had been established in sociological analysis of crime. It was a bridgehead which Edwin Sutherland soon occupied with great effect to bring much attention to the 'white-collar' criminal (Sutherland, 1940, 1941, 1949). But it was Tannenbaum (1938: 25) who neatly observed that the 'distinction between the criminal and the community drawn in sharp contrast – a distinction between good and evil – is a false distinction and obscures the issue'. He continued:

> The amount of crime in the United States responds to all the factors and forces in American life – it is one way of describing our politics, our police, our civil and judicial administration, our immigration policy, our industrial and social conditions, our education, our morals, our religion, our manners, our culture. It is just as much one aspect of America as is baseball or divorce or anti-union industry or unemployment or Fords or movies.
>
> (*ibid.*: 25)

The issue, then, was not crime or the delinquent, but American society itself. America had to look to its history to find the causes of extensive crime, and therein also lay the answers to the problem. 'It is by regulating these forces that we may ultimately achieve a control and redirection of the energy that goes into criminal conduct' (*ibid.*: 25–6).

Tannenbaum's account of the criminogenic forces in American history is still extremely pertinent to any analysis of crime in modernity, and certainly in the USA. He highlighted the conflicts endemic in American history, conflicts which reflected its dynamic qualities. He pointed to the rapid growth of industrialism and cities, the influx of immigrants from all quarters of the globe and the high degree of individualism, acquisitiveness and insecurity. He emphasized the lack of stability that this produced, and the fact that law appeared to be a foreign and external imposition. He spoke of pioneer values in a frontier culture, values such as self-assertion, competitiveness, self-dependence and success:

> The individual had to succeed or be lost, forgotten, thrown upon the scrap heap. The individual who could not make a fortune or secure a niche for himself had to face poverty, isolation, neglect, unemployment, and possibly scorn and abuse. Therefore friction was the

essence of life . . . Against such a background of experience law is a feeble instrument indeed, and custom has no roots.

(*ibid.*: 28)

In such a harsh context, the 'philosophy of individualism' would flourish, and of course still does, to produce a massive overemphasis on success. Older legal forms based upon the household and the neighbourhood (see Pound, 1930) were simply unable to withstand the tide of problems flowing from rapid industrialization and urbanization. A flood of new legislation followed in the early part of the century, only to compound the difficulties by reflecting narrow economic interests and by often being inconsistent with older principles. Large immigrant populations, 'helpless and friendless in a new environment, unacquainted with the democratic technique and indifferent to it', had made for 'the growth of machine-controlled politics' in the big cities (Tannenbaum, 1938: 34). Alliances were struck between immigrant power-brokers and big business; a system of patronage and corruption was forged. The stakes were high so the building of a political machine drawing upon immigrant 'labour' was worthwhile, but it was unfortunately also a way of mechanizing dishonesty. Crime was mass-manufactured, like cars, and politics became integrated with crime.

A 'habit of violence' had been spawned earlier in fierce conflicts between capital and labour, intensified by cultural and racial divisions, and it supported the growth of criminal gangs and rackets. Further waves of immigration, xenophobia and ethnic conflict compounded the growth of habits which strengthened the hold of crime within urban communities. Or so Tannenbaum argued. To be clear, he did not attribute high crime rates to immigrants themselves, but he did believe that crime could grow behind the 'veil' of ethnic division (*ibid.*: 43). Pioneer culture had encouraged the crude legal suppression of such phenomena as prostitution, fornication, gambling and drunkenness. In modernized, urban, America that approach simply worked to nurture the field of crime and the profits of the criminals. All these conflicts and problems were compounded by the over-arching set of conflicts between federal and state authority, between one state law and another, and between urban and rural moral-legal predilections. There were too few common standards. More uniformity in legal rules, sentencing policy and enforcement practice was urgently required.

All in all, Tannenbaum concluded, there had to be changes in the community if there was to be a restraint on crime. His arguments cry out for the creation of a genuinely social system of regulation in the USA and the supersession of a violent frontier culture. As we shall see in Chapter 7, such a system was to be proclaimed by decree in the 1950s, once the war was over.

Juvenile Delinquency and Urban Areas

Shaw and McKay's book of this title appeared in 1942 and provided the demonstration of all that Tannenbaum had said. Its significance rests in its clear shift within Chicago sociology to a more structural analysis of delinquency, and thus in its closure of an era of optimistic, Chicagoan, research focused upon the inner workings of the city and the community. The broader vision discussed in this chapter was now registered in a major piece of criminological research. As Harold Finestone, who worked with Shaw, has observed:

> The central theoretical problem confronting Shaw and McKay had now subtly changed. Instead of seeking to relate juvenile delinquency to the processes of social change in the inner-city areas, it had become that of accounting for a relatively stable structural feature of these areas – the pattern of rates of the delinquents. Not surprisingly, the new emphasis upon the role played by structural forces originating in the larger society was accompanied by a reduced emphasis upon the etiological significance of processes occurring in the local community ... From stress upon personal and primary group relationships – that is, upon the local milieu – they had moved to attribute priority to the impersonal pressures originating in the larger social system.
>
> (Finestone, 1976: 92–3)

Shaw and McKay concluded that, in areas with high delinquency rates, there was a wide diversity of norms resulting from the cultural diversity and lack of assimilation of immigrant groups, and that these low-income areas contained the greatest degree of economic deprivation (see Beirne and Messerschmidt, 1991: 363–76). Crime was thus a rational attempt to succeed, according to the values 'generally idealized in our culture', in an environment where legitimate facilities and opportunities were barely available (Shaw and McKay, 1942: 319). Organized crime was identical to legitimate business in goals and organization (*ibid.*: 173). Yet despite this they also talked of 'deviant values' being symbolized by criminal and delinquent gangs and businesses (*ibid.*: 171). Clearly, while Chicagoan sociology had finally changed, to examine the 'larger economic and social processes characterizing the history and growth of the city' (*ibid.*: 14), it was still not ready to draw the logical, but politically awkward, inference that the only thing that differentiated criminal from legitimate enterprise was the official censure of crime in the criminal law. The East Coast, more cosmopolitan, work of Sellin and Tannenbaum had already taken that step: the centre of gravity in sociology had indeed shifted.

Ford's *Social Deviation*

The first book in our field to have the phrase social deviation in the title, as far as I know, was published in 1939, in New York, by a professor of social administration at the Harvard Institute of Social Ethics, James Ford. The East Coast location is unsurprising, and so is an Institute of Social Ethics, but how appropriate that a man named Ford got the honour!

Social deviation was truly a concept of the era of mass production, systematic social organization, the automobile, social mobility, scientific direction and popular psychology – an era which Henry Ford's car factories did so much to launch.

The book itself is curious and a major disappointment. Inside its covers, the whole of the subject material specified by Laughlin's old, paternalistic but encyclopaedic, concept of social inadequacy (see pp. 38–41) was dealt with, but in a language which exhibited many of the trademarks of twenties and thirties sociology. What a confusion! It began well. All human behaviour was seen as social. The 'bio-organismic' concept of society was recognized as dead. Problems like war, strikes, slums, illiteracy, ignorance, crime, deviations, delinquency and 'misuse of leisure time'(!?) were seen as social problems, as signs of social pathology. But the discourse kept returning to the same old people, and some very old ideas:

> The angle of approach is the deviation or inadequacy of the individual, its sources, consequences, and correctives. Physical or mental abnormalities, antisocial behaviour and delinquency, low standards of living and dependency, and the interrelations of these various maladjustments and of their social treatment and prevention are thus treated together under the caption of social pathology, or the sociology of substandard statistical groups.
>
> (Ford, 1939: 6)

Substandard statistical groups? Come back Quételet, all is forgiven! At least with him we were spared all this casual condescension and mindless jargon justifying full intervention into the lives of the powerless and poor. What nonsense Ford came out with at times! Another key example:

> Failures to conform to the rules of the group, whether customs, mores, or statute law, and positive revolt against the forces which make for social unity and stability, as well as evidences of degeneration or decay at any point in the social structure, are listed as types of social disorganization ... In terms of human interest and aspiration, social disorganization consists of those threats to or changes in social structure, institutions, rules, or even attitudes which thwart man's socialized desires or endanger his health, growth, freedom, or achievement. Utilizing either definition it is clear that social organization may be weakened by relative increase in the number of its handicapped citizens, or by increase in the volume of poverty, because of the reduction in standards of living which such increases entail. Increases in dependency and social parasitism, or in delinquency and antisocial behaviour, may menace social organization still more.
>
> (*ibid.*: 8–9)

It was as if, in many ways, the theoretical advances in American sociology during the 1930s had not happened. Yet, in a bizarre twist, Ford's text clearly reflected all these advances at an unconscious level. Sociology was suddenly turned upside down in the hands of a social administrator: the theoretical advances became mere subliminal references and the old concepts and prejudices openly structured the surface text.

Ford did not even sustain the emergent concept of social deviation: his title is very misleading. In fact, although he insisted that the sociologist must always define the normality 'from which a given condition deviates' (*ibid*.: 13), it was the sociologist, or social worker, who was to define the categories of health, adequacy and progress against which social deviation was defined. So, for example, within this utopian framework, crime was seen as a form of social deviation from healthy normality as defined by the new 'social' professions, as well as a breach of the criminal law (*ibid*.: 498). Overall, Ford suggested an ethical definition of deviation, based on the social scientist's (or social worker's) value-judgement of 'optimal standards' (*ibid*.: 14–15, 56–67).

> Since human beings look for guidance in their undertakings from the scientific groups concerned, it is natural and proper that social pathology should follow its analysis of human and institutional deficiencies with appraisals of the group's devices for social organization or social control, making use in such appraisal of the standards of reference employed by specialists in social amelioration.
>
> The remaking of the deviate and the overcoming of inadequacy have thus led not only to social work and restrictive legislation but to constructive legislation and broad-gauge planning.
>
> (*ibid*.: 65)

In so doing, he completely missed the point made by Wirth and others that, in a state of cultural diversity, deviation must be relative to the norms of a specific social group and thus polymorphous, and that, therefore, there was no established entitlement for one group to assert or enforce a transcendental norm – even if they were 'specialists in social amelioration'. Any such assertion of moral superiority was in effect normative fascism.

Ford's position was redolent of a new 'social' authoritarianism. All doubt and critique was swept aside in an unreflexive, poorly written, reassertion of moral absolutism and middle-class paternalism. Yet it was well-meaning and thoroughly sociological. It was a strange, paradoxical and theoretically warped ending to a decade of conceptual advances. But then, as we noted earlier, dumb yearnings must have their food.

This was, in many ways, the 1939 American equivalent of German national socialism and Soviet communism. Exhibiting the faith in science so pervasive during this bleak moment of human history, Ford outlined a number of guidelines for the elimination of poverty and the establishment of true social control. But always his starting point is the individual: 'The first principle of improvement in social organization is to so reorganize individuals that they will be interested and equipped to serve the interests of the group' (*ibid*.: 566). A dominant class or hegemonic group which directs the operation seems to be assumed throughout, and the precise individuals in need of 'reorganizing' were not an issue. Ford's standpoint was thus in truth that of the older, liberal-paternalistic, East Coast Establishment. The need to win hegemony through the successful promulgation of some popular core values seems to have eluded him. This was social control by scientific fiat. Its methodology was that of the authoritarian personality surfacing on the world stage.

Its Orwellian moral and political conservatism is obvious to us today, and was a sign of things to come, but the text is still useful in reiterating the political and ideological linkages between the concept of social deviation and the forceful establishment of a social-democratic welfare state. The spirit of liberal-bourgeois paternalism changes little over the ages, but now the terminology, and the policies, had changed greatly. This was the age of state social-ism. Social problems indicated social pathology and had to be dealt with by a social administration using a scientific social policy. Degeneracy, poverty and parasitism were to be planned out of existence by unilateral social administration. Existing societies were pathological, filled with socially handicapped populations and more than a few pathological individuals. They required massive reform.

In Ford's text of 1939, we were witnessing the entry of a thoroughgoing state 'social control'. A wave of textbooks called *Social Pathology* was emerging in the USA (Mangold, 1932, 1934; Gillin, 1933, 1939; Queen and Gruener, 1940; all quoted in Mills's essay of 1943 in Lefton *et al.*, 1968), and our story moved on to another stage. Ford's text is a permanent monument to the fact that the sociology of deviation emerged amidst a widely felt need to establish a firm societal system which relocated social control in regulatory apparatuses of state. Once it was accepted that society was in a pathological condition, the only cure was social reconstruction. Sociologists and social administrators varied in the degree to which they desired popular participation, but almost universally they seemed to agree that a dominant moral code should be re-created which would keep people interested in voluntarily behaving themselves while not inflating their expectations. It was a question of balance, but a question that most seemed to assume must be resolved by the state. As Chapter 7 of this book shows, there was an authoritarianism inherent in some of the founding texts of the sociology of deviation which was to come to fruition in 1950s structural-functionalist sociology.

Notes

1 This might be usefully contrasted with Gramsci's analysis of hegemony. Gramsci's ideas share a common concern with American sociology in their focus on unifying world-views and ideologies, but the connections run little further than that. For Gramsci, hegemony was always being rendered unstable by the explosive contradictions of class.

2 Having worked with boys and girls from gangs in Chicago in 1968, I can from personal experience vouch for the tremendous significance of organized gang life to ghetto kids (of both sexes) in big American cities; kids who are often severely socially distanced from their parents and relatively anonymous, not to say isolated, with only peer group support in a highly individualistic, privatized, society.

3 There were still some who believed that 'criminals' lacked 'social intelligence' (e.g. Young, 1938). Ford's book (1939), along with other signs, suggests that an ancient prejudice was making a come-back, re-scientized and legitimated by the use of the word social.

6 Deviance, degeneration and social democracy

The history of the formation of the sociology of deviation reveals a close connection between labour migration, cultural conflict and social democracy. The concept of social deviation was a more socially aware way of stigmatizing the disapproved, dissident, rejected, costly or unwanted, while protecting them from the harsher side of the criminal law. Social deviation was initially a liberal improvement on the rightist concept of racial degeneration. It specified society's oppositions, charges or miscreants as socially produced rather than individually degenerate. Nevertheless, it still rested within a problematic of capitalist domination and did not challenge the political-economic constitution of society. The notion of the purity of the master race may not be as popular as it once was, but still people have a strong preference to protect what they have rather than do what is morally right or politically just. In Germany in 1992, thousands of *Ausländer* from all over the world were discovering the recurrent social fact that people who are unwanted soon become censured as worthless, deviant or criminal; while millions of east Germans were discovering that the western Germans are loath to pay the price for the joys of unification and that their clothes, speech and attitude are often regarded as 'funny' or peculiar. Social deviance is one thing that has not lost its roots. It is a censure of unintegrated or unintegratable social fragments that are perceived as a threat to the unity (or desired unity) of the social whole – a censure precipitated and recurrently activated by cultural conflicts following major labour migrations in societies aspiring to social democracy.

As the Nazis displayed their abusive exhibition of 'degenerate art'

(*Entartete Kunst*) in Munich in 1937, American sociology began to adopt the clinical-sounding concept of social deviation to replace the last vestiges of the theory of degeneracy. The 'victories of art' had indeed been bought by the loss of character. It was a striking contrast. The strange union of psychiatry and sociology in the USA, which precipitated the concept of social deviation, combined a sense of personal angst with an appreciation of culture conflict in a multicultural society. Not only did Roosevelt try to rescue capitalism through his social welfare programmes, the intellectuals of his time tried to rescue the unwanted, unemployed, dislocated and estranged from the worst kinds of rejection, criminalization and persecution. It may only have been a very partial success, but the German route was a holocaust. Millions were eliminated by the latter, as if they were not even human enough to be managed as deviants. The Jew, the communist, the homosexual, the critic and the avant-garde were hounded and slaughtered as the psychic Other: that alternative world that could not be allowed its difference.

> Society's power to define the Other was articulated through an explanatory model of human pathology. But all of this distancing reflected only the deep-seated anxiety stemming from the consciousness that power (including the power to stigmatize) can be lost, leaving its erstwhile possessor in danger of becoming the Other . . . The magic of any overarching explanatory model such as degeneracy disguises, but does not eliminate, the potential loss of power. The only buffer 'science' could provide against the anxiety that remained because of this inherent flaw, the fear of oneself eventually being labelled as degenerate, was to create categories that were absolutely self-contained. Thus disease-entities were invented which defined a clearly limited subset of human beings as the group solely at risk . . .
>   In the mid-1930s there was a purge of Jews from all state and academic functions . . .
>   The new perception of the insane as unable to communicate on any level permitted the Nazis to begin their first experiment in mass murder, the 'euthanasia' of the inmates of the German asylums.
>   (Gilman, 1985: 214–15, 235, 236–7)

In America, even under Roosevelt, the difference of the Other could only be clinically captured as social deviance, and its threat only contained by a burgeoning dominant culture of social control. The victories of art recognized in late thirties America, stimulated by the migration of European artists, were bought by a loss of political innocence. Ending its isolationism, America became part of the global struggle in the forties, eventually launching a movement to eradicate the global deviance of communism and reduce the threat to free enterprise. Its methods were to be no more effective than those of the fascists, but they at least represented modernity rather than a terroristic archaism.

Social deviation, ultimately and complexly, is not just a sign of modernity's toleration of a greater degree of difference, but its attempted conversion of threatening difference into a socially controlled object. It represents an academic disciplinary matrix intertwined with the political attempt to regulate cultural conflict without amplifying it. The growth of the concept of social deviation is not just a sign of the desire to live peacefully with ambiguity and contradiction, or with other cultures. It is also the conceptual indicator of the crisis in the theory of degeneration and the crisis of society which activated fears of social degeneration. It is thus an indicator of a liberal, modernist, mode of crisis resolution within the confines of a corporatist culture of capitalist domination. It is a sign of the recognition that the eugenic and psychiatric theories of degeneration were non-rational, unscientific, unfair and ready for consignment to the archives of history, while holding tight to the idea that fractious, dependent or hostile social fragments had to be subject to social control. It is a sign of an emerging system of social control, of the social-scientific management by governments of the tensions, conflicts and contradictions inherent in modern capitalist, multicultural societies. It registers the growing recognition that unemployment, crime, dissent, drug abuse, sexual diversity and racial antagonism are products of the social structure both in their existence as practices and in their existence as categories. As such, it was a recognition that a disapproved phenomenon was a category as well as a social practice. As such, it was a sign of modernity's self-doubt, a sign of uncertainty about what was normal and about the healthiness of normality. But it was also a sign within a utopian discourse which was involved in the cultural reconstruction of the normal, which itself was a key moment in the political-economic project of establishing a stable, corporate, society. It registered cultural diversity while simultaneously signifying the drive to normative consensus. It was thus a pragmatic holding concept pregnant with its contrary.

In short and in summary, the question of how much deviance could be tolerated in a society became a form of the question of how long is a piece of string. The string is as long as you cut it. To rephrase Foucault (1977b: 154), knowledge is as much for 'cutting' as for understanding, and so the amount of deviance in a society from the thirties onward was simply and openly a question of how much the social system could tolerate. It became a question of calibration and balance. A little more tolerance, by definition, meant a little less crime and more social deviance; a little more repression meant a little more crime and less social deviance. Deviance was part of the movement to social regulation; a concomitant of the regulatory project and a rejection of the older project of suppression. In this way, it expressed a guilty awareness of the psychically repressed Other and a sense of ambiguity or fear about the open acceptance of that Other. It was, therefore, fundamentally concerned with a balance between repression and acceptance.

The sociology of social deviation, in conclusion, seems to emerge along with the beginnings of social democracy. Like social democracy, it was somewhere in between two extremes and pregnant with the offspring of their contestation. It harboured latent hints about degeneracy at the same time that its obsession with the culturally exotic suggested an ambiguity about the value of conformity. Equally, it flaunted a rhetoric of permissiveness and a philosophy of moral relativism resonant of those who were too comfortable and conformist to fret about the material consequences of social censure, while at the same time never doubting the need for state-led social control. It is a sociology that can also be seen as an ideological reflection of, and upon, the international expansion of capitalism, in that this expanded field of vision created by imperialism demanded that the dominant Western consciousness come to terms with its colonized or repressed forms of life, whether these be female sexuality, the working-class delinquent, the culture of Africa, homosexuality, madness or communism. The cultures of Others could not be continually suppressed or ignored. One victory of art, in its avant-garde forms, was to bring such cultures to light and to challenge conventional vision. The sociology of social deviation, to its credit, began to do the same.

It will still be many years before it can be said that criminology has fully come to terms with the 'dark continents' of Western consciousness and the new visions (and techniques of seeing) required to see them properly. Sociological studies of the crime and deviance of women, underdeveloped societies, children and the insane are still in their infancy. The world of unreason, as Foucault called it, remains a secret, and will continue so unless there is a revolution in the ways of seeing criminologically. Instead, what we have is a criminological knowledge of this 'dark continent' which is still crippled by its archaic vision, its natural-scientific methodology, its positivist philosophy, its refusal to learn new languages, its subservience to the power of the state and its massive philosophic and political naiveté in accepting the laws and norms of society as the definers of what is unreason. A sizable chunk of criminology today remains locked in the emotional–conceptual–political prison within which Lombroso did a long sentence.

The formation of the sociology of social deviation was at least a sign of the times, and not a relic from the past. It was one consequence of the modernist's doubt, one effect of the realization of ambiguity, one spirit in search of the lost soul of character. It did at least realize that all was not what it seems. Liberalism was of course flawed. It never severed its ties to the capitalist patriarchal state which gave it so much to study. It was still in the business of management and social control, rather than liberation from the blinkered categories and practices of oppression. But at least it could see that society needed a doctor and that to accept the targets of its abusive pathological raving as really, scientifically, criminal or degenerate was somewhat mistaken.

Of course, it was a sociology with its own left, right and middle, and it was rarely to be a unified force after reaching the age of majority. Its childhood had been an uncertain one of change, disruption, war, emigration and orphanages. Its teenage years were spent trying to find an identity on some very mean streets of a foreign country which itself had no clear identity. Adulthood had thus been reached in a state of profound ambiguity, not to say neurosis and conflictful cultural identity. Subsequent chapters will illustrate, for example, the differences between the conservative wing concerned with an effective social system focusing on juvenile delinquency and a liberal wing concerned with equity and focusing on the fairness of social control. The sociology of deviation registered the human authenticity of the oppressed cultures and the internality of these forms within the white, male unconscious, but it never liberated them from the categorical prison which prevents an accurate reassessment of what we as a species are all about. Some of these forms, namely the female/feminine and pre-capitalist cultures, were largely ignored and remained in their cells until the seventies and eighties, when radical criminology began to give them some attention. Women, and female sexuality, like blacks, revolutionaries and homosexuals, were powerful, determinant, agitators of the discourse on deviation, but they did not effect their agitation at a conscious level very often, their work went on behind the scenes, as part of the 'dark stirrings of the unconscious' – as part of the historical object of social control, the suppressed populations and forms of being which threatened the dominant moral–epistemological–political ethic.

Roosevelt had offered a New Deal to the American people, which the sociologists in our field felt should be applied to those formerly stigmatized as degenerate members of the species. These sociologists, in partnership with some critical psychiatrists, adopted the concept of social deviation, gave it some distinctively American and distinctively middle-class clothes, and put it to work in the service of the welfare state. It was a strange marriage and a strange adoption, truly deviant in fact, but it was of more than passing significance to the wider society, even though the latter in practice preferred to ignore it. It was a social event, like a gay marriage, which provided a wider window on the world. It was soon to help open the eyes of many in sociology, from 1937 onwards, to the fact that society itself was constituted very much by a coalition of agreements and disagreements, approvals and disapprovals, consents and conflicts, prohibitions and punishments, censures and supports.

PART TWO

Regulating deviance: fantasies of social control 1941–1967

7 Beyond the frontier and into fantasyland: deviance, social control and the end of ideology

> European social theory since the Enlightenment has in
> general been an attempt to secure a coherent liberalism on
> the ruins of a crumbling and decreasingly legitimate
> patriarchy. American social theory has been an attempt to
> secure a coherent liberalism on the basis of nothing at all.
>
> (Hawthorn, 1976: 216)

By the outbreak of war in Europe, no new social system, no normative or political consensus, had emerged or been constructed in the USA. Raw capitalism and its concomitant tragedies had been only mildly restrained. Elements of a welfare state had been launched, despite great opposition from the conservative establishment, but the New Deal still had much to do. The right saw Roosevelt as a class traitor, a 'red', who had installed state social control, individual dependency upon excessive federal power and a large national debt (Sitkoff, 1985: 6–9). The left and the progressive movement documented the failure to eradicate poverty, racism, excessive corporate power and the political disenfranchisement of the powerless, and felt that all that had been achieved was a temporary rescue of capitalism from its harsh internal flaws. American social reality in 1939 was not a good foundation to secure a coherent liberalism.

Piling paradox upon paradox, the worldwide war of 1939–45 forced the USA to abandon its parochial isolationism in both politics and sociological theory, and, indeed, gave it an opportunity not only to establish its might on a world stage but also to project its internal needs as the universal sociological laws of human development. The need for a moral and political consensus was acute. One could not be found in reality, nor readily constructed in practice. It had to be fabricated in political ideology and the sociological imagination, and foisted upon some recalcitrant publics by propaganda, backed up by the new, improved, hardware of coercive power. In parallel, the concept of social deviation was about to be generalized and aggregated as social deviance, an object of an elaborated sociological theory.

The empirical details of different deviations were to be sacrificed on the altar of abstraction in the drive for a general theory which would unify the field. Inspired by the social search for an elusive normative order, that general theory was fired by a utopian desire for the elimination of social deviance in general, or at least for the successful state management of its more disturbing effects. However, as we shall see, this development could not ultimately shake off the fact that America was divided and hetero-geneous. Many were still committed to the progressive liberalism of the Roosevelt period, and had no desire to lump all types of social deviation together as a sign of social disintegration or the need for moral consensus. Two different approaches to the sociology of deviance emerged as a result: one which saw the (re-)socialization of deviants as an integrative mechanism for equilibrium in the new social system, and another which portrayed deviance and tolerance as hallmarks of cosmopolitan, pluralist, social democracies. The theoretical tensions between the two distinct sociological perspectives, referred to in Chapters 4, 5 and 6, were now to come to the surface. The sociology of deviance was thus about to experience a neurotic adulthood in post-war America, one which was comfortable but divided, liberal but ethereal, and established but subversive.

From parochialism to JFK

The Japanese and German imperial campaigns of aggression in China and Europe had failed to dislodge the forces of unilateralism, pacifism and isolationism within the USA. Roosevelt was only finally enabled to declare war by the Japanese onslaught on Pearl Harbor in 1941. American public opinion was outraged and converted to intervention. A few months earlier, Roosevelt had begun to push industry towards a military production system, and had acquired the powers to give military aid to anyone 'in the interest of national defence'. The creation of a 'superpower', with a Presidency of enormous strength and influence, was under way.

As Brogan (1985: 585) comments, 'The war replaced the Depression with a boom to dwarf the twenties.' Workers' wages boomed along with the GDP. Defence industries snowballed to transform the economy irre-versibly. The 'permanent arms economy' had been born, as America supplied the Allies with ships and planes. Millions migrated from the East and Mid-West to the new jobs in California and the South-West, 'the sun belt'. America's centre of gravity was shifting, from Chicago to California, a fact that was soon to be reflected in the location, tone and line of its leading sociologists (e.g. Lemert). The economic basis of a middle-class society had been launched. After the war was over, cars, college education, good housing, medical care and regular work were to become the norm for many. California became the most populous state, stocked with univer-sities quickly growing fat from research contracts with the Defense De-partment. A Pacific Rim economy emerged, underpinned by the affluence of the 'warfare state' (Brogan's nice phrase), sustained by high-technology industry and trade with a revived Japanese economy under American influence, characterized by a conformist individualism and committed to 'enjoy' (as Westcoasters so often say). The blacks were again to be left behind, to be later followed by an increasingly large immigrant Hispanic population.

The war very much affected the black population. Jobs were available in the South, many were conscripted and segregation in the armed forces created massive tensions. Gradually, a degree of desegregation in the forces began to occur, and the reforms established by Roosevelt in the thirties (e.g. enabling some black judges in the North) were reinforced. Perhaps more importantly, black consciousness was mightily heightened; things were no more going to remain the same in the USA after the war than they were in Britain's African colonies. *Brown v. Topeka Board of Education* gave the Supreme Court imprimatur to the demand to desegregate schools, and a revolution in race relations in the USA was gradually getting under way. That court in 1956 outlawed segregation on Alabama's buses, after a struggle in Montgomery which saw the rise of the charismatic black leader, Martin Luther King. In 1960, Kennedy (JFK) helped to get King out of jail in Atlanta and won the black vote and thus the election. The black vote was becoming important in an America reluctantly dragging itself into line with its own Free World propaganda, for, as the war ended, America, as Myrdal (1944) commented, had a split 'moral personality'.

With American support, the Allies slowly began to regain ground against the fascist imperialists. In 1944, the Allies invaded continental Europe and the Bretton Woods agreement was signed. German imperial intent and an exhausted British empire were simultaneously on the retreat in the face of their successor. Bretton Woods set up the International Monetary Fund (IMF) and a new world monetary system tied to the dollar. American capital was expanding, its reliance on federal support revived, and the global conditions for the safety of the American profit system were now secured. The alliance with Stalin, the Soviet Union's need for national security after the shock of German invasion, the devastation in Eastern Europe and the concessions at Yalta made the growth of the other empire, the Other Superpower, virtually inevitable. As Stalin gradually colonized Eastern Europe after the war, the anti-communist fear in the USA generated support for the Marshall Plan which revived an equally devastated Western Europe. That American aid left huge amounts of European currency in American hands. Reinvested in European industry, it gave American capital an enormous hold over Western Europe in the ensuing decades. The formation of the United Nations, like the IMF very much under American control, completed the picture. The dice were now loaded to win any fight against the possibility of new communist regimes around the world.

Roosevelt died in 1945 and the Truman doctrine, 'to support free peoples . . . resisting attempted subjugation', provided an early ideological legitimation of the new imperial strategy. Brogan comments:

the memory of Munich was repeatedly going to distort Western policy in the next thirty years. The trouble was that in the process the peaceful prospects of the world were sacrificed to American self-righteousness . . . It is possible that the Americans were more enthusiastically ideological, more missionary-minded than the Russians . . . Americanism . . . is a crusading faith, anxious to liberate the peoples of the world, to expose and confound their enemies, and forestall any ideology and revolution which threatens the continuance of the liberal, capitalist, individualistic system.

(Brogan, 1985: 601)

The atomic bombs Truman decided to drop on Japan were soon reproduced in the Soviet Union, and the Cold War scene of sustained insecurity in the face of potential annihilation and an infinite arms race was firmly established. That arms race fuelled American prosperity and what became known as the American way of life.

During 1938, the House Un-American Activities Committee (HUAC) had been set up and it was to operate for twenty years, causing much misery and demoralization. In 1946, the Republicans had regained full control of Congress, riding in on a rhetoric of anti-communism. In 1947, the Taft–Hartley Act curtailed the freedom to strike, outlawed the closed shop, banned strikes by the likes of government employees, made unions liable to lawsuits for breaches of contract, revived the use of the labour injunction and forced union leaders to swear they were not communists. Combined with the extensive number of strikes in 1946–7, these events showed the degree of division in American politics. Truman was re-elected in 1948, as the Democrats regained Congress, to provide a Fair Deal to the American people. The New Deal was extended in certain respects. The minimum wage was raised, social security expanded, and slum-clearance and public housing programmes were launched (*ibid.*: 614). However, the anti-communist lobby was not to be squashed. In what is for us a most consequential development, Senator McCarthy in 1950 rescued his own flagging career by beginning an anti-communist campaign which was to destroy those of many others.

According to Brogan (1985: 617–18), McCarthy was an inveterate liar, bribe-taker and drunk. He took advantage of the political situation and the new power of the mass media to engage in a demagogic set of character assassinations. Reds were now to be found under every bed. The campaign was fired by the conviction of Alger Hiss for denying under oath that he had sent state documents to the Soviet Union.[1] Money flowed in to McCarthy's pockets from anti-communists as he made his accusations and initiated hearings through the HUAC. Encouraged by other Republicans, such as Taft, he took on the State Department, the army and even the Presidency. FDR, he said, should have got twenty years for treason. The hearings of the HUAC are now famous of course, as is McCarthy's haranguing and innuendo. The effects on American sociology are less discussed.

For sure, we know that many actors, journalists and scholars were subjected to the 'great fear' (Caute's phrase), and that their lives were made miserable. Many lost their jobs, some went to prison for contempt of Congress, and many just remained silent in private for fear of exposure. Vigilante groups were set up, and blacklists. A university employing a suspect might find it was losing its government research contracts. 'A grey fog of timid conformity settled over middle-class life' (*ibid.*: 620).

It would not be a remarkable thesis to suggest that the liberal wing of the sociology of deviance, following on from the writings of Tannenbaum, Mills and Lemert, remained quiet in American sociology throughout the fifties because of McCarthyism. In consequence, the final emergence of the field in the early fifties had a misleadingly conservative look to it. The Harvard and Columbia scholars, Parsons and Merton, had it all to themselves for far longer than their work warranted. Lemert wrote from Los Angeles in the late forties, but it was only in the sixties that his work got its full recognition. Only in the sixties was a West Coast liberal perspective fully represented in the textbooks, and neo-Chicagoan scepticism fully expressed. McCarthyism created a hiatus in our field. It greatly slowed the full flowering of the liberal wing of the sociology of deviance. It would not have been easy in a period of accusation, pillory and slander to have produced a book demonstrating that deviance was merely a moral-ideological label located within a web of conflictful social relations, and that those who labelled others deviant were in most cases hypocrites acting out of self-interest. The proof was all around, but who could speak up in the Land of the Free?

The political impact of McCarthyism was enormous. The campaign once and for all established character assassination, via the mass media, as a prominent feature of American politics. Even worse, any policy which had even a tinge of being soft on communism, such as recognizing Mao's new China, would have few public adherents. Rational debate about the Soviet Union was no longer possible, and the vested interests in the arms industry had little opposition to their acceleration of the arms race. Inevitably in such a climate, 'By the end of the fifties the United States was committed to propping up any number of weak and worthless régimes' (Brogan, 1985: 622). In such a climate, there could be no serious debate about the merits of sending in troops to liberate South Korea from North Korean aggression, or even about allowing General MacArthur's troops to threaten the Chinese border. NATO was formed in this same period as a military bulwark against the imagined threat from Stalin. Expulsion from North Korea by the Chinese and a growing casualty list, rejection of most of Truman's Fair Deal plans, and news stories of official bribe-taking meant that the Republicans were heading back to power, which they duly took in 1952 under the former Allied Commander in Europe and first Supreme Commander of NATO, General Eisenhower. Eisenhower won by a landslide. *En route*, he had endorsed McCarthy's re-election, and McCarthyism continued until 1954. Big business was back in power and, to an extent, the USA went back to the regimes of the twenties. Tax was cut and government reforms were rolled back; the CIA overthrew the Guatemalan regime to protect the United Fruit Company. The slander of deviance on a global scale was beginning to pay out.

Eisenhower's administration was domestically lethargic. The most noteworthy event for our purposes was the Interstate Highways Act of 1956, which linked all America's big towns and cities. Parsons's theory of social systems in 1951 interlinked all the roles, values and institutions of American society; it found its concrete reflection in the new highway system. Twenty years of modern government, media, population movement, war and military-style discipline had rendered Americans a little more homogeneous; the Interstate Highways Act subjugated them all to 'the ascendancy of the private car' (Brogan's phrase). By the end of the fifties, Republicanism was jaded and could only offer a bleary-eyed 'Tricky Dicky' Nixon, the Vice-President, as opposition to Kennedy in the 1960 elections. Nixon's disastrous appearance on a televised debate with JFK sealed his fate – for the moment. As Kennedy said in his inaugural, 'the torch has passed to a new generation of Americans'.

The Cold War of the fifties had been a sustained defence of the fantasy of the American way through a constant ideological attack on anything that could be labelled as communist. It was a paranoid phase that frequently lost touch with reality; a phase where America became the world's policeman and thus completed the transition from one extreme to another, from isolationism to global domination. In a world of ubiquitous reconstruction under American hegemony, conservative American ideologists could perhaps be forgiven for thinking that a total social system inspired by a single set of values was being created. But it was wishful thinking. Nevertheless, it was a wishful thinking that was inextricably and concretely intertwined with the reality of post-war American imperialism. The 'other' America, the black world within that its rulers strove to forget, was soon to make its voice heard in the fifties, and the later war in Vietnam was to reveal the full extent of the moral schizophrenia that had been established in the new social system. But, as many have noted, the old order of inequality and discrimination that emerged from the New Deal and the Second World War remained essentially intact right up to the present. It is thus little wonder that the character of that order was to deliver social deviance as a central ideological problem.

Abstract Expressionism and the search for universals

The horror of the German concentration camps had impacted deeply on the American consciousness, as had Hiroshima and Nagasaki. What had happened was beyond belief. The parameters of normality had been shattered. If this could happen, then anything could. Realism was permanently mocked. The imagination and the unconscious had been unleashed. To a certain extent, this explosion of feeling created a desire for peace, reconstruction and healing, but still the question after the war was how to make sure the Pandora's box of the unconscious could not be opened again: how best to put the lid back on? One part of the answer was not so much to put the lid back on but to accentuate the visions of the positive side of imagination. Unleashed, the imagination could also be positive; it could dream; it could invent a new utopia beyond capitalism and communism. To this end, social projects of reconstruction abounded and, in American art, visions of the universal and the popular unfolded in an abstract expression of the new desire to rebuild on universally valid foundations.

There was an impulse to be free from memory. Some, as in Germany, simply put their heads in the sand. Others recounted their tales, and those of the deceased. One survivor of Auschwitz described it thus:

> Even if they had paper and pen, the submerged would not have testified because their death had begun before that of their body. Weeks and months before being snuffed out, they had already lost the ability to observe, to remember, compare and express themselves. We speak in their stead, by proxy.
>
> I could not say whether we did so or do so because of a kind of moral obligation towards those who were silenced, or rather in order to free ourselves of their memory.
>
> (Levi, 1988: 64)

Psychoanalysis was not competent, Levi argued, to explain this impulse to tell. It was a 'civilian' knowledge, built up in civilian circumstances. In contrast, the physiological and psychopathological states of the *Häftlinge* (prisoners) often defied existing medical and psychiatric knowledges – it was a world without, for example, colds and influenza where death could suddenly strike for no obvious reason. It had been a 'deserted and empty universe . . . from which the spirit of man is absent' (*ibid.*: 65). In a very real way, Levi's observations capture a crucial element of post-war consciousness: civilian knowledges and imaginations had been proved to be limited, there was a wider and deeper world now to be explored and constructed, and, this time, psychoanalysis, while still important for some, was not to be taken by liberals as a science of universals so much as one tool among many to enable us to grasp our roots.

The dream, in general, was now not to be sidelined as mere sublimation but to be celebrated as a valuable vision of what could be. As Levi said, because of the acute nausea about the Holocaust, there was a certain immunization effect against it ever happening again in the Western world, Japan and the Soviet Union – so positive fantasies could roam freer than ever before. Moreover, the desire to tell the whole world of the irrevocable horror and its lessons was unstoppable – no one could be untouched by the shame or ignorant of the need to create a brave new world.

Memory had been permanently altered. The war had been a consciousness-altering state far beyond anything social deviants could muster up in the late sixties. Levi wrote:

> We have bored our way through all the minutes of the day, this very day which seemed invincible and eternal this morning; now it lies dead and is immediately forgotten; already it is no longer a day, it has left no trace in anybody's memory. We know that tomorrow will be like today.
>
> (Levi, 1961: 121)

It was a feeling that was to pervade the post-war consciousness for some time to come. It was a feeling, later heightened by mass society consumerism and one-dimensional existence, which was also to colour the sociology of the post-war age. History, with all its pain, was to be forgotten and abstract sociological (California) dreaming could commence – in a world of absolute uncertainty about what could happen next. As Levi noted, no one in a concentration camp says the word never. As Bob Dylan put it some years later, 'yesterday's just a memory, tomorrow's never what it's supposed to be' (*Infidels* album, 1983). Abstractionism was, perhaps, ultimately a retreat from the pain of the war. Walt Disney's cartoon *Fantasia* (1940) was to become one of the most popular films of all time, and Parsons one of the best-known sociologists.

Roosevelt's avowed national culturalism, and the surrounding circumstances, had given birth in the 1940s to an intensely personal abstract expressionism in art. The intent of the abstractness was to convey feeling – good feeling. For example, Stuart Davis's jaunty humour in his abstractionist canvases combined all kinds of urban elements in a new and positive way. Davis himself commented that this feeling rested on a faith that people within a common culture have a rapport that does not depend on outward representational form[2] (Lawson, 1985: 173). His art was consciously intended to be 'popular art'; he had already introduced to painting the picture of the commercial product (e.g. *Odol*, 1924). In 1950, he declared: 'I like popular art, Topical Ideas, and not High Culture or Modernistic Formalism. I care nothing for Abstract Art as such, but only as it evidences a contemporary language of vision suited to modern life' (quoted in Hughes, 1981: 330). The artist, he said, was 'a cool Spectator-Reporter at an Arena of Hot Events'. Davis reported for the 'common man'. Art from life, but a life in mass metropolitan society which was either glued existentially to the fleeting present or in search of universal human values.

Abstract Expressionism seemed to break from Dewey's view that 'direct experience is the stuff of fully realized art' (Lawson, 1985: 173), and social realism was already outdated by the early forties. The patronage of the New Deal had become an embarrassment to the artists. Mass culture made the artist feel like an outsider,[3] and there was a great fear that art would become just another piece of mass entertainment. Once severed from New Deal projects, some artists lost energy and drifted away from avant-garde modernism (such as Davis's). A poetic naturalism had given way to some very mysterious abstractions. Propaganda took over from documentary;

system from process. The concrete, reflexive, self, in control of, and directing, events, was giving way to an appreciation of unconscious psychic and cultural universals which might drive a world potentially well out of control.

The artistic interest in the psyche, nature, anthropology and religion, which developed during the 1930s, came to full fruition during the 1940s in the USA. Idealized nature and transcendentalism have a long history as cohabitants. The mysterious abstractions of Mondrian and Kandinsky were much mimicked by New York artists (Kandinsky was famously exhibited in that city in 1939). As Hughes comments, Kandinsky could hardly have foreseen that his metaphysical ideas of 1910–14 would combine with a distinctively American vision of the transcendental character of the natural landscape. This combination was best expressed by Jackson Pollock in the late forties. Pollock was influenced by his experience of Jungian analysis (1939–41) as well as by Kandinsky's idea of the *Geist*. His *Guardians of the Secret* (1943) is described by Hughes (1981: 265) as 'a rummaging for the authentic residue of the self'. Timeless archetypes of human consciousness were to abound at a time when many wanted to grasp for universal values, or the unchanging nature of things. Parsons's abstract expressionist sociology was foreshadowed by Abstract Expressionism in art – the latter explains Parsonianism much better than either Parsons or his critics did. Too often, Parsons's unrealism is simply dismissed as stupidity when it is very much part of its time. Realism was now insufficient. 'Representation no longer meant looking' (Taylor, 1979: 205). Expressive form was superseding realistic representation. Picasso and Kandinsky were 'proof that form could carry human meaning in a profound and curiously timeless way' (*ibid.*: 207). Surrealism became very popular, and stayed so well into the late sixties.

In 1943, the Abstract Expressionist Rothko stated that 'the subject is crucial and only that subject matter is valid which is tragic and timeless' (quoted in Hughes, 1981: 259). Hughes comments:

> Painters like Pollock, Rothko, and Still wanted to locate their discourse beyond events, in a field not bound by historical time, that went back to pre-literate, 'primitive' tribal antiquity. Somewhere in the back of every viewer's head, an ancestor crouched in the shadows of the cave; he was the audience their art wanted to address . . . Barnett Newman . . . harped on the need to re-primitivize oneself to obtain cultural wholeness, by regression as it were: 'Original man, shouting his consonants, did so in yells of awe and anger at his own tragic state, at his own self-awareness, and at his own helplessness before the void'. That phrase, 'helplessness before the void', sums up the period style.
>
> (*ibid.*: 259)

The artists themselves were suspicious of Surrealism, with its sado-masochistic fantasies, but still held on to Breton's concept of art as 'psychic automatism'. So, the Abstract Expressionists were open to the effect of drips (e.g. Pollock's drip technique) and other chance effects of unintended combinations. As Rothko said, the 'familiar identity' of things had to be 'pulverized' so as to destroy the finitude of sensations surrounding all aspects of the environment. The later work of the sociologist Goffman was to emulate such a celebration of chance in the construction of what we took as so solid and eternal, and, equally, to emulate the deconstruction of the familiar to discover the deeper truths of the environment. The superficial level of the social world was no longer obvious. Its meaning was mutable. Positivism had little in common, spiritually, with this new movement in thought: 'all he believes are his eyes, and his eyes they just tell him lies' (Bob Dylan, *Infidels*, 1983). However, paradoxically, its practical value in providing the statistics of the newly systemic state of surveillance, legitimated by scientism, had increased dramatically.

In Pollock's work, 'painting became, for both spectator and artist, a detached object that invited endless participation and discovery' (Taylor, 1979: 208) – like, we must add, social theory and the whole of that sociology based on Parsons's own drip technique. 'If one attempts to follow a single line of motion in one of Pollock's paintings, he is quickly absorbed into the complexity and must eventually be content to follow many paths at the same time' (*ibid.*). Time and distance seem to be of no consequence. Rothko's paintings 'seem to be composed of positive yet insubstantial forms of colored light hovering in a dimensionless space' (*ibid.*: 210). But more of Parsons and Goffman later. The first response of post-war American sociology was to try to express cultural universals in a very formal abstract way. Deviance was becoming abstractly conceptualized as a universal feature of societies.

The professional ideology of social pathologists

For obvious reasons, there was little apparent development of our subject during the forties. The operational research techniques, the cybernetic thinking, and the propaganda jargon so marked in fifties sociology were emerging and being applied to more external matters (the war). However, the intellectual–political divisions of the thirties were polarizing. Some sociologists, such as Cuber, rejected the critique of the concept of social disorganization. Stressing the importance of institutional or systemic organization, as opposed to local or specific instances of disorganization, and noting that social change often brought out imperfections or latent, alternative ways of doing things in organizations, Cuber (1940: 486) argued that value conflict, diversity or divergence were not in themselves to be taken as signs of institutional disorganization. What was crucial, echoing Parsons's work later, was that the value dissensus did not affect 'the integration of social roles'. By this cute phrase, which was later to become so popular, Cuber seems to have meant 'the hierarchy of functionaries', 'the system of subordination–superordination and the perquisites of position', and the absence of a replacement system. As he so obligingly put it, to confirm our worst suspicions, the 'essence of "organization" seems to be a consensus relative to how one role relates to another and what a given person filling a given role should and should not do' (*ibid.*). America could have diversity and conflict in values, in other words, as long as it did not alter the power structure. Sociologists were becoming more aware of system structure, and it was the preservation of that which mattered, not cultural pluralism, variations in taste or even divergences of ideology.

Developments in the theory of social control

In similar vein, Hollingshead exhorted sociology to exhume what he incorrectly took to be the neglected concept of social control. Ignoring and implicitly rejecting Park's corporatist–assimilationist model of social control and its importance to the whole Chicagoan project, he stressed that the essence of social control was not the formal mechanisms of control, or even the informal norms structuring personality, but the organization of the society as a whole, binding its parts into 'a more or less coherent unity' (Hollingshead, 1941: 220). Society, in this sense, 'from the viewpoint of social control is a vast, multiform, organized system of appeals, sanctions, prescriptions, usages and structures focused upon directing the behavior of its members into culturally defined norms' (*ibid.*). What made it 'organized' was the 'system of reciprocal values and usages inherent in a culture', that is, the coherence of the links between values, mores, roles, ideologies and institutions (*ibid.*: 221). Again, Parsons's work was prefigured.

What is striking during this period is the way that the notion of social-systemic integration was coming to the fore. Social control was being redefined as a scientific, system-management exercise from above rather than the two-way process of negotiated assimilation of cultural and ethnic pluralities. Correct state monitoring and management of the social system would sustain its equilibrium, and in turn this equilibrium would induce the appropriate individual personalities and behavioural responses. Such positions of course begged all the profound questions raised by Wirth, Tannenbaum and Sellin. They amounted to a revised conservatism, an attempt from the establishment right to recover the moral ground abandoned so blatantly in the *laissez-faire* twenties. They assumed a cultural unity *ab initio*, and they supposed that scientific management could somehow spoof away the intrinsic contradictions and difficulties of capitalism, democratic pluralism and cultural diversity. Memory had been repressed. Nevertheless, in retrospect, the sociological ideology of the welfare state was clearly evolving further during this period. It was now concerned less with hegemony or a genuine moral-political consensus than with formal or contractual consensus and mass-society management of a Fordist type. The workers could have their cultural and political diversity as long as they produced the goods and did not rock the boat.

This was an important period for developments in social control theory.[4] As we have seen, in the thirties formal legalism had been criticized by progressive sociologists. It now warranted the attention of the conservative system-builders. In 1939, Timasheff (1974) had outlined the premises of a structural-functionalist sociology of law, and the latter was taking off as a distinct field of enquiry. What clearly mattered to structural-functionalist writers like Hollingshead and Timasheff was how the law functioned within the whole social system. In the forties, therefore, the question of justice slowly gave way to an ethos concerned with the efficacy of law as a means of social control: with the structure and function of law, a phrase that was later to grate on the ears of a whole generation of young sociologists and lawyers. For example, despite the influential sociological and anthropological realism of Llewellyn, Frank, Arnold and Hoebel, the famous jurist Roscoe Pound now extended his earlier ideas on the dependence of law upon a universal home-based morality and informal normative foundations (Pound, 1942). His response to the dangers of modernity was to argue for the installation of a positive natural law: an idealism above, and restrictive of, the unlimited and brutal positive law of Hitler and Stalin which was also to transcend, organize and unify the moral diversity of urban pluralism. Others insisted, like W. G. Sumner, that definitions of social problems were often expressions of cherished values vital to the operation of the society (e.g. Fuller and Myers, 1942; Fuller 1942). They were thus not invalidated by being shown to be value-laden. This 'positivization of natural law' (a phrase coined later by Habermas) was very much a 'standpoint . . . of cognitive and implicitly ethical monism, a reaction against the suspect pluralism of the previous period' (Melossi, 1990: 133). It amounted to a classically conservative reassertion of 'traditional values', but one which was combined with the New Dealers' sense of the need for a firm, directive state. It also involved a new political claim: namely, that mass societies can be governed without ideology or an ideological blueprint. Pragmatism was now to be combined with scientific system-management and traditional values in a new alliance. Of course, today the internal contradiction seems obvious. None of these components of the prototype American welfare state are free from ideology – they are all subtly, or even openly, loaded with the concepts, sentiments and structural imperatives of the social relations and social (dis)order which gave rise to them in the first place.

Nevertheless, this conservative revival of a univocal consensus, a discredited natural moral order, did not represent the only response of American sociology to the hegemonic crisis of the late thirties. Nor was it the only reading of Durkheim to gain adherence. It is important to emphasize that there was an alternative, albeit one which was subdued and subordinate in the fifties. The seeds sown by Wirth, Sellin, Tannenbaum and Mills were to bear fruit in the work of Lemert from the forties onwards, and especially in the 1960s in the work of Becker, Goffman and Matza. This was a view which refused to ignore the ideological and cultural diversity of modern societies and to gloss the question of recalcitrant social divisions in favour of a fantasy social contract induced by repression of memory, state propaganda, post-war affluence and imperialist adventures against the communist enemy. This view refused to suppress recent memory and instead was to portray social control as all too often irrational. The conservatives were to retain the notion of social deviation but dismissed it as a non-rational product of inadequate socialization, a residual obstacle to the final triumph of a complete system of consumerist conformity. The progressives also retained the notion of social deviation, but enriched its meaning as a sign of moral diversity in a culturally pluralistic world and of the continued existence of a tolerance which sustained a sphere between serious crime and trivial difference.

The continuation of the progressive line in the forties began with an attack by Lemert (1942) on the essay by Hollingshead. Noting the plenitude of discussions of social control and folkways in the twentieth century and thus demolishing the fantasy that social control had been neglected, Lemert pointed out that W. G. Sumner's conception of folkways portrayed them as 'the fulfillment of natural laws inherent in the universe' (Lemert, 1942: 395), thus indicating that Hollingshead's claims were a back-handed way of resurrecting natural law. As Lemert stated, Mead's social psychology had avoided the cruder implications of a structural-functionalist analysis which supposed that there was a static, deterministic relation between the structure and function of cultural forms and individual behaviour. That relation was always mediated by indeterminate symbolic interaction between the ego and the significant others. But, Lemert continued, a complete sociological account required an analysis of the processes whereby authorities and individuals were able to 'shape the responses of others'. As he said, it was important to distinguish between 'the regularities in behaviour and the techniques employed to induce these regularities' (*ibid.*: 396). Moreover, it was necessary to distinguish between passive or unconscious adjustment to contexts and active adjustment. Tentatively, Lemert was suggesting that we all frequently passively adjust to contexts, whether they be climatic and geographical or normative and regulatory, and therefore folkways, popular morality and institutions were not necessarily any more 'means of social control' in this sense than the weather. Therefore, the true sociological sense of social control must recognize that it arises out of 'undefined or crisis situations' and that its success requires active not passive adjustment of individuals to conflicts. In this way, social control is as much about conflict, regulatory technique and symbolic reorganizations as it is about folkways, shared morality and conformity.

This critique defended the progressive work of the thirties in an acute and sharp manner. It also laid some foundations for Lemert's future analysis of secondary deviance (see Chapter 8). Its subtle suggestions are, like Tannenbaum's book, resonant of the conflicts of the 1930s and their role in the demand for an assimilationist social control. Moreover, they strongly suggest the active and determinant role of agencies of social control in defining, regulating and thus calibrating the exact degree of social deviance officially recorded within a society.

This concept of the societal calibration of deviance was developed further by Lemert in 1945. Lemert had by then moved from Michigan to Los Angeles, and this was the first of a number of significant contributions from West Coast sociology which by the late 1960s were to alter considerably the content, tone and style of the sociology of deviance. It was the beginning of a laconic, laid-back sense of irony. Lemert's general position was much stronger and clearer than in 1942, and he was using the concept of social deviation with great frequency and significance. He saw that the best analyses of social control must recognize categorically that it was about *power*, its size, distribution, purpose and methods (see Lemert, 1945: 751). More specifically, the central issues in social control, said Lemert, surrounded the relation between power and customary behaviour. So, 'the amount of deviation in any situation is determined by the point on the continuum of norms . . . at which an agency of control identifies itself . . . Thus if an agency of control identifies with modal norms it automatically decreases deviation . . . This action gains much personal and group support for the control agency and neutralizes potential opposition' (*ibid.*: 752). Complete lack of identification with customary norms denied power any support and gave us a situation where the amount of raw institutionalized power could be measured sociologically. The degree of deviation in any given control situation was, therefore, a completely relational question. It was completely dependent upon the power balance.[5] It was produced by the overall structure of the situation:

> As deviation between controllers and controllees increases, through action of either, a point is reached where the situation gets structured as a struggle for power. Often this is as much a problem of semantics or putative (spurious?) deviation growing out of a superimposed pattern of institutionalized conflict as it is a problem of genuinely gross or cumulative deviation . . . When deviation reaches a point where power relations must be changed it is unrealistic to assume that any groups will liquidate themselves out of rational considerations.
>
> (*ibid.*: 752, 758)

In short, deviance is a social fact produced by normative conflict between defining agencies of social control and controlled populations, and is not necessarily a rational outcome. For the first time, deviation was conceptualized completely in structural and collective terms – the concept of pathology, individual or social, is nowhere to be seen. The pivotal question is the degree of identification between the control agency and the norms of the group controlled.

Of course, this is still tentative and begs the question as to why the control agency was involved with the group in the first place; it begs the issue of motivated ideological surveillance and the total societal relation between the group and the agency. But it was a major analytic advance in the field. Deviation could be seen clearly to be a relatively impersonal matter dependent upon the field of power relations and normative-ideological differences and conflicts. It was a relational effect of some sort.

Lemert's analysis was the precursor of much that was to follow in the 1960s, although the relational quality of deviation was never conceptualized clearly as such, by him or by others, as clearly as, for example, the relational theory of power in Poulantzas and Foucault. But more on Lemert later.

The themes of Tannenbaum's work were also to be found in Elliott's essay of 1944. Like Tannenbaum, she attacked frontier culture, and like Lemert she attacked the romanticism inherent in the notion of folkways as the normative bedrock of social control. Folkways were important all right, but more as a bedrock of crime than as a basis for conformity. Culture was indeed the 'matrix out of which much of the modern crime problem emerges' (Elliott, 1944: 185), but this culture was often rooted deeply in the past. Noting the historic role of gangsterism, piracy, opportunism and 'exaggerated individualism' involved in the conquest of the wilderness, and the shelter it provided for Eastern ex-convicts and outlaws, Elliott stressed the lawlessness and rough justice of frontier culture. She concluded that while social legislation was truly a sign of increasing 'social consciousness', it also created new crimes by redefining practices still tied to frontier culture. Thus, Sutherland's emergent work on the 'white-collar criminal' (1940, 1941, 1945) could be seen as a testimony to the 'lawless heritage' of frontier culture, to the consequent degree of resistance to any government restriction on industry and the big corporations. Crime, she concluded, was indeed writ large in American mores, and social control was not something that was going to come readily in a culture of excessive individualism.

Sutherland's essays on 'white-collar' crime apparently caused a stir, but they were really no more than the extension of the ideas coming out of the thirties (to which he, of course, was a regular contributor). At last the robber barons and the fraudsters in the banks and industry were receiving attention, as the lessons of 1929, and of the previous hundred years, began to sink in. Sutherland's own explanation in terms of differential association, exposure to an excess of criminal norms, was unfortunately quite superficial and begged more explanatory questions than it answered. Like theories of slum delinquency which blamed the culture of the slum, this explanation is purely descriptive and therefore is no explanation at all. But Sutherland's work was a start, and it did have the undying merit of forcefully feeding the new scepticism about taking the legal definition of crime as a scientific starting point, a practice so trenchantly criticized by Sellin. Essays began to appear questioning the concept of crime itself (notably Tappan, 1947; see also Sutherland, 1945). Tappan's essay asked 'who was the criminal?' and registered the increasing feeling among sociologists and lawyers that when they delved into crime by looking at the criminals convicted by the courts they found that they were not 'studying the real criminal at all, but an insignificant proportion of non-representative and stupid unfortunates who happen to have become enmeshed in technical legal difficulties' (Tappan, 1947: 96). The superficially obvious was no longer so obvious.

Capone's immunity from conviction had not been in vain as it combined with Sutherland's indictment of white-collar criminals to form a huge moral question which began to pose itself in the 1940s. Who were the criminals? And what does the definition of crime amount to if it is thoroughly embroiled in politics and culture? At this stage, sociologists were only prepared to condemn the legacies of frontier culture and none of them subverted the concept of crime at its roots. For example, Tappan, fearing the condemnation of anything and everything as crime, and displaying a touching faith in the morality of state officials, concluded that a man may be 'a boor, a sinner, a moral leper, or the devil incarnate, but he does not become a criminal through sociological name-calling unless politically constituted authority says he is' (*ibid.*: 101). Somewhat missing the point that such a state of affairs is a damning indictment of the legitimacy and morality of state authority, he stated that the sociologist must 'avoid definitions predicated simply upon state of mind or social injury and determine what particular types of deviation, in what directions, and to what degree, shall be considered criminal' (*ibid.*: 100). So Capone was not a criminal, and nor were white-collar law-violators such as Insull and Yerkes, because they were not so defined by politically constituted authority. The positivism of the conservatives was not dead.

This open attack on Sutherland demonstrated the conflict then emerging within American criminology. The conservatives were fighting back. Law was held to be a useful and major means of social control and the latter was possible through law (but not through the informal condemnations of the sociologists). Even if this meant legitimating corruption, the conservatives upheld the law as the great symbol and pillar of order. Roosevelt's defeat on constitutional issues and on the political constitution of the Supreme Court was reaping its ideological harvest. For a time, it would not be too wise to broadcast a really radical critique of the legal system.

Looking back on these debates, one irony is very striking: the progressives had agreed that folkways were after all important, in stimulating criminal behaviour, and the conservatives were now in fact conceding that behaviour was not sociologically criminal until it had been so defined by the law. Everything had turned upside down. What both sides clearly shared, however, was a recognition that the criminality of an action lay in its official definition by the legal system, or that deviation was only so defined by the dominant culture of the day, a position which was to become the anchor for all post-war American sociology of deviance, whatever inferences different political animals were to draw from it.

One other thing was clear: the older problematic was now transcended. The issues now concerned the interaction between law-makers and law-breakers. The 'nature or nurture' debates were falling into the background, and rejuvenated conservative faith in the abstract positivity of law was not going to escape the established realist critique. Indeed, the earlier proponents of social disorganization and criminal pathology were now to be roundly condemned by Mills in another magisterial essay.

Mills's critique of the social pathologists

Mills's essay of 1943 was a study of the professional ideology of social pathologists as displayed in their textbooks (including that of Ford, discussed in Chapter 5). To this day, its criticisms summarize the progressive objection to the conservative/liberal view of crime and deviation as a learned cultural response to the social pathology of disorganized, inner-city areas, and its constructive postulates undoubtedly contributed to the formation of the labelling perspective which was to follow. These same criticisms have also been rehearsed many times in attacks on the labelling perspective without any acknowledgment that Mills outlined them all in 1943. It is important to recognize that this essay was as much a critique of symbolic interactionist work as it was a critique of more conservative approaches. It might be fair to note that Mills occupied a rare and lonely position in American sociology at that time.

The criticisms surrounded the essential point that the work of the social pathologists contained a low level of abstraction and thus displayed a variety of poorly linked evidence. Such work inevitably failed to analyse the total social structure and presented a fragmentary picture. It was oriented to practical problems and away from a totalizing philosophy of history. It was journalistic, descriptive and apolitical (or aspiring to a democratic opportunism). Such explanation as it provided was multi-factorial and over-focused on 'a structureless flux'. It focused on the waves of immigrants, and their status, rather than class positions and the limits on mobility. Implicit concepts of order and pathology were not reflexively analysed and exposed, and the rural scene remained neglected as if it was an implicit haven of conformity. In short, and pointedly, Mills saw the picture of crime and the criminal portrayed by these sociologists and criminologists as the view from 'the norms of independent middle-class persons verbally living out Protestant ideals in the small towns of America' (Mills, 1943, reprinted in Lefton *et al.*, 1968: 23).

Mills's essay had a precisely defined target, a large sample of textbook writers on social pathology. Most of these 'social pathologists' turned out to be born in small towns, or on farms near small towns, most of which were not in industrialized states. They were academic men who moved within the professional and business classes. This kind of class critique made Mills's essay a landmark text. In my view, however, its major intellectual contribution lay in its connection of that class analysis with the concepts of the social pathologists. His remarks on the question of social deviation were far ahead of their time. They effectively planted a huge question mark over the emergent sociology of deviance *in all its varieties*, a mark which was to remain in place for the next thirty years, like a dark inexplicable shadow which everyone duly ignored for fear of touching it. No one ever demolished the Mills thesis which we will now discuss, and indeed I know of no significant critique of its positions. Yet it became a widely read reference.

What was really distinctive and radical about Mills's essay was that he challenged the new concept of social deviation at its roots. He pointed out that the whole notion of social deviation, as the substance of social problems and as the index of social disorganization, was dependent upon a set of norms which expressed a particular, sectional *Lebenswelt*, not a societal consensus or a universal morality as was claimed:

> One of the pervasive ways of defining 'problems' or of detecting 'disorganization' is in terms of *deviation from norms*. The 'norms' so used are usually held to be the standards of 'society' . . . This mode of problematization shifts the responsibility of 'taking a stand' away from the thinker and gives a 'democratic' rationale to his work. Rationally, it would seem that those who accept this approach to 'disorganization' would immediately examine these norms themselves. It is significant that, given their interest in reforming society, which is usually avowed, these writers typically assume the norms which they use and often tacitly sanction them. There are few attempts to explain deviations from norms in terms of the norms themselves, and no rigorous facing of the implications of the fact that social transformations would involve shifts *in them*.
>
> (*ibid.*: 8)

Rosenquist's textbook on 'social problems' provided a clear and classical example. Mills quoted a passage from it which simply stated that 'Perhaps we may be on solid ground through a recognition of the capitalist system and its accompaniments as normal. We may then deal with its several parts, treating as problems those which do not function smoothly. This, it seems, is what the more reputable sociologist actually does' (*ibid.*). In fact, as Mills noted, writers like Rosenquist often simply took popular definitions of social problems and social deviations as their criteria. This is in fact not necessarily the same as accepting capitalism as the norm, and Mills thus avoided the problem of the distinction between popular and radical definitions of social problems, which is the difficult one of defining social problems outside of popular understandings and still retaining political purchase or referential clarity.

The reference to democracy in the passage quoted above is interesting, and indicated that Mills, like other critics, was sceptical about the politics of some of the New Dealers. He accused the social pathologists of '"democratic" opportunism'. They conflated 'the political' with the action of legislators and avoided addressing the relation between 'total structures of norms' and 'distributions of power', or the political implications of particular 'normative structures' (*ibid.*: 9–10). Their understanding of social entities focused on local 'situations' and 'milieux', using a 'paste-pot psychology' to describe the interactions within – a perspective which was 'intellectually tied to social work' and other institutions of social discipline. This occupational tie, the social origins of the pathologists, and their 'probable lack of any continuous "class experience"', much reduced their capacity to see social structure as a whole, rather than as 'a scatter of situations'. The focus, Mills argued, was so often upon individuals not classes, upon details and change, rather than the broad recalcitrance of more general structures such as private property. Individuals were said to be maladjusted, a term deriving from the neo-Darwinist concept of adaptation, as if they had accepted the goals and values of small-town America but failed to apply them properly. 'Maladjustment' obscured the moral content, and the arbitrary character, of the judgement involved. The social pathologists 'do not typically consider whether or not certain groups or individuals caught in economically underprivileged situations can possibly obtain the current goals without drastic shifts in the basic institutions which channel and promote them' (*ibid*.: 21).

In short, social pathology had been dominated by a piecemeal, liberal tinkering with individuals or specific milieux; a tinkering which has little capacity for reforming a society which had well-entrenched, and divergent, structures of economic, political and cultural life. Like Merton, Shaw and McKay, and others, Mills argued that the broader system or structure had now to be recognized and analysed. Like them, he also called for the analysis of structural tensions and condemned the assumption of equilibrium or a tendency to equilibrium. The drive for a system analysis was now on, whether from the left or the right.

Social deviation was and is a central concept for any kind of social-systems thinking. Quite separately from its psychiatric connotations, deviation has a root in the modern concept of system. The notion of a smooth, well-ordered, reliably running set of patterns or organizations inevitably implies a notion of what is deviant from these patterns. For example, the concept of language as a system or structure means we can clearly identify deviant usages or connections. Part of the reason the sociology of deviance came into full view in 1951, a period of system-building and cybernetic thinking, was because of this connection with the scientistic approach to social-system management. It may be an obvious, although undiscussed, fact that this approach to social deviation was derived directly from the experience of fast-moving, focused, large-scale organizations during the war. It was clear to many that the success of 'running a tight ship' was administrative partnership, cooperation and understanding between the classes, clearly stated and agreed common goals, and an efficient but humane disciplinary system to regulate deviation. The horrors and idiocies of the war proved that the left hand often did not know what the right was doing, that the old class distances now had to melt in favour of cooperation, and that there could be universally shared system objectives. Such was one of the fundamental elements and features of post-war social democracy.

What Mills had grasped about the concept of social deviation suggests to us its intimate ties with 'democratic opportunism' and the basic components of the social-democratic social system forming in the decade after the war was over. He had understood that the concept of social deviation was partly ideological (a word Mills used for it; *ibid*.: 17) in that it was derived from a specific vision of order and health (a rural vision of intimacy, slow pace, community, sobriety, hard work, capitalism, marriage and thrift), and partly 'utopian', in that some deviation was seen as 'culture-lag', practices out-of-touch with the new technological, modernist sensibility and which needed to be integrated into the new order or system. This imperfect distinction helps us see both the static and dynamic qualities of the normative criteria for defining social deviance; both were fired by the rural conservatism suppressed and, eventually, brought back to life in opposition by the roaring twenties, the Depression and the urban social democracy of the New Deal. Indeed, Mills's arguments, however undeveloped, help us see that these two dimensions of the ideology behind the concept of social deviation, the rural ideological and the utopian systemic, suggest the exact forms of social control necessary for its 'integration' and re-socialization and a new language of penality. The forms are regulatory rather than exclusive; the language is scientistic and integrative rather than rhetorical and rejective. The forms are technically apposite, generalized and social-system oriented, rather than amateurishly *ad hoc*, parochial and personal; the language is technical, professional and not meant to be comprehensible, rather than an open, moral denunciation. Such attitudes and ideas had of course been born many years earlier, but what was distinct now, in the aftermath of war, was that they were now harnessed together to restrict the worst excesses of *laissez-faire* capitalism *and* the New Dealers, and to building a social system from the farm but beyond the farm, a system which could unite the whole people as a nation – and ultimately the globe.

We should be clear that Mills himself wanted to detach the concept of social deviation from *both* the normative commitment to the small-town, farm values of middle America *and* the progressivist-careerist federalism of the upwardly mobile urban academic committed to a notion of progress. He was no more impressed with the demand that we all fall into line behind the new technological society than he was with the ideology of moral puritanism. The advocates of the former, progressive, line forgot that change affects different sectors unequally and that industry itself is no better than farmers at letting go of entrenched practices. However, he felt that the progressives' sense of deviation from the social system did at least have 'structural anchorage' (*ibid*.: 18). In retrospect, it is striking how long the normative, usually puritanical and legalistic, criterion for defining deviance and crime has lasted. In the last decade of the century, normative criteria are still predominant over system criteria. The failure of system criteria for defining deviance, evidenced so clearly in Nazi Germany and the Soviet Union, is very evident, but let us register the fact that, even today, we are still generally unsure, despite all our cynical modernism, whether we want to abandon the normative way of defining deviance and immorality, or whether we want to abandon legalism for efficient system regulation.

In any event, by the end of the war, the theoretical developments launched in the 1930s had produced both conservative and progressive beliefs in the production of social deviation by the social system itself. Both tendencies merged to some extent, and to a degree they conflicted. The 1950s, however, belonged to the conservative version, as America began its imperialist phase of building a social system of internal and external controls and alliances which was intended to be the foundation of a lasting, capitalist peace and the bulwark against a more fundamental structural change in power relations.

Imperialism, system-building and the call for consensus

The scientistic social-system builders were given an authoritative boost and an official sociological mandate in 1948 by none other than Louis Wirth. In his essay of 1940 (see Chapter 3), Wirth had exposed the normative-political component of the old social disorganization theories. Drawing upon Mannheim, he had deployed the concept of ideology to assess the weaknesses of cultural pluralism and the dangers of the growth of sectional propaganda as a means to secure a new moral-political consensus. By 1948, he was President of the American Sociological Society and in his presidential address, 'Consensus and mass communication', he defined the problem for post-war American sociology in a somewhat different manner:

> The many problems of the present-day world call for a kind of knowledge of the physical world which led to the atomic bomb, on the one hand, and which promises to lead to the harnessing of atomic energy for peaceful purposes, on the other hand. The great task before us is to discover the ways and means of mobilizing human action to prevent the suicide of civilization in the face of the new physical power which has recently been discovered to make that eventuality at least a threatening possibility.
>
> (Wirth, 1964: 19)

As Smith (1988: 164) comments, before the war Wirth was calling for sociological understanding to enable politically effective action by others, whereas after it he was calling for political action by sociologists in order to shape the understandings of others – and, indeed, the war had been a watershed for the relationship between sociology and politics. By 1968, sociology was at the forefront, on the barricades – but on 'the other side'. In 1948, sociology, through Wirth's address, was merely announcing that it had the technical knowledge and that it wanted the power to save civilization before it was too late. Unfortunately, Wirth's atomic bomb metaphor was all too accurate and ominous: sociology had the technology – it was becoming highly 'operationalist' and mathematical – but only a technology for a military strategy against recalcitrant populations (Lazarsfeld's work was very important here, both on communications and propaganda during the war and later in the development of 'operational' or empirical sociology;

see also Lasswell, 1966; Sumner, 1979: 99). After its place in the industrial-military complex was secured during the war, the potential of sociology, alongside the mass media, for constructing artificial universals within civilian society was enormous.

Wirth now redefined the project of sociology as the study of the conditions for consensus and signalled its imperial intent to free the world from authoritarianism. Mass societies, the creation of the modern age, he declared, had achieved some democracy and some consensus. They had a double-pronged tendency to produce mass organizations alongside a proliferation of diverse, highly individualized, social groups. Sociology's task was to ensure effective communication between the leaders of these vast new organizations and their members. It could provide the knowledge of public opinion needed by decision-makers to meet this task, for rule by force would no longer be accepted. After all that had gone before to produce a general scepticism and disenchantment with 'all dogmas and ideologies', a non-ideological consensus was clearly vital to mobilize the energies of the mass. The future of democracy depended on it.

He forewarned that, as in the war, the mass media were a crucial institution. They could reflect the moral and political consensus, and thus bind the society together. Or they could reflect the huge monopolistic interests which now controlled them, and misrepresent 'minority' views (Wirth, 1964: 37). Control over the mass media was now one of the principal sources of economic and political power. This 'new force' had 'the power to build loyalties, to undermine them, and thus by furthering or hindering consensus to affect all other sources of power' (*ibid.*: 38). Then, noting conflicts between management and unions, Wirth, ever the social realist who was still very aware of the multiplicity of conflicts in contemporary societies, laid down the tactics of the new social democracies:

> Propaganda appeals directed toward the larger public, toward government, and toward organized bodies in society are among the indispensable elements in the strategy of collective bargaining, arbitration, labor legislation, and the conduct of strikes. The means of mass communication play no less significant a role in the maintenance of mass production and mass markets.
>
> (*ibid.*: 39)

The goal, then, was consensus and the tactic propaganda. Yet, he himself had, before the war, warned that propaganda undermined the consensus at the same time that it constructed it, through contributing to the belief that all symbols lacked intrinsic meaning and were just the tools of powerful manipulators. Nevertheless, his statement captured the spirit of dominant post-war American sociology. The task was to stem the tide of dissent and disintegration to preserve freedom and democracy, even if it meant that the projected consensus was a lie, a utopia not a fact.

When Wirth proclaimed that America had learned to live with its diverse racial and cultural groups to produce a 'fairly orderly, productive, and peaceful society' (*ibid*.: 40), we could predict that imperial intent was about to show itself. It did. Declaring American sociology's new-found interest in the 'interaction between national states', and ending its period of isolationist sociology, Wirth said that 'we' now recognize the economic interdependence of states and have made 'some progress in the building of world consensus', 'we' now even have some 'incipient international institutions', 'we' have 'some semblance of world loyalties', and 'we' have the means of mass communication 'for the furtherance of understanding across the borders of sovereign states' (*ibid*.: 41). 'We' do not have 'a monopoly of power to coerce all the other nations and peoples of the earth into our way of life' (did the possibility even cross his mind?), so compromise, persuasion and negotiation are the only alternatives. Besides, he said, if 'we' used coercion 'we' would destroy 'our' own values. As they say in Canada today, who's this 'we', white man? It was true, he continued, that American freedom and democracy were irreconcilable with 'the only other remaining power constellation in the world', thus ruling Europe and Japan out of the new 'superpower' game. This conflict looked irresoluble, but:

> The uncomfortable but at the same time reassuring fact . . . is that today in this shrunken world there are more effective ways of interfering with the internal life of any society by those without through the instruments of mass communication . . . these products of mass communication have a way of reaching the great inert masses of the world, for making them restless and mobilizing them for action, or at least for making the dominant groups in their respective societies more responsive to their pressure.
>
> (*ibid*.: 42)

Thus spoke the Voice of America. If it could not be isolationist, then this was now to be the American way of socializing with other nations, or should we say socializing other nations? Gangsterism and protection rackets, overlain by campaigns for moral purity, had now been elevated from domestic disgrace to international foreign policy. For what? 'nothing less than the building of a world consensus, for a social-psychological integration of the human race commensurate with the interdependent far-flung and rich material resources and human energies of the world' (*ibid*.: 42). For what? 'to allow the fullest use of the world's resources to meet human needs under freedom, order and peace' (*ibid*.). That is, the free-market economy without disturbance from political opposition. Its fear? What people might do with the products of science. As Wirth put it, 'The only defense we have is social' (*ibid*.: 43). The Voice of America now seemed to think that Hiroshima had given it the moral authority to lead the world and become its police force; to turn its own domestic incoherence, intellectual vacuousness and violent immaturity into the principles of global hegemony. It had gone beyond the frontier all right, not by transcending the chaos of frontier culture but by shifting the frontiers of chaos beyond its own borders. It was now at one with its dominant sociological voice. Both now proposed to interfere in the lives of other cultures, internal and external, to resocialize deviation from the Norm, the American view of Freedom and Democracy, through the means of mass propaganda, persuasion and negotiation, backed up, where necessary, by coercion. American imperialism had found its sociological voice, and sociology had found the voice of American imperialism.

Until the 1960s, American sociology was to abandon the navel-gazing of the 1930s, all that uncertainty floating on a sea of cultural diversity, and any conception of deviation as healthy cultural difference. It now had a Norm and a Consensus – by arbitrary fiat. Perhaps, we should remember Norm, the boring, conservative, conformist, sexist, middle-class husband in Marilyn French's *The Women's Room*. Norm represented the Norm all too well, and the heroine ran off with a radical social scientist.

All deviation was now to be measured against the Norm. It was a new absolutism, that of liberal democracy in consumer America. For a time, the fine-tuned appreciation of minute cultural differences was mostly submerged. The USA in the 1950s was not the place for symbolic interactionism. Apart from the essays by Becker (1963: Chapter 3) and Finestone (1964), it seemed to go underground – now was not the moment to question the Norm, merely to study its subterranean flouting. Significantly, these two essays were on the subjects of learning to smoke marijuana and black drug addicts, respectively. Lemert's book (1951) proffered a developed deviancy amplification thesis, but there was nothing about it that was critical of the Norm, as we shall see in Chapter 8. McCarthyism must have had its effect on liberal sociologists.

Instead of 'appreciative' ethnographies stuffed with trivial detail and totally devoid of crucial macro-economic context, what 'we' were now treated to was a frequency of abstract rhetorics with virtually no empirical reality in them whatsoever (frequency has to be the collective noun for an aggregate of rhetorics during the era of Voice of America). This frequency found its drone in the writings of Talcott Parsons; he played Norm to C. Wright Mills's Bogart. But Parsons and his clones were never allowed to have the stage completely to themselves – when Parsons's *The Social System* came out, it was accompanied by Lemert's *Social Pathology*. The concept of social deviation was finally fully integrated into systematic social theory by these two books of 1951. Both Parsons and Lemert, like Durkheim, adopted and developed a systematic approach to sociology which attempted to present a complete, explanatory picture of their object and its context. Both of them followed Durkheim closely, yet the two books are quite different and represent the two versions of the sociology of deviance which emerged from the forties. One was the view of progressive conservatism and the other of conservative progressivism. They extended the two lines we have discussed in this chapter, and which Mills had already condemned.

The Parsons fantasy

The American attempt to impose an artificial consensus upon itself and the rest of the world was expressed beautifully in ideology by Parsons's *The Social System*. Mills's criticism of its ugly jargon ('a clumsy piece of irrelevant ponderosity'; Mills, 1970: 34) missed the point to an extent. The fact that it is almost unreadable because of its turgidly deployed jargon is precisely its exquisite beauty as an abstract art form of its time. It is abstract expressionism; the spectacle as reality; the advertising fantasy taken seriously. It has all the hallmarks of classic propaganda. The book is another Cold War Voice of America disguised in long, apparently scientific, words. It says virtually nothing. Mills (1970: 36) said it all when he paraphrased the sociological message of the book: 'people often share standards and expect one another to stick to them. In so far as they do, their society may be orderly.' It is extremely difficult to read Parsons's text in order to make that message clear. To do so in itself is almost to concede that reality is no longer the point, merely one's position and its proximity to the Norm – and that of course has been the failing or preference of many sociologists ever since. However, respect for the enormous impact of Parsonian sociology throughout the world, especially the Free World of the Economic Miracle, and its importance for the sociology of deviance, compels us to enter the text, even though it is almost as tasteless as going to Disneyland and assessing the realism of Mickey as a mouse. I doubt if social realism was Parsons's objective; like Durkheim's work on the division of labour and the state, so much of it was wishful thinking. Disneyland was built in 1955; two of its areas were, and are, called Frontierland and Fantasyland. Like Parsons, it fared less well in Europe.

Like Mills, I do believe, however, that Parsons said something of substance, albeit in a foreign language and albeit very little. One commentator said that *The Social System* expressed a theory of the workings of societies, drawing much from Durkheimian inspiration but also providing an optimistic American version of Weber-inspired German romanticism (Gouldner, 1970: 139). Gouldner's view of the book was that it had less stress on the energizing character of values than Parsons's early work, and that it put the emphasis upon the utility of 'certain social or cultural arrangements for system equilibrium' and upon the 'importance of the gratifying outcome of individual conformity with values' (*ibid.*). Values, however, were very much the sources of the systematicity of the social system and thus order: 'It is only by virtue of internalization of institutionalized values that a genuine motivational integration takes place, that the "deeper" layers of motivation become harnessed to the fulfillment of role expectations' (Parsons, quoted in Mills, 1970: 39). Why conflicts and dissidence arose was not addressed, nor was why and how social change occurs, but the mechanics of a social-system-integration based on conformity are detailed at great length, in the most abstract terms. After the Holocaust with its ultimate expresssions of human conflict, it can be seen as a kind of Marshall Plan for societies which did not want to talk of the past but rather of the future, for societies which wanted to forget the old social reality.

So what of social deviation? Logically, it was an important problem for such a project. As Parsons himself stated, 'It has been evident from the beginning of this work that the dimension of conformity-deviance was inherent in and central to the whole conception of social action and hence of social systems' (Parsons, 1951: 249). Indeed. If the reader has followed the argument and intellectual lineages observed in the present book, she or he will immediately grasp that what Parsons said about conformity and deviance is profoundly true, more than even he seemed to realize. The whole construction of the concept of social action as opposed to merely individual behaviour, discussed earlier in Chapter 3, had supposed all along that conformity through internalized or learned cultural norms and values was crucial. Deviance, on this view, was a central feature in the development of social systems. Parsons was the first to articulate this clearly and systematically in his chapter entitled 'Deviant behaviour and the mechanisms of social control', although he changed it from a feature to a problem. Conformity with cultural patterns was now expected; it was no longer something to be negotiated democratically through social work and community development schemes. Indeed, global post-war reconstruction under the hegemony of imperial American capital demanded it, and recalcitrant deviants were met with considerable force, pervasive surveillance, strident rhetoric and extensive intervention into their private lives. Deviance was now entering the ranks of the major concepts in American sociology.

Motivated deviant behaviour, Parsons argued, was an outcome of the individual's past interactions (*ibid.*: 249–50). Deviance, like socialization, was rooted in interactions between ego and alter, situated within specific normative and cultural contexts or expectations. The individual's orientation and feelings towards significant others, as affected by interactions, were crucial. None of this was at all different from Mead and much of the sociology of the 1930s. Social interactions were basic for Parsons – the textbooks assert too much divergence between the structural functionalists and the symbolic interactionists. In this sense, he substantially modified Freud. As Weinstein (1973: 31) put it, 'Once Parsons understood that erotic patterns were structured by external forces, he was able to conclude that a theory of motivation had to be in the first place not instinctual and personal (i.e., private), but subjective and social, and that all levels of personality are related to social structure and are "open" to socialization processes.' Where Parsons went from this starting premise, however, was quite typically functionalist and quite typical of sociology just after 1945: *deviance, when observed from the standpoint of the interaction system, was defined by its tendency to disturb that system, or to generate social control efforts against it.* From the standpoint of the individual, it was a motivated tendency to contravene institutionalized normative patterns. Moral content was now more or less irrelevant, the challenge to the system everything. Social deviance was to be understood as the aggregate of behaviours which disturbed the system.

Such formulations were perfect examples of the post-war amalgamation of conservative, functionalist, thought, which defended established institutions as functional for order or the social system, and symbolic interactionist work, which had established the principle of social interaction as the starting point in analysing the emergence of social deviations. What was so strikingly different from the thirties was the blatant and unashamed assumption that conformity equalled equilibrium, or as Parsons (1951: 250) put it: 'It is presumed here that such an equilibrium always implies integration of action with a system of normative patterns which are more or less institutionalized.' This assumption proceeded with no sense of a need for self-justification, sustained by the mood of the late forties and early fifties, which was one of optimism, determination and militarism. Yet only ten years earlier, it seemed generally agreed by all sociologists that there were major flaws and problems in 'the normative system' and all that was institutionalized: namely, (a) that there was little that was systemic about the normative situation – cultural diversity in the melting pot was the usual description; (b) that not enough of the common good had been institutionalized – that was the whole point of the thirties critique of *laissez-faire*; and (c) that such normative consensus as existed had been exposed by Merton and others as in stark contradiction to the recalcitrant class structure. So how could Parsons say what he said? The belief that conformity equalled equilibrium had no empirical basis; it was but a mere dream, a propagandist's rhetoric, a post-war fantasy. Nor did Parsons imply that there was any empirical basis; just that this was logically true and wouldn't it be nice? This is abstract expressionism at its peak, or 'grand theory' as Mills called it.

Parsons went on to admit that deviance had 'a certain relativity', even when conceived of as system-disruption. It depended upon the nature of the system referred to. Indeed, he readily admitted that in reality the 'structure of normative patterns in any but the simplest sub-system is always intricate and usually far from fully integrated' (*ibid*.: 251). In addition, he recognized that everyone played a plurality of roles with a complex range of expectations and tensions. Beyond this, he wisely noted, it is also a question of timing: deviance can amount to doing routine things at the wrong time or in somebody else's time. Despite all these observations, which point overwhelmingly to the social reality of pluralism, change, conflict and relativity, Parsons insisted that the norms orienting action must 'to a degree' be common to the 'actors in an institutionally integrated interactive system'. In short, never mind reality, let's concentrate on what is true by definition. Parsons's analysis was confounded from the start because it begged all the questions so rightfully and painfully addressed by sociologists in the 1930s.

The detailed analysis of the logistics of deviance-producing interactions was of the same type. All true by definition – but saying nothing about reality, and being dumbly unreflexive about its own fantastic assumptions.

For example, the analysis began with the immortal words 'Let us assume that, from whatever source, a disturbance is introduced into the system' (*ibid.*: 252). The peaceful equilibrium of capitalism is disturbed by deviance from the outside – the classic conservative ideology about difference and dissent (see Sumner and Sandberg, 1990). In any case, the conservative view of the logistics of conflict does not logically require sociology to study the deviant who introduced the disruption into this Disneyland of conformist equilibrium. Logically, it is just as apposite to study the norms which were infringed to see if they were worth keeping, to see if they existed, to see if they had been applied correctly, or to see whether conformity to them was itself a socially desirable state of affairs. Indeed, if Parsons had been faithful to the German historicism of Dilthey and Weber, he would have readily realized that his own ideas were very much creatures of the Cold War age: 'let us suppose that we all now agree, and define anyone who doesn't as a deviant, or, if they disagree a lot, as a dissident'. In retrospect, Parsons's writing on deviance looks like a manifesto for McCarthyism.

Deviation was thus rendered non-rational and the deviant as in need of re-socialization. After all, why would anyone reasonably introduce disruption into a perfectly equilibrating, integrated normatively institutionalized, interactive system? (Which normal person would recognize such a monstrosity if they saw one?) Clearly, deviants or dissidents were rebels without a cause. James Dean was an important figure for a definite ideological reason, and *On the Waterfront* touched the same raw nerves. Clearly, such a deviant must be suffering from lack of socialization, or a lack of security (to recall the title of Fyvel's book, *The Insecure Offenders*, of 1961).

To do full justice to Parsons, we must also recognize the Americanized Freudianism in his analysis of the logistics of deviance production within social systems. Not only was deviance defined by the patterns and norms of the system, but the conformists to that system were often deeply ambivalent or neurotic about their adherence to the norms because it 'cost' them the price of conflict with the deviant. The need to repress or punish is always part of an ambivalent attitude, while conformity and equilibrium may not be. Indeed, Parsons noted, one reaction to the feelings of hostility to deviance is fantasy. Therefore, deviance presented the system with a problem of remaining in a permanent state of ambivalence and neurosis, because there was no way of ignoring it. The need for security was built into the need for stable collectivities; deviance by definition created insecurity – on Parsons's logic. What Parsons could not see was that it was the very insecurity of the post-war peace which compelled it to try to search out deviance and exorcise it from the social whole. Instead, what Parsons went on to do was to identify the feeling of adequacy with the need to live up to the standards of the system, and the feeling of insecurity with the need to be independent or aggressive. So, the compulsive deviant, or the compulsive punisher, evidenced insecurity, while the liberal conformist was the epitome of adequacy and balance. On both sides of the social control equation, insecurity and inadequacy were root sources of system imbalance. Here Parsons sounded exactly like Durkheim, with his search for a controlling tolerance, admitting, logically, that deviance could be produced by insecure, compulsive punishers just as much as by insecure offenders. Logically. In fact, the sociology that followed almost never studied the compulsive-neurotic-repressive types in the police, the legislature, the church and the prison.

What was axiomatic here was the assumption that 'Probably a stable interactive relationship without common value-patterns is not empirically possible' (*ibid.*: 261). This openly confessed the psychological problem of Parsons's generation after the war. They could not conceive of a peaceful relationship with people they despised, feared or could not understand. Parsons looked at the world from the standpoint of insecure rulers and policy-makers trying to build a new world under one system. He could not see that the enforcement of the Norm of a single system was the prime cause of that insecurity. In this sense, the conservative progressivism which Parsons stood for needed Deviance, like it needed the Cold War and the Soviet Union, to reassure itself that it really did have a collective normative system, and to make sure that some semblance of it would actually come to pass, if only in opposition to carefully constructed ideological enemies. Parsons's analysis was so abstract and so ethereal that even he did not notice that he himself said:

> Rationalization is an adjunct and instrument of repression in that cognitively it denies the existence of conflict and attempts to present a consistent picture in accord with approved normative standards of proper motivational orientation. There are many possible 'devices' to which rationalization may resort in order to make the actor's behavior and attitudes plausible and acceptable, such as the appeal to 'extenuating circumstances', the imputation of exaggerated deviance to alters and the like, but they have in common an element of cognitive distortion of what, in terms of the cognitive culture which is predominantly institutionalized, is the appropriate and adequate explanation and justification of action. Again the relevance of these considerations to the genesis and structuring of ideologies needs no further comment at this time.
>
> (Parsons, 1951: 266–7)

Precisely. Parsons had inadvertently acknowledged that the rationalized attribution of deviance to alter made ego feel better because real conflict could then be denied. He had also undercut the dominant ideology of social work in brutally observing that the 'excuses' it made for the manufactured deviant were incompatible with the dominant philosophy of Free Will, and therefore glossed the reality of persistent social conflict.

The end of ideology: rebels without a cause

Logically, the sociology of deviance could have followed Parsons's formulations and studied values and their institutionalization, value conflicts and
role inconsistencies, the relation between deviance-attribution and ideology,
and the insecurity of dominant groups. But logic is a different thing from
ideology, and, for the next decade, sociology was to follow the ideological
spirit of Parsons's line rather than its theoretical logic, and thus analysed
the deviant as a distinct kind of person lacking in adequate socialization,
as someone without good reason to deviate who had simply not learned
the rules properly – as a rebel without a cause. That ideological spirit is
clear on a close reading of Parsons, but it was announced with great clarity
by Daniel Bell around the same time. As Matza (1969: 33) has also noted,
Bell is the perfect link-man between the Chicago school and the functionalists
(although previous chapters herein have shown that Wirth had a very
strong claim too), and what Bell's collected essays, *The End of Ideology*
(1962), had to say about crime corresponded exactly to the dominant
voice of the emergent sociology of deviance of the 1950s.

Bell and the laundering of American ideology

A former socialist and ex-journalist, Bell (1962: 402) declared that the
utopias of communism and fascism were 'exhausted'. The Moscow trials
of the thirties, the Hitler–Stalin pact, and the concentration camps of
Nazism and Stalinism had sealed the fate of these two utopian ideologies,
and even ideology as such. If, as Mannheim had argued, ideology was a
vision of the future tied to a critique of the present, then, Bell concluded,
the way to heaven was now clearly not to be found through faith but
research, notably small-scale empirical studies uncontaminated by grand
visions of social change. A Keynesian consensus now ruled:

> In the Western world, therefore, there is today a rough consensus
> among intellectuals on political issues: the acceptance of a Welfare
> State; the desirability of decentralized power; a system of mixed
> economy and of political pluralism. In that sense . . . the ideological
> age has ended.
>
> (*ibid.*: 402–3)

Before becoming a sociology professor, Bell had been managing editor of
the *New Leader*, which organized 'a weekly meeting of minds for professional anti-Communists' (Fletcher, 1978: 191). Its executive editor had
worked with Trotsky and fled from Stalin's prisons in the twenties. This
Cold War magazine published articles calling for a commission of enquiry
into subversive influences in the USA, and the use of democratic institutions to destroy them (*ibid.*). It also advocated the infiltration of foreign
socialist parties. In 1950, in line with *New Leader* doctrine, the Congress
for Cultural Freedom (CCF) was launched, with American money and

top-level political support. The CCF attracted membership or support from several leading lights or promising talents in the British Labour Party, notably Crosland, Healey and Gaitskell. Bell was one of the CCF's brightest stars, organizing seminars frequently attended by these political notables. Denis Healey, a close friend of Bell's, wrote many pieces for the *New Leader*, as did Hugh Gaitskell, later the Labour leader. Healey has since written that Bell's path was always one which steered 'to the right of the left, and to the left of the right, seeking always the road of freedom and intellectual decency' (Healey, 1990: 201). Anthony Crosland's influential book *The Future of Socialism* seemed to owe much to the ideology of the CCF, and of Bell in particular, as Fletcher comments:

> Bell and his colleagues argued that growing affluence had trans-formed the working class in Europe – and Britain – which was now virtually indistinguishable from the middle class, and thus Marx's theory of class struggle was no longer relevant. Future political progress, they thought, would involve the gradual reform of capitalism and the spread of equality and welfare as a consequence of continued economic growth.
>
> (Fletcher, 1978: 193)

Gaitskellism now acquired the academic respectability conferred by the theories of Crosland and American social science, and Labour's defeat in the 1959 election saw Gaitskell, Jenkins, Crosland, Jay, Rodgers and others turn this theory into the new social-democratic manifesto of a Labour Party reborn without its cloth-cap image. It took power in 1964 under Harold Wilson. Some of these same people were of course later to form the short-lived Social Democratic Party as a breakaway from the Labour Party. The CCF had benefited from large subventions from the CIA, and Fletcher hints broadly that other CIA monies played a part in the rise of the social democrats within the Labour Party. Healey later became aware of the CIA's funding of the CCF, commenting in his autobiography only that the CCF 'made a useful contribution to the quality of Western life at that time' (Healey, 1990: 195). What is important here for our story is that Daniel Bell had played a major role in the formation of buffers against communism, in both stimulating and encouraging, at a very high level, the growth of (a) the social-democratic wing of the British Labour Party and (b) a firm commitment to NATO. In a very real sense, therefore, the emergence of the sociology of deviance in Britain during a long period of Labour government in the 1960s is no coincidence. Of course, it developed a distinct, European form of its own far removed from many of Bell's ideas, but more of that in Chapter 10. For now, suffice it to say that Bell's role in our story is clearly pivotal. The concrete connections between academic theory and the world of professional politics surface regularly during the history of the sociology of deviance, but rarely with such clarity.

Bell had devoted attention to the crime question, because he regarded it as part of the American way of life. Serious crime had played a crucial part in the formation of American society, as had some, equally extreme, moralistic campaigns. It was not just the expression of 'a hunger for the "forbidden fruits" of conventional morality' (Bell, 1962: 129), but also an integral part of the jostling for position between classes and ethnic groups in a socially mobile world. Crime was functional for American society, he argued, and Durkheim's echo was deafening. Crime, for Bell, was a 'route of social ascent', an inevitable concomitant of the passion for gain. Like Merton, he stressed that crime was tied up with the passion for gain and that the crime problem depended upon how the methods of securing that gain were organized and distributed. So, as American society became more 'organized', more 'civilized', less 'buccaneering' and more oriented to consumption than production, American crime became more organized, more integrated with 'legitimate' institutions and more oriented towards consumption. For example, Bell noted, the gambling rackets became big industries, systematically organized, concentrated in fewer hands and locked into the structures of respectability. The mobsters 'had immigrant roots' and just wanted respectable success like everyone else (*ibid.*: 138).

Bell's account of the changes in the American way of crime was a startlingly optimistic one, not to say another fantasy. It runs something like this: (a) as the mob found more legitimate ways of making vast sums of money, notably through gambling, and became increasingly integrated with mainstream American capital, homicide, prostitution and kidnapping declined; (b) as industrial relations became federally or socially regulated, labour racketeering by the mob declined too; (c) the above merely involved the development of new social agencies for regulating matters that had been regulated by the mob – yes, even labour racketeering had been functional for society; (d) the concept of an omnipotent Mafia was a complete myth – the Italian involvement in organized crime was merely a temporary and natural device to enable their upward mobility (after all what were they to do when the Jews controlled city commerce and the Irish ran the political machines?); (e) crime was just a natural resort for the under-resourced in the sequences of ethnic succession so characteristic of a society dominated by immigration; and (f) the Fair Deal of the fifties was bringing about the passing of the slums and the rise of Middle-class Life. From all the work we have discussed in the last few chapters, the composition and sources of Bell's account should be very familiar. It was very much a mixture of Durkheim, Park, Merton and Davis, written with great verve and a journalist's knowledge of the dirty details. The figure of Sinatra mixing with the mob served well to symbolize Bell's thesis and its tone – the mob, its music and its sociological account, like its money, had been laundered.

Bell went on to dismiss the official rise in crime of the fifties as a media-constructed scare, claiming that there was less crime in the USA than ever before. Juvenile delinquency was prime fodder for the newspapers, he said, and besides the rise in the new crime of juvenile auto theft was explicable by the sheer number of cars now available to be taken. He had spoofed away serious crime and now he spoofed away the juvenile delinquency of the fifties. He admitted that the rise in black crime was very striking too, but again brushed it under the carpet with the following astonishing comment:

> Crime of this sort represents a form of 'unorganized class struggle' . . . it follows the business cycle. Crime is a form of resentment, a desire for gain, an act of violence against a person who has more. These are lower-class crimes, and the Negro makes up the bulk of the lower class. There is nothing racial about this fact. At the turn of the century, the majority of such crimes were committed predominantly by the Irish, later by the Italians, then by the Slavs.
>
> (Bell, 1962: 156–7)

This was the very stuff of conservative, functionalist sociology in the 1950s: 'reverse muckraking' as Matza so aptly called it. This is the spirit of their whole approach, from Durkheim onwards. It was repeated frequently in many studies (see, for example, Davis, 1961; Bensman and Gerver, 1963).[6] Again, it boomed forth as social democracy built its welfare–warfare states. Nothing was going to blur or besmirch the purity of the new utopia. Now, in the form of Bell's bold pronouncements, it could even openly accept the persistence of class in order to downplay the growing size of the racism issue, it could map the cycles of crime against the cycles of legitimate business and document their periodic integrations without any sense of a need to reflect on the implications of this for the evaluation of capitalism, and it could even deploy concepts from Engels, such as 'unorganized class struggle', in its determination to assert the submergence of the 'real' class struggle. Again, women's issues were nowhere to be seen, and nothing was said about the massive growth of crime in the underdeveloped countries colonized or invaded, or just simply underdeveloped, in the name of Freedom. The institutionalized racism sustaining black underprivilege was glossed over in the name of the acceptable inequities of 'the natural succession of the races', so that there was no preparation for what was to come in Watts or Chicago in the sixties, in the Hispanic slums of the seventies and eighties, and of course in Vietnam. What the fifties functionalists did talk about, endlessly, was juvenile delinquency, as if it was the last remaining blot on a copybook whose dirty reality had been largely erased by the new utopia.

Juvenile delinquency was like an irritating spot that had to be scratched continually. Blacks, mobsters, crime-ridden client states like Cuba and women could all be brushed under the carpet, presumably because they were now seen as integrated into the American social order or in the process of integrating, or at least under control. But the likes of James Dean and Elvis Presley represented something very different. Broad sectors of youth were refusing to be integrated into the new WASP middle-class society. Born and raised with a plastic, welfare-state, spoon in their mouths, freed from the need to deviate socially in order to gain upward mobility, the new juvenile delinquent committed the ultimate sin: he or she rejected the lifestyle of the middle-class society without a material cause. Motorbikes, rock and wrecked coffee bars represented something well out of control's reach . . . and the functionalists could not understand it. Such things were beyond the reach of their concepts and outside of their utopia. Bell (1962: 157) openly admitted that he knew less about the crimes of juveniles than of adults, nor could he see a clear pattern in their crime rates. He could see that juvenile delinquency had increased drastically since 1940, and blamed that on the effects of war (broken homes, lack of parental supervision, etc.). His account from there onwards is incoherent and poor, for a sociologist of Bell's obvious ability. The only sense he could make of middle-class juvenile delinquency was that it was a reflection of 'psychological disturbance' (*ibid.*: 159), whereas with poor kids from the slums one could apply sociology. He even played with the possibility that the Gluecks' study might explain juvenile delinquency, by reference to body type and temperamental characteristics, and that some of it must be due to the youthful search for independent identity. That a sociologist of Bell's quality should produce such incoherence and lapse into biologism and psychologism is a clear sign of the bankruptcy of his theoretical perspective. His theories had rendered juvenile delinquency as quasi-political resistance without any underlying social pathology to generate it – the kids had indeed become rebels without a cause.[7]

One might also consider that, during this time, the notion of cause as an epistemological concept was also going through a bad patch. Philosophers and social scientists were increasingly rejecting models of causation. Realism of any kind was philosophically in the cold. This exclusion took two forms. The first was a kind of epistemological McCarthyism, drawing on Popper's work, which saw causation as a metaphysical or ideological concept owing more to faith than to observation. This positivistic view satisfied itself with the establishment of statistical associations which would be useful for social-democratic government, and completely abandoned Grand Theory. It produced the kind of small-scale statistical research which Bell had called for, and which still dominates the social science departments of the Western world. It was a view which put theory, passion and politics into the Gulag, only for their conservative shadows to roam freely within the interstices of research procedure as 'conjecture' and 'middle-range theory'. It produced what the grey men of state wanted. The second form of exorcizing realism was a relativistic, existentialist denial of the permanence or substance of phenomena. Drawing on phenomenology, Kant, Hegel and later Nietzsche, this view denied the reliability of observation and the mechanical character of causation in order to replace them with a literary critic's sense of the complex, elusive, contextual and changing character of everything. This view satisfied itself with nothing less than the subversion of all taken-for-granted realities in the new society of the middle class, producing the vaguest and grandest of theories at the expense of any sustained observation. In short, the juvenile rebels of the fifties were not only denied their cause, but their academic observers denied themselves a belief in causation. Not for the first time, middle-class society had somehow generated a sense of meaninglessness.

By the end of the fifties, Bell's views reflected the conservative's typical dismay at the acceptance of avant-garde art and the growing 'conviction' politics of angry young men of the intelligentsia. Quite rightly, he discerned at the end of the fifties 'a disconcerting caesura' (*ibid.*: 404). A new tune was blowing in the wind, and Bell identified it as prophetically as anyone, albeit in his own terms:

> In the West, among the intellectuals, the old passions are spent. The new generation, with no meaningful memory of these old debates, and no secure tradition to build upon, finds itself seeking new purposes within a framework of political society that has rejected, intellectually speaking, the old apocalyptic and chiliastic visions. In the search for a 'cause', there is a deep, desperate, almost pathetic anger . . . They cannot define the content of the 'cause' they seek, but the yearning is clear.
>
> (*ibid.*: 404)

The 'wastelands' of the West were generating a sense of meaninglessness and, Bell astutely observed, it was to the East that young intellectuals would look in the sixties to find outlets and sources for their spiritual need for self-definition.

What happened in the sociology of deviance in the 1950s corresponded very closely with the ideas and spirit in the writings of Parsons and Bell. Teams of sociologists now descended upon the street corners of working-class America to attempt to discern whether there really was a delinquent subculture now emerging whose life revolved around delinquency and the rejection of middle-class values (see Short and Strodtbeck, 1965). They produced a battery of articles linking delinquency to lower-class socio-economic status, thus proving, in their own eyes, the immutability of the desire for gain, or, in our eyes, the persistence of class in the welfare state. This small-scale, quantitative, research, taking for granted its own utopian ideology, was by far the biggest and most prominent tendency. The more liberal, progressive line to emerge from the thirties, reflected in a development of the ideas of Tannenbaum and Lemert, was submerged underground, its proponents perhaps talking to the people whose ideas and force were blowing in the wind. This tendency produced only two studies of note after Lemert's *Social Pathology* of 1951: Becker's study of learning how to become a marijuana user and Finestone's fine-tuned ethnography of black juvenile drug users. Neither of these studies seemed to prove anything much, except, to paraphrase Bob Dylan, that 'there's something going on down there, Mr Parsons, and you don't know what it is'. The fifties was a time when liberals had to exercise discretion. Their reticence was deafening and only occasionally did their concerns hit the surface: these two studies demonstrated their sense of the growth of an alternative culture, which at this time had to remain a 'subculture' and which glossed over the enormous black influence upon its tone, texture, music and style.

The sociology of boredom or the boring sociology of post-war delinquency

The textbooks written in the fifties waltzed to the sober tune of the Parsons dirge. Parsons had established a frequent and distinct usage of the terms 'deviant' and 'deviance'. But his was not the only voice. Bloch and Prince's totally neglected book *Social Crisis and Deviance*, finally published in 1967 much after Bloch's death, articulated the same problematic. Drawing inspiration from an unholy combination of Frank and Parsons, they saw a world in malaise producing much social deviance, mainly via the strain within the conventional family structure, a subject of much concern to sociologists after the war as divorce followed divorce. Like Bell, they clearly felt that the family was the focus of post-war societal tensions, resulting in the inadequate socialization of the new generation. Like many, they saw adolescent rebellion as a breakdown in the normative binding of society and in social control. As Fyvel (1961: 18, 24) said, 'there was something new afoot' that resisted old, poverty-focused explanations and suggested 'the break-up of traditional authority'.

The classically functionalist textbook by Bredemeier and Stephenson, *The Analysis of Social Systems* (1962), put the sharp point of the Parsonian message this way: 'The socialization process, in short, is the process by which people, who at one time do not define situations in accordance with institutional prescriptions, are brought, at a later time, to do so' (*ibid.*: 61). The authoritarianism in this definition is extraordinary. Moral values did not come into it (socialization into what value system?), conformity with authority was all. It is easy to see from this why there was a rebellion and why social deviance was deemed to be a product of faulty socialization if socialization is defined as bringing people into line. The definition also highlights the intimate ties between the theory of deviance and the theory of social control. Deviance and social control can be seen, in semiotic terms, as two sides of the binary code of 1950s sociological discourse. Bredemeier and Stephenson went on to argue that 'deviant socialization' can occur if the child is exposed to inefficient conditioning from the parents or if the parents disagree. Additionally, they were concerned that in heterogeneous, modern societies there were many different patterns of conduct, and many models of socialization. Yet they still concluded, somewhat counterfactually, that 'deviant types' resulted from 'atypical biological factors and atypical group experiences' (*ibid.*: 89).

In general, the textbooks of this period emphasized 'undersocialization' or 'inappropriate' socialization as the cause of deviant behaviour. High rates of social deviation were said to occur in those areas of society whose families suffered the greatest stress or societal 'strain', namely working-class families. The textbooks rarely questioned the moral value of institutionalized expectations: conformity was an unqualified good. Bell's sense of the ambiguity of crime was absent and so also any attempt to spoof it away. In textbooks, there were few remarks such as Bell's (1962: 161) comment on the Gluecks' work that 'many of the factors associated with the delinquent' make up 'the drive-image of the businessman'.

Instead, sociology students were confronted with the amoral authoritarianism of textbooks like that by Bredemeier and Stephenson, whose chapter 'Deviation from culture patterns' began by emphasizing that they were not discussing what was good or bad in evaluative terms (Bredemeier and Stephenson, 1962: 121). They agreed that sometimes deviance was more healthy or moral than the system it infringed, and that some systems should be abandoned, but refused to explore the implications of this for the theory of deviance. They argued that 'there is no such thing as "deviance" or "conformity" ... only deviance *from* someone's expectations or conformity *to* someone's expectations' (*ibid.*: 122). Deviance lay in the eye of the beholder. If a person's goals were seen by others as legitimate, then the behaviour itself could be seen as normal and not deviant. Moreover, it was accepted that not all deviations amounted to social problems. Then, instead of this leading to a discussion of the normative validity of legitimate motives and institutionalized goals, the authors simply proceeded to expound the socio-psychological mechanics of the emergence of deviant behaviour *à la* Parsons and Merton. They drifted unquestioningly into an analysis of why people sometimes did not conform to cultural prescriptions, 'the most obvious reason for which' was that they were not adequately or appropriately socialized to these prescriptions (*ibid.*: 126). But, if Bredemeier and Stephenson were truly trying to be neutral about the moral worth of norms and deviations, why did they not discuss the reasons why authorities sustained particular moral ideologies and cultural expectations? Logically, it was as pertinent to ask why the Norm of the new Middleclass Society demanded conformity, property acquisition, upward mobility, an obsession with social status, the subordination of women, racial segregation, the brutal suppression of communism in the underdeveloped world, nuclear families of two adults and two children working for Freedom within an ideology of teamwork, a limited range of lifestyles, music and art, and, of course, heterosexuality. No doubt President Eisenhower and Senator McCarthy would not have approved of such questions, but what then of the much-vaunted Freedom? Or the enquiring, objective sciences of Popper's 'open society'? If this was the end of ideology in the Western world, why did university professors make such ideological moves in the course of their argumentation?

Bredemeier and Stephenson stated that 'inadequate or inappropriate' socialization 'may be' randomly distributed in a society (*ibid.*: 127). However, they proceeded to observe that this was not the case – without considering why that would be a mathematical miracle while oppressions of class, race and gender persisted. They observed that 'whole *groups* or *categories* of people are inadequately or inappropriately socialized because of their particular position in the social structure' (*ibid.*). Clearly, American sociologists had not learned from the extermination of six million Jews in the war that it was morally wrong to judge a person by their social group. So much for the wisdom passed on by sociology to the next generation! They seriously expected us to respect their norms, when they were intellectually unable to draw such basic moral lessons from the worst genocide in human history, one that had occurred only a few years earlier in Europe. Had all memory been erased?

In Bredemeier and Stephenson's book, whole sections of the population were now effectively branded as unsocial creatures, just like the Jews had been, as beyond the pale and in need of correction. If you were working class, you were now inappropriately socialized for a middle-class school system (as many of us were to discover in painful detail). If you were an 'urban middle-class female' you were probably inadequately socialized for the role of 'housewife and mother'. If you rebelled in some way, or were 'deviant', the reason for your deviance was your lack of suitable socialization (and the remedy was presumably to be sent to a social worker, i.e. a young, graduate, middle-class conformist, who had probably studied sociology under Bredemeier and Stephenson and who would tell you what the correct rules of behaviour were – as if you did not know). This lack of socialization helps us understand, said our kindly and wise teachers, why different positions in the social structure account for 'differential rates and types of deviance among various groups or categories of people' (*ibid.*). Actually, the only thing it really helps us understand is why sociologists of this period published so many studies linking, or investigating the link between, lower-class background or milieu and recorded delinquency – this was the theory behind them.[8] Because otherwise this is just insulting nonsense. To talk blandly in the 1950s of it being a social fact that whole sections of the population are 'inadequately or inappropriately socialized' is morally hardly any different to talking blandly in the 1940s of it being a social fact that a few million Jews had just been systematically exterminated because the Nazis did not think they were fit to live. Was it really none of Bredemeier and Stephenson's business to evaluate the pattern of deviance attribution? For example, should not a non-evaluative position have described the norms applied to intelligent women forced into a housework-only lifestyle, or the norms applied to working-class kids in middle-class schools, as inadequate or inappropriate? Should it not logically have asked why schoolteachers and the male community adopted such blatantly discriminatory systems of rules? Should it not logically have asked why such schoolteachers had been inadequately or inappropriately informed or trained on the subject of working-class culture, or why male authority figures were so inadequately informed about women's needs? Would not a truly non-evaluative position, however conservative, match its studies of working-class delinquency with studies of class-cultural bias within teacher-training colleges, or of gender bias within male socialization? Despite our awareness of each generation's habit of accusing the previous one of moral laxity, it seems reasonable to describe the position adopted by the Parsonian sociology of deviance in the 1950s as one of amoral authoritarianism. Thirties sociology had at least been morally critical.

Differential rates of social deviation could not, according to Bredemeier and Stephenson, be explained by the thesis that deviants were subject to exceptional social strain. Firstly, stress does not necessarily lead to deviation; secondly, effective social control and diminution of the opportunities to deviate would channel the frustrated energy into acceptable directions (presumably the theory behind youth clubs and evening flower-arranging classes for housewives). The logical weight of their analysis of juvenile deviance lay upon faulty child-rearing and lack of suitably controlled channels of expression, which of course occurred more often in areas of high social strain: a conservative tendency that reappeared with a vengeance in the 1980s. It inevitably kept the focus of the sociology of deviance upon delinquent slum kids and immigrant or black families.

It really is not part of our purpose here to describe all the statistical studies that followed from this type of analysis. There were many between 1940 and 1962 (see, for example, Monahan 1957; Nye *et al.*, 1958; Reiss and Rhodes, 1961). Noting them is worthwhile because attention is usually given only to the subcultural studies, yet these statistical analyses are more indicative of the sociological focus of the fifties. The fieldwork studies of so-called delinquent subcultures were of course truly indicative of the belief that there really was a youth culture beneath the mainstream culture developing a rebellion around delinquent behaviour. The funny thing about both these sets of studies was that, eventually, they produced conclusions which did not sit well with their orienting theoretical–political assumptions. It turned out that middle-class kids seemed to get into virtually as many minor scrapes as their working-class counterparts, and all that hanging around on street corners by tweed-jacketed sociologists, with their notebooks in their hands and their eyes in their pockets, produced very few subcultures of delinquency. The kids, it turned out, were just 'hanging out' or 'doing nothing' (see Paul Corrigan's later study, 1979). Delinquency was not central to their lives or their groups (see Short and Strodtbeck, 1965); or, at least, not as important as it was to those of the sociologists. By the early sixties, the conservative wing of the sociology of deviance was running out of credible things to say.

The most famous study of the conservative wing of post-war sociology of deviance was Cohen's *Delinquent Boys* (1955). Its title perfectly captured the focus of that tendency in the 1950s, although, in highlighting class contradictions, Cohen came dangerously close to an early 1930s realism. It has become well known within criminology as a book which argued that working-class boys attempting to succeed in schools or societies suffused by middle-class, masculine, values were likely to suffer severe 'status frustration' because their working-class values and methods were likely to produce constant failure in a system alien to them. What has been glossed over is the fact that Cohen was, quite openly, combining a creative version of Sutherland's theory of the cultural transmission of delinquency with psychoanalytic theories of delinquency which saw it as a symptom or sublimation of latent frustrations or anger (*ibid.*: 13–19). Cohen openly acknowledged his debts to Sutherland, Parsons and Alexander. Reflecting the attempts to unify sociology with psychiatry begun in the 1930s, Cohen explicitly declared an interest in seeing how 'psychogenic and subcultural factors' combined to produce delinquency (*ibid.*: 17). He had no doubt that the 'Social control of juvenile delinquency' was 'a major practical problem of every sizeable American community', that such control had been very unsuccessful, and that a better understanding of the roots of the 'delinquent subculture' would aid social control. His view was anchored in the belief or fear that 'a delinquent subculture' was a 'normal, integral and deeply rooted feature of the social life of the modern American city' (*ibid.*: 18–19).

Seen in its intellectual context, Cohen's book was almost the apogee of the conservative sociology of deviance. It was an almost perfect composition of the ideological themes of its day. In retrospect, it seems like another piece of scientistic, system-management sociology which takes for granted the legitimacy of the dominant norms and does nothing to subvert the paranoia of the day about the danger of the slightest deviance within society. Juvenile delinquency was the last speck of black dust on the ideological horizon and even that was to be eliminated. However, at the time, and for some years to come, some criminologists regarded it as a subversive study in that it 'provided an excuse for delinquency'.

Cohen steered away from any policy recommendations, remaining content with having demonstrated that delinquency had origins in social tensions, namely between different class value-systems. Perhaps the power of McCarthyism cast its shadow, but it seems that Cohen's book, like the essays of Davis and Merton discussed in Chapter 3, looked class and class ideology in the face and then bolted for the cover of scientific tension-management. There is a deep ambiguity in its interstices which he himself saw: should the working-class male have his values changed, or should middle-class teachers be retrained to modify their approach? The merit of his work lay in its willingness to problematize the imposition of middle-class values. Its little-discussed implication was the idea that deviance was just as much a product of the norms and values enforced by the agencies of social control as it was a function of the behaviour of the controlled. Nevertheless, his study, along with Garfinkel's essay (see below), suggested that in the centre, between Parsonian conservatism and Lemertian liberalism, there was a growing area of overlap of concerns around the question of balance within social regulation. It was a space that Goffman was decisively and creatively to occupy very soon (see Chapter 9). Arguably, it was the very centre of the sociology of deviance in general.

More than anything else, however, Cohen's book firmly established the term delinquent subculture within the language of sociology and criminology. For the next two decades it was to become axiomatic in these disciplines that there were such things in reality as subcultures and that the United States was full of them. It took about thirty years for it to be respectable to believe that these so-called subcultures were just mere concepts, phantoms or products of the paranoid imagination. For that is all they were. The concept of the subculture is simply part of the Parsonian fantasy: the red under the bed, the deviant or underground culture growing in our midst threatening to shatter truly American values. No one seemed to notice the point that if the delinquent culture was so common in US cities perhaps it was not so 'sub', and few made anything of the fact that its occupants were mostly black. Their blackness, and the blackness of the so-called subculture, was completely glossed over in the theory. It was not seen as a fact of any theoretical significance. The subculture was truly an abstraction from reality; it was not a descriptive concept. It measured the depth of the ideological need to believe that there was an enemy within that could subvert the drive to consensus. It did not measure the stark reality of the position of blacks in American cities: that would have been too much for the fantasy to bear. There was to be a stark awakening in the sixties; one which would render the abstraction of the subculture somewhat farcical.

Systems thinking, social work and social control

During this period, social control remained a central concept, as the other side of the coin from deviance, and as the keyword for the utopian project of an integrated, consensual society. However, the meaning of the concept shifted subtly from the assimilationist or incorporationist notion held by Park to a more defensive idea. It began to mean 'social defence', a phrase that became popular after the war. As Bredemeier and Stephenson (1962: 146) commented, the various types of social control could be regarded as different ' "lines of defense" against deviance'. Social control, in conservative sociology, became ways of preventing social 'strain' occurring or of preventing strain from producing deviance. It became a profound intervention into the details of everyday social life in order to defend the social system against the perceived attack upon it from deviance. The resonances of Cold War ideology here need hardly any comment. Paranoia was normal in the 1950s; peace meant engaging in war to prevent the spread of subversion; and society was so insecure and fragile it could not tolerate the free expression of social deviance.

Social control thus now included 'tension management' (*ibid.*: 157) as well as basic socialization. This might involve allowing a certain amount of innocuous free play in the system so people could let off steam. For example, 'Banter and a certain amount of free interplay among workers is permitted, coffee breaks are arranged, music is piped in, and routine, monotonous tasks are rotated' (*ibid.*). The development of the 'youth club' system would fall under the same category. What is important here is the shift to a negative or defensive posture against the perceived potential tide of deviance that might sweep the system away. Park's attitude was always a positive one of creating social control through voluntary participation in society's structures; this new view was strictly defensive in creating structures which would effectively manipulate behaviour to sustain active system equilibrium. Social control now turned the idea of the welfare state into a series of barriers against deviance and revolution. As Gramsci had argued, the role of the organic intellectuals of the bourgeoisie was to dig the moral trenches and build the administrative bunkers which constituted the ideological front in the twentieth-century war of position.

Social work no doubt played a pivotal role in the fantastic strategy imagined by the followers of Parsons, whatever his scepticism about that profession. It must have done much to anticipate the emergence of deviance and to prevent it becoming a systematic challenge to the system. But Orwell's *1984*, published in 1949, was being proved prophetic. Welfare was only being provided at the expense of freedom to criticize and think independently. It was a high price to pay. The amorality of system tension-management was well demonstrated by the fact that Bredemeier and Stephenson footnote a study of a lynching in Texas which 'presents a useful illustration of the function of mob action for the management of tension of some of its members'; in addition to a study of anti-semitism which they say 'suggests the "scapegoat" role that minorities play in American society' (*ibid.*: 161, notes 19 and 20). Scientism ran riot, as conservative sociologists expressed their values in descriptions of effective social control techniques. Such a mood later produced many studies in the sociology of law concerned with the effectiveness or impact of law as a device for social control, or with the merits of extra-legal methods of social control. It was a mood which was perfectly consistent with the jurisprudential drive to produce a new natural law which articulated the norms and values necessary to bind a pluralistic, capitalist society together.

Durkheim's arguments about the dangers of excessive punishment and criminalization had now found their fullest expression in the welfare state era. Bredemeier and Stephenson articulated his undeveloped implications about the tolerant society with perfect exactness. The modern ideology of social work was first outlined (support the person as an individual while refusing to approve the deviant act) and praise showered on the value of leniency for first offenders, probation, the avoidance of stigma and keeping a door open for conformity. Then they pose the classic question flowing from the Durkheimian problematic: 'How much toleration, under what conditions, and at what point does tolerance cease to motivate conformity and begin to reinforce deviance?' (*ibid.*: 175). The field of enquiry produced by Durkheim's ideas had now reached full maturity.

Finally, Harold Garfinkel in 1956 (reprinted in Rubington and Weinberg, 1968) unwittingly provided the most bizarre parody of the Parsonian functionalist perspective, before it was assaulted with critique after critique in the 1960s. Apparently quite seriously, his short essay 'Conditions of successful degradation ceremonies', which was later to become widely quoted as a forerunner of ethnomethodology (the study of people's methods of making sense of the world), considered the questions 'What program of communicative tactics will get the work of status degradation done?' and 'How can one make a good denunciation?' (*ibid*.: 188, 189). Reflecting on the period of McCarthyism, these questions take on a stark and brutal meaning now. Garfinkel's detailed conditions for successully degrading someone are of little importance in comparison. Whether Garfinkel intended a parody I do not know, but there is no sign of awareness in the article that the essay was a contender for the Orwell prize for amoral, authoritarian, technocratic discourses of the 1950s. Functionalism, scientism, Parsonianism, scientific social-system management, call it what you will, all stood naked – degraded and reduced to sycophantic passivity in the face of power. At worst, their proponents became the technocrats of the tactics of domination; at best, they were active collaborators.

Notes

1 The trial of Hiss joins those of Dreyfus, Sacco and Vanzetti as political trials of special note for our tale. It seems that the political denunciation of the enemy in the national courts is a key sign of the beginning of a campaign for moral solidarity.
2 Davis always remained devoted to Léger's work, as is very clear in the *Mellow Pad* of 1945–51. Léger's work was, of course, the inspiration for the abstract book covers in our 'New Directions in Criminology' series.
3 This gives new meaning to Becker's analysis in his *Outsiders* of 1963.
4 Indeed, the term social control itself now became used with much greater frequency.
5 There is no evidence that Foucault was aware of Lemert's work, but the similarities in the analysis of power and its moral effects are obvious. Both began their academic lives, indeed spent the late 1940s, with a great interest in the social psychology of the abnormal and the findings of the structural analysis of myths and custom. Lemert was an anthropologist and Foucault was very influenced by Dumézil, a historian of religions.
6 Davis's study is a classic. Prostitution was held to be 'the oldest profession' because it was functional for the family as the social institution which tied sex to reproduction: it was 'the most convenient sexual outlet for armies and for the legions of strangers, perverts and physically repulsive in our midst' (Davis, 1961: 288). Bensman and Gerver's analysis was much more sophisticated and made the very Durkheimian point that if rules were tightly enforced, in this case the rules governing aeroplane production, the social costs were too high (in this case, the loss of profits by the manufacturers), and there had to be a negotiated balance between rule-enforcement and rule-breaking.
7 Later on, Taylor *et al.* (1973) were to revive this old concept of quasi-political resistance against authority as a socialist theory of deviance. We will look at this

in Chapter 10. Suffice it to note here that they made no reference to Bell's analysis of 'unorganized class struggle', just as they glossed Merton's wrestle with Frommian concepts.

8 They also published many studies attempting to discover whether unrecorded crime or delinquency was as class-distributed as the officially recorded (see, for example, Short and Nye, 1958; Voss, 1966; Gold, 1966).

8 Sociopathy and secondary deviance: regulation as measurement and balance

The liberal tendency within the emergent sociology of deviance, the true inheritance of the Durkheimian legacy, produced two major texts immediately after the war, before going very quiet during the McCarthy period. Both were written by Edwin Lemert.

In a paper to the Pacific Sociological Society in 1948, Lemert outlined the beginnings of a very distinctive approach to deviance, developing his earlier statements on the calibration of deviance as a measure of social control activity and extending the work of Tannenbaum and Lindesmith. As usual, Lemert was ahead of his colleagues and his time. He had realized the elasticity of the attribution of deviance, and its intrinsic vacuousness as a concept. He illustrated this by observing that if one used textbook categories of social pathology as many as 80 per cent of the population could be counted as 'sociopathic deviants' (Lemert, 1948: 23). This figure was so low because he deliberately excluded white-collar criminals, 'the obese and ugly', and those who engage in extra-marital sexual relations. Had these categories been included the figure would have far surpassed 100 per cent.

Instead of defining society as sick, Lemert refused to infer that this was 'a dismal commentary upon the true state of the American population' and concluded that his figures demonstrate 'the absence of any usable distinction between normal and abnormal human behavior' (*ibid.*: 24). This is a much underquoted classic statement in American sociology.

To redress the balance, Lemert declared:

We may pertinently ask at this juncture whether the time has not come to break abruptly with the traditions of the older social patho- logists and abandon once and for all the archaic and medicinal idea that human beings can be divided into normal and pathological, or, at least, if such a division must be made, to divest the term 'patho- logical' of its moralistic, unscientific overtones. As a step in this direction, the writer suggests that the concepts of social differentia- tion and individuation be rescued from the limbo of the older text- books on sociology, dusted off and given scientific airing, perhaps being supplemented and given statistical meaning with the perfectly usable concept of deviation.

(ibid.: 25)

By merely posing the question, Lemert retreated from the idea that we actually do not need a division between normal and pathological individu- als. He reached the brink of a revolution in the sociology of moral judge- ment and then lost his nerve. His analysis was far-sighted but not courageous enough. Instead, he settled for a liberal emphasis on the way that modern society renders us all very different, and argued that social pathology can be treated as 'a special phase of social and cultural differentiation and individuation' *(ibid.)*. As such, his analysis was absolutely true to Durkheim's thought; as opposed to the functionalist distortion which portrayed Durkheim as an advocate of social control or socialization into conformity to integrate society and shore up its moral boundaries. Lemert's analysis went on to define social pathology, or the 'sociopathic phenomenon', as

differentiated behavior which, at a given time and in a given place, is socially disapproved, though the same behavior may be socially approved at other times and at other places, and for our society as a whole there may be no consensus as to whether the behavior is desirable or undesirable.

(ibid.: 25)

In short, said Lemert, there is a 'tolerance quotient'.

On this view, some disapproved behavior may be symptomatic of 'deep-lying, intra-psychic conflicts in individuals', but the great bulk of it is a manifestation of social situations, notably those involving culture con- flict *(ibid.: 26)*. In addition, there is a third category of deviant behaviour: 'namely, systematic role- and status-oriented deviation, or professional pathological behavior' *(ibid.)*. The present state of analysis, Lemert said, did little to explain this third type, or the conversion of the situational type of deviation into the systematic. In this way, Lemert followed Wirth and others from the thirties on the importance of culture conflict but added a wholly new field of analysis (one that Tannenbaum and Wirth had out- lined but not developed): the analysis of 'secondary deviation' *(ibid.: 27)*. He took the Meadian concept of interaction from the Chicago work of the 1930s, making the valuable insight that it was not so much a theory or an explanation as a mere condition of enquiry, and applied it to the transformation of situational deviance into systematic deviance. Through symbolic interaction between the offender and his or her significant others, offenders take different courses: some interactions lead to the normalization or acceptance of the deviation as peripheral to identity, others lead to the full reorganization of the offender's identity around a self-understanding as deviant. Deviant behaviour based upon such a symbolic reorganization of identity, Lemert argued, tends to be systematic and significant. As such, secondary deviation

> may be said to exist when the person begins to employ his defiant behavior or a role based upon it *as a means of defense, attack, or adjustment to the overt and covert problems created by the societal reaction to it*. In effect, the original causes of the deviation recede in importance or give way to the central importance of the disapproval and isolating reactions of the community.
>
> (*ibid.*: 28)

Lemert had given the arguments of Tannenbaum, Wirth and Lindesmith a very precise shape. Their interpretations had been moulded into an operational theory of the production of systematic deviance by the agencies of social control under specific social conditions.

It should be clear from Lemert's statements in 1948 that this was not a critique of social control, or its methods, but rather an attempt at a scientific explanation of the social production of deviance. In a nutshell, the thesis was that social deviance was primarily produced by culture conflict in highly differentiated, highly individuated, multicultural societies, and secondarily by social control itself. Essentially, Lemert was holding on to the insights of the thirties and using them to formulate a new dimension of analysis. It was not a new theory, nor was it a revolution in the field. However, it was an argument of pristine clarity and sharpness. Lemert's elevation of the argument into book form in *Social Pathology* in 1951, alongside Parsons's tome *The Social System*, marked the full maturation of the sociology of deviance into a branch of sociology which was fully theorized and consistent with much of mainstream sociology, and which threw new light on to existing sociological analysis.

Social Pathology

Lemert's *Social Pathology* actually only moved his 1948 argument on a little further. Mainly, the book outlined the conditions under which 'social reaction' worked to convert situational deviance into systematic deviance and illustrated how the argument worked in certain empirical areas. However, the thesis was given a harder form. Mills's condemnation of the professional ideology of social pathologists was supported and deployed to make the claim that reform movements and public reactions 'may create more problems than they solve' (Lemert, 1951: 4). Lemert now clearly made public reactions to deviation a central part of the sociological analysis of deviant behaviour and social problems. Noting the indifference to corporate crimes and to the depletion of natural resources, he emphasized the selectivity of moral indignation. Again ahead of his time, he went on to register what is now taken as the fact, that public indignation, or the diagnosis of experts, is no guide to what is truly a social problem. Any consensus among authorities as to what is a problem 'may prove to be a projection of moral beliefs or special interests of certain power groups in the community, with little to distinguish them from the moral judgments of the uninformed laity save, perhaps, a more convincing top-dressing of rationalizations' (*ibid.*: 5). Wirth's reflections on the ideological character of social problems were not in vain. However, while Lemert contended that science itself contained moral and ethical values, unlike the sociologists of the sixties he did not believe that the sociologist 'must break out his colors and show whose side he is on in public controversies' (*ibid.*). Rejecting the view that science was authoritarian, Lemert felt that it was more 'congenial to nonauthoritarian leadership' and that social science should be used more in social planning and public administration (*ibid.*: 6, n. 3). His book can then be reasonably taken to be aimed at informing 'policymakers what the consequences of certain lines of social action are likely to be' (*ibid.*: 6). For Lemert himself, it was an attempt to set up 'a systematic theory of sociopathic behavior'.

For present purposes, what is really important about Lemert's book is that he made a clear break with all pre-existing ideas of moral deviation as an expression of some kind of psychopathology. Since it is a rare person who has never committed a felony, Lemert observed:

> The designation of crime as a psychopathic symptom obscures rather than clarifies how criminal activity becomes integrated into forms of social organization which are participated in by persons with a wide variety of personal motives and psychological orientations. Criminals may operate illegal gambling establishments but their patrons include the respectable citizens of the community. Bankers operate banks for non-criminal use, but many such bankers in the past have knowingly accepted deposits of money gained by criminals. Lawyers, labor unions, insurance companies, and newspapers have been known to enter into collusion with criminals. Even presidents of the United States have appointed members of criminally corrupt political machines to high offices. Unless we wish to diagnose all their patrons or customers and those who cooperate economically and politically with criminals as psychopathic, we are driven to the conclusions that 'reductionist' psychiatric theories of organized crime in terms of abnormal mental processes are insufficient.
>
> (*ibid.*: 20)

This very American statement, which of course merely develops Lemert's earlier formulations, illustrates the sharpness with which Lemert now broke with the sociological dalliance with psychiatry. For most deviations, psychiatry was now irrelevant and even dangerous to a scientific account of their origin and organization. The wheel had turned another crucial degree.

The liberal wing of the sociology of deviance had now completely abandoned the baggage of the nineteenth century, the problematic of degeneration, and had completed the Durkheimian revolution in the analysis of moral judgement. In so doing, of course, it also abandoned the Frank-type critique of society itself as degenerate, as a patient needing a fundamental cure, as a deeply pathological structure generating some deeply pathological individuals. The consequent analysis in the sociology of deviance tended instead to a bland liberalism which emphasized the social expansion of difference in a pluralist society, and the unfairness of severe punishment or stigmatization in cases where little harm was done by the crime except to the perpetrator himself or herself ('crimes without victims'). Lemert's book was the forerunner of much that followed in the sociology of deviance of the 'swinging' sixties. Its West Coast sense of individualism, differentiation and tolerance was very evident.

Sophisticated and cogent as it was, Lemert's book was pregnant with an unresolved contradiction: if deviance was mostly situational, and could range from mass murder to being a movie star, and if deviance owed little to psychopathology, then the term pathology was totally inappropriate here. Indeed, the whole concept of social pathology was no longer meaningful. Lemert had rendered it a misleading and archaic category. He was really now talking about difference and systematic difference, and the self-interested censorious labelling of some difference as crime or social deviation.

What an oddity! His book is called *Social Pathology*, it talks continuously about social deviation, yet it is actually all about two other things: (a) the social production of difference, and (b) the social censure of some difference as deviance. It might be an understatement to call this a text of a transition.

In fact, to his great credit, Lemert actually addresses the question of terminology. Rightly criticizing criminology and sociology for borrowing terms like crime from legal or medical discourses, he tried to find a meaning for the term deviation which would avoid the problems with the concepts of crime and psychopathology. Noting that Fuller had, in a book review of 1943, commented that the concept of deviation could have little meaning in a 'multi-norm' society (Fuller, 1943), Lemert went on to fudge the issue by arguing that moral norms vary in their intensity and that social deviations tend to be those behaviours which breach norms people hold as important, e.g. those governing rights and privileges. He discussed a wide range of social deviations before seeming to conclude that the degree of moral indignation elicited by deviance really depended very much on the exact social context. While this may be true, and while it may be true that most attributions of deviation occur in a situation of culture conflict, this did not address the issue of the vacuousness of the concept of deviance which it implied.

The vagueness of his conception of social deviation clearly bothered

Lemert, but he could not see that what he had done was to begin negating the analytic validity of the term for further theoretical advance. Essentially, his starting point was his finishing point: there was no basis for distinguishing conformity from deviance in the behaviour of the actor in question, the only distinguishing feature was the censorious attribution of deviance. That social censure was, as he effectively admitted, usually rooted in socially established rights and privileges connected to power, and its application was dependent upon the exact interactive context, but that context was usually one of significant conflict between the parties in question. The concept of deviance is of little help in describing or capturing the processual twists and turns of this human phenomenon. Indeed, since it is one of the censorious labels applied to the offender, i.e. a weapon within the conflict, it could hardly be the basis for a scientific sociology; especially since the failings of the concept of crime in this respect had already been noted. Lemert took the field to the point where it required a concept of social censure, but he himself did not deliver it. Nevertheless, his book did advance the field further and took it to a point where it could begin to conceptualize many of the contradictions and political features of social censure which appeared in the 1960s.

Lemert also retained the concept of subculture developed in the thirties by the symbolic interactionists in Chicago, and indeed developed it further. Subculture was a concept that had a firm, longstanding, place in liberal thought and fears; it was not a conservative or functionalist invention. The functionalists may have redefined it to mean a pocket of urban resistance to the system, a sector which was in need of 're-socializing', and this may have had a lasting effect on its popular meaning, but liberal sociology had always conceived of it as a system of group support in lower-class, urban areas which enabled its members to survive in a rat-race favouring the rich and white (see Finestone, 1976: 156–86). It had, of course, in both traditions long referred in actuality to ethnically defined groupings, particularly black communities. Whites, according to this ideology, do not exist in subcultures, they live in clubs, groups, companies or associations. Essentially, subculture was always the white liberal's term for lower-class ethnic communities or groups. Lemert's use of the concept to explain systematic deviation, unlike that of the functionalists such as A. K. Cohen, somewhat distanced it from these historic, racist, meanings. He began to see a subculture as the necessary accompaniment to systematic social deviation; as a 'special social organization' with definite roles and mores which involved a 'definite professionalization of conduct by deviant group members' (Lemert, 1951: 44). It fostered a certain 'craft pride', sustained a distinct identity, served to protect the group against attack and taught the neophyte the tricks of the trade. In this way, it was very little different to a craft union, a freemasonry or a religious sect.[1] Indeed, Lemert so generalized the concept that he concluded that modern societies contained 'hundreds of thousands' of such deviant subcultures. Deviant subcultures had now been conscripted into a fully pluralistic analysis. 'Their appearance and growth is a response to the drive of individuals to achieve tension reductions in a chaotic and conflicting culture' (*ibid.*: 46).

An inherent and logical part of the liberal-pluralist analysis of the adjustment of individuals to life in a multicultural, highly differentiated, mass society full of conflict, the concept of subculture, for Lemert, helped to describe the processes of group formation in modern life and therefore the process of becoming a systematic or secondary deviant. Visible, repeated, deviation combined with indignant, moralistic, public reaction to produce an aggravated need for subcultural support, which in turn became one of the necessary preconditions for future systematic, and more organized or professional, social deviation. Subculture was a vital tool in the account of the emergence of secondary deviation.

The strongest development in Lemert's book was the analysis of secondary deviation. This gave real meat to the points made in outline by Tannenbaum. Social control was now rendered not only as the clear calibrator of the social rate of deviance but as itself a direct cause of systematic deviance. Noting the variability of social reaction to a single type of action across the various states of the union, Lemert discussed various dimensions of the importance of social reaction not only in defining deviance in the first place but in structuring its development and in ultimately producing the phenomenon of secondary deviance. His discussion is not as sophisticated and cogent as his later one (Lemert, 1972), but it is still remarkable, although not quite as remarkable as the number of criminologists who have not read it or subjected it to detailed commentary. Briefly, Lemert focused on spurious or disproportionate social reaction to a deviant act. He was probably the first to deal clearly with social reaction to deviance as an independent variable; to treat it as bearing little necessary relation to the deviant act committed. Many 'factors' could produce an over-reaction by social control agencies, but 'a factor of supervening importance which very often introduces a spurious element in the societal reaction is the rivalry or conflict of groups in the situation as they aspire to power or struggle to maintain their position in a hegemony of power relations' (Lemert, 1951: 56). This was a formulation that was more sophisticated than some in the wave of radical criminology following 1968; its similarity to later statements by Foucault perhaps owes something to the profound interest of the two authors in cultural anthropology. It could also be said that the analysis in *Policing the Crisis* (Hall *et al.*, 1978) was a direct successor to Lemert's position of 1951. Indeed, Lemert's observation was prescient in that it foresaw one of the prime roots of the McCarthyite over-reaction in the 1950s. McCarthy's accusations rescued his ailing political career and sustained the revival of the Republican Party.

Lemert went on to observe that:

the situation in which deviation is present becomes structured in conflict terms and values. This is not an uncommon occurrence in our culture. The institutionalization of conflict and factionalism as a means of intergroup adjustment frequently leads to an amplification of the societal reaction in the presence of the minutiae of deviation. Trivial or insignificant departures from social norms are stimuli for hair-trigger public reactions, 'storms of protest' and 'controversies'. Closer inspection of these reactions often reveals that a political alignment within the community is seeking to embarrass the party in power and has seized upon some otherwise unimportant deviant event – a crime or a license violation – for this purpose.

(Lemert, 1951: 56)

These words thus captured the McCarthyite nightmare to follow. But Lemert was also talking about the typical moral reform campaign which criminalized many 'small fry' in a wave of moral indignation, before leaving the basic situation alone – unaltered. The concept of deviance was thus irrevocably changed, and in a way which brought politics to the fore. The selection of at least minor social deviations for public labelling and stigma was clearly a policy or political decision subject to the vagaries of hegemonic politics. Criminal statistics were from here on forever tainted. It became clear that they were not so much the official statistics as the statistics of the officials.[2] Many essays were written subsequently in the 1960s on the senselessness of using the officials' statistics as the foundation of a scientific explanation of deviant behaviour, and the real significance of those statistics as indices of social control policies or agents' decisions (e.g. Kitsuse and Cicourel, 1963).

The social rate of publicly defined deviance in a particular area was, for Lemert, clearly a function of a number of societal, political and organizational variables. As such, deviance was less clearly a purely moral question, and much more a matter of politics than previously portrayed. Lemert's American pluralism gave a different tone to Durkheim's conception of crime and deviation as censures defined by a collective sentiment. Now, clearly, the notion of a collective consensus, of an undisputed hegemonic ideological unity, was challenged by a post-immigration, post-1945, American concept of the heterogeneity and multiculturalism of modern societies which stressed the multiplicity of competing power groups and moral views. In such a light, the conception of deviance was beginning to look inappropriate at the very same moment that it was being elevated to the status of a full-fledged sociological concept; for how could substantial social difference in a context of multicultural pluralism be translated as social deviation?

The scientism of the term deviation, derived from its psychiatric connections, made little sense given the logic of Lemert's arguments. While Lemert himself did not address the issue directly, his thesis had unfrocked the psychiatric heritage. Now the question had only been implicitly posed. It was later to be asked with vehemence by the anti-psychiatrists and a variety of ethnic/women's pressure groups, as to whether the profession of psychiatry itself was merely the province and product of white, male, middle-class Westerners. Lemert's anthropological fieldwork experience in 'other' cultures had forced out a very new question, at least in embryo. The differential concept of culture and the unconscious or repressed world of the oppressed were continuing to make their presence felt.

Lemert's book said so much more in the way of providing a detailed analysis of the emergence of secondary deviation and of the role of the societal control culture in producing it. It repays reading even today. But our focus is on the concept of deviance and its journey through the world. As such our tale has reached another watershed: the field of the sociology of deviance was fully formed and theorized by 1951 with the publication of the books by Parsons and Lemert. It was, for the moment, dominated by the conservative wing and thus by a functionalist mode of analysis of 'non-rational' deviation from the post-war consensus. It contained a liberal wing which was beginning to ask some fundamental questions about the character, values and efficacy of social control, but which was to remain largely underground until the early sixties. The Durkheimian heritage had been adopted and developed in a faithful, critical, manner by this wing, and thus had begun to expose the unconscious discriminations involved in the public definition and stigmatization of deviants. It thus seems appropriate to end this chapter by briefly recording the other two most significant liberal contributions coming out of the 1950s. Their focus and tone speak volumes for the power of the smouldering underclass culture which was to force its attentions upon American sociology and society in the 1960s. The propagandist's veil of ignorance and intolerance was being lifted, but slowly, and in the heat of the night.

In the heat of the night: cool cats, drugs and the black underground

Both essays concern the suppressed black culture of the fifties, and both concern drug use (and jazz). The first was a paper by Becker in 1953, 'Becoming a marijuana user' (Becker, 1963, Chapter 3). It followed the tradition of illicit drug use research established by Lindesmith, and charted the processes whereby initiates to marijuana smoking were acculturated to perceive and reproduce its pleasurable effects through association with experienced users. The essay is very descriptive and leaves most theoretical questions well alone. Its main contribution to the field was to make the point that the motive to deviation may well be learned after the praxis of deviation rather than being a prerequisite for that praxis; although it is a point that Mills had made and that was at least implicit in Lemert's account of the many possible sequences of becoming a systematic deviant. It drew heavily upon Becker's own attachment to the underworld of jazz musicians, in that the latter constituted half of his sample of interviewees.

The second essay was much more important, substantive and prophetic. It was by Harold Finestone on the subject of 'Cats, kicks and color'

(1964), and based on research done in the early 1950s. It reported his study of young, black, heroin users from Chicago's 'asphalt jungle'. The study was supervised by Shaw, McKay and Kobrin, and is very much within the tradition of Chicagoan, appreciative–ecological, research. Finestone's essay is a masterpiece of fine-tuned observation; a classic of its kind. Drawing on all the gains made by the sociology of deviance since Thrasher's book of 1927, it documents the dress, style, language, music and attitude of the 'cool cats' as the responses of a 'sacrificed generation' to their profound frustration and rage. Without romanticizing that culture, whose thefts, pickpocketing, drug use and exploitation of women (through occasional pimping) hardly qualify it as a model of moral health, Finestone began to tap the world beneath the American consensus fantasy and to present an image so distant from the 'failure' figures of Cohen's delinquent boys. After describing the sartorial elegance and aesthetic style of the 'cool cat', expressions of the cat's perceived sense of superiority over the 'square' world, he spoke of the significance of heroin for the cats:

> It was the ultimate 'kick'. No substance was more profoundly tabooed by conventional middle-class society. Regular heroin use provides a sense of maximal social differentiation from the 'square'. The cat was at last engaged, he felt, in an activity completely beyond the comprehension of the 'square' . . . the cat as a social type is . . . a manifestation of a process of social change in which a new type of self-conception has been emerging among the adolescents of the lower socioeconomic levels of the colored population in large urban centers.
>
> (Finestone, 1964: 285–6)

He provided an account of a section of black culture which posited cool and kicks as an adjustment to the 'blocking and frustration' created by 'the policies of social segregation and discrimination' maintained by 'the dominant social order'. There might seem a passing similarity to Cohen's analysis, but really they have little in common except the assertion that the frustrated 'dispositions' were derived from dominant white society. Finestone's analysis owes more to Frazier's *Black Bourgeoisie* than to Parsonian functionalism.

At last, black resistance was beginning to be placed within the context of institutionalized white racism. At last, the structural rationality of 'deviance' was being put on to the agenda, and, at last, there was little talk of heroin use as 'deviant'. Instead, heroin use was put into context as an integral part of a confident, new, rejectionist culture developed by people whose exploitation by white society was massive and historic, and whose growing aspirations were still being sidelined or suppressed. In this context, the term deviance does not readily suggest itself as appropriate. Instead, Finestone talked about play.[3]

The cat as a social type, said Finestone, is a personification of 'an expressive social movement', focused on the 'hustle' and the 'kick', which indirectly attacked the values of the dominant culture. Survival based on this kind of cool, enjoyable, play, or fun, successfully evaded the harsh reality of economic exploitation and cultural/legal discrimination. It is play because it is fun, it is voluntary and it is an escape. It sustained a pretend world, an oppositional fantasy against the oppressive one of the dominant society. It was not an attack on property so much as fun; the former being more common among delinquent white youth.

The cool black cat 'came from what were externally the drabbest, most overcrowded, and physically deteriorated sections of the city and yet discussed his pattern of living as though it were a consciously cultivated work of art' (*ibid*.: 282). Cohen's findings were thus exposed as more applicable to white kids. Status frustration is only a relevant explanation for people who have the potential to go somewhere. The young black heroin addicts Finestone talked of were going nowhere. They were not even part of the mob; a fact that may have driven some kids into more violent responses (Cloward and Ohlin, 1960). They faced only increased demoralization in the face of growing white affluence and their own continuing exclusion. They were, and are, part of the sacrificed generations. Heroin was an adjustment to a dead-end.

The cat was nevertheless part of a movement which was producing a new self-conception among poor blacks. That movement had perhaps begun back in the twenties and thirties with jazz, Marcus Garvey and the collapse of King Cotton. In any case, Martin Luther King was now soon to announce that he had a dream, and things were about to change. America was beginning to attend to its unfinished business. But slowly. For as I write large parts of Los Angeles have just been razed to the ground yet again, as black people predictably reacted to continuing police racism and the years of constant economic and political regress in their world under President Bush. As Nathaniel Playthell (1992), the black journalist, commented, 'virtually every Afro-American urban community has a fairly recent case of gross police brutality which inspired a widespread identification with the outrage of black Californians.'

To use the concept of social deviance today to describe the Afro-American rage in Los Angeles would be a joke. To Playthell, on television the black mayor of Los Angeles seemed 'quite out of touch', and the governor of California 'looked like a man from another country'. The blacks did not deviate from their norms; their norms are so far apart from daily black reality as to constitute satellites in an outer space. At its best, the concept of deviance registered the fact of multiculturalism in thirties America and the death of the concept of degeneration; after McCarthy and Eisenhower, the concept registered the fact of WASP social control and the stillborn character of American social democracy. Deviance had not lost touch with its Durkheimian heritage, but that heritage was proving to be a blockage preventing an understanding of discriminations entrenched and rooted in the history of oppression. Where the Durkheimian connection was particularly strong, in Lemert's work, the concept of deviance had begun to display its inherent weakness: there can be no science of social deviance where the judges of normality use only the norms of the white male middle class, where groups live in worlds apart, and where the relativism, factionalism and cultural bigotry intertwined with modernity's moral judgements constantly undercut its drive to order. Deviance began to outlive its usefulness the moment American social democracy refused to get a grip of its institutionalized racism. Its value lay in the drive to multicultural incorporation; its decay began in the imposition of an artificial moral consensus.

Notes

1 Lemert's argument was the forerunner of many in the 1960s which were to treat deviant subcultures as objects amenable to analysis by the sociology of occupations. Some, grasping the importance of communication, teaching and graduation within this group-formation process, applied the sociology of education to it (such as Becker, 1970, for example).
2 After my experiences in Africa, and studies of crime in the underdeveloped societies, I personally now always use the phrase 'the officials' statistics' in the course of teaching.
3 Yet how many sociology teachers use A. K. Cohen to talk about delinquency and how many use Finestone's essay? Unfortunately, the standard way of teaching the sociology of deviance, as I hope I have shown throughout this text, tends to neglect several key works, and tends to concern itself with the problems of white adolescent males.

9 The labelling perspective and the flowering of social deviance

So much of what is referred to as labelling theory had already been developed in Lemert's work before the 1960s explosion of what its exponents preferred to call the labelling perspective. Chapter 8 demonstrated that, in bringing forward and developing many themes from the thirties, Edwin Lemert had brought to maturity a perspective on the sociology of deviance which stressed six major arguments:

- that there was little scientific basis for dividing people into the normal and the pathological;
- that most deviation was inconsequential for individual and social organization, because it was an inevitable daily feature of life in pluralistic, multicultural, societies full of conflict;
- that systematic social deviation is usually the product of the individual's adoption of an identity and orientation to life centred on the fact of his or her socially established deviance;
- that social control creates as much deviance as it deters in pluralistic, multicultural, societies full of conflict, not least because it is a reflection of sharp conflicts of values and interests;
- that the labelling of deviance is an independent phenomenon, not necessarily linked to the detail of the deviant act, and can therefore be an expression of the partisan motives and interests involved in moral reform campaigns, political advancement or economic advantage;
- that the above five arguments do not constitute an explanation or theory of deviant behaviour but a useful orientation or perspective for analysing specific instances.

What happened in the sixties was little more than a flowering of this perspective. The sociology of deviance had already matured. It had got its driving licence and the vote; its liberal wing now needed 'wheels' and a social movement to vote for. It already had a sceptical attitude to social control and the established consensus, it just needed some encouragement and it would decry the whole system. History dutifully supplied it.

As a preface, however, it is valuable to remember that the notion that 'social control' creates as much 'deviant behaviour' as it deters has a much longer history. In the same way that much of the observational fieldwork of the Chicago school was prefigured by the documentary studies of Mayhew and Booth in nineteenth-century England, so too the labelling perspective had been prefigured frequently in nineteenth-century writings in Britain. For example, as early as 1818, the Reverend Hunt wrote in the Report of the Bedfordshire Jail Committee of Magistrates: 'the administration of the criminal law, in so far as regards minor offences, has notoriously contributed to, rather than diminished, delinquency throughout the country, by its tendency to corrupt, rather than to reform' (quoted in Stockdale, 1977: 124). Many other such comments could be found. So why did we take so much notice of American sociology from the sixties? Why did 'labelling theory', as it was mistakenly called, seem so radical? Why was it so opposed by 'established' criminology? Because it rocked the boat of post-war complacency which was still holding on to the end of ideology, the rise of political consensus in the welfare state and the fantasy of a unified culture. The thinking of 'the labelling theorists' was not new, but they systematically developed some old ideas to the point where they attained the status of theory.[1] The labelling perspective represented a renewed liberalism. It picked up the liberal themes from the 1930s, and Lemert's work, and took them to centre stage, after the dull drone of post-war conservative hegemony within sociology resulting from the McCarthyite purges.

Discrimination, dissent and the smell of power

The Rooseveltian state was essentially still intact in the 1960s yet the radical changes necessary to rescue the poor, notably the blacks, were not forthcoming. The great American dream and the dream of Luther King were a long way from fruition. JFK offered more dreams, as his youthful charm and idealistic rhetoric caught the desires for change that were blowing in the wind. As we saw in Chapter 7, however, an American superstate had been formed since 1945, based on some very powerful military-industrial interests. Integrated with organized crime and its key forces growing fat from the arms economy, this organized, massive, power was not about to tolerate a great deal of internal dissent. Social and global equilibrium was about to be maintained, whatever it took – as JFK was to find out for himself. Even the President of the United States was disposable. Kennedy's fate, to this day, remains the major symbol of all that was wrong with the American dream of social democracy in the sixties.

The inroads made by the blacks into industry, the military and the administration during Roosevelt's time had hardened conservative opposition and sharpened their worst fears. The blacks, in turn, had learned to use political and economic pressure, the courts and the tactics of resistance. On attaining office, Kennedy did not give black demands, now well articulated by various organizations, urgent priority. He proclaimed a 'new frontier', within which all would feel his helping hand. It seemed to extend across the world. The Bay of Pigs was a humiliating failure, although the 1962 blockade seemed to succeed in preventing Khruschev from installing nuclear missiles in Cuba. It meant little new for the blacks. The Freedom Rides of the early sixties, the Birmingham riot, King's frequent arrest and violence in Mississippi all testified to that. Kennedy was converted to the cause of civil rights but did little of lasting impact. Instead, the American commitment to preventing a communist takeover in South Vietnam was hardened, although not decisively.

Nevertheless, it may well be that Kennedy did too much that was liberal and too little that was in the interests of the militaristic conservative élites, for who now does not believe that his assassination in 1963 was inspired by sources within the American imperialist state? Many books, and the film *JFK*, suggest that his murder was certainly covered up by the Warren Commission in a scandalous manner. The official account of the murder simply lacks credibility. In a book on deviance, it has to be said that so many people suspecting that even the President of the United States was not safe from rogue forces within government, representing the old frontier culture, must have been consequential for their allegiance to any notion that social deviance was confined to the inner-city ghettoes. The subsequent murders of Bobby Kennedy, Martin Luther King, Lee Harvey Oswald and various people associated with the enquiry into the murder of JFK were ample testimony to the immensely volatile divisions within American society. Inevitably, they fed a scepticism about the neutrality of official moral-legal judgements.

Kennedy's successor, Johnson, rapidly launched civil rights legislation aimed at racial discrimination. But, as Brogan comments, the 'savagery lurking in American life was welling to the surface'. Three civil rights workers were murdered in Mississippi and no one was convicted. Johnson's landslide win in 1964 had probably hardened Southern resistance to change, but more legislation to encourage the black voter brought even more black presence in state legislatures. As Brogan says, after years of what was now called Third World poverty, blacks became firmly established in the cities across America, and some even began to share in the post-war boom which rolled on until the early 1970s, only to find that 'urban slums were worse than rural ones' (Brogan, 1985: 657). Appropriately, it was in the new epicentre of America, California, that the inevitable explosion eventually occurred. The Watts ghetto blew up in 1965, as the contradiction between the incredible wealth and spectacular consumption at the centre of the Sun Belt arms economy and Hollywood, Los Angeles, and the overcrowded relative deprivation of the newly arrived black population finally broke its bounds.

Johnson launched a 'war on poverty' and continued passing laws aimed at reducing disadvantage, but, as Brogan affirms, the American inner city continued to decay at an alarming rate, and crime rates boomed. Immigrant gangs fought it out in asphalt jungles, and *West Side Story* looked prophetic. King's assassination in 1968 accelerated the increasing militancy and militarization of black politics: it was not obvious to many that entering institutional politics was an efficient way of gaining real change.

The sixties was a time of growing resistance on all fronts to the edifice of power and the one-dimensionality of hyper-consumerism. Even the youth of the educated middle class revolted, and in droves. Haight-Ashbury, in San Francisco, became the mythic centre of a rejection of utilitarian-militaristic values, as youth congregated to express their retreat from or rejection of a way of life that was spiritually vacuous. 1967 was the 'summer of love'. At this stage, before 1968, the 'revolution' was primarily cultural (see Young, 1973; Larkin, 1979). The ethos of productivity was rejected in the age and society of leisure (see Young, 1973: 195). Mind-expanding drugs, permissive sexuality, the new rock music and transcendental poetry all articulated the peaceful principles of a 'flower power' whose opposition was committedly non-violent. Social deviants, with a growing political consciousness, sprouted all over America, creating new communities committed to 'dropping out' and a 'hip' lifestyle.

The avant-garde was back, drawing on all the best modernist traditions of Greenwich Village and the culture of black jazz from the first third of the century. Marijuana use became common, and there were subsequently calls for its possession to be legalized. Howard Becker's moment had come and he took it, writing a famous book called *Outsiders*, whose title alone expressed the mild, even bland, but peaceful scepticism of a subterranean world he had long been part of. Many now adopted the philosophies of existentialism, surrealism and transcendentalism. The straight world which made them feel like outsiders seemed totally surreal.

The art of this period was primarily popular and musical, and the adoption of black rhythm and blues was a notable feature – however, this phase reached its high point with The Beatles' *Sergeant Pepper* album, an openly surrealist exercise in the classic tradition (discussed in Chapter 3). 'Pop art', like 'pop music', was the fashion in the sixties in America. Most existing art was identified with 'highbrow culture' and the world of the élite. McCarthyism and the new world of the mass media had spawned a philistinism which was hardly revolutionary. On the other hand, this was an age when people wanted to produce culture, and identify with a home-grown culture, rather than worship the culture that was foisted on them, however 'good' it was. Moreover, the television age was upon us. We lived in a culture of distractions. Inevitably, the meaning of the word culture had to change. It was a consequential shift for our purposes in this book, because it undercut one of the fundamental concepts of the interdisciplinary matrix behind the concept of deviance. If anything could be culture, then nothing was left of the differential concept of culture (see Chapter 3), and therefore very little of the culturalist impetus behind the concept of deviance. We were all cultural deviants now in a society without any shared definition of culture. This was really fundamental, and unstoppable – because the mass media rolled on with ever greater vigour, popularizing a new art form, and all art forms, and, while the authorities could enforce conformity of outward behaviour they could not stop people listening to the Beatles (although they tried in some of the states).

Andy Warhol was perhaps the most widely known 'pop artist'. Like Dalí, a great self-publicist in the media age, Warhol strung together disparate images in a new way. His unique focus was death, and his position was that of the uninvolved spectator (Hughes, 1981: 351). Death was anathema to the beat generation, for they saw it as installed in their lives and in the boredom of the social structure – and this was art in the society of the spectacle (Vaneigem, 1977). Warhol, says Hughes, treated all events as a spectacle. In that way he mirrored his society. The medium was becoming the message as one spectacle vied for popularity with another in a meaningless parade of disconnected images projected by teams of anonymous producers. I doubt if this is what Wirth had in mind when he talked of the propagandistic power of the media (Chapter 7). He did not foresee that the power of the mass media would undercut the power of all propaganda and transform culture and discourse into very popular, and sometimes trivial, pursuits.

This was also a time of the growth of the movement to 'self-reconstruction', finding yourself, rather than organized political revolt. Consciousness of the self was painfully explicit. Few youths in the sixties wanted to be seen to be like 'The Man', in any way, and great energies were spent trying to expunge all uncool facets of the self.

> The beats possessed deviant tastes in language, literature, music, drugs and religion. Profoundly alienated from dominant American values, practising voluntary poverty and spade cool, they rejected materialism, competition, the work ethic, hygiene, sexual repression, monogamy, and the Faustian quest to subdue nature.
>
> (Matusow, 1984: 287)

Eventually, of course, the widespread interest in Eastern philosophies should have revealed that this was a distinctly uncool preoccupation in some ways, and more of an obsession of an individualist society in torment; however, a more externally directed, more political, mood was not to take off until the end of the sixties, generally speaking. The political tenor of this period was more of a mocking of the hypocrisy and discrimination of the insanely complacent and boring culture of power. Abolition of repression was on the agenda, but, for most, it was conducted in Dionysian mode and aimed at the self. It was a kind of cleansing of the soul of an infected generation. It was a truly Dalínian revolt. America, as Matusow

(1984) put it, was 'unraveling'. The insanity of the hyper-materialist, super-conformist, social system constructed after 1945 was self-evident, and Ken Kesey parodied its definition of lunacy in *One Flew over the Cuckoo's Nest*.

American social reality had now evolved to a state which made Dalí seem like a realist, and surrealist painting enjoyed a sustained after-life. The violence flowing from the conservative American unconscious in the 1960s mirrored some of that in inter-war Europe, but amidst such stunning affluence it seemed bizarre – and the heavy weight of established power made direct violent resistance a pipe-dream. Many dreamt instead of joining the guerrilla revolutions in Cuba and Latin America, and some actually did go into the hills to fight the imperialist forces, but mostly the flowering of social deviance remained a flower power.

The conservative fantasy of social control on a global scale found its sublimation, and later nemesis, in the far-off lands of South-east Asia. The illusions of post-war power produced a view that the South Vietnamese were really different from the North, that their government was a legitimate one and that they were in need of rescue by an anti-communist crusade. In 1965, Johnson sent the Marines to Saigon and the Vietnam War was on. Of course, this was only one escapade among many, as American mega-wealth was poured into propping up client dictatorships across the globe, invariably the countries topping the table in any list of human rights violations. But it was a massive enterprise of an old imperial type, and one that history had already proved was bound to fail. As if Lemert's thesis needed further proof, South Vietnam was turned into a pit of corruption, torture, prostitution, illegal drugs, crime and violence.

Labelling and the power to regulate

The labelling perspective, the liberal wing of the sociology of deviance, also flowered in the 1960s. It not only became the dominant school of thought within the sociology of deviance, it also became a strong influence within sociology as a whole, in both the USA and Europe. Consequently, of course, there are now many accounts and collections of its main themes, strengths and weaknesses (the following are among the best in my opinion: Rubington and Weinberg, 1968; Schur, 1971; Taylor *et al.*, 1973; Becker, 1974; Finestone, 1976; Downes and Rock, 1982; Pfohl, 1985). However, very few of the many published textbooks put the labelling perspective into its historical context and read it historically. When we do this, I believe, we can see more sharply what was actually being registered in the 1960s by the labelling perspective. It is one thing to describe and criticize what it said literally; it is another thing altogether to describe what it effectively did intellectually and what developments it forged in the history of the analysis of social deviance. The rest of this chapter is devoted to this question: what did the labelling perspective mean in the way of analytic change?

The first and most striking point about the sixties labelling perspective, and this was true for me when I first began to read this material in 1968, a fateful year, is that it registered the importance of power and the political in the labelling of deviance. In effect, it showed how moral concepts, well embedded in everyday life and apparently 'natural', were often the product of institutional political decisions and processes. Lemert had, as we have seen, already stressed the importance of politics in the social control agencies' selection of which primary deviance to target and punish. However, there were many more things to be said about power, and these came out in the sixties. *The whole discussion of power at this time amounted to a recognition, I would say, of the enormous power of social control agencies to shape people's identities, behaviour and lifestyle; to restrict people's ability to 'do their own thing'.* That capacity, however, remained conceptualized in a 'flower power' mode, until the seventies, because young, liberal, American sociologists, like their generation in the sixties, were not out to demonstrate that it was inextricably linked to the more fundamental, less flowery and more bloody, power of the military-industrial complex and its ruling élite.

Liberal American sociologists in the post-McCarthy era seemed to have been struck by the capacity of social control, and the whole new 'social system' ideology of the 1950s, to invade people's private lives, even their most minor moral preferences, with the effect of reshaping their personal worlds, either positively or negatively. As Goffman (1968a: 121) said: 'It is thus a tribute to the power of social forces that the uniform status of mental patient cannot only assure an aggregate of persons a common fate and eventually, because of this a common character, but that this social reworking can be done upon what is perhaps the most obstinate diversity of human materials that can be brought together by society.' The disapproval of or scepticism about the character and value of this powerful interference with the population's mores was compounded by the recognition that such interference was frequently highly discriminatory. All too often it seemed that the targets of the various 're-socializing' practices of the criminal justice and social welfare systems were the same old historic faces: the faces of the underclass, the inner-city poor, the lower-class immigrant, the avant-garde, the homosexual, the bohemian drug culture, the sexually deviant female and rebellious young men. The power of social control was not just intrusive, it was biased. In fact, the hegemony of the social system it was helping to mould was rooted in some longstanding economic, political and ideological value-judgements. This was recognized by sixties sociologists as 'discrimination' in the identification and selection of 'deviants'.

If it is true, as Gibbons (1979: 21) wrote, that the Progressivism of the early part of the century 'contained a spirit of optimism born of the conviction that people could solve most or all of their problems simply through the application of reason and sincere effort', then sixties liberalism was fired by a spirit of idealism born of the conviction that reason would recognize bias and inequity, and reduce or remove it. Consequently, the political inference drawn by the adherents of the labelling perspective was not that longstanding economic, political and ideological value-judgements were rooted in some very entrenched power structures, but rather that through enlightenment the bigotry of the parochial could be transformed into a more tolerant generality. As in the film *In the Heat of the Night*, the black federal liberal could try to show the parochial Southern racist the way to tolerance and truth.

While there was no doubt more than an element of the historic American liberal tradition of celebrating the originality, obstinacy, authenticity and freedom of the grass-roots, this sixties liberalism more strongly represented the socially aware, social-democratic, welfare-oriented, sceptical wing of the New Deal. It did not share James Ford's complacency about centralized power, or about the wisdom of the state's social administration policies, but it did support federal intervention against local prejudice and it did care about the reform of inequitable institutional procedures at all levels of government.

Its aim could be said to modernize and rationalize the operation of power; not to subvert the historically established structures of power, but rather to make them fairer or more tolerant. The labelling perspective thus challenged the extension of social control into morally ambiguous areas, those areas of 'crime without victims' (Schur's phrase) or of relatively harmless deviance. Its focus was always on the borderlines between crime and deviance, and between deviance and difference. It did not really challenge the social management or definition of serious crime, but focused on minor crimes and social deviations. This involved questioning the value of the criminalization of such practices as sexual prostitution and marijuana use, the value of stigmatizing as deviant such matters as homosexuality, nudism and mental disturbance, and the moral propriety of picking on, and punishing heavily, the minor crime and deviance of subordinate social groups. In this way, the liberal sociology of deviance became a systematic intervention of Enlightenment philosophy into the technocracy of social control, but, it should be added, with a touch of the surreal about it which quietly mocked the absurdity of any notion of consensus or convention.

The second most striking thing about the labelling perspective is a very sixties thing indeed. It noticed, indeed focused upon, the impact of moral regulation upon everyday life. Radical literature of the sixties, in general, is distinguishable from orthodox Marxism and orthodox sociology by its concern to show how the grand structures of power, such as class, capitalism, the family, imperialism and the death wish, were reproduced in, and impacted upon, everyday life (see, for example, Brown, 1959; Vaneigem, 1962, 1977; Mills, 1970). Social powers were not just abstract forces 'out there', beyond the control of the individual. As Mills (1970: 205) argued it, the very task of the social scientist was to reveal the meaning of 'structural trends and decisions' for 'everyday milieux' and thus to show the connection between 'personal troubles' and 'public issues'.

Of course, such a perspective had been the general approach of many good sociologists since Park had correctly drawn the inference from Durkheim that social structure existed nowhere else than in routine social interactions, and was, in fact, constructed within such routines. And the Chicago school had long documented the intimate details of mundane existence on the street. But what was different in the sixties was that sociologists started to demonstrate the detailed everyday consequences of being labelled as deviant, such as unemployment (see e.g. Schwartz and Skolnick, 1962), rather than documenting the effects of infrastructures, such as 'social disorganization', or the responses to those infrastructures, such as teenage gangs. The intimate effects of labelling, especially in relation to the self, had come to the fore. The practices of social control and regulation, the superstructures, had now become subject to the process of empirical sociological analysis. Deviance and crime were no longer just the effects of social-structural tensions or contradictions but also the practical products of practical processes of regulatory labelling with practical effects on the everyday lives of targeted populations.

This was no minor development. It was one thing to show that the contradictions between the class structure and the acquisitive society ethos effected great everyday frustration among the modern poor; it was wholly another to show that the processes of social control effected considerable everyday restraint on the freedom, personality and sanity of the individual. By the nature of this difference, the weight of attention now moved away from economics and culture towards politics; from capitalism to power. The freedom of the individual, his or her speech, dress, hair-length and taste in music, was ultimately a political question. It belonged to a political discourse stemming from the Enlightenment; a discourse which celebrated freedom from state interference, especially if you were not hurting anyone else, and freedom from arbitrary or discriminatory state intervention. The 'rebels without a cause' from the fifties had grown up, and studied social science, and they could not see that they, and others such as prostitutes, teenage gangs and illegal drug users, were actually harming anyone else, so why, they asked, were they so frequently the targets of police surveillance?

The answer their question clearly begged was that the state had other agendas, beyond the technical regulation of social welfare – ideological agendas which had no political legitimation from post-war social system ideology and could in theory, therefore, be junked as unjustifiable uses of power. From its inception, the whole problematic of the labelling perspective in the sociology of deviance is fired by the drive to protect everyday life from unnecessary intrusion by the state. It is thus a fundamentally political perspective. Not necessarily a very radical one though. For the above argument makes it abundantly clear that this is the politics of the West Coast, Haight-Ashbury and the hippie: it is not an aggressive politics committed to the overthrow of anything, but a defensive politics to justify the enjoyment of some personal space . . . man. The space cadets of the sixties were exactly that: children of the space age; personal space, spaced out half the time and awed by the journey into space. Theirs was the self-protective politics of the harmless; it was flower power. When 'all you need is love', the inadmissible tired old moral agendas of the élite seemed like alien forces from outer space, and their police agencies were thus experienced as beasts from beyond.

Contingency and cooling out the mark

Erving Goffman's contribution to this attempt to modernize, liberalize and 'de-culturalize' the reach of power was a subtle but very important one. With some elegance, his achievement was to combine the concern with the intrusive role of the power to regulate with the recognition of the everyday collusion of ordinary citizens in the weekly reproduction of grander social structures and institutions. He did not directly scrutinize the great systems of power, or the grand patterns of human conduct; what he did was to put their daily detail under a very focused microscope. The mores were thus given a fuller, richer, meaning. Not so much 'natural laws' of human existence, they were more the ritual expression of a daily accommodation to social forces. To use the sixties phrase, the population had 'sold out', and Goffman documented its compliance. It had been 'a mark' which had been 'stung' and 'cooled out' by the crooks, who were now clearly in the establishment, and the establishment itself, which had always been crooked anyway. Goffman observed this process with all the relish of any student of the post-war casinos of Las Vegas. Cynically, the word mores now seemed very apposite to refer to the new shared desire in the post-war age to get as much if not *more* for oneself out of any situation as one could negotiate.

After a Chicago PhD, his earlier work in the 1950s had shown how social roles and expectations were not fixed and were always negotiable. The collection of essays called *Interaction Ritual* (Goffman, 1972) provides us with a direct link with Lemert, who is singled out for his helpful criticisms in the acknowledgements, and a direct parallel with Garfinkel's work around that same time. Goffman argued that normative structures merely organized the 'co-mingling of persons' and 'temporary interactional enterprises', 'occasions' which were 'shifting' and 'necessarily evanescent'. This existential argot meant that the fleeting character of 'moments' was the determinant thing in explaining social phenomena, not the fixity of normative structures. Of course, this was very Chicagoan and resonated strongly of Simmel and Dewey. But, crucially, Goffman also followed Durkheim in believing that mundane interpersonal interactions contained systematic ritual support for collective representations and symbols. This became the distinctive hallmark of his sociology, combined with an acute, anthropologist's, ability to observe in detail the normative rituals and power dynamics involved in the most routine social occasions.

In the essay 'Where the action is', Goffman underlined the 'fatefulness' of actions which were both socially problematic and consequential, or which made ritual support for collective norms very difficult. Bank robbery would be a reasonable example, and its popularity with film-makers illustrates Goffman's point that we all recognize its fateful charm; although huge stock market take-overs, mountaineering and hang-gliding would also qualify as fateful. The risk element in these situations constitutes a central feature of 'real action'. Such special action offers opportunities for expression of character not available to those who practise 'safe and momentless living' (*ibid.*: 260). Fateful action creates moments when the individual is not easily able to keep 'cool' and display adherence to regulatory norms; it is risky. But, only within the fatefulness of such risky 'action' can we fully express, discover or prove fundamental strengths of character, the features that distinguish the human being from 'a simple machine': 'Serious action is a means of obtaining some of the moral benefits of heroic conduct without taking quite all of the chance of loss that opportunity for heroism would ordinarily involve' (*ibid.*: 262). Many, of course, as he said, reduce their costs by taking vicarious pleasure from the fatefulness of others portrayed daily in the mass media; others maximize the gains by making a business out of it. Not many of us can become racing car drivers or 'high rollers' in a casino. Consequently, there is a strong social need for the media construction of an array of stereotyped risky practices, daredevils, character contests and 'serious action'. It is a short step from here to understanding one reason why society needs its stereotyped delinquents, bank robbers, adventurers, explorers, charlatans, perverts and whores. Delinquents can thus be seen to 'cooperate' with society 'by staging a scene in which we project our dynamics of character'. The more they drift to the edges of society the more they cooperate: 'Their alienation from our reality frees them to be subtly induced into realizing our moral fantasies' (*ibid.*: 267). Durkheim would have been delighted with such sentiments, and with the sense of irony.

Durkheim had observed that the suicide, or the drop-out, were in society's grip even as they cut their bonds to it. Goffman had taken Durkheim and updated him beautifully. Crime and deviance were now more than behavioural responses to social tensions or even moral categories of condemnation. Now, they were also identikit pictures of immorality, interesting but carefully specified instances of exciting and characterful action, safely distant projections of conformity's profound lack; or as the 'punk' poet John Cooper Clarke once exquisitely put it, 'delightfully disciplined, dumb but de luxe, deliciously, deliciously, deranged'.

Degeneracy had become delicious, inverted and popular; symbolized above all by those leather-clad 'cycle sluts', the 'twin wheeled existentialists steeped in the excrement of a doomed democracy' whose 'post-Nietzschean sensibilities reject the bovine gregariousness of a senile oligarchy' (Cooper Clarke's delightful and delicious phrasing from his poem 'Psycle sluts', *Disguise in Love* album, 1978). Degeneracy was also very frequently and powerfully symbolized by the smoking of 'the joint'. Becker's 1953 essay on becoming a marijuana user, drawn no doubt from experiences in an earlier jazz culture, was recycled in the sixties by teachers who wanted to reach out to their students' direct experience of 'becoming deviant'. The successful film *Easy Rider*, of course, combined a leather-clad biker with the fetishism of learning how to smoke marijuana, the fantasies of the hippie commune, and the repressive reactions of the 'rednecks', to become the cult film of the decade. As Goffman portrayed such fateful moments, the contrast between the safe but lifeless and the risky but characterful was the source of our simultaneous condemnation of and drooling over the deranged but delicious deviant. And Jack Nicholson, by stealing the show in *Easy Rider* as the alcoholic lawyer experimenting with marijuana, became everyone's favourite actor – the devil was indeed worshipped.

Such a powerful neurosis was bound to become industrialized, and it happened in post-1945 imperial America, to an extent still not yet seen in Europe, through the film studios, casinos, strip-joints and topless serveries of the newly buoyant Sun Belt. Timing, location and form were in perfect congruence:

> Commercialization, of course, brings the final mingling of fantasy and action. And it has an ecology. On the arcade strips of urban settlements and summer resorts, scenes are available for hire where the customer can be the star performer in gambles enlivened by being very slightly consequential. Here a person currently without social connections can insert coins in skill machines to demonstrate to the other machines that he has socially approved qualities of character. These naked little spasms of the self occur at the end of his world, but there at the end is action and character.
>
> (Goffman, 1972: 269–70)

Sinatra did it his way, as Las Vegas came to symbolize the full absorption of deviance into 'the system'. The newly imperial American social order dealt with degeneracy in an inimitably American way: it turned it into a big business employing a lot of not-so-ex-crooks, morally tut-tutting all the way to the bank, comforted by its conclusion that the rackets, along with ideology, were now past history. Degeneracy had been capitalized, democratized and domesticated, turned into tinsel sex, one-armed bandits and petty risk as it was institutionalized into a sanitized social blur.

Goffman, for a time a professor at Berkeley, in effect adroitly conceptualized what was going on in American society as 'cooling out the mark', the title of a famous essay of 1952. Blumer had already alerted us to the importance of the explosive and sensitive processes whereby respectable identity was transformed into deviance, but Goffman gave the account an edge by comparing such transformative processes to the ways that confidence men cooled out their mark before taking it to the cleaners (Goffman, 1962) – the laundry business had long been in the hands of the mob, that paragon of the new, conservative, confidence. Again, gambling provided Goffman's main illustration. Role transformations of various kinds, for example from marriage to divorce, were said to require a 'cooling-out', or even 'cooling-in', of the mark to enable a smooth transition and to neutralize the 'sting'. The target of the rejection, enforced change or demotion was seen as in need of diplomatic assistance in adjusting to a new and less favourable position. Sometimes, even offering a consolation status or permitting an explosion of anger were appropriate cooling-out tactics. Cool was vital in the society of the bland sting, which post-war America had become.

Again, Goffman drew no conclusions about how healthy a society it was which (de-)generated such manipulative con tricks to conduct its everyday interactions. Perhaps he might have reflected that Bell's claimed integration of the rackets into 'straight' society meant that the 'legitimate' world had now been absorbed into the rackets rather than vice versa. If Capone was the Godfather of the sociology of deviance, Sinatra was probably the singer at its wedding to imperial Amerika.

The astute detail of Goffman's analysis almost conceals the complete lack of criticism of the forms of interaction and forms of power which are displayed in these quasi-fraudulent, social confidence tricks. Gouldner later accused Goffman of producing the 'sociology of soul-selling' (1970: 383). Certainly, Goffman's work is a laconic account of how people can be accommodated by others to the fact of their total failure or social death. It is, in my view, the sociology of the salesman in the anonymous media age; a salesman selling life policies to the inmates of death row, or anyone. As Gouldner said, it is not really about morality at all but about appearing to be moral. It is a sociology concerned with 'passing', appearing to be 'wise', managing or controlling interactions, keeping face, selling the goods and accommodating to the ever-present and always fateful intrusions of power into everyday life. It is a dramaturgy where

> All the world's a stage,
> And all the men and women merely players:
> They have their exits and their entrances;
> And one man in his time plays many parts,
> (Shakespeare, *As You Like It*, II. vii. 139)

It is a dramaturgy, however, in which there is only a passing collusion with the script and no choice of rejecting it or the director. It is also a dramaturgy that feigns to deceive, for there is no real play in the production.

The play, Gouldner argued, only concerned style and not substance, and style 'becomes the strategy of interpersonal legitimation for those who are disengaged from work and for whom morality has become a prudent convenience' (1970: 381). To view life as a play, he said, is to see it as an 'arena of limited and tentative commitments'. As such, Goffman's sociology was 'a complexly articulated theoretical expression that resonates the new experience of the educated middle class' (*ibid.*: 389).

Well, class origins of themselves never made a theory right or wrong, useful or useless, but in this case the characterization is a telling one because Goffman merely showed how deviance had become a trade in identities for social advantage. That's all. Gouldner's comment is one-sided though, because Goffman's portrait was clearly an accurate and acidic micro-critique of the new American social relations. The enormity of Goffman's contribution can be measured by the fact that the symbolic interactionist or labelling perspective of the sixties was widely known as the transactional perspective. Deviance had become part of a social contract; it was about trading. It was a deal, supposedly a Fair Deal. 'You can rob, cheat and chisel, but just do it through legitimate channels, OK? If you cheat illegitimately, *and* then don't play ball by admitting guilt and complying with the system, we'll cut you out of the script altogether.' That was the new role for deviance – in social exile – and it was no bit-part. The industrialization of the hustle was integral to a post-war society committed to sanitizing itself from all its sins, even the most minor, and to the ideological laundering of the much bigger crimes.

The sad tale of the mental patient

Asylums (Goffman, 1968a), first published in 1961, was, I believe, a bestseller. Well, contingency was lucky for Goffman and the book was an outstandingly good contribution to the sociology of deviance. It was in line with its times in highlighting the meaningfulness and normality of the social world of the mental patient. 'In line with its times' because these were days when many mental patients were living testimony to the insanity of the sanitized world which had exiled them from main street. Ken Kesey made a similar point in *One Flew over the Cuckoo's Nest* (1962). The highly acclaimed film from that book starred Jack Nicholson, who, curiously, was born in that fateful year of 1937. Nicholson went on to play many deviant characters in his career in films, including the devil himself, a role he once said he had been practising for all his life.

Goffman's book was based on a year's fieldwork within the social world of the mental patients within a big Washington hospital, and is openly committed to a partisan view in favour of the patients' perspective and against the discipline of psychiatry. It marked a major decline in the alliance between psychiatry and the liberal sociology of deviance forged in 1937; although the symbolic interactionists' continual concern with psychiatry and the social identity of the deviant was a constant reminder of the impact of psychiatry on the field.

In terms of the general development of the sociology of deviance, *Asylums* was an important book because it took the old view that an individual's movement from normality to deviance can be fruitfully analysed with the concept of the career, and claimed that the most crucial career changes were as much a result of contingency as anything else. Delinquency had long been seen as a product of, first, predilection, second, criminal association and, finally, the perfection of good technique (see, for example, Shaw and Moore, 1931). But, now, Goffman emphasized that the deviant could psychologically accommodate to the impact of social control, or even turn back, and also that there was a constant movement between the 'straight' world and the realm of social deviants. Nothing was black and white. The contrast between good and evil was compromised and confused.[2] The popular fantasy of systematic deviance was being further divorced from the reality of deviance as fluid contingency. The fantasy of reality was becoming even more alienated from the reality of fantasy – and what better illustration than the world of the mental patient where the relation between fantasy and reality was the nebulous subject of so much unresolved contestation.

Goffman described the continual, but phased, interrelation between the straight life and the world of deviance within the biography of any given individual as a moral career. To his credit, Goffman was aware of, and acknowledged, earlier versions of his conception – in this case in social anthropology, criminology and Lemert's work particularly. The concept of the career enabled Goffman to move back and forth between the personal world of self-image and identity and the public world of certification and access/exclusion. The boundaries of the normal and the pathological were now blurred. However, Lemert was surely right to argue later that Goffman was mistaken in supposing that the individual is always able to accommodate to social reaction or labelling and that all stigmas are equally negotiable (Lemert, 1972: 63). Some moral dichotomies are extremely powerful and awkward, and entry into the negative can transgress a pivotal point of no return, e.g. treason. Indeed, at different points in history, or in different social contexts, even the transgression of lesser categories can lead to social or physical death. Not all careers are open to all and not all openings are structured like careers; and some careers are irreversible.

For Goffman, the psychiatric attribution of mental illness to a person is only relevant if it alters that person's fate, notably through hospitalization. Therefore, logically, he saw his subjects not as 'really' mentally ill people but as people who had suffered the contingency of hospitalization and who thus had to adjust their self-conception and behaviour to this new stage in their moral career. They may or may not have suffered from some degree of mental sickness; they may have included people, 'however robust in temperament', who somehow got 'included in the heavy machinery of mental-hospital servicing' (Goffman, 1968a: 120). Having examined the offences leading to hospitalization, Goffman felt obliged to conclude that luck was crucial in determining the likelihood of commitment. His statement on this is a classic:

> The society's official view is that inmates of mental hospitals are there primarily because they are suffering from mental illness. However, in the degree that the 'mentally ill' outside hospitals numerically approach or surpass those inside hospitals, one could say that mental patients distinctively suffer not from mental illness, but from contingencies.
>
> (*ibid.*: 126)

'There but for the grace of God go I' had now become a social-scientific fact, and deviance a socially but randomly attributed status. In effect, the social acquisition of the status of deviant was reduced to a question of chance. It was one of the less fortunate pay-outs of society's one-armed bandit. But the message from Goffman was clear: if we play the fruit machine of life some of us will occasionally get the big lemon. It was a matter of fate: life is fateful.

Clearly, however, the fruit machine of life was fixed by vested interests in Goffman's eyes, to an extent, since he also observed that

> since inappropriate behaviour is typically behaviour that someone does not like and finds extremely troublesome, decisions concerning it tend to be political, in the sense of expressing the special interest of some particular faction or person rather than interests that can be said to be above the concerns of any particular grouping, as in the case of physical pathology.
>
> (*ibid.*: 317)

Fate was politically loaded. Unfortunately, the politics of deviance attribution was not one of Goffman's main concerns.

Getting caught up in the 'heavy machinery of mental-hospital servicing' was unpleasant, and it illustrated a broader point: the construction or reconstruction of a moral career was a matter of the effects of socially constructed fateful moments. Certain kinds of fateful moment were common to members of certain social groups and so each social group had specific career patterns and possibilities which were integral to its evolution. Career, in this sense, was a concept derived directly from Chicagoan neo-Darwinism – it was a strand or phase of a person's life which was part of the 'natural history' of that person's social group. Goffman's debt to Park was clear. Moral careers were thus destined never to be brilliant or disastrous, merely social (*ibid.*: 119). In a deep irony, the accentuated focus on the individual and the microscopic, so central to Goffman and the interactionists, was never to betray a commitment to sociology and the power of the social to forge individual moral development. Biography had now acquired a clearly two-dimensional quality.[3] So, in the case of the mental patient, there was the history of the 'effects upon a person's life of traits a clinician would view as psychopathological', and there was the history of 'the effects of being treated as a mental patient' (*ibid.*: 120). The latter was a thoroughly social affair and not at all unique to the individual. Once launched on a moral career as a mental patient the phases of stigmatization and processes of adjustment were common to the whole social group of mental patients. As Goffman astutely observed, the similarities in response among mental patients to the processes of induction, treatment and deprivation do not so much come from mental illness, 'they would seem to occur in spite of it' (*ibid.*: 121). Being a mental patient was thus not a function of individual propensities but a social status acquired by persons who had to live with it whatever their individual propensities.

It is doubtful if anyone had ever made it clearer why deviance was a social possession and not an individual property – not because the labelling process was necessarily selective, discriminatory, ideological or political, but because being branded as a deviant entailed a common set of everyday effects and responses. Goffman generously acknowledged Lemert's work, but he gave it a new slant. He could be said to have de-politicized it in some ways, because he had made the political bias of conjuncturally 'interested' labellers secondary to the more universal meaning of social deviance as a social status or category typically subject to certain negative processes of stigmatization, exclusion and punishment. Lemert had stressed temporal interests, Goffman pointed to a more fundamental anthropological process. Neither of them, unfortunately, moved beyond all this to recognize that the category of deviance was itself a profoundly historical category, albeit one instance of a longer history and anthropology of censure, stigmatization and exclusion, and that, while they talked of biased labelling and demeaned social status, they had overlooked the category of the meaningful social censure, the ideological or moral discursive formation, which was the necessary intermediary between bias and changed status. The study of historically specific moral censures interlinking longstanding processes of negative labelling and exclusion with sociologically conse-quential statuses, demonstrating that the censures were an integral part of both the labelling process and the structure of status, had not yet been opened up. However, it was getting closer.

Goffman, like all symbolic interactionists, highlighted the passages from one social status to another, from normality to deviance, from freedom to constraint. His personal hallmark was an acute observation of the details of these journeys, laden with irony, cynicism and pathos. With Lindesmith and others, he perceived the danger of deviance to reside not in reality (e.g. in the toxicological properties of substances) but in 'culturally derived and socially engrained stereotypes as to the significance of symptoms' (*ibid.*: 123). The sense of 'losing one's mind' is as much a culturally loaded conception as is 'getting high' on marijuana. Indeed, for Goffman, it was one of 'the questionable privileges of the upper classes' to belong to a subculture which gave them a capacity 'to take this disintegrative view of oneself without psychiatric prompting' (*ibid.*: 124).

Asylums shows the detail of the 'phases' an individual has to move, or be put, through in order that the transition from sane status to the status of confirmed insane can be achieved by those who wish for, or whose job it is to produce, this transformation. Such difficult and drastic involuntary changes, from having relationships and rights to having neither and nothing, are eased by certain *rites of passage*; for example, the haircut, shower and imposition of uniform undergone by the entrant into prison. The shift from unique citizen to anonymous inmate does not just happen, the interactionist sociologists' achievement was to show how it was constructed and managed. Drawing on Garfinkel's (1956, reprinted in Rubington and Weinberg, 1968) essay on the mechanics of successful degradation ceremonies, Goffman described the various processes involved. The 'mark' has to be 'cooled out' to get him or her to hospital – offering a cigarette is more appropriate than imposing a straitjacket. The fact that relatives are, of course, essentially betraying the individual 'in his or her own interests' needs to be spoofed away or managed with various pretences or rationalizations. Just as the organization of the court is driven by the need to conduct orderly and systematic degradation ceremonies, so too the process of hospitalization is structured by the need to effect and conceal a managed betrayal of a close relative. Society today, Goffman observed, was a little embarrassed about admitting its expulsions. But that was what was happening. Hospitalization as a mental patient was and is social death – there is no recovery, a social identity dies. Full execution of the process extinguishes the patient's former self and the contacts, interviews, diagnoses and records produce the verdict that he or she was always mad. Any resistance to the process confirms the correctness of the verdict. Besides, resistance to the definition as mad makes it hard work for the staff to conduct the everyday life of the hospital smoothly and efficiently, so it is suppressed. The patient eventually comes round to accepting, or no longer resisting, the hospital staff's view of him or her as a mental patient.

Patient and outside society thus collude, in the perfect case, to deny the continued existence of the patient's former self. That self is literally mortified. Everything in the patient's pre-history is re-worked in the psychiatric reading of biography to be a proof of permanent, irresistible, madness; no sane self existed. Such a mortification of the self is the frequent concomitant of life within a *total institution*: 'here one begins to learn about the limited extent to which a conception of oneself can be sustained when the usual setting of supports for it are suddenly removed' (Goffman, 1968a: 137).

Total institutions and the critique of institutional authority

Not only did Goffman demonstrate that the construction of deviant status is a thoroughly social or collective process, requiring cooperation, collusion or at least bodily participation from both sides, he chillingly reminded us all that the self is so thoroughly a social construct that it can be demolished, reformed, reconstructed and expunged in powerful social institutions geared to the mortification of unacceptable selves. This was truly a work of the sixties.

The classic example of such a total institution, mentioned by Goffman, was the concentration camp – and the memories of the war finally entered the concepts of sociological theory directly. In the most total of total institutions, all the techniques, rituals, tricks and processes for stripping individuals of their liberty and identity are gathered in one place, systematized, coordinated and focused into a laser beam of liquidation. Faced with the possibility of being killed every second of every day, robbed of all personal identity and disciplined in the most extreme detail – where even not making one's bed precisely could lead to a lethal beating – human beings, we, sadly, now know, usually lose their dignity as social selves in a human world and start to behave like wounded or desperate animals.

Goffman not only demonstrated that the construction of deviants involved the mortification of the rejected self and the perfectly legal trade in identities whereby peace could be purchased by buying society's deviant mask, he vividly alerted us to the fact that, even in peacetime society, this daily mortification of selves was achieved by institutions like the prison and the mental hospital. His work amplified the growing view that institutions in general crushed the free spirit or the original soul and replaced it with a mass-produced social mask (as mental patient, for example, rather than human being). The critique of 'institutions' by sixties sociology, so consequential in feeding the demonstrations and rebellions of 1968 and beyond, was under way. The welfare–warfare state had spawned its antithesis – a critique of 'bureaucracy'.

All institutions had some control over people's lives, and thus all institutions capture and separate individuals from their community to a degree, but total institutions effected a considerable separation from the outside world. Their hold on their 'inmates' was more total. The production of deviants was not just a social process, it was a highly professional, highly systematized, bureaucratic piece of work.

Goffman elucidated something which every student of criminology soon discovers, namely that it really is so odd that laypeople usually see labelled criminals and deviants as biologically defective when occupations actually exist, with public codes of conduct, handbooks, rules, 'sciences', textbooks, diplomas, degrees and charters, for the specific purpose of systematically identifying, capturing, understanding and treating people as criminals and deviants.[4] A lot of work goes into the professional and bureaucratic production of social deviants. It must – because it is not at all obvious who they are. If they were all atavistic degenerates *à la* Lombrosianism, then it would be no problem – the dinosaurs' heads could be easily spotted above the trees, without any special training. No, societies are embarrassed by their exclusions and rejections; such violence needs legitimating. Never has an occupation so public and so social been mystified by an ideology so obscure and so biological; yes, the production of deviants is work, social work. It really is odd – the people who carry out this occupation even call themselves by perfectly accurate names which announce their sociological function, like 'social worker' and 'police officer', yet the public still rarely seems to get beyond the view that deviance 'just happens' and these public officials just respond to it. The 'sad tale' of the mental patient is just one version of a much bigger tragedy.

Authoritarianism was no longer neglected, as in essays such as Garfinkel's; it was now described in anthropological detail – in the form it took in total institutions. The 'sad tale' in Goffman's account of mental hospitals was a routinized, socially acceptable, stock story told by patients to explain their tragic 'fall from grace' – a rational account of the changes in status which of course denied the existence of permanent biological defect (e.g. 'my business went bust') – but the really sad tale was that American society was still only held together by a handful of recently discovered moral imperatives and the constant threats of authority to uphold them to the letter. Serious deviants, and the seriously incapable, in the post-war welfare state world of efficient mass production, teamwork and militarism, had to be excluded yet regimented. They could not be left to the whims of free enterprise, whether it be for private justice or local philanthropy. With echoes of Orwell, they had to be 'institutionalized'.

Normative integration or moral binding was the cement which, Parsonian sociologists claimed, was holding America together, but the truth was that the plentiful commodities of the post-war boom were more adhesive. Moreover, it was a recurrent fact of American history in the twentieth century that moral imperatives had to be backed by the threat of considerable institutional force before they carried much weight. Capone's cement shoes were a mightier metaphor than Gramsci's moral cement in a society where the dangers of frontier 'justice' – authoritarianism, arbitrariness and excessive punishment – were ever-present. Since a multicultural melting pot organized around barely diluted free enterprise and a corrupted civic ideal was always in danger of boiling over, the risk of random overcorrection and the need for institutional provision were permanent. The moral totalitarianism within this inherent tendency of American society was not wasted on Goffman. His analysis of total institutions was powerful. A critique of the combination of stifling bureaucracy and moral intolerance was begun, and a new derogatory term entered the language – institutionalization – bemoaning the effect of losing one's independent vitality through constant residence or captivity within institutions.

The institutional stigma is so powerful it retroactively constructs the patient's biography, as a patient. Former selves disappear or diminish in favour of the self which serves the interests of the hospital staff and the next of kin. As Goffman wrote in *Asylums*,

> until the point of hospitalization is reached, he [the patient] or others may not conceive of him as a person who is becoming a mental patient. However, since he will be held against his will in the hospital, his next-of-relation and the hospital staff will be in great need of a rationale for the hardships they are sponsoring. The medical elements of the staff will also need evidence that they are still in the trade they were trained for. These problems are eased, no doubt unintentionally, by the case-history construction that is placed on the patient's past life, this having the effect of demonstrating that all along he had been becoming sick, that he finally became very sick, and that if he had not been hospitalized much worse things would have happened to him – all of which, of course, may be true.
>
> (Goffman, 1968a: 134–5)

What Goffman did was to illustrate elegantly and in some detail a point first made plain by Lemert: namely that there are various people or groups in society who, in any given case, have a vested interest in securing the application of a deviant label to an individual. This vested interest is so substantial that its owners are quite prepared to ensure that offending individuals are locked away in institutions, stripped of civil liberties, given completely new biographies and told that any resistance is proof of their problematic status.

Deviance is thus a social phenomenon in a very strong sense – it is a status collectively organized and enforced by groups with a particular interest. To a certain extent, therefore, it is also a self-perpetuating form – because one of those interest groups is the professional class of deviance-producers (police, psychiatrists, social workers, etc.) and it is always in their interest to appear to be doing their job and to identify the risk they are paid to watch for. Later in the sixties, the film *Catch 22* wittily captured some of the lunacies of bureaucracy: the bureaucracy of lunacy was no exception. Goffman was perhaps the first to demonstrate clearly what a 'Catch 22' social control was: once a regulatory agency is set up, it will regulate, and therefore it will find targets somewhere, anywhere; once the number of targets, or 'instances', is recorded, it is discovered, inevitably, that this number is higher than the figure before the agency was set up, and this finding sets off a little panic in the community and the agency demands greater resources to deal with 'the rising tide' of targets; this in turn, of course, increases the number of recorded instances.

In short, sociological work from the labelling perspective demonstrated, in a very real way, that if an institution was set up to identify or catch deviants it will, assuming everyone is doing their job, and thus by virtue of its foundation it will expand or amplify the number of recorded deviants and the officially defined field of their deviance. I would formulate the law this way: deviance grows exponentially to the number of institutions established to deal with it.[5] But, apart from the productivity of the deviance-producers, there is another factor. Once a regulatory agency is founded, someone will resist its operations and thus a new category of deviance is created, namely resisting the new institution. Humanity is always sufficiently diverse and obstinate to provide endless fodder for moral watchdogs, police, crusaders, vigilantes and entrepreneurs – if only because, once moral crusaders start moralizing, a section of humanity will, thank goodness, resist them just for the sake of it. Definitions of deviance are, to a certain extent, self-fulfilling prophecies:

> From the patient's point of view, to decline to exchange a word with the staff or with his fellow patients may be ample evidence of rejecting the institution's view of what and who he is; yet higher management may construe this alienative expression as just the sort of symptomatology the institution was established to deal with.
>
> (*ibid.*: 268)

There was something really scary in discovering the power of the deviant label during the sixties – apart from the fact that by 1970 we had all realized the truth of Mushanga's dictum that the power to regulate was in the hands of 'vandals, hooligans, nitwits, and anomic delinquents' (Mushanga, 1976: 18), not to mention some seriously anal-retentive moralists and matrons. It revealed how hard it was to resist, and what little was being done against, that power. Being labelled as socially deviant and physically attacked, by people who still destroyed Beatles records and saw the Rolling Stones as revolutionaries, was one of life's lesser trips, and could lead to social death. *Easy Rider* revealed the great fear of my generation of being either discredited (at considerable social cost) or destroyed (like Peter Fonda and Dennis Hopper, for ever). It was a very sixties perception. Its constitution required a really revolting subculture and a really reactionary response, and both existed at that time. Thus, allegation and stigma were proof and evidence in the totalitarian world of moral management. We knew that. We had no faith in, or money for, lawyers to protect us – they were part of the management. Basically, if the authorities wanted your skin then they could get it. The rule of law was of marginal value as self-defence. As any street-wise citizen would confirm, the best defence was to pass (as one from the straight world) or trade (information, for example – see Skolnick's 1966 study of street prostitutes' negotiations with the police).

Goffman was the first sociologist to convey the true depth of the horror many of us felt at realizing the extent of institutional power. He did not make much of it, nor did he connect greatly with the social resistance movements of his day, but his *Asylums* hit more than a few raw nerves as the battle of the generations which so dominated the sixties began to warm up. He alerted many to the fact that power did not just reside in the military-industrial complex, or in the barrel of a gun, but also within the institutions designed to care for us all in the post-war welfare state. Power lay in institutions, Goffman was interpreted to say, and many, whether they had read Goffman or not, rejected all institutions, precisely because they held so much power. Power was used to intrude, restrict or prevent, so it was bad, and if institutions had a lot of it then they too were *ipso facto* bad. The sixties had this anarchist streak throughout, and one of its key features was the rejection of all institutions. *One Flew over the Cuckoo's Nest*, which could have been the film from Goffman's book if it hadn't been from Kesey's, did not get public attention so much because it was a critique of the handling of mental illness but because, like *Catch 22*, it was a devastating exposé of the self-justifying, self-perpetuating, irrational, bureaucratic and moralistic character of institutions which, in theory, were supposed to be caring, neutral and devoted to the removal of the causes which brought them into being. But, of course, to reject institutions was to become a discreditable revolutionary overnight, and to invite the wrath of the institutions.

Like the mental patients, we survived, we 'made out'. Like a university, the mental hospital worked with inmates with a varying capacity to play the role socially offered to them. And like university students, these inmates of varying origins and talents, to adjust to their context, developed a social world of their own with all the features of any meaningful community. Such a community, for the symbolic interactionists, is a subculture which provides the materials for its members to survive as human beings with a distinct social status. In Goffman's study, it was a community of social exiles. It became a metaphor for our generation. We were all in social exile from a very crazy world that said that to preserve peace it had to drop thousands of tons of bombs on a poor underdeveloped country thousands of miles away, and that our protests against this genocide were subversive violence.

Crime as a verb and the rigged fruit machine

Two contradictory points were established firmly and loudly by Goffman's work: (a) deviance and crime were socially constructed and (b) labelled deviants were unlucky. Institutions systematically identified and processed deviance, yet given labelled individuals may or may not be deviant. Few have noted it, but there is something deeply contradictory about this: if institutions were so organized how come their targeting was so erratic? Or, to put it another way, if patients suffered more from contingencies than deviance, how come the world's jails are full of poor people? Why did the rich accumulate capital and the poor accumulate bad luck? Had Goffman rediscovered the old aphorism that if shit was money the poor would have been born without arseholes? Didn't his position imply that the dice are loaded, but for no obvious reason other than that's the way things are?

If Goffman had taken his own analysis further, he would have recognized the profound consequence of seeing deviance as a social product: namely, that crime is more of a verb than a noun. In some British police forces, that is actually the nature of the usage. Officers decide whether to 'crime' a case or 'cuff' it (cuff, as in the old bobby's cuff round the ear, rather than formal sanctions). Working police officers recognize that to make something into a crime requires work. The facts, the accused, the law and legally acceptable evidence all have to be packaged up in such a way that the court will readily see the case as an instance of a socially recognizable crime (a 'normal crime': Sudnow, 1965, reprinted in Rubington and Weinberg, 1968). In this sense, cases are crimed. Criming a case is something a police officer does.

Now, if criming cases is a very active, creative, process involving some social and legal skill, and much awareness of what magistrates and judges will accept, then presumably the fact that cases are crimed in a highly patterned and predictable way, leaving the world's prisons full of poor people, is hardly an accident. To believe otherwise would be to imply that police officers are stupid pigs, and that of course was a very popular but highly naive belief in the 1960s. Given that the police are 'wise' in Goffman's terms, wise to the ways of the world and to their own position in it, he should have gone on to analyse the great structural forces which skew the legal process so much that what should be a random process, like the shake of a dice, manages to produce an almost wholly working-class, mostly male, clientele. For if deviants only suffer from contingencies, how come these contingencies pick so disproportionately on black, working-class males between the ages of 16 and 21? If criminals suffer mainly from contingencies, why doesn't contingency pick on women as much? Is fortune really a dame? If 'there but for the grace of God go I' is true, then, given the prevalence of males in the official criminal statistics, either God is a woman (and an ultra-feminist) or the dice are loaded. To mention one other important example: why would North America have such an astronomically high homicide rate, compared to Europe, if murderers merely suffered from contingency? Was bad luck so culturally biased?

Goffman's work indicted institutional self-justification and exposed the self-interest involved in the attribution of deviance, but it really made no attempt to study the deeper structural processes behind the institutions and the systematic biases in law enforcement and moral judgement. Laurie Taylor's comment on this point is justifiably treated as a classic – it was made in a critical discussion of Mertonian anomie theory:

> It is as though individuals in society are playing a gigantic fruit machine, but the machine is rigged and only some players are consistently rewarded. The deprived ones then either resort to using foreign coins or magnets to increase their chances of winning (innovation) or play on mindlessly (ritualism), give up the game (retreatism) or propose a new game altogether (rebellion). But in this analysis nobody appears to ask who put the machine there in the first place and who takes the profits. Criticism of the game is confined to changing the pay-out sequences.
>
> (Taylor, 1971: 148)

Goffman (1968a: 115) did claim to be concerned with the 'underlying structural design' of total institutions, but he understood this to be the internal logic of the total institution and he derived this from the manifest features of its functioning. Goffman, in this respect, closely adhered to the classic functionalist method of deriving social functions from the apparently continuous features of institutions. Just as Davis (1937) derived a universal human need for prostitution from its apparent longevity as a 'profession', so too Goffman (1968a: 17–22) seemed to see the inherent limitations of the wage-system and of solitary living (as opposed to 'batch living') as requiring total institutions – to deal efficiently with large numbers of people who need forcibly 'warehousing' in some way. So, not only did Goffman ignore the wicked selectivity of contingency in the stigmatization of deviance, he also seemed to accept that total institutions are functional for modern society as a whole rather than attacking their class/gender/ethnic biases, or questioning the merits of any society that needs to warehouse so many people by force, or doubting the actual success of total institutions as warehousing systems.

As we now know, what purpose, if any, some total institutions serve is very unclear indeed, so Goffman's apparent belief that they function in the business of 'changing persons' (*ibid.*: 22) seems very complacent today. This is all the more so when we remember that his own evidence strongly suggests that (a) hospitalization causes the individual more mental illness than he or she brought into the establishment in the first place (*ibid.*: 310), and that (b) since individual psychotherapy was so rare in state mental hospitals, and therapy sessions so valuable in alleviating the inmates' lot (e.g. in enabling better living conditions and enabling contact with the opposite sex), by actually getting what 'the institution formally claims to offer, the patient can succeed in getting away from what the establishment actually provides' (*ibid.*: 274). Today, it is evident that the stated purposes of such institutions as the school and the prison are only marginally achieved, and that their actual social function seems to be containment, within varying degrees of civility. As Goffman said, 'Mental patients can find themselves crushed by the weight of a service ideal which eases life for the rest of us' (*ibid.*: 336).

The concentration camp, the prison, the school, the hospital, the university and the home for the elderly perform the function of housing large numbers of people who receive subnormal wages. It is one of the things they have in common. Goffman describes their workings with rich irony, biting cynicism and sharp pathos, but this account does not take him to an explanation of why the total institution was becoming a frequent feature, and even a symbol of what was wrong, with post-war welfare societies. I would tentatively suggest that total institutions are common today in so far as: (a) they soak up surplus (i.e. unwaged) populations cheaply; (b) they are effective and minimally costly in dealing with prisoners or casualties in any of the civil or external wars continually around us; and (c) they provide humane but minimally meaningful containment in an age of high unemployment, extensive policing, frequent wars, massive refugee problems, great demand for education and huge government fiscal problems. In short, many institutions today are tending towards the total institution model, although rising costs may stimulate de-institutionalization in the post-welfare age. But Goffman did not pursue any such analysis, and left his work rooted in the sixties.

Nevertheless, whatever the limitations of his analysis, Goffman did advance the sociology of deviance. With an exquisite sense of the absurd, he extended and elaborated Lemert's thesis that social control created deviance. He did this, like Lemert, by showing not only that social control amplified deviant behaviour and made it worse, but also that control agencies' definitions of deviance were crucial in marking off deviance from other apparently identical behaviour. These are two distinct arguments. One could be called the empirical amplification thesis and the other the constitution-by-definition thesis (see Fine, 1977). Students often confuse them. But one really is a claim about the unintended bad effects of some forms of social control, whereas the other is a point about the arbitrary character of social censure.[6]

Deviance was, indeed, not what it seemed any more. In fact, it was looking very close to an arbitrary and counter-productive moral judgement, made by people with a vested interest and resulting in a range of unintended, unhappy and fruitless effects.[7] None too cool.

Goffman summed it all up in one devastating indictment of the moral pretensions of the fifties, a nice ending to a book which effectively demolished the legitimacy of sociology's dalliance with psychiatry:

> Mental hospitals are not found in our society because supervisors, psychiatrists, and attendants want jobs; mental hospitals are found because there is a market for them. If all the mental hospitals in a given region were emptied and closed down today, tomorrow relatives, police, and judges would raise a clamour for new ones; and these true clients of the mental hospital would demand an institution to satisfy their needs ...
>
> Professional psychiatric staff [have] one of the firmest claims to deference and regard available in our society ... yet in the mental hospital their whole role is constantly in question. Everything that goes on in the hospital must be legitimated by assimilating it or translating it to fit into a medical-service frame of reference. Daily staff actions must be defined and presented as expressions of observation, diagnosis and treatment. To effect this translation, reality must be considerably twisted, somewhat as it is by judges, instructors, and officers in other of our coercive institutions. *A crime must be uncovered that fits the punishment, and the character of the inmate must be reconstituted to fit the crime.*
>
> (Goffman, 1968a: 334; emphasis added)

McCarthyism obviously left its mark on Erving Goffman as well as Edwin Lemert.

'A crime must be uncovered that fits the punishment', 'the character of the inmate must be reconstituted to fit the crime' ... what is clear throughout *Asylums* is that the deviant is 'fitted up', to use a deliciously accurate expression used by the British police, for his or her role by interested members of society.[8] Whether or not the accused is guilty, Goffman and other interactionists were saying, he or she is 'fitted up' by interested parties, according to the social script for the role of deviant. *So, the criminal, in truth, is someone who has been crimed.* We do not have the language to express the same thought easily regarding deviance – 'deviantize' would be too ugly – but we can say that, for the interactionists, deviance is in the eye of the beholder and that a deviant is someone scripted as such in a moral judgement. The deviant is someone so labelled and portrayed. He or she is someone whose biography has been rewritten to exclude the relevance of all factors and considerations other than the deviance.

The social deviance is taken to be 'a master status' (Everett Hughes's phrase) explaining and describing everything about the individual. It negates and overshadows any other characteristics or connections the individual has. So, for example, the fact that Nolde was a Jew far overshadowed his longstanding membership of the Nazi party, and led to the attacks on his art and then his self. The same went for communists in the McCarthy period. Later, it was true for anti-war protesters, and it has always been true for homosexuals and sex offenders.

Making someone deviant is indeed an active process warranting a verb. Deviance is not a self-evident category. It does not just float down from the skies applying itself to people who quite obviously are deviant. Deviance is a historical term and its application and/or adoption can create a status which dwarfs all others in its consequences for the individual's existence. Even the most deviant of all deviants does not just 'happen'; someone has to pass judgement, to portray, to stigmatize, to insult, to heap abuse, to exclude or to reject. The symbolic interactionists made a great contribution not only to sociology but also to human thought in general in recognizing and studying the active character of moral attribution.

Because the end result of moral attribution can be described as criminality, deviance, immorality or just plain poor taste, we could use several verbs to refer to the active element in the branding (e.g. criming, disapproving, moralizing, disavowing, etc.) – so it is useful to have one all-encompassing verb to describe what is going on in this practice. In my own work, I have argued for the value of the term censure (Sumner, 1976, 1981, 1983, 1990a). Deviance, like criminality and shame, is a concept used in the practice of social censure; if we say 'the censure of deviance', then we can see that it is a practice as well as a moral concept. In Goffman's day, however, the various practices of social censure were only just beginning to be put under the spotlight. A concept used in censuring, namely deviance, was still being used by social scientists to describe the status of the censured person – as if it was behaviourally and morally valid. The term censure itself, at that time, was mainly used within the discourses of politics, and politics was only just being brought into the analysis of 'deviant behaviour'. But times they were a-changing. Events in the USA and Europe conspired with sociology to ensure that never again would moral judgement be separated from its place within power relations; never again would social science tolerate a field which would uncritically accept that those officially adjudged criminal or deviant were the best or the only examples of true criminality and deviance in the society, or that the moral judgement as to what was criminal or deviant was entirely devoid of political considerations.

Stigma and the politics of social deviance

Goffman had demonstrated that making a deviant label stick was essentially a power-play, and that the microsociology of human interactions revealed a nasty tendency to self-interest and the betrayal of others. What could be more political than the Machiavellian cooling out of the mark before nailing it to the cross of a state mental hospital? Like Lemert, Goffman drew attention to the politics of stigma. Branding people as witches, communists, perverts or lunatics was fired by vested interests and moral crusades, people with an interest in the censure. It was not the course of the disinterested bystander.

It is rarely observed, however, that Goffman also saw deviance as political in another way – one which refers more to the censured behaviour than to the interest in censuring. In *Stigma* (1963; reprinted 1968b), he was concerned with the public character of social stigma, how people 'managed' stigma, how they lived with it, and what happened to an individual's identity. Clearly, Goffman was again fascinated by the universal forms and rituals of social life, but he was also focusing on the politics of public morality. Right from the beginning, he noted that the Greeks used the word stigma to refer to

> bodily signs designed to expose something unusual and bad about the moral status of the signifier. The signs were cut or burnt into the body and advertised that the bearer was a slave, a criminal, or a traitor – a blemished person, ritually polluted, to be avoided, especially in public places.
>
> (Goffman, 1968b: 11)

Today, we use it to refer more to the disgrace itself than to any bodily evidence of its justification.

Did it follow that the stigmata defined the stigma? Did the public signs of stigma define the private truth of the stigma? Did stigma reside only in its (outer) sign? What of the relation between the sign and its referent, between the stigmata and the stigma?

These were vital questions for the sociology of deviance, and they have been absolutely central in debates in the field ever since. Indeed, the answers to these apparently abstract questions determine the very viability of the field as an intellectual enterprise. Goffman's answers not only constituted the first major doubt about the integrity of the field as a branch of sociology, they also signalled the entry of the sociology of deviance into its next phase, the phase where deviance became highly politicized. As we shall see, like Lemert, Goffman was not yet ready to abandon this wayward émigré whose rise to notoriety was marred by intrinsic character flaws. His discussion is of some considerable interest.

Early on in *Stigma*, Goffman recognizes that stigmata do not define stigmas and that, therefore, there is a problem – what does? The sign is not the full story of its referent. There can be smoke without fire when it comes to moral tales. Indeed, when it comes to moral discourse and judgement, there can be an awful lot of hot air, much imagination, great miscarriages of justice, and the same sign can mean totally opposite things in different contexts. When it comes to morality and gossip, there can not only be smoke without fire, but even fire without smoke. So it was that Goffman recognized that, for example, having a university degree might be a plus in some occupations and a minus in others. Going to a library might be a sign of normality in one class culture and a sign of oddity in another. He could have given simpler examples. Killing is murder in some contexts and heroism in others. Sex in some contexts is a sign of deep love, and in others a sign of profound hate. Fatness is attractive, a positive sign, in some cultures, whereas in others it is an unattractive signal. So, when it comes to morality, there is no necessary relation at all between the signifier and the signified, between the stigmata and the stigma. The same item which is a sign of stigma in one context is a sign of merit in another.

Therefore, Goffman correctly concluded, 'a stigma . . . is really a special kind of relationship between attribute and stereotype' (*ibid.*: 14). That is, stigma follows where attribute fails to meet stereotype, where reality does not come up to expectations. Stigma is a negative relationship between attribute and context; it explains why we 'use cripple, bastard, moron in our daily discourse as a source of metaphor and imagery' (*ibid.*: 14). Like power, stigma is a relational phenomenon.

A stigma is established, to paraphrase Goffman creatively, when societies or social groups have to construct successful rationalizations for their punitive disapprovals. Such a rationalization or moral justification is a 'stigma theory' or an 'ideology' to explain the inferiority and dangerousness of the stigmatized ones. Sometimes, Goffman observed, such ideologies rationalized 'an animosity based on other differences, such as those of social class' (*ibid.*: 15). Only 'sometimes'? My own theory of social censures suggests that it is rare that a stigmatization or censure is anything other than an expression, sublimation or rationalization of larger social divisions, such as class, gender and ethnicity (Sumner, 1990a). Goffman still seemed to hold out the possibility that a sizeable number of social censures were unmediated by wider ideologies of inferiority stemming from fundamental social fissures along class, gender, ethnic, age or regional fault-lines; as if deficiency, disability and degeneracy spoke loudly and only for themselves; as if these dreaded Ds were the self-explanatory root of social conflicts and not the effect.

Goffman's rough typology of stigmas illustrates his perspective, and is helpful in indicating the continued legacy of the three Ds in even the most sophisticated sociology of deviance of the 1960s (see above, pp. 38–40). Type one was 'physical deformities'. The second sort were the character weaknesses (and presumably their physical concomitants) associated with 'social deviance' (mental illness, suicide, addiction, homosexuality and radicalism are examples given by Goffman), and the third were the 'tribal' stigma of 'race, nation, and religion, these being stigma that can be transmitted through lineages and equally contaminate all members of a family' (Goffman, 1968b: 14). This typology indicates that the sociology of deviance was increasingly about normative resistance to the established moral order, and much less about physical handicap. So it was no surprise when, at the very end of his book, Goffman openly defined the 'core' of deviance in this manner and declared that the subject had insufficient to hold it together as a coherent field. In fact, I would argue, Goffman had implicitly recognized that there were types of social deviation which were not really 'socially deviant' any more – physical handicap, in a post-war era, was moving faster and faster towards moral acceptability – but he was reluctant to accept explicitly that they were not social deviations. After all, physical handicap still carried social stigma.

Clearly, if all that really held deviance together as a coherent concept was normative difference from or resistance to the established cultural order then there could be little objective or physical commonality to actions stigmatized as deviant. Deviance, in that case, would merely describe a myriad of highly subjective, highly contextual, highly political, alleged infractions or rejections of the dominant norms. What Goffman actually said was that he preferred to avoid using the term deviance, which he described as 'currently fashionable' (*ibid.*: 167). He could see the convenience of the term, but then made the devastating observation that

> It is remarkable that those who live around the social sciences have so quickly become comfortable in using the term 'deviant', as if those to whom the term is applied have enough in common so that significant things can be said about them as a whole. Just as there are iatrogenic disorders caused by the work that physicians do (which then gives them more work to do), so there are categories of persons who are created by students of society, and then studied by them.
> (*ibid.*: 167, n. 1)

Goffman did not think deviants had very much in common. They had more differences than similarities, he said. After all, deviation could occur in every social group, and that covered a vast spectrum of human existence. Like Parsons, he saw deviation as specific to each social group, but unlike Parsons he had little concern for dominant value-systems. Goffman's view is of highly pluralistic society and, therefore, the only thing deviants seemed to have in common was that they had been so labelled by sociologists. But then Goffman made the following remarkable statement:

> If there is to be a field of enquiry called 'deviance', it is social deviants as here defined that would presumably constitute its core. Prostitutes, drug addicts, delinquents, criminals, jazz musicians, bohemians, gypsies, carnival workers, hobos, winos, show people, full-time gamblers, beach dwellers, homosexuals, and the urban unrepentant poor – these would be included. These are the folk who are considered to be engaged in some kind of collective denial of the social order. They are perceived as failing to use available opportunity for advancement in the various approved runways of society; they show open disrespect for their betters; they lack piety; they represent failures in the motivational schemes of society.
> (*ibid.*: 170–1)

Back to square one with a list of degenerates? Not really. Goffman was merely focusing the field. He had the sociological imagination to see many kinds of social deviation (see Goffman, 1968b: Chapter 5), and simply saw the above as central characters. What is significant about these passages for the history of the field is that social deviance was now being defined as (a) multiform and (b) grouped around a core of urban ghetto dwellers who 'flaunt their refusal to accept their place and are temporarily tolerated in this gestural rebellion, provided it is restricted within the ecological boundaries of their community' (Goffman, 1968b: 172). Core social deviants, for Goffman, are 'disaffiliates', people who reject their place and 'act irregularly and somewhat rebelliously in connexion with our basic institutions' (*ibid.*: 170); and disaffiliates who live together in a specific community or milieu are 'social deviants', a distinct type of 'deviator'.

Goffman had initiated a new phase in the sociology of deviance by defining its central characters in political terms. Theirs was no psychiatric deficiency. It was a chosen, 'unrepentant', lifestyle. These beach bums and bohemians did not subscribe to the profit motive, the 'rat race', or the war on communism. They had committed the cardinal sin. They were not motivated by property or power. None of the insider-dealers, the genocidal generals or the corrupt politicians had violated fundamental social norms as seriously as this. As Simmons's survey (1969) of the Californian public at the end of the sixties showed, homosexuality was more socially deviant than mass murder. In line with the culture of his day, Goffman defined core social deviance as community-sustained disaffiliation from the mainstream. Deviance was now a political position. It was a vote for the opt-out party, for no party, for one long party. It was a politically aware rejection of the social system.

The attribution of political perspective to deviants is usually a position associated with *The New Criminology* and British deviancy theories after 1968. Some would also say that Becker began the politicization of the field, when in fact he never developed any theory of the commonalities of social deviants. However, it was in fact Goffman who, in *Stigma*, was the first to articulate a theory of core social deviance as community-sustained disaffiliation from the system.

Goffman did not take this view very far, for the obvious reason that he regarded deviants as too diverse a group to warrant a branch of sociology or a general theory of their existence. He regarded social deviants as one group of stigmatized persons, and the latter was the only generic or group category Goffman had any time for (see 1968a: 174). So, clearly, it cannot be said that he launched a political theory or a general theory of social deviance. What he did was to point to the huge gap between the public stigma and the variable and multiform private reality of stigmatized persons, to show that all that was held in common was stigma and to assert that core social deviants were social rebels. But he had sown some corrosive seeds. Both the suggestion that deviants were too diverse to warrant a general theory of deviant behaviour and the claim that core deviants were politically self-defined were radical departures from all that had gone

hitherto. The sociology of deviance had begun its long process of dissolution. Its very existence supposed some commonality in behaviours
labelled socially deviant, and its fundamental assumptions supposed from
the outset that its core subjects did not consciously disaffiliate from the
mainstream. The original psychiatric connection, so central to the field,
had now been stretched to breaking point – after all, some of the people
now defined as core deviants consciously rejected and criticized the psychiatric establishment. Indeed, before too long, the anti-psychiatry movement was to suggest that it was the psychiatrists who might be the ones
in need of treatment (see Chapter 10).

What Goffman had also effectively exposed in *Stigma* was the in-
appropriateness of the term social deviation to describe physical handicap
and ethnic difference. Such handicap and difference were now seen as
physically and historically given, and not as effects of any psychological
deficiency or deficit. Moreover, if core social deviation was a form of
normative or cultural resistance to the established order, the term deviance
was ultimately inappropriate for it. Resistance or disaffiliation is not a sign
of psychiatric dysfunction, but a sign of political tension and of the healthy
functioning of democracy in a pluralistic society. For all types of stigma,
the term social deviation had become very inappropriate and, in fact,
politically discreditable by the 1960s, and, logically, some more general
conception of social censure was needed to describe and explain the fact
that physical handicap and ethnic difference were still the subjects of
condescension, stigma or disapproval yet not seen as intrinsically socially
deviant.

The psychiatric connotation had actually become redundant in the age
of cultural politics. A new and politically significant term was required.
But, first, a rebellion against the establishment had to occur – to make the
space needed to move forward, to put politics firmly on to the academic
agenda. The debris of the McCarthy period had to be completely removed
before progress could resume. The dead hand of history had to be lifted,
and this meant exposing and challenging existing moral categories. So,
what actually happened in the sixties was that deviance was retained but
politicized and sometimes inverted. Deviants did not recast the normal–
deviant dichotomy, instead they came out of the closet and inverted it. So,
for a while, black was best and gay was greatest. The categories of social
deviation were put in quotation marks for about a decade while they were
examined, rejected, overhauled, revised and recast. The long march through
the moral categories had begun.

In fact, deviance had been substantially democratized in Goffman's work.
There were only faint traces of the old distinction between the normal and
the deviant. Like Lemert, Goffman regularly observed that we all move
between the two worlds, that in fact every sphere of life contained its own
normality and deviance and as we move from one sphere to another we
regularly cross the borders of normalcy/deviance. Life's realms were not
perfectly coordinated or systematized; societies were heterogeneous and

pluralistic; cultures, regions and communities bloomed with the diversity of a thousand flowers, especially in the Sun Belt. Therefore, our identity often changed as we crossed boundaries between realms or between regions (and certainly countries).

> stigma involves not so much a set of concrete individuals who can be separated into two piles, the stigmatized and the normal, as a pervasive two-role social process in which every individual participates in both roles, at least in some connexions and in some phases of life. The normal and the stigmatized are not persons but rather perspectives.
>
> (*ibid.*: 164)

This is why deviance had, in effect, been democratized – *we were all deviants now*. Well, at least those of us who were spiritually and emotionally alive – Goffman did not discuss the phenomenon, which was to become so noticeable later in the 1980s, and so discussed by the anti-psychiatrists, of killing oneself softly by trying to be 'good' or 'respectable' or 'safe' on all fronts.

In complex, pluralistic societies, the very heartlands of modernity, deviance had to be a commonplace because of the continual discrepancy between 'virtual and actual identity', as Goffman put it. All is very rarely what it seems in modernity. People seem one thing and are another. Our expectations are stereotypical because we lack direct experience, and, therefore, our eventual experience is so often a disappointment. As diversity proliferates, so experience lessens and stereotypes rule OK. It is a necessary contradiction or paradox of modern existence.

This was, and is, especially true in America, the imperial kingdom of modernity. America has made as its own the paradox that bewildering and raging diversity relentlessly breeds a stunningly totalitarian and wildly evangelistic moral uniformity. The Land of the Free has patented the one-line stereotype which consigns anything it chooses to the dustbin of history, in an instant. The allegedly greatest freedom of speech on the globe had by the sixties produced the minimum vocal emission – the sound-bite – produced compulsively and with a minimum of cerebral involvement. Reality had been condensed into a bunch of one-liners, and knowledge was the prime province of the stand-up comedian. Indeed, intellectuals of today increasingly realize that to get through to a big audience they too must become stand-up comics and mistresses (or even masters) of the one-liner.

In the sixties, we had a quaint fondness for the variety of speech and thought, no doubt because it was much more suppressed than now. Speech became a political topic (free speech movements, the Dirty Speech Movement and the celebration of local dialects), and we created a highly distinct language as we got our act together and dug the sounds. At that time, as America emerged from McCarthyism to rediscover its moral and political diversity, 'driving along in their automobiles' along the great new highways, Americans naturally crashed into some very, very, different people every day of the week, producing, as Goffman (*ibid.*: 164) put it, a 'need for tension management' (nothing was said of the great increase in automobile accidents). Everyone had become a deviant in some respect. The multiform and fragmented characters who emerged naturally in this high-speed kaleidoscope exhibited all the moral schizophrenia one would expect from individualistic people with little moral or political glue to bind their personality fragments together. It was no wonder my generation talked of 'getting it together' and creating 'good vibrations' – there was a need for spiritual unity and for a recognition of the unity of the whole. The classic example used by Goffman is that very often he or she 'who is stigmatized in one regard nicely exhibits all the normal prejudices held toward those who are stigmatized in another regard' (*ibid.*). Black men, for example, sometimes exhibit some classic stereotypes against women or against Asians. And nothing matches the outraged moralism of prison inmates; their condemnations of all and sundry more than compensate for the tainted moralism so frequently dumped on them in the past.

Naturally, therefore, the term social deviant now emerged within the sociology of deviance to describe the people who Goffman called the core deviators, and whom Lemert had described as secondary deviants; people who were systematically disaffiliated in some way from the dominant cultural system. These individuals were seen as being deviant to the core, their deviance overshadowed any other characteristics they had, their lives were seen as centred solely on deviance and they were not capable of any degree of normalcy. So, just as we shout loudly when we talk to the dumb and treat them as idiots, the communist, the homosexual and the hippie were treated as complete devils. The old prejudice that lesbians cannot be good parents is another example – as Everett Hughes said, serious deviance becomes a master-status swamping all else.[9] My generation responded by announcing that 'the kids were all right' and that we were all completely communist, gay, promiscuous, dope-smoking, hippies – totally and utterly deviant. It wasn't true, but it was just so funny to see the outrageous social reaction of the establishment. Even funnier, but not so ha-ha, was the fact that they never really did get the point, and it was at root not so much a claim for the value of different lifestyles as a point about the dubious politics and morality of labelling people with these totalizing stereotypes, thus preventing the free exploration and discarding of ideas, sexual preferences and lifestyles. The previous generation had still not grasped one of the key reasons why the German fascists wanted to exterminate the Jews, namely that their conception of deviance or degeneracy was a *total* one – if you were deviant in one respect you were totally bad and totally dangerous. Deviance, in this respect, showed its ancestry; it carried the implication of degeneracy, the fouling of the whole being. Yet, surely what is wrong with racism (or nationalism, sexism and regionalism) is not so much that we should never observe racial (or national, or gender or regional, etc.) characteristics but that historically we have been very prejudiced indeed, and sloppy and unscientific, in our attribution of characteristics to races, and that we have reduced whole individuals or races to one or two crude and prejudicially attributed characteristics. Even today, long after the labelling perspective has been assimilated into the establishment, criminology has only partly dealt with the implications of this point about the political and unscientific nature of the concept of the secondary or total (or social) deviant.

Becker, social deviance and the politics of labelling

Howard Becker's work had a very powerful effect on the sociology of deviance, propelling it to the centre of the sociological stage by 1970. Lemert and Goffman had already advanced the sociological theory of deviance considerably, and their writings were innovative, incisive, laconic, detailed and witty, but Becker is probably the one name every student of this field has read. Yet his research presentations on becoming a marijuana user and on the Marijuana Tax Act have very little depth at all. Even more strangely, the man seen as the leading 'labelling theorist' of deviance never produced a systematic theory of the labelling process, or becoming deviant. In fact, he never wrote much at all about the labelling process, and, indeed, never claimed to be a theorist. So why the popularity? Quite simply, it is probably because Becker had the great merit of being able to express the ideas of the labelling perspective with great simplicity and clarity. He was a translator and a communicator; he was the field's popularizer. He connected the academic ideas with their age. Crucially, as a jazz musician and an activist in the campaign to legalize marijuana, he was a social deviant, in Goffman's sense of that term, and you could feel it in his writing, whereas Lemert and Goffman always read like straight, albeit cynical, academics. More committed to being a jazz musician than a sociologist (see Debro, 1970), and more committed to the sociology of education than to the sociology of deviance (see Becker, 1970), Becker expressed the spirit of defiance within social deviance and the commitment to disaffiliation from dominant values. Consequently, his writings capture the political spirit of the labelling perspective better than anyone else's. Lemert and Goffman had both initiated analysis of the politics of deviance, but it was Becker's politicized formulations which really captured the imagination.

Becker made one statement which everyone in the field quotes:

> *social groups create deviance by making the rules whose infraction constitutes deviance*, and by applying those rules to particular people and labeling them as outsiders. From this point of view, deviance is *not* a quality of the act the person commits but rather a consequence of the application by others of rules and sanctions to an 'offender'. The deviant is one to whom that label has successfully been applied; deviant behavior is behavior that people so label.
>
> (Becker, 1963: 9)

Lemert had said this, more or less, in 1951 in relation to his concept of secondary deviance, and Goffman in 1961 in relation to his insight into social contingencies, but there was something uniquely striking about Becker's formulation. What he emphasized strongly was that the social character of deviance lay in the labelling, not in the law or the target of the labelling. Neither law nor evil explained the social character of the stigma or label. This emphasis was so strong that it launched a theoretical and political drive to distance the labelling process from the offender (see Becker, 1974: 47 – 'I intended my own original formulations to emphasize the logical independence of acts and the judgements people make of them'). The signifiers of disapproval, and the branding agencies, were socially independent, autonomous and self-justifying; the law and the evil committed were merely resources for rationalizing moral and political censure in specific, culturally unique, societies. The behaviour or practices labelled as deviant contributed little to explaining the nature, tone and targeting of the censure. Mass murder may have been illegal and distasteful, empirically and according to some transcendental morality, but, as Simmons's (1965) study showed, it was those 'long-haired, homosexual, drug-taking, commie bastards' that really got society's back up.

What Becker was forging was a sharp break with legalism. His formulations represented a rejection of the view that law expressed popular morality and was enforced fairly and equally. One could no longer breezily assume that the tenets of the criminal law were an accurate guide to what was legitimately suppressed by authority, or how.

Lemert and Goffman had stressed that minor deviance was structural, everyday and normal in a pluralistic society with many groups and many value systems, that secondary deviance was a result of social control agencies repeatedly labelling certain primary deviance as serious, and that the labelling practices of social control agencies had institutional imperatives all of their own. In short, they had perceived that being labelled as a social deviant was a result of the institutional work of the social control agencies. Becker clearly saw this too but emphasized the important implication that, taken across the board, the labelling process was a political process drawing upon political/moral ideology, and that there is really no social deviance outside of the label. In short, his position was virtually indistinguishable from those of Lemert and Goffman in asserting that judgements of deviance arose from value-conflicts rather than from any universally disapproved features of behaviour, or the principles and codes of the criminal law, but, unlike them, Becker drew the conclusion that this left social deviance as mainly a political function of moral ideology. Social deviance, therefore, in sociological theory, was becoming seen as an ideological category driven by political interests; and social deviants were seen as people who do what they do 'for much the same reasons that justify more ordinary activities' (Becker, 1974: 51).

Like the other sociologists writing from the labelling perspective, Becker recognized that people break social rules all the time without being labelled as deviant, and, conversely, that a person could be labelled as a social deviant without having broken any moral rules. In that way, Becker was saying that crime was not necessarily deviant and deviance was not necessarily criminal, although he never articulated it that openly. Durkheim's hierarchy of morality, the trichotomy of crime/deviance/difference, was being given a severe challenge. Becker's view supposed that moral censure was simply not that consistent or logically organized; morality was a messy matter subject to the laws of politics in a pluralistic society. Like Wirth, Becker (1963: 8) did not see much moral consensus around him. All social deviance was a result of somebody 'making something of it'; the emergence of a deviant status therefore generally depended upon political action or the exercise of power.

This was a much more political definition of deviance. It fitted well with the spirit of the sixties. In true anarchical fashion, the sixties ethos was to challenge all existing morality and authority. Becker's definition of deviance supposed that the labelling and marginalization of deviants was a matter of political caprice, which sometimes overlapped with what deviants actually did or threatened but which largely bore little logical relation to legal or moral principle. Politics was seen as a seedily corrupt business which had little resemblance in practice to the idealized process of representing the people democratically. The people, implicitly, were paragons of virtue who 'really had their thing together', as that evocative phrase from the sixties proclaimed.

Deviance, Becker said, restating Goffman in more blatant terms, was not a quality present in some behaviours and not in others, 'it is the product of a process which involves responses of other people to the behavior' (Becker, 1963: 14). Deviance lay in 'the interaction between the person who commits an act and those who respond to it'. In these formulations, Becker made it clear that one could see social deviance as a collective phenomenon. 'In its simplest form, the theory insists that we look at all the people involved in any episode of alleged deviance . . . the collective activity going on consists of more than acts of alleged wrongdoing. It is an involved drama in which making allegations of wrongdoing is a central feature' (Becker, 1974: 45). Deviance really was a product of contemporary social interaction, an interaction primarily governed by individuals' interpretations of the meaning of each other's actions or appearances. It was thus very much an effect of *symbolic* interaction, or the clash of ideals, lifestyles and cultures. The great question of whether deviance really was completely social or historical and nothing at all to do with transcendental moral values was left completely unaddressed, as it had been throughout the work of the symbolic interactionist sociologists. Jurisprudentially, their work followed, and contributed to, the Realist movement of Pound, Llewellyn, Olivecrona and Arnold.

Becker observed that social responses to individuals' actions varied greatly, and, prefiguring future developments, he even once used the term social censure to refer to that type of response which labelled an action as deviant (*ibid.*: 13). Using a variety of examples, he demonstrated that the likelihood of censure typically depended on the social character of the actor, whether he or she is black, working class, powerless, etc., and on the social character of the person who feels harmed by the action, for example whether this person or entity has an economic interest. The likelihood of censure also depends on timing; for example, it increases when there is a drive to eradicate a certain kind of action or attitude. In short, it was one thing to break current legal rules, but another to be labelled as deviant.

This was the beginning of the sixties and liberal sociology was well aware of the long-neglected long history of discrimination against black people in the United States. Becker's work rested on a familiarity with facts like those confirmed in later studies which showed, for example, that in the 821 homicides found in ten North Carolina counties from 1930 to 1940 none of the whites convicted of killing blacks received the death sentence, while 37 per cent of the blacks killing whites did (Overby, 1972: 271). The fact that women usually comprised only around 15 per cent of those arrested in the USA, and only around 3 per cent of those in federal prisons, drew less attention and awaited the efforts of feminist criminology before it was harnessed to a similar argument about discrimination against women (see, for example, Chesney-Lind, 1978).

Consequently, Becker (1963: 15) saw social rules as 'the creations of specific social groups' in highly differentiated societies. Echoing Durkheim and drawing examples from immigration problems, he saw that modernity had brought with it the proliferation and conflict of rule-systems within societies. 'The lower-class delinquent who fights for his "turf" is only doing what he considers necessary and right, but teachers, social workers, and police see it differently' (*ibid.*: 16). Becker not only felt that there was little consensus in attitudes to rules and their appropriateness in specific situations but also that in the case of behaviour usually labelled as deviant the rule-breakers are very likely to have a different perspective on the rules being applied; they are typically likely to see them as outsiders' rules, as rules forced upon them. Now this was a strong formulation, and it anticipated much of what was to follow in the 1970s even though it retained strong links with the culture-conflict approach from the 1930s. Its strength lay in its suggestion that deviance resided not only in the label applied to the offender but also within the 'attitude' of the offender. Unfortunately, this suggestion did not command much weight within Becker's broader formulations, and, in his work, deviance often remained a function of the attitude of the labellers. Unlike Goffman, Becker was not careful enough to resist consistently the fallacy that just because people became deviants more from contingency than pathology it did not mean that they were not pathological, rebellious or difficult in some sense. His deviants never seem to have 'an attitude problem' whereas his labellers always had one. This was no accident. Given Becker's (1970) well-developed methodological positions, which insisted on the need for value-choices in research in the

selection of whose viewpoint to explicate and the impossibility of empath-
ically expressing both the ideology of the underdog and the 'overdog'
within the parameters of qualitative fieldwork, once he had decided to side
with the underdog in the 'hierarchy of credibility' it was always likely that
those in authority would appear to be the ones with the attitude problem.
Yet to understate the difficulty certain attitudes posed for parents, police
and authority was really to understate the interactionist case. Labelled
social deviants often did pose, and consciously so, a threat to the established mores and interests of authority: that was sometimes the whole
point of their attitude. Because of this, Becker, and other interactionists,
were sometimes guilty of understating the degree of social conflict involved
and of neglecting an important dimension of the subjectivity of labelled
offenders, conscious rebellion or rejection.

The much-quoted essay by Piliavin and Briar (1964, reprinted in
Rubington and Weinberg, 1968) captured much of the spirit and impact
of this politicized symbolic interactionism, at the same time as it evidenced
its theoretical weakness. Their study found widespread police dislike of
blacks, 'immense latitude' in the police disposition of apprehended juveniles, a much greater likelihood of black youths being stopped and in-
terrogated, even in the absence of evidence of an offence, and a greater
chance of black youths receiving a more severe disposition for the same
violation as a white youth (*ibid.*: 143–5). The demeanour of apprehended
youths was found to be the factor most likely to induce a police officer
towards a severe disposition. Piliavin and Briar acknowledged that this
police attitude to black youth may have been based on 'accurate statistical
information' but argued that the whole process was one of self-fulfilling
prophecy. Greater suspicion and dislike led to greater chance of arrest and
conviction, which led to greater statistical support for suspicion and dislike,
and so on. Whatever the statistics say, this was a process of racial discrimination, a self-reproducing cycle of prejudice. Piliavin and Briar
concluded that their study supported the fact that the official delinquent
is 'the product of a social judgement . . . He is a delinquent because someone in authority has defined him as one, often on the basis of the public
face he has presented to officials rather than of the kind of offence he has
committed' (*ibid.*: 145).

From his position on rules within modern societies, Becker (1963: 17)
concluded that normally rules were forced upon people, and the ability to
force rules upon others was a question of 'political and economic power'.
Elders forced rules on the young, men upon women, whites upon blacks,
the resident WASP minority upon the immigrant foreign majority, and the
middle class upon the lower class. Typically, he observed, these rules were
not made with regard to the problems of the subordinate group, as if such
'problems' could ever amount to anything other than a demand for more
power from established élites. Such 'power differentials' could be legal but
just as often they were 'extralegal'. Moral and legal rules were thus the
objects and sites of much conflict; they were part of 'the political process

of society' (*ibid.*: 18). The modernity of Becker's political and moral pluralism could not be in any doubt.

Becker's view of the interested and partial process of making rules or 'laying down the law' was firmly registered in his concept of the *moral entrepreneur*. Gusfield had already been developing the idea of the symbolic or moral crusade (see Gusfield, 1955, 1963), extending Lemert's earlier formulations on the political character of reform campaigns and drives against crime. In *Outsiders*, Becker coined the succinct phrase 'moral enterprise' to describe organized activity to enforce a rule or alter the moral constitution of society. He saw such enterprise as a 'key variable' in rule enforcement where there was agreement on the rules to be enforced; 'if no enterprising person appears, no action is taken' (Becker, 1963: 128). Moral enterprise was characterized by 'personal interest, armed with publicity, and conditioned by the character of the organization'. It was absolutely crucial in the shaping of rules to deal with specific 'problematic situations' (*ibid.*: 131), and thus in translating values into current social practice. It was also very likely where deviance was socially oppositional rather than repentant or pathological and, in those cases, involved a major restatement of dominant social norms in legal terms (Gusfield, 1967: 188). The moral entrepreneur is thus a key player in the definition of social deviance; rules rarely applied themselves. Their moral crusades are often humanitarian missions in spirit and intent, fired by reforming zeal for the good of all, but they are often economically driven, concerned with securing profit. In either case, they try to make or enforce rules which serve their ends and thus concretely shape the meaning of social deviance. Whether an action is labelled as deviant at a particular time, therefore, is often dependent on whether the 'offender' happened to stand in the firing line of a piece of moral enterprise. The economic, political or organizational needs and whims of moral entrepreneurs determine what is deviance. Deviance, Becker (1963: 162) concluded, was 'always the result of enterprise', both because someone had to get the rules made in the first place and because someone has to apply the rule. That enterprise is clearly a highly political exercise in both the large and small senses of the word political. It involves a continual reinforcement, restatement, reform or re-presentation of the practical meaning of society's most powerful moral codes and political/economic interests.

In these ways, to sum up, Becker politicized the field of the sociology of deviance; or, more accurately, he established its profoundly political character. Deviance had become a site and object of moral and political conflict. The earlier political formulations of Lemert and Goffman had been extended and clarified. Not only was McCarthyism still registering theoretical effects within sociology, but the burgeoning civil rights struggles waged by blacks were also making their mark. What Becker had alluded to, but did not theorize, was that the 'social deviants' of American society were people who resisted or fought against their economic, political and cultural suppression. Blacks, delinquents, women, immigrants, drug users, homosexuals, jazz musicians and youth generally were all part of a piece – and that piece was the lot of the inner-city powerless, the underdog and the minority within a society systematizing itself since 1945 around the moral and political values of an industrial and military WASP élite minority.

Normal crime: professional categorizations of social deviance

Social deviance by the middle sixties was, therefore, not just seen as a political label, it was also a business for some people. Moral enterprise was not always a one-off campaign, but was usually a daily and professional matter. It was work. The social reproduction of the existing moral order was the business of police, social workers, judges, probation officers and prison guards. The crime control industry had become a multi-million dollar enterprise, and criminology itself benefited financially in no small measure during the sixties. Moreover, the whole 'true confessions' industry, the publicization of private matters, had become so much part of the mass media archipelago, especially with the growth of television, that the social reproduction of the existing moral order was arguably at least as much in the hands of the media proprietors as under the direction of the crime-control people. The symbolic restatement of the moral values supposedly holding the social system together was by now very much a drama, a crime drama lasting for hours of prime-time and in full colour, but this was of course less of a symbolic interaction in the classic sense than a symbolic reassurance (see Sparks, 1992). Unfortunately, the symbolic interactionist sociologists very much neglected the significance, or significations, of television in the sixties, but what they did do was to register the fact that social deviance had been packaged up into significant images by the crime-control professions. No longer a simple slur in an abusive tirade against long-hairs, commies, blacks, prostitutes and homosexuals, social deviance, through professional use, had become a series of stereotyped pen-pictures, or identikit scenarios. The demonic panorama had been divided into workable stereotypes. The folk devils had their rogues' gallery.

The conversion of deviance into professional, stereotyped, packages was well captured by Sudnow in his essay on normal crimes. Beginning from the position that the categories of the criminal law, their interpretation by crime-control agencies and the statistical rates produced by their operationalization are valuable sociological data about the official process of assembling crimes and about the workings of the control agencies themselves, Sudnow demonstrated that professionals in the criminal justice system work not so much with the legal categories of the penal code but with a set of 'normal crimes'. These normal crimes are stereotyped images or packaged scenarios of the typical instance. So, for example, the normal burglary 'is seen as involving regular violators, no weapons, low-priced items, little property damage, lower class establishments, largely Negro defendants, independent operators, and a non-professional orientation to the crime' (Sudnow, 1965, reprinted in Rubington and Weinberg, 1968: 163). These stereotypes were vital, Sudnow's research concluded, to the possibility and practice of mundane plea bargaining whereby, for example, burglary is reduced by lawyers' negotiation to petty theft to gain a guilty plea. The point of great sociological significance which emerged from this was that, legally, petty theft was not necessarily included, situationally or logically, within a burglary so the everyday reduction of a burglary charge to a petty theft rap in the course of plea bargaining could not be deduced from the legal code. The rule justifying such reduction lay elsewhere – in the ideological hierarchy of normal crimes.

This was a major point in the sociological break away from legalism, a break which gained in speed during the sixties. What Sudnow had shown was that the rules governing which legal category could be used to frame a workable conviction were not in fact legal but sociological; they were the rules of a common-sense criminology, rules specifying the hierarchy of offence packages. Law, therefore, on this analysis, was merely a written rhetorical resource available for professionals to legitimize the practical, common-sense decisions they had to make within given organizational settings, budgets and constraints. In this instance, the need to arrange regular guilty pleas was determined by the imperative of fast processing of cases in courts with a heavy load, and facilitated by the deployment of an easy but superficial common-sense criminology. The final legal conviction simply supplied a legitimate label for what had been commonsensically or ideologically processed.

The essays by Piliavin and Briar, Sudnow, and Bittner (1967), along with the books by Skolnick (1966) and Cicourel (1976), convincingly illustrated the proposition developed by Goffman and Becker that the legal description of the crime (or moral account of the deviation) was rarely the true reason for the arrest, apprehension or conviction. Bittner (1967: 714) put this neatly when he said that 'the real reason behind an arrest is virtually always the actual state of particular social situations'. Realism, in the form of a grounded sociological analysis aiming to be true to the everyday reality of the participants in the social drama, was reaching its logical conclusions. Bittner's own elegant contribution was to remind everyone that the job of the police was essentially to keep the peace and that they used the law as a resource to do precisely that. They were not compelled to act by the infraction of the law; their first priority was the judicious use of their discretion and training to ensure the keeping of the peace. Their work was therefore a craft involving great social and human judgement rather than an automated enforcement of abstract legal categories. In short, the police officer's work was defined by its sociological objective not its legal description. The informal rules which translated a problematic situation into one requiring an arrest, a diplomatic caution or even a wise silence were the fundamental skills of the trade, only learned on the job and not evident in any training manual.

Which demeanours or actions required labelling as deviant was now, therefore, seen very much as a situated, practical, question of the degree of social problematicity of a person, act or situation rather than the apparent legal infringement. The revolution wrought by the labelling perspective was beginning to detach deviance from norms as well as the labelling agency from the offender. Which were the norms that now defined deviance? The norms of society or the organizational norms of the policing or labelling agencies? The fundamental assumptions in the labelling perspective – of high individuation, ethnic and moral pluralism, institutional relative autonomy, societal differentiation, contemporaneity rather than historicity, and the individual action as the basic unit of analysis – were beginning to produce an analytic sense of social and moral dislocation. Morality had become unbounded by principled praxis in interdependent communities and was running loose, lost in pragmatically oriented organizations committed to nothing but keeping face against the tide of challenges to a technically oriented social system committed only to its own continued functionality.

Paradoxically, these tendencies to moral dislocation were amplified by ethnomethodology, a form of sociological analysis focused upon the methods whereby people ascertained social reality or truth and thus maintained social order. Sudnow's essay had benefited from comments by the ethnomethodologists Sacks and Schegloff, but its real debt lay with Garfinkel, the founder of ethnomethodology. Garfinkel's work took sociology into the most microscopic of micro-analysis, teasing out the most intimate assumptions about normality which undoubtedly help to structure an otherwise fast-changing, amorphous and bewildering social world. Following Parsons closely in many respects, Garfinkel demonstrated that the world was indeed profoundly structured by norms and informal micro-rules and that really nothing made much sense without an understanding of these norms. Macro-rhetorics were but sophisticated rationalizations for situated, highly contextualized, accounts which made individual actions intersubjectively justifiable to relevant social audiences. Action was thus incomprehensible without an understanding of these normative accounts, which were built into action at the very moment of its conception. To dismiss official rationalizations of discriminatory actions as prejudice or dissembling was thus to miss the point sociologically. Such rationalizations were but coded rhetorics expressing, sometimes inaccurately or misleadingly, the situated accounts which were truly the key to explaining the logic of officials' action.

Members of social groups were thus reflexive people whose daily tasks usually precluded the need to display constantly the justifiability of their actions; the excavation of the normative bedrock of daily praxis was the task of the ethnomethodologist. Members took much for granted, otherwise life would be impossible; the ethnomethodologist described exactly what they took for granted. The ensuing studies therefore naturally excavated much which was apparently trivial or microscopic. To criticize ethnomethodology for that is to miss the point – social life is deeply textured and no macro-analysis of social structure worth its salt should underestimate the importance of these 'trivia'. In practice, however, too much ethnomethodology made little of the social dust it excavated.

A good example of this concerns a piece of research whose political sensitivity meant that it is confined to rest on library shelves on restricted access. That in itself, of course, tells the story. Social research which penetrates deep into the rich texture of social control often threatens significant political and individual interests. This example involved a very sharp student who had worked within a control agency for well over a year and who, as a devotee of ethnomethodology committed to sticking close to his data and loyal to his subjects' perceptions, had systematically documented the details of the informal rules which enforcement officers relied upon to focus their activities. These informal rules operated as a kind of common-sense criminology of the kind described by Sudnow and Cicourel. The rules involved considerable discrimination against the weakest members of the society concerned and seemed to give the richer members a certain immunity from apprehension. To his great credit, the student was restless with a mere description, despite the challenge to his ethnomethodological principles any further explication might bring. He was reluctant to draw upon any abstract model of class or political economy which might lead him away from the principle of making his study 'adequate at the level of meaning' to his subjects (a Weberian principle of social science method). So I suggested that he consider that his enforcement officers may just be following policy guidelines from above (a more Marxian principle recognizing the hierarchy of power within organizations) and that the senior officers may well have a developed sense of what the social system required of them; in short, that members might themselves have a taken-for-granted sociological understanding of the social structure. Consequently, he returned 'to the field' and ascertained that there was indeed considerable disaffection within the ranks about the inherently discriminatory guidelines handed down from above. Moreover, on my suggestion, he then interviewed the head of the organization. When asked whether he had noticed that the informal working rules of his officers tended to support and reinforce the political economy of the society, the man retorted, a little indignantly no doubt, with words to the effect of 'what do you expect?' He observed to my student that if one read the constitutional parameters and prescriptions for his office it was specified clearly that the prime directive was 'to safeguard the revenue'. QED. Clearly, as Bittner also showed, deviance is specified not so much in legal codes as in the political-economic objectives of social control organizations. As for my student's research, it demonstrated to me at least that, without sensitivity to members' awareness of political and economic features of society, ethnomethodology merely provided a morass of interesting data with little persuasive explication.

We must understand that it is one thing to remain close to members' perceptions and accounts and make detailed descriptions of the norms intrinsic to walking in an acceptable manner (Ryave and Schenkein, 1974), or to behaving 'normally' within one's own home (see Garfinkel, 1967: 47–9), or to making a justifiable arrest of a juvenile (see Cicourel, 1976), but it is wholly another to exclude the possibility that these situated norms were not themselves richly textured by members' understanding of the workings of an altogether too external, impersonal and powerful social structure well beyond their control. In short, the incredible micro-detail of ethnomethodology paradoxically revealed very clearly a general problem with the subjectivism of post-war American sociology: it was neglecting the structuring power of its own fundamental taken-for-granted norm, namely the political economy of the social system. Demystifying the rhetorics of law and order by reference to the concrete, everyday, workings of the criminal justice system was all well and good, but it proved nothing on its own. We all know, as a matter of common sense, that people are reflexive, 'smart', perceptive and self-protective beings whose actions only fully emerge through interaction with others – so what? That is like describing the flow of fluids in an engine without telling us about the vehicle, its normal functions and the direction it travels in – or about the driver and what he or she has in mind for the passengers. What ethnomethodology, ironically, proved was that we needed more substantive knowledge of the general functioning and direction of social relations. Without that contextualization of the micro-logics of everyday life, it appeared, at its worst, as the most neurotic form of the modern search for the inner psychic truth of social order, a neurotic digging for the secrets of Eldorado in specks of dust whose significance could not be read with the tools being deployed.

So, indeed, ethnomethodology added to sociology's understanding of deviance by showing that its recognition, identification and labelling by society's members was dependent on many unexplicated, taken-for-granted, normative assumptions about the way the world is supposed to work, and about their own precious accountability within that precarious existence. It might be true to say that it took interactionist sociology to its logical extreme. But, in so doing, it revealed the fundamental weakness of post-war American sociology in its refusal to question the workings of the goal, fantasy, matrix, *Grundnorm* and bedrock of its own society, the military-industrial complex of post-war American capitalism. What it took for granted was precisely the key to what 'wise' social members took for granted.

Matza's *Becoming Deviant*

David Matza's book deserves attention here partly because it was one of the best books ever produced in the field, partly because it summarized many of the problems inherent in the sociology of deviance, and partly because it came very close to addressing the question of the state. Ultimately, it was a book that stated the most developed all-round position possible within the framework of interactionist or phenomenological sociology of deviance, but not a book which moved the field beyond existing parameters. Written in Berkeley and London, it hinted at things to come; these locations again being significant – notably regarding the coming impact of a renewed European social theory on the whole field of enquiry, and the place of Berkeley in the history of New Left politics and criminology in the USA. The book is indebted to Goffman, Lemert, Becker and Skolnick, but also to David Downes and Stanley Cohen. The field had moved a long way from Chicago and was returning to Northern Europe to sustain its intellectual momentum.

Matza's earlier book, *Delinquency and Drift* (1964), had been similarly progressive in posing the value of a concept of drift into delinquency against positivistic conceptions of causal necessity, thus developing earlier Chicagoan awareness of the fluidity, ambiguity and conflict inherent in individual growth. Now, he drew more emphatically upon European existentialism, especially that of Sartre and Genet, to suggest the openness and flexibility of the deviant career. In his view, there was no more certainty about the processes of deviancy amplification than there was about the processes engendering delinquent behaviour. The individual could always turn back and go straight. Certainly, social circumstances may produce a predilection to deviation, an affinity; certainly, affiliation with people sharing similar problems or predilections could lead to repeated deviation, and, certainly, repeated labelling by the agencies of social control could lead to the adoption of deviant identities and lifestyles, but none of this was pre-ordained. The individual always made a choice and reigned sovereign over social forces. This sovereignty was, in true sixties style, very much in the head and not in the social structure; the ability to adjust one's head-set was sufficient to reconstruct an individual's reality for all practical purposes. The resonances of Haight-Ashbury were clear, but so too were those of Foucault, Sartre and Garfinkel.

Even though he acknowledged that Leviathan could capture a subject within its spell and, for a while, make that person believe in his or her true deviance, Matza believed that, through the imaginary, semiotic and philosophical deconstruction of the language of the spell, the subject could free himself (or herself?).[10] The following passage captures well the intellectual space Matza had forged at the very limits of phenomenological interactionism, a space which contained some of the most potent seeds of future debate and development in the theory of deviance:

> the perception which converts a person playing baseball into one who refrains from doing bad things because he has been forcefully told to . . . is unusual and warrants full appreciation . . . because it is a real spell and not theatrical, the bind of Leviathan and the magic it works can be undone by the subject. He can be *dis*-spelled. Thus, the subject may try to disspell himself, rid himself of an unformulated sense of dis-ease . . . *the magic of words*, the capacity of words first to juggle reality by boggling the mind and subsequently shape reality

by directing the mind. By a manner of speaking and the construction of words, the baseball player can be transformed into one who is primarily behaving himself . . .

Reason points us away from an understanding of word-magic and the potent spells it can help produce by rendering wholly imaginary – useless in the world – the direct and explicit approach to detection and discovery. Reason does that by enunciating the *non-sequitur* and banning it, by defining madness and confining it . . .

Because he is in the world, the subject is effectively sealed off *by reason* from this method of breaking the spell . . . His entire heritage . . . has seen to it that the escape of imagination is sealed from him . . .

The subject has been left hanging in this book . . . because, currently, that is where he is, and for a time that is where he will be . . .

The spell can be broken easily even though no exact moment of being freed from its bind can be visualized, and even though the sorcerer – Leviathan – keeps its hand hidden throughout. The spell is broken when the subject comes to terms with the *actual*, the *objective* relation between Leviathan and himself: when, in other words, he concretely realizes that he is a *subject of Leviathan*.

(Matza, 1969: 175–7)

Matza was quite sanguine about the likelihood of the subject breaking the spell; many simply give up and accept Leviathan's definition as deviant. The deviant self-image was thus self-ordained, albeit because it made life simpler to accept rather than continually resist the labelling. What was important here was that not only had Matza persuasively asserted the fact of openness in the deviancy amplification process, but the importance of language, will and imagination had finally re-emerged long after Mills's early essays.

More prosaically, Matza offered a neat analysis of the deviancy amplification process as one of affinity, affiliation and signification; when it was carried to completion. Affinity and affiliation had been well documented, of course. What was striking was Matza's version of the final stage of repeated labelling and the adoption of a deviant identity. The thief had to be prepared to stand for theft, but once he or she was, he argued, Leviathan employed the thief as a collective representation, an employee who symbolized evil. Thus fitted up, using the method of suspicion of known offenders, but by no means necessarily framed, the deviant becomes employed as a folk devil, the bad that is supposedly so starkly different from the good:

In its avid concern for public order and safety, implemented through police force and penal policy, Leviathan is vindicated. By pursuing evil and producing the *appearance of good*, the state reveals its abiding method – the perpetuation of its good name in the face of its own propensities for violence, conquest, and destruction. Guarded by a collective representation in which theft and violence reside in a dangerous class, morally elevated by its correctional quest, the state achieves the legitimacy of pacific intention and the appearance of legality – even if it goes to war and massively perpetrates activities it has allegedly banned from the world.

(ibid.: 197)

So, a concept of the state finally entered the sociology of deviance. However, its introduction was timid and unclear. The passage quoted above, on the last page of the book, hints at an analysis that is not actually present in a book which really does no more than elegantly present a phenomenological version of the deviancy amplification process. But the future was signposted. Collective representations of crime and deviance were now suggested to be state tactics in some kind of self-justifying process. Previously, the discriminations of social control had been portrayed as patterned by prejudices which were not in any sense part of a coherent picture of domination but simply a reflection of local ignorance or institutional self-interest.

However, once the state entered the scene, even if coyly disguised as 'Leviathan', in Matza's language, deviance as a field was conceptually undercut – for if deviance was really a system of signs used to sustain state power and legitimacy then it had no coherent logic as a general concept intended to describe a class of internally deficient behaviours. Deviance had thus become a signifier disconnected from its constituent referents. Its coherence was now seen to be rooted in the social logic of state proscriptions rather than in any ideologically supposed commonality within its reference. The emperor had shed his clothes. The psychoanalytic, social-democratic, sociology of the thirties had been de-frocked and its invention exposed – from the left by Matza, with great caution, and from the right, with much plain speaking, by Turk (1969).

Cleansing the body politic: Turk

So much of the sociology of deviance from Wirth, Sellin and Mills through to Lemert, Vold, Becker and Quinney had pointed up the political character of labelling and the profound cultural conflicts frequently involved. From its very roots in the late thirties, the labelling perspective had a politics. Wirth and Sellin had emphasized the increasing likelihood of conflicts between different cultural groups as societies became more complex. Wirth once said:

> One of the most convincing bits of evidence for the importance of the role played by culture conflict . . . is the frequency with which delinquents, far from exhibiting a sense of guilt, made the charge of hypocrisy toward official representatives of the social order such as teachers, judges, newspapers, and social workers with whom they came into contact.

(Quoted in Pfohl, 1985: 342)

Mills had continued his critique of the élite character of general cultural norms: 'National establishments tend to set the relations of culture and politics the important tasks, the suitable themes, the major uses of the cultural apparatus. In the end, what is "established" are definitions of reality, judgements of value, canons of taste and of beauty' (Mills, 1959, in 1967: 410). Vold had treated officially defined criminals as 'losers in a social struggle for power' (Pfohl, 1985: 341). Becker had insisted that we cannot describe a 'higher reality' that makes sense of both the views of the socially defined deviants and the labelling agencies, and that the research sociologist had to take sides. Lemert had developed his view of society as a competition between a wide and ever-changing range of associations, sub-groups and coalitions to 'advance their values or maintain them in favoured positions' (Lemert, 1972: 54), and openly hoped for the time when the administrative judgements of moral turpitude 'may crystallize a wider democracy for deviants' and when organizational devices evolve 'for hedging the process by which degradation is translated further into denials, suspensions, and revocations of the right to follow one's livelihood' (*ibid*.: 92). And Quinney had argued that the chance of social groups influencing 'the formulation of the law is related to the power positions of particular groups' and that 'the criminal law changes as the values and norms of the dominant groups are modified and as the place of these groups is altered in the power structure itself' (Quinney, 1965: 135). But these were all sociologists on the liberal wing of the sociology of deviance. Now the conservative strand was to declare its hand on the rising tide of resistance to the American social order in the 1960s – and who better than a South African white, Austin Turk, to articulate the position at its strongest and clearest?

Turk, like the liberals, saw social order as a fragile affair:

> not as a system of inevitable and necessary norms challenged by unruly and anti-social people, but rather as an always tenuous approximation of an order, more a temporary resolution of conflicting notions about right and wrong and of incompatible desires, than either any sort of automatic equilibrating mechanism or any kind of spiritual harmony among right-thinking minds. Order such as we find is basically a pattern of conflicts and resolutions of conflict that lead to new lines of struggle.
>
> (Turk, 1969: xii)

Conflict rather than consensus was now seen as the primary principle of social life. For Turk, it was a conflict among 'parties seeking to protect and improve their life chances', a conflict which assumed the need for some limits on the use of violence and for some compromise (*ibid*.: 31). The conflict was between the authorities who make the decisions and the subjects who are affected by them. Subjective idiosyncrasy meant that behaviour always only, at best, approximated group norms and thus the potential for conflict was ever-present. For 'students of criminality', the main concern was with the 'challenges to relatively explicit structures of authority' and the responses to those challenges. The impact of political demonstrations in the sixties was clearly felt, but also the generalized rise of social deviance connected to that increased politicization of the body politic. It was not simply overt political dissent that challenged authority but the whole range of social deviation. The following statement revealed the essence of Turk's concern and the growing new mood on the right:

> There are indications that some authorities are beginning to understand that such norm violations as juvenile misconduct, family disorganizations, indifference to hygiene, personality disorder, and lack of available work skills constitute insoluble problems until and unless a total, determined, attempt is made to destroy the structure of values and social relationships ... creating and perpetuating the unwanted patterns of language and behaviour, and to force people (impolitic phrasing!) into structures that lead to 'good'.
>
> (*ibid.*: 58)

Impolitic phrasing indeed! Social democracy had reached the limits of its tolerance. Even 'indifference to hygiene' ('the great unwashed', as the media constantly described the welter of social deviants at the end of the sixties) was now a sign of the profound threat to authority. Foreshadowing the rise of the right in the 1970s, Turk called for a 'total' destruction of the structure of values and relationships breeding this cancer. Deviance had now been politicized by left, liberal and right. Any core of sense it might have had in the Rooseveltian drive to mitigate the worst aspects of *laissez-faire* capitalism had now disintegrated. It was no longer a metaphor for the liberal management of disadvantage and difficulty but a symbol of political resistance and revolt. As such, its meaning as an infraction of generalized social norms collapsed, and, quite plainly, it became a social censure of threats to authority.

Nemesis

The sociology of deviance had thus reached its nemesis. Nemesis was the Greek goddess of vengeance, personifying, in this case, the remorseless logic whereby the full extension of a social theory brings down on its own head the critique which it fundamentally neglects. What was to follow was no accident. It was directly connected to the silences which had preceded. On reaching maturity, the field had climbed its own personal heights and achieved its limit; its middle age, like so many, produced a crisis which demanded a radical re-orientation and re-conceptualization that could not be contained within the parameters of the existing *modus vivendi*. It began to be haunted by its own repressed unconscious.

The labelling perspective's critique of discrimination, heavy-handedness and bigotry was indeed an expression of flower-power. It was lightweight. Its gay, free-thinking, creative and elegant exposure of the discriminatory character of social control had certainly moved the sociology of deviance into another space altogether. We were now well beyond the elementary debate about the dangers of heavy-handed policing. Social control had been so dissected, excavated, explored and demystified that it had become virtually impossible by the end of the sixties to see it as in any way a coherent expression of collective values and sentiments. It had become the authorities' struggle to contain the challenges posed by the disadvantaged, the dissident, and the different.

Durkheim's trichotomy – crime/deviance/difference – was racked with dis-ease. It had run its course. Crime could no longer be seen as a more serious form of deviance. Deviance was not necessarily less serious than crime. And difference was all too often the biggest crime of all. The agencies of social control could not easily be seen to be coherently enforcing a collectively agreed normative system or *Volksgeist*. Moral multiplicity seemed more evident than spiritual unity. Each institution and each individual increasingly seemed to be heading for a world where the pragmatic defence of the realm took precedence over collective self-realization and where the pursuit of individualism raced ahead of social obligation. Deviance had thus lost its moorings. Detached from modernity's early self-justificatory ambiguity and increasingly blatantly connected to the ideological, political and economic predilections of a predatory and over-inflated élite, it had become exposed as a political censure – as just another way of handling the enemy within. Once revealed, there was no turning back. Either it somehow reconnected itself to a new justificatory norm or it went the way of all hegemonic apologias and exploded on exposure to light. But there were no new justificatory norms in sight.

Notes

1 The view of theory and theorizing popular around that time in liberal American sociology is well treated by Alan Blum, one of many professors trained in Chicago. Blum (1974: 180) says this: 'The modern attitude toward theory then sees it as the method for creating a new thing out of two, instead of as a way of making the unity of all things transparent and Reasonable . . . Genuine theorizing can never overcome difference.'

2 It was not the only thing that became confused. Lemert's later comments on Goffman's use of the career concept completely miss Goffman's point and accuse him of arguments he was specifically against (Lemert, 1972: 78–9). Goffman never imagined that moral careers involved fixed phases or that individuals always went through each phase in a fixed order; contingency and interaction were always his watchwords. Nor did his writings suppose that all forms of deviance involved professionalization, or some such similar process.

3 We had to wait until the 1970s for the introduction of the history of societies, a move which finally made the analysis of social deviance three-dimensional.

4 Goffman's work obviously mirrors the later work of Foucault, in so far as Foucault talks of discourses producing social practices and social reality through the operation of their rules, codes, specifications and readings within determinate discursive practices. I am unaware of Foucault having read Goffman, or of any acknowledgement of any intellectual debt to Goffman. Of course, the debt is not large because Goffman is trading in identities whereas Foucault was in the discourse market. The former dealt with what passed for character these days, the latter dealt with what passed for knowledge.

5 If one more institution is created to regulate the deviation, then the rate of deviant manifestations will increase by 100 or 200 per cent. If, then, three more institutions are added, the rate will increase by 500 or 600 per cent. But if far too many institutions get created then the rate of instances, or 'sightings', will decrease. It's like fishing. Increase the fishing fleet and you catch more fish, but increase it indefinitely and you over-fish the water and the rate of catch declines. (This is an extension of E. H. Carr's (1961) fishing metaphor for doing history in his *What Is History?*, published the same year as *Asylums*.)

6 Contrary to the positivist myth, both propositions are empirically testable and both are amply evidenced by 'sad tales' running back to the very beginning of human history.

7 Nietszche had argued the same thing in his *Genealogy of Morals* in 1887, but American sociologists didn't read Nietszche – they were more likely, like Matza for example, to have read Genet's version of the argument.

8 The American slang 'framed' has a slightly different and unfortunate meaning, implying lack of guilt.

9 On the concept of the master-status, see Becker's discussion (1963: 32–5). I have suggested that the 'master' element is no historical accident and that it reflects the dominant masculinity of most censures (Sumner, 1990b).

10 Again, the frequent use of the masculine pronoun unfortunately obscures much of real importance here. Official crime is a singularly male phenomenon, but no one has really explored the question of whether men are more under the spell of reason and therefore less able to break the semiotic prison of state signification; a question I once tangentially approached (Sumner, 1990b).

PART THREE

Crime and power:
the re-politicization of
moral judgement
1968–1975

10 Resistance and resentment: morality, politics and subjectivity

Freedom, just around the corner from you,
but, with truth so far off, what good will it do?

(Bob Dylan, *Infidels*)

The heart of darkness and the corruption of absolute power

The My Lai massacre in 1968 divided America even further than it had been divided before. The number of American casualties was also growing to unacceptable proportions. Television showed the full horror of war for the first time. The means for mass propaganda were backfiring on all cylinders. The insanity of the great new social system was obvious to many. The draft brought it all back home. What now of household mores? The moral core of America had been conscripted and decimated. The Tet offensive of 1968 made the technical–strategic futility of the exercise even clearer. Corporate, militarized, America was failing at what it was supposed to be best at – social control. The fall of Saigon in 1975 marked the end of an era. If America's actions were to be euphemized as social control and the North Vietnamese derogated as deviants, then the terms were meaningless.

This national failure was compounded by the disgrace President Nixon brought upon himself in Watergate. America's bad habits had caught up on its ruling class, and were fully exposed in public. The law was even more tainted. By the time of Nixon's downfall in 1974, the morality of the cybernetic social system had been frequently discredited. Corruption stories abounded in relation to the CIA, the international arms and drugs rackets, and city hall (see Block and Chambliss, 1981). The bloated multinational corporations had blotted their financial and environmental copybooks more than once or twice. Absolute power was being seen to corrupt absolutely. The disgrace was apocalyptic. At a minimum, the grounds for taking the view that law enforcement was a totally political question seemed solid.

The Vietnam War had been widely opposed in Europe and had prompted many large demonstrations. It fed into a burgeoning radical student politics. The 'issues' abounded. The Soviet invasion of Prague and the barricades in Paris were testimony to a watershed in the history of post-war power relations. Both Superpowers were under attack. America's massive bombing of a poor Third World country paralleled the gulags of the Soviet Union in the wave of revelations about the dark heart of super-power.

Art, many said, was now dead. Hughes (1981: 365) commented that 'The seventies are gone, and where was their typical art? Nobody seems to know.' By 1979, he said, the idea of the avant-garde had gone. It was a time of politics and party lines, not cultural differentiation. The meaning of culture had been exploded, and all that were left were sign-systems. The study of semiotics now came into its own, and we all reached for Roland Barthes to try to decipher the age.

The cultural revolution had blended into a political confrontation all over the globe. Battle-lines were being hardened, and a certain kind of realism was back in vogue. Romanticism was dying fast. The surreal was all too real. It really was now a question of 'whose side were you on?' (Becker's famous question for social researchers). A hard neo-Marxism was resurgent in the universities of Europe, and even strong within American criminology. Liberalism was discredited.

Social deviance now either was individualistic navel-gazing or else it declared its hand. Zen gave way to theoretical practice as Marx's texts were exhumed for a thoroughly theological re-reading. Maybe we had missed something. It turned out that a lot had been missed, and for a while the new political realism was Marxist. Frittering about with lifestyles was all very well but the point now was to change the world, not just to philosophize about it. Street-fighting man, as in the Rolling Stones song, entered the fray in a big way, and the weekends were full of demonstrations. As the song suggested, it was the resurgence of a hard man's struggle. The masculinity of the left was yet to be reconstructed. However, many Other forms of politics were, thankfully, emerging on the streets at this time. A new wave of feminism was an increasingly vibrant force, as were the anti-racist, gay and nationalist movements. Indeed, it was a time for political 'movements' as such. A whole new politics was emerging in the seventies, one which was not content to leave things to the vanguard party – large organizations with hierarchies and systems, codes of rules, party lines and set texts were one of the biggest reasons the world was in this mess in the first place. Society had all too many total institutions, so there was a new respect for any form of radical politics.

A critical sociology of deviance emerged after 1968 and it hung its hat on the peg of any kind of radical politics for a while. The central thing was that some people at least had finally started to resist the post-war authoritarian blur politically, and that was to be the essence of the new developments in deviancy theory: any sign of resistance was to be welcomed as political and meaningful. Insanity had been rehabilitated. Deviance was politicized, and since we were still talking the language of a general theory of deviance, it was politicized completely. The excitement of European politics persuaded it to take a tour. The field was about to implode. It could not handle its domain assumptions being returned to the cradle of the politics which precipitated them. It was to stand exposed.

Power and definitions of deviance

Once weakened by its overt politicization, the sociology of deviance was ravaged by its own internal contradictions and savaged by outside forces beyond its control. So much of this was effected in 1968 and then onwards. The field was explosive and vulnerable to fundamental reconstruction. This is not mere rhetoric. The volatility, dynamism and instability of the field were felt regularly in the often explosive or controversial exchanges at academic conferences, especially in Europe.

Gouldner's critique of Becker

In 1968, Alvin Gouldner anticipated his later attack on Western sociology with a virulent assault on Becker's work (Gouldner, 1975), right at the heart of the liberal sociology of deviance. Social democracy's strongest ideological articulation within the field was about to fall. Washington was making yet another assault upon Chicago, this time on the work of the man taken, by Gouldner, to be representative of neo-Chicagoan sociology of deviance.

Gouldner first denounced Becker's partisan sociology as 'glib' and ultimately unclear in its political allegiance. Becker, he says, did not openly admit he was on the side of 'the cool' and 'the underdog'. The Meadian tradition demanded empathy with the research subjects, and Becker's sentiments were clearly in favour of the cool and the underdog. There was a contradiction, however, and it was underpinned by an unclear theoretical foundation for the sentimental affiliation with the 'under-world'. Gouldner asked: what is the basis for assuming that the underdog is more virtuous than the authorities? Is suffering enough to suppose virtue? This was a Nietzschean question, without any reference to Nietzsche. Gouldner's own answer to this question, in this particular essay, was minimal: the suffering of the underdogs received far less attention and was frequently unknown to the general public. The 'Becker School' gave an even less satisfactory answer, he argued: theirs was primarily a devotion to 'cool' which was afraid to confess the passion of the sentiment in favour of the suffering of the deviant. Instead, their 'cool' held them back and left them as liberal zookeepers:

The Becker School's view embodies an implicit critique of lower middle-class ethnocentrism, of small-town respectability, of the paradoxical superiority one ethnic can feel toward another. Indeed, one might say that theirs is most especially a critique of the uneducated middle classes. Now this is no mean thing, for the piety of these strata is certainly pervasive in the United States. Becker's rejection of their smug narrowness is wholesome and valuable.

At the same time, however, Becker's school of deviance is redolent of romanticism. It expresses the satisfaction of the Great White Hunter who has bravely risked the perils of the urban jungle to bring back an exotic specimen. It expresses the romanticism of the zoo curator who preeningly displays his rare specimens. And, like the zookeeper, he wishes to protect his collection; he does not want spectators to throw rocks at the animals behind the bars. But neither is he eager to tear down the bars and let the animals go. The attitude of these zookeepers of deviance is to create a comfortable and humane Indian Reservation, a protected social space, within which these colourful specimens may be exhibited, unmolested and unchanged. The very empirical sensitivity to fine detail, characterizing this school, is both born of and limited by the connoisseur's fascination with the rare object: its empirical richness is inspired by a collector's aesthetic.

(Gouldner, 1975: 37–8)

The resonances with my earlier analysis of the roots of cultural relativism and the relation of deviancy theory to the cultural anthropology of the 1930s are very clear (see pp. 78–91). Neo-Chicagoanism had simply dropped the pretence of complete neutrality without abandoning the essential distance between white liberal anthropology and the cultures of the dominated; a distance which was, in my view, both political *and* epistemological, in short, fundamental to the domination of WASP imperialism.

Gouldner went on to claim that, in fact, the 'Becker School' approach amounted to a 'rejection of unenlightened middle-class bigotry' which emphasized that the deviant was a victim and product of society rather than a rebel against it (*ibid*.: 38). This he saw as inherent in their theory of deviance generation, which tended to portray the deviant as 'a passive nonentity who is responsible neither for his suffering nor its alleviation'; as someone who has been badly treated by the bureaucratic establishment. As such, deviance was denied its roots in 'the master institutions of the larger society'. Gouldner did not see deviants as always in rebellion, and noted their frequent adherence to the norms of the dominant culture, but he argued in this essay that it was insufficient for the 'bureaucratically dependent middle-classes', the 'young men with friends in Washington', to criticize small-town bigotry without daring to question the power élite and the 'master institutions', or to recognize the now many forms of overt political deviance. Becker's sociology was a sociology 'of and for the new welfare state' (*ibid*.: 49). It was 'suffused with an air of complacency' (*ibid.*: 38) and 'complacency is the mind's embalming fluid' (*ibid.*: 54). It was a complacency derived from an 'unexamined, comfortable, commitment to political liberalism' and 'much of liberalism today is the well-financed ideology of a loosely organized but coherent Establishment' (*ibid.*: 55). Deviancy sociology hitherto had its biases towards the underdogs because it was politically liberal; it had been political from the beginning.

Frankly, in the light of the life of the field described in this book, Gouldner's critique seems very tame: he refers to Mills's critique of the power élite but hardly mentions the 'master institutions' by name; nor does he draw any actual connections between, for example, deviance and capitalism. Moreover, it did not specify the exact history which tied the sociology of deviance to the welfare state. Nevertheless, it was widely read and outlined a new direction which was soon to be developed by others.

Conflict theory and the politicization of deviance

As a part of the emergence of a pluralistic conflict theory perspective in the USA, Quinney (1970) and Chambliss and Seidman (1971) stated the point more clearly. Quinney argued that the social reality of crime was defined by those in positions of power and that the rest of us tended to accept this reality as our own. So, again, clearly, empathic fieldwork allowing subjects to speak for themselves, as Gouldner said, would not tell us much apart from the influence of the powerful in defining the subjective reality of crime. Quinney, in this book, saw conflict as eternal and force as the recurrent form of binding conflictful societies together. The police, therefore, were always instruments for the status quo:

> The use of the police to control political protest clearly shows the extent to which police are the representatives of the powerful interests of the society. Law enforcement in this context consists of the selective application of criminal definitions on those who protest against the established government in ways that are regarded by the government as illegitimate. Behaviour that is regarded by the government as illegitimate may, consequently, be defined as criminal . . . The very emergence of the police in the last century was a response to conditions of unrest and mass protest.
> (Quinney, 1970: 134, 135)

Quinney was clear that structural advantage in defining public policy and definitions of crime was related to 'economic production' (*ibid.*: 38, n. 22), as well as to the élites at the top of the six institutional orders of society (a concept borrowed from Gerth and Mills). The bottom line was that those 'behaviours that violate the sensibilities and interests of the powerful segments of society are the behaviours that have a high possibility of being defined as criminal' (*ibid.*: 217). This type of formulation was repeated many times at the end of the sixties in the USA, and clearly the emphasis was now shifting to structure rather than interaction, although the conflict theory perspective was very much an amalgamation of interactionist and structural approaches (and much time was spent trying to make the two seem either totally polarized positions or logically compatible dimensions of the same thing). Chambliss and Seidman (1971: 504) provide another illustration. Their conclusion about law in action was that 'the law represents an institutionalized tool of those in power which functions to provide them with superior moral as well as coercive power in conflict'.

Pfohl (1985: 343) comments that 'pluralistic conflict theories were extremely influential and paved the way for a more historically and structurally informed critical perspective' but that they failed 'to adequately examine the historically based structural context in which power struggles occur'. Indeed. But, for our purposes, the fact that this prevented them from moving beyond the category of deviance was also important. The historical significance of the ideological category of deviance was difficult to see within such a perspective, I think. Typically, deviance was retained as a valid general category of good social science and its contents explained as the result of powerful contemporary interests and ideologies. The theoretical struggle, at the end of the sixties, was not about the concept of deviance so much as within the concept of deviance. The concept of deviance itself was not directly under attack. Its underpinnings were being eroded, but the overt deconstruction of the concept in the USA was only to begin with the essays by Liazos (1972) and Thio (1973).

Before we turn to those essays, however, we should note that the new understanding of social deviants as a distinct social group of marginalized people, initiated by Goffman, was developed and well articulated by Horowitz and Liebowitz (1968). Adopting a conflict perspective which saw deviance as a conflict between superordinates who make the rules and subordinates who violate them (*ibid.*: 282), and which drew on the insights of Mills, Lemert, and Becker, Horowitz and Liebowitz grasped the essential point about the various rebellions and voices of defiance at the end of the sixties, namely that there had been a blurring in reality of the usual academic distinction between political marginality and social deviance. As they observed, McCarthyism had already broadened the definition of radicalism to include even minor forms of dissent, but now political radicalism was adopting the new tactics of civil disobedience and Third World guerrilla movements, and often the cultural lifestyles of oppressed or progressive groups; politics was melding with the avant-garde. It was becoming more socially deviant, as well as more militant. At the same time, social deviants were becoming increasingly politically aware, forming self-help groups, anti-professional therapy groups, pressure groups, communities and communes, and taking increasingly politically coherent positions on the roots of their stigmatization. Moreover, 'a new set of cultural heroes, dance forms, art forms, coalesce to define not just a classic generational revolt for the rage to live, but for a particularistic expression of immediate personal liberation as a prelude to a distant public equalitarianism.' Deviants were increasingly politicized, increasingly ideologically self-conscious;

art forms had melded with life forms. The result of this twin-pronged development in politics and culture was 'the disruption of the legitimation system of American society':

> It is becoming increasingly clear that these marginals threaten to destroy the fruits of general affluence, and indeed threaten to disrupt the entire system . . . it might well be that the extent of deviance in the past was not sufficient to cause more than a ripple in the political system. In the emerging system, with automation and cybernetics creating greater dislocation and marginal employment, personal deviance may generate a distinct transformation in normal political functions; it marks the point at which the political system cannot cope with deviant expressions of discontent.
>
> *(ibid.: 293, 295)*

Horowitz and Liebowitz, like many others around this time, made the Marcusean point that this melding of social and political deviance revolved around the lumpenproletariat which was growing larger every day within American cities – and especially its black component, as expressed in the followings of Fanon and Malcolm X – replacing the working and middle classes as the deciding political force in America. Watts and Newark had brought black rage, and state repression, to the surface. The distrust of formal politics and increasingly centralized government was obvious, so too the political and military character of riots as forms of guerrilla warfare, and the inability of the political system to maintain equilibrium between increasingly polarized classes; many, consequently, feared that 'totalitarianism is the perfect solution to the problem of disorder' *(ibid.: 295)*. 'Political legitimacy is itself subject to change in order to meet the demands of a society in which social deviants and political marginals have become more, rather than less, important in determining the structure of American society' *(ibid.: 296)*.

The importance of Horowitz and Liebowitz's essay is that it makes it clear to us today why the concept of social deviance could not be overhauled at the end of the sixties, even though the developments described above compelled 'social scientists to reconsider their definitions of the entire range of social phenomena – from deviance to politics'. Social deviance was being celebrated by many liberals as an innovative critique of the worst elements of the American social order. Indeed, today, its ethos has produced a President of the United States who once aligned himself with the anti-war movement and was probably not averse to the occasional joint. Moreover, social deviance was being celebrated in a way that was fully aware of its psychoanalytic significance as a breach and rejection of unwanted repressions:

> toward an extreme and libertarian ethos replacing Puritanism . . . The ideology of the New Left . . . is based on freedom from repression: freedom for the Negro from the effects of racial discrimination;

freedom for the student from the constraints of university regulations; freedom for the young generation from the demands of their
elders; and freedom for politically powerless groups from the growing
authority of the centralized State. In this sense, Freud feeds the ideology of the New Left at least as much as Marx defined the ideology
of the Old Left.

(*ibid.*: 289)

The psychoanalytic dimension of the concept of deviance was now explod-
ing in full colour; the contradictions within psychiatry fully exposed to
general political light. The Norm, both internal and external, was under
attack.

Social deviance really was in full flower; it *was* one of the 'fruits of general
affluence' (it even celebrated its fruitiness), not a big threat to those fruits;
and it was frequently very middle class and educated. It celebrated its own
defiance; it developed its own music, dress and language; it parodied itself
and derided WASP culture. The political problem it posed was 'how to
avoid social disorder while at the same time avoiding the problem of total
social control', said Horowitz and Liebowitz, in true Durkheimian style.

This was hardly a time for sociologists to declare that deviance was a
dead concept. Far from it, it was all too tempting to take the concept and
give it a new behavioural meaning as a political rejection of the established
social order. *In this sense, the late sixties gave the concept of deviance a
whole new lease of life, a second wind.* Theoretically, it may have been
riddled with contradictions as an attempt to conceptualize the gap between
crime and difference, but, when it was effectively adopted by so many in
their ordinary social practice, liberal sociology simply adjusted its sails and
went with the wind. Deviance now became mainly a mode of emancipation and a healthy form of critique; a reduction of the Durkheimian concept
to its liberal component. The liberal-pluralist version of deviancy theory
could thus adopt the idea of deviance as social dissent and give it new
meaning as both a powerful label and a cultural-political practice of
refusal or dissent to repression and élitism. It was that theoretical impetus,
among several others, which was to produce the development of the central idea of *The New Criminology* (Taylor *et al.*, 1973) that deviance was
a quasi-political form of social practice; an idea which was clearly emerging,
albeit loosely, in American sociology at the end of the sixties.

This new lease of life was based on borrowed time, and was therefore,
inevitably, short. For the political reality that emerged in the seventies was
that there was really very little in common between the various groups
assembled under the banner of social deviance; their 'long march through
the institutions' was to be diffused and confused by the fact that they were
assembled under a banner defined by their opposition. Ultimately, deviance
was not their category and it did not amount to a substantial basis for
sustained collective rebellion. Not for the first time, it was soon to become
clear that deviance as a general category, as a way of grasping a collection

of human practices and social censures, was totally unstable, empirically unworkable and logically incoherent.

Inverting its social evaluation and making it a positive form, however, was in effect to enable social deviance to serve a purpose as a rhetorical justification for the rebellious unity that prevailed at that time. But it did not, and could not, alter the fact that the category of social deviance could never be intellectually sufficient for the task it was now being asked to perform. It simply could not function for long under the weight of the obligation to describe both bank robbery and political dissent, gay culture and rape, or insanity and corruption: there was simply no general behavioural unity describable as deviance other than the social censures that constituted its definition. The Great Revolt of the late sixties and early seventies was mainly a revolt for freedom and creativity against repressive stigmatizing norms; it had no single, new, theory of life without repressive norms or of which norms could be retained to found a new life with order. It had no theory of excess, or of the limits of unreason. Deviance was turned on its head; not rethought. It was ultimately a negation of a negation, as Marcuse might have put it, not a re-constructive moment.

The higher immorality

The new lease of life could not last long. Plainly, the concept of deviance did not so much describe a generality of dissenting practices as express a series of selective censures by the powerful groups of society. The overt deconstruction of the concept of deviance in the United States began with the essays of Liazos (1972) and Thio (1973).

Mills had already established a powerful critique of contemporary morality in his book *The Power Élite* (1956), foreshadowed by various earlier essays. The essence of his position now became axiomatic as American sociology entered the seventies, although all too often remaining unacknowledged. Mills had observed in acute detail the 'higher immorality' of the power élite: the corruption, the sinecures, the privilege, the crime, the clinical exploitation and the dissembling. His phrase, the higher immorality, captured his point well, although it was clear that he saw 'white-collar crime' as a problem of 'structural immorality' (Mills, 1967: 331). In his essay of 1952, 'Diagnosis of our moral uneasiness', we see the kind of analysis which was to take the stage in the early seventies (*ibid.*: 330). The black market of the war, the post-war integration of gangsterism into big business, the regular use of bribery to gain ascent and the corruption of public life were all noted as Mills asserted the corrupting character of the institutions of modern society. As he prophetically observed, the question was not whether Senator Nixon was 'morally insensitive' but whether any politician who had risen so fast could have done so without 'a somewhat blunted moral sensitivity' (*ibid.*: 331). Older values no longer grip us, he argued. We have not rejected them, they have just become hollow and the morality of rejecting them is also unclear: 'No moral terms of acceptance are any longer available, but neither are any moral terms of rejection' (*ibid.*: 332). Many personal relations have become part of public relations, 'a sacrifice of selfhood on a personality market, to the sole end of individual success' (*ibid.*). The power élite wields enormous power, yet has never had to win the moral consent of those over whom it rules. Old moralities are trotted out and mass-marketed as 'decorous excuses' or moral justifications, which leads to the 'banalization' of older values. Modernity, he argued, strips values of their meaningful content in the anonymous, market-oriented, individualistic, battle for ascent. As Bob Dylan once put it, 'money doesn't talk, it swears'. Money, said Mills, was the one thing that was regularly valued. 'Practical' now meant private gain, and 'common sense' denoted financial sense. In short:

> If there *is* a genuine moral aim, it will continuously be made relevant to practical policies and operations. Mere *profession* of 'ultimate moral aims' is simply cant, the repetition of which, in an immoral context, increases the amoral cynicism of half-intelligent people...
>
> Where there are moral men in immoral institutions, you seek to improve the institutions. When there are immoral men in moral institutions, you kick the rascals out. When you are confronted by immoral men in immoral institutions, you follow Jefferson's advice and revolt.
>
> (*ibid.*: 337)

The essay by Liazos (1972) did not develop the argument very far, but it did register several crucial blows in the deconstruction of the concept of deviance. He observed, after perusing the textbooks, that:

(a) the 'continued use of the word "deviant" (and its variants), despite its invidious distinctions and connotations, ... belies our explicit statements on the equality of the people under consideration' (*ibid.*: 105). Deviance implies difference *and* inferiority, as Szasz had emphasized:

> Words have lives of their own. However much sociologists insist that the term 'deviant' does not diminish the worth of the person or group so categorized, the implication of inferiority adheres to the word. Indeed, sociologists are not wholly exempt from blame: they describe addicts and homosexuals as deviants, but never Olympic champions or Nobel prize winners...
>
> The term 'social deviants' ... does not make sufficiently explicit – as the terms 'scapegoat' or 'victim' do – that majorities usually categorize persons or groups as 'deviant' in order to set them apart as inferior beings and to justify their social control, oppression, persecution, or even complete destruction.
>
> (Szasz, 1973: xxv–xxvi)

As Liazos noted, by 1972 several textbook writers had expressed uneasiness about the continued use of the category of deviance, but it did not stop them continuing to use it, usually, he discovered, to refer to delinquency, addiction, prostitution, suicide, homosexuality, mental illness and political radicalism.

(b) The textbook use of the word deviant usually excluded the crimes of officials, the crimes of the powerful, institutional deviance, corporate crime.

(c) The texts still focused upon the subculture and identity of the deviant rather than upon the persecutors, the agencies of social control.

(d) The texts failed to register the point, so acutely felt by Liazos after the killing of George Jackson in San Quentin in 1971, that 'most prisoners are *political prisoners*' because their actions result from 'current social and political conditions', not psychopathic personalities (Liazos, 1972: 108).

(e) Sociologists tended to take current definitions of deviance as the only ones worthy of attention.

(f) The sociology of deviance tended to ignore the fact that 'the corporate economy' is much more violent than so-called criminals and that 'the most destructive use of violence in the last decade has been the war in Vietnam'.

In short, Liazos concluded, the sociology of deviance was the study of nuts, sluts and perverts rather than the study of 'covert, institutional and normal' deviance. It was thus biased and perpetuated the concept of deviance, and many other moral judgements too. The daily violence of the capitalist economy, in condemning so many to poverty, ill health and exploitation, and the daily violence of institutional racism, for example, were ignored because their agencies were the ones with the most influence in defining deviance publicly as the province of nuts, sluts and perverts. Instead, the field was guilty of broad, meaningless, generalizations and confusing abstractions which effectively served to avoid the specification of the people who committed the worst sins and of the structural forms which perpetuated serious, daily, violence. It was thus an ideological smokescreen which relativized morality, blamed everybody and specified little.

Thio's essay (1973) also criticized the neglect of the crime and deviance of the powerful, and argued that this showed a class bias in the field. Unlike Liazos, Thio thought that the problem lay with the users of the concept of deviance rather than the concept itself. More so than Liazos, he developed a clear position, albeit a crude one, which saw deviance as a violation of élite rules and the power élite as the main *causal* agency of deviance through their sustenance of the unequal power structure that gave rise both to 'deviant behaviour' and the dominant definitions of deviance. Thus Thio concluded, like Liazos, that the sociology of deviance in the USA had hitherto been profoundly ideologically biased. It had been a servant of the power élite, and this had resulted in 'no breakthrough in the field' because this relation had 'seriously delimited the phenomenon of deviance to be studied by professional sociologists' (*ibid*.: 9). Explicitly, therefore, he retained a belief in the validity of the search for a general theory of deviance while holding that the search had been conducted too narrowly.

These two essays took American sociology of deviance to the brink of a dissolution of the field of study, but held back from the crucial theoretical steps of *superseding* the concept of deviance and abandoning the search for a *general* theory of deviance. And there things were to remain, right up to the present. Meanwhile, the concept itself had gone on tour to Europe – with profound consequences.

Deviance, politics and street-fighting man: the European tour

Until 1968, British sociology, and European sociology generally, had not taken much notice of the American sociology of deviance. Typically, its analysis was of crime, and it focused on inner-city relative deprivation and juvenile delinquency, drawing on American functionalist sociology in a pragmatic, uncommitted, sort of way. Then, in 1968, a group of young sociologists in Britain formed the National Deviancy Conference (NDC). The concept of deviance had come home to Europe.

Folk devils, the mass media and the NDC

Conceptually, the NDC had no shared view, and made few theoretical advances beyond the position reached within American sociology. It represented a dynamic hotchpot of interactionists, anarchists, phenomenologists and Marxists. Nevertheless, right from the beginning (see Cohen, 1971: 15), it was clear what it was against. This opposition was important since it provided a platform for the changes which followed in the mid-seventies. It represented a point of no return for the concept of deviance. The NDC was to stretch the meaning and viability of the radical conception of deviance to its absolute limit – so far in fact that it collapsed under the strain.

At first, the sociology of the NDC members was little different from American deviancy theory and quite derivative of American sociology generally. However, one clear, sophisticated and valuable development emerged and that was a version of deviancy amplification theory which was much more collective than the American variant (see Young, 1971; Cohen, 1973; Cohen and Young, 1973; Hall, 1974; Hall *et al.*, 1978). The latter had tended to focus upon single institutions, like the police, dealing with single individuals; the late 1960s British version, notably in the work of Cohen and Young, had much more of a collective flavour about it. We saw a sociology grappling with the collective clashes between deviant groups and the rough alliance of hegemonic groups and forces we British think of as the Establishment. Cohen and Young did not theorize these collective clashes in terms of the Gramscian concept of hegemony – Stuart Hall accomplished that a little later – but what they did was to analyse and describe the more collective features of the conflicts between a deviant group or subculture and the establishment forces aligned in disapproval against it. The issue was not so much a Lemertian concern with the

reorganization of individual identity but a rather more macroscopic interest in the whole society's ability to sustain and reproduce some kind of
order in the face of recurrent cultural conflicts. This was very much a
reflection of the cultural character of the 1968 renaissance in Britain with
its unique youth subcultures and musical innovation. It was an interest
that was to throw much attention on to the role of the mass media in
signifying that social movement in terms of a deviant threat to social
order.

Stan Cohen's book *Folk Devils and Moral Panics* (1973) illustrated well
the general characteristics described above. It was particularly significant
because of one conceptual development, Cohen's formulation of the concept
of moral panic:

> Societies appear to be subject, every now and then, to periods of
> moral panic. A condition, episode, person or group of persons emerges
> to become defined as a threat to societal values and interests; its
> nature is presented in a stylized and stereotypical fashion by the mass
> media; the moral barricades are manned by editors, bishops, politi-
> cians and other right-thinking people; socially accredited experts pro-
> nounce their diagnoses and solutions; ways of coping are evolved or
> (more often) resorted to; the condition then disappears, submerges
> or deteriorates and becomes more visible. Sometimes the object of
> the panic is quite novel and at other times it is something which has
> been in existence long enough, but suddenly appears in the limelight.
> Sometimes the panic passes over and is forgotten, except in folklore
> and collective memory; at other times it has more serious and long-
> lasting repercussions and might produce such changes as those in
> legal and social policy or even in the way the society conceives itself.
>
> One of the most recurrent types of moral panic in Britain since the
> war has been associated with the emergence of various forms of
> youth culture (originally almost exclusively working class, but often
> recently middle class or student based) whose behaviour is deviant or
> delinquent.
>
> *(ibid.: 9)*

Clearly, at one level, this was a very Durkheimian formulation, stressing
'societies' in general, the apparently voluntary character of the panic, the
interaction and deep interconnection between signifier (the discourse of
punitive reaction) and signified (juvenile delinquency), the moral aspect of
panic, and the almost random episodic nature of moral panic. Yet there
was also a clear sense of class and power, suggesting that we could rely
on Durkheim for insights into general societal change/evolution and on
Marx for the internal, detailed, dynamics of that change; an approach that
was not uncommon in British sociology in the 1960s. Of course, the
overall picture presented is not far removed from Lemert's analysis in
Social Pathology, work Cohen acknowledged, along with that of Becker,
Gusfield and the American sociology of collective behaviour. But what is

of special interest to our story is the very strong way that the collective character of deviance was understood. Cohen, more clearly, and more elegantly, than any of the American sociologists of deviance, presented deviance as a recurrent and structural feature of all forms of social organization. All hint of individual pathology was erased and all that mattered was societal evolution and group dynamics. The picture was unequivocally societal, albeit very little removed from Durkheim, and even the 1930-ish psychoanalytic sense of a deep, unconscious, irrationality, embodied in Cohen's use of the term panic, was located at the collective level.

Cohen deployed a deviancy amplification model to explain how the petty delinquencies of groups of (mostly working-class) youths on brief moral holidays at seaside resorts close to London were identified, symbolized, policed, dramatized and blown up into serious threats to life and limb, law and order, and business-as-usual, by the agencies of the 'control culture'. The social reaction had the effect of polarizing the groups into types (Mods and Rockers) and hardening their opposition to the older-generation culture of the Establishment. As is so often the case, the author himself provided a revealing and honest description of the bulk of the book: 'So far, in a series of somewhat mixed metaphors, we have viewed the objects of the moral panic as Rorschach blots, folk devils, actors on a stage, images flickering on a screen. This was, after all, how they appeared to society: as processed images' (Cohen, 1973: 177). Cohen balanced this up in his last chapter with a well-grounded account of the sociological bases of 'expressive fringe delinquency', arguing that the signifier was connected to the signified. He emphasized the angst of urban working-class and lower middle-class youth, its sense of 'personal redundancy and waste', and its alienation from expensive, conventional, leisure outlets. With echoes of Finestone, and Downes (1966), Cohen saw the kids manufacturing their own excitement and leisure, and 'doing nothing', in a stylized way, as a teenage subcultural and sub-political way of having fun while expressing identity. Both instrumentally and symbolically, the kids expressed an undirected resentment against the culture of the older generations of all classes. Songs from The Who and The Rolling Stones said it all: 'I can't explain', 'The kids are alright', 'My generation', 'Get off my cloud' and 'I can't get no satisfaction'. The Mods in particular captured the spirit of modernism with their moody, passive, class-less, resentment against an affluent society which had offered them consumerism yet had failed, until the commercialization of *their* music and *their* styles in clothes, to offer their values a significant place in the social order. Cohen paid full attention to the significance of music, clothes, scooters, bikes and style and thus fully represented the current convulsions of British culture in his sociology. It was a very balanced amplification thesis, which expressed well the liberal interactionists' sense of deviance as very much a collective transaction, but in a distinctively British, late sixties, way.

As in Young's work, such an analysis threw the attention of the sociology of deviance on to the mass media, while retaining the focus on cultural conflicts around style and values. Cohen's book was significant in the history of the sociology of deviance in that, while not particularly conceptually innovative, it demonstrated how images of deviance were mediated and deeply structured by collective ideological conflicts. Sociologists of deviance were now thinking not simply in terms of conflicts of interest and power differentials but in a more complex fashion about the way that deviance was a site and expression of a real struggle over certain collective representations or images. Cohen's analysis has a lasting power, possibly greater than that of *The New Criminology*, because it did not foist an overly or falsely political consciousness on to the actors in the drama. Concepts of projection, envy, resentment, anger, inexplicable change and angst are at least as valuable as concepts of critique, emancipation, ideology, rejection and resistance. Cohen's combination of Durkheim, the 1930s vision of cultural irrationality, symbolic interactionism, the class contradictions within the leisure culture of the welfare state, the signifying power of the modern mass media, and an acute awareness of the general significance of the Mod, effected a renewed expression of the most penetrating features of modernist analysis.

At the end of the day, it may be that the bewildering deceptiveness, contradictoriness and speed of modernity might make the politicization of deviance at the end of the 1960s into another merely insubstantive and fanciful blip of opposition against modernity's relentless march towards the elision of any residual sense of structure, form and control from the collective unconsciousness. Socialism may have had its last fling in the 'new' criminology and the general resistances of 1968; they may have been a brief burst of realist critique and organized resistance in a much more powerful maelstrom of irrational and disorganized angsts. But, then, they may not have been. It may be, on the other hand, that Cohen's rich modernism was the last fling of a science of representation against the agnostic forces of disintegration; the last stand of the Mod, like the smooth images of middle-class life in Hockney, in the face of a decreasing sense of meaning and connection within a white middle class, increasingly surrounded on one side by a relative surplus population of immigrants, redundants and anonymous monads and, on the other, by a mini-class of super-rich purveyors of disconnected images of disconnection. (Certainly, the next major empirical study in this line of transition from the American labelling perspective to neo-Marxist sociology of crime was *Policing the Crisis* (Hall *et al.*, 1978), a study of the moral panic about urban black delinquency.) Caught in the middle of these two classes, which appear locked in a polarizing dialectic of commercial exploitation, political incorporation, surreal rejection and sublime violence, the Mod may have been neither a Rorschach blot for society's fearful confusion nor a representative of a 'new wave' of heroic space-creators, but just another moral icon in the history of social censures. As capital expands, speeds up ever faster, dissolves new technologies in favour of hyper-technology and converts us all into images with or without value in a rapidly de-materializing materialism, it may be that the Mod was at one and the same time the last stand of a coherent representation of the devil and the first form of an insubstantial flicker on a perpetual screen of daily denunciations in a world where the screen is more significant than the signifier or the signified.

To Cohen's credit, his analysis enabled such thoughts, and indeed, I would say, through his particular focus on the mass media, provoked them. Something in the text suggests an inchoate forerunner of post-modernism, even though Cohen himself presented a coherent connection between signifier and signified. That something is perhaps captured in this recurrent theme from Cohen's work:

> We are dealing on a large scale – and therefore the problem is infi-nitely more complex – with what Laing and the anti-psychiatry school are concerned with on a small scale. The argument is not that there is 'nothing there' when somebody is labelled mentally ill or that this person has no problems, but that the reaction to what is observed or inferred is fundamentally inappropriate. The initial step is one of unmasking and debunking: an intrinsic quality of the sceptical and transactional perspective on deviance.
>
> (Cohen, 1973: 203–4)

Cohen said that the media were important carriers and producers of moral panics and imagery of folk devils. Images of deviants in industrial societies were, he argued, 'invariably received at second hand', 'already processed by the mass media' (*ibid.*: 16). Noting that the mass media spend a lot of time on deviance, he claimed that when media moral indignation coincided with a generally felt need to protect certain values there was a basis for the creation of a new rule or social problem. Of course, the more visible or vulnerable the stigmatized group the more likely it is to adopt an identity provided by the mass media and collude with the process of deviance amplification. In any case, the mass media dramatized, denounced, dis-sociated and exploited deviance – a process not likely to induce accuracy of coverage. In a moral panic, easy targets were picked, whether actual or merely putative (*ibid.*: 138), and portrayed as recognizable folk devils. The media thus had a crucial role to play in the definition, stigmatization and amplification of deviance. Clearly, the more powerful and inaccurate the media coverage, and the more the labelled deviants respond to its imagery, the greater the distance created between the social images of deviance and the concrete social contexts of the original individual deviation. Amplifi-cation was also distanciation from sociological reality.

What was to follow in the 1970s in Europe began to disconnect signifier and signified, but Cohen, like Laing, had already begun to suggest that the relation between signifier and signified was 'fundamentally inappropriate'. Insanity seemed sane and sanity seemed lunatic. Deviance was being seen as at least as normal as normality, and the latter looked very deviant indeed. The signifiers were becoming unhooked. They were being rendered as parodies of themselves. Reality was mocked up, and mock-ups became reality. Deviance became politics, politics became deviant. Connections between images of deviance and actual social practices became less coherent, less clear, less persuasive. The media spectacle was taking over at the expense of any dialectic with reality. What was deviance became less clear. Who were the deviants became less clear – was it the corporate rich, with their corruptions, client genocides, tax evasions and environmental destruction, or the kinky transvestites and swingers, with their creative play on the corpses of disappearing sexual norms? By the time of the de-regulated eighties and the enterprise culture, deviance had gone. Drowned in a sea of amoralism. Cut loose from its moorings in polarized but coherent opposed moralities, and awash in a ubiquitous mass circulation of de-moralized images, it became just another d-word, alongside daily, de-regulated, diversity divorced from any deep dalliance with deity and diabolism. Symbolically displaced in the postmodern vista by death, drugs and dependency.

Jock Young's *The Drugtakers* was important, in my view, for its clarity of presentation of two particular themes in British sociology of deviance: (a) moral relativism, and (b) the role of the mass media in the deviance amplification process. In relation to psychotropic drugtaking (some legal, some illegal), Young's subject matter, his position on relativism (see Young, 1971: Chapter 3) can be summarized briefly:

- Firstly, he observed that drugtaking is not necessarily deviant, but is deviant to those who condemn it. Thus, there is a social conflict over the subject. The definition of taking certain drugs as a form of individual pathology is thus unfounded and may often be a function of the threat posed to the middle-class value system and lifestyle by the drug subculture.
- At a minimum, such derogatory definition reflects differential socialization patterns in modern society. Drugtaking is, in fact, an individual solution to problems of modernity which is chosen, often because adequate alternatives do not exist. It is meaningful in terms of the (sub)cultural values which the user subscribes to, and its authenticity for the individual cannot be spoofed away by the attribution of the influence of a small group of 'evil pushers'.
- The psychiatric and sociological jargon of 'psychopathy', 'social disorganization', 'undersocialization', or 'retreatism' pretends to objectivity but does nothing other than reflect the values of middle-class professionals. Yet deviants, unless they are 'highly ideologically buttressed', are very vulnerable to the influence of these experts. Given the degree of artificial disciplinary divisions and the narrowness of their middle-class world, the 'experts can, from the vantage of their cloistered chauvinism, scarcely grasp the totality of the social world even in terms of their own values let alone take a critical stance outside of these values' (*ibid.*: 73).
- 'Experts' therefore have the dangerous power to negotiate and change reality so that it fits the fantasy of their theories and proposed controls or reforms. They also have the extremely dangerous and more concrete

power to conduct neurosurgery and administer very powerful drugs to diagnosed deviants (*ibid.*: 78–9).

- Through the deviance amplification process, the reality of the censured individual is reconstructed and treated, for example through medicine and total institutions, so that eventually it can begin to appear as a justification for the theories and programmes of the experts.

The echoes of Goffman and Laing were explicit in the last part of Young's assessment, and we will return to the significance of Laing's critique of psychiatry shortly.

What was distinctive and valuable in his comments on relativism, apart from their clarity, vitality and succinctness, was the fact that whereas American sociologists such as Becker had actively defended the deviant's right to be different in a pluralistic world, Young, like other European social scientists, openly poured scorn on the knowledge and power of the judges and experts of morality and health. It was less a case of recognizing equality of perception in a confused and pluralistic world, but rather more a matter of developing a forceful critique of therapeutic and moralistic knowledges which claimed to be sciences yet contained monumental errors and bigotry. The sociology of deviance, in its British guise, was becoming more confident and more radical. It challenged the epistemological and substantive claims of the doctors, lawyers, psychiatrists, judiciary, journalists and criminologists with a greater depth and ferocity than it had in the USA. At the risk of a slight exaggeration, the judges of morality were now being presented as the ones who had the strange views, values and practices.

So, again, the question was sharply posed: who was the deviant? Who was the bigger danger – the drug addict or the surgeon who imagined that neurosurgery could and should be used to deal with the 'primitive emotions' (quoted in *ibid.*) of the addict? American sociology had arrived at the economic and political delinquencies of the powerful; British sociology of deviance began with severe scepticism about the validity of established knowledge about crime and deviance. It went right to the root of the concept of deviance itself. Perhaps, as a foreign visitor, that concept was more exposed for what it was when it was abroad. If its scientific proponents could be presented as mistaken, misguided, self-righteous, blinkered, dogmatic and dangerous, as well as self-interested, the concept itself could not possibly survive long.

In terms of the mass media, Young's work was a source of inspiration for Cohen (1973) and the two later put together an anthology on deviance and the mass media (Cohen and Young, 1973). In *The Drugtakers*, Young drew upon the work of Leslie Wilkins to outline the thesis that deviance amplification was much less likely in small-scale societies and that the 'significant information drop' in modernity produced a very different way of dealing with deviance (Young, 1971: 175). In the former type of society, information was 'rich and multidimensional' and less likely to permit individual status and identity to be reduced to a single trait such as deviance.

In modernity, however, where there is severe social segregation, lack of direct information about labelled deviants creates a great reliance on information from the mass media, and the media's need to give the public what it wants, to maintain circulation in a competitive market, means that they constantly play upon the 'normative worries' of large sectors of the population, often utilizing 'outgroups as living Rorschach Blots on to which collective fears and doubts are projected' (*ibid.*: 179). Young's *tour de force* on the conference circuit was to show how the 'stereotypical distorted image of the deviant' was contrasted by the mass media 'against the overtypical, hypothetical "man in the street", that persistent illusion of consensual sociology and politics' (*ibid.*). Again, the Durkheimian theme is strong. The boundaries of normality and order are reinforced through the censure of the deviant and disordered; but in this case, Young, like Cohen, was emphasizing that this process only occurred effectively in modern societies through a considerable distortion of social reality. The forte of radical British deviancy theory seems to have been its capacity to demonstrate that, in divided, conflictful, societies, normative censure and the reproduction of dominant morality tended to be economic with the truth. Its first implication, therefore, was always that one should be sceptical today about the truth value of any censure of deviance; the second was perhaps that such censures were constantly open to becoming the playthings of the economic and political needs and biases of powerful groups – and sublimated expressions of the fears of subordinate and insecure populations.

Like the work of Cohen, and other members of the NDC, Young's analysis was also notable because of its 'engagement with the enemy'. It is perhaps one of the striking features of radical sociology of deviance in the late sixties and early seventies in Britain that it was constantly, and vigorously, engaged in a detailed critique or assault on the established orthodoxies of what Young called moral absolutism. The involved passion and detail of that critique gave the work considerable dynamism and verve. It contrasts sharply with the more clinical, detached and abstracted radical sociology of the 1980s, a world where the validity of moral difference is now intellectually axiomatic. In the late sixties, it had to be fought for. Cohen and Young had done a lot to show that it was not simply that deviance was a category of the powerful but that claims about deviance were short on truth value, and, indeed, could amount to 'rank misperception' (*ibid.*: 183).

Stuart Hall's seminal paper 'Deviance, politics and the media' (1974) advanced and broadened these themes, arguing that there was a fine line between being defined as a political minority or being condemned as a deviant outgroup. This was an important step in the argument, because, although much was owed to Horowitz and Liebowitz (1968), Hall was arguing, very clearly for the first time in the sociology of deviance, that the process of rendering a social group deviant was a question of open political struggle. It was not a simple, given, fact that a group was deviant, but a matter of hegemonic contestation. Drawing on Althusser and Poulantzas, and espousing the positions of the then recently translated Gramsci, Hall dragged the implicit political assumptions of the existing sociology of deviance into the glaring spotlight of contemporary debates in political science. The concept of ideology was deployed to the full, and the concept of hegemony was introduced into our field with great consequence. Hall demolished the assumption of a normative consensus, so common within post-war American sociology, with the argument that 'consensus politics' had been a phase of 'institutional politics in managed capitalism' (Hall, 1974: 272). The welfare state had not involved a decentralization of élite powers, merely an incorporation of organized subaltern powers under the umbrella of the national interest and 'the end of ideology'. All alternative politics were thus marginalized and rendered politically deviant. The Rooseveltian welfare state which had spawned the formation of the sociology of deviance had amounted to a development of the ideological state apparatuses and state economic mechanisms which had only contained the threat from the organized working class at the expense of the creation of (a) a new lumpenproletariat of excluded groups and (b) a new set of political deviants of the hard left. These groups were the ones who were making demands on the hegemony of the ruling-class bloc at the end of the sixties and in the early seventies. These demands were 'proto-political' and insufficiently developed to be 'pivotal to revolutionary political transformation'.

Consensus politics had thus directly produced 'the politics of deviance' (*ibid.*: 273). 'The drive to install consensual forms of domination at the heart of the political process itself' had engendered a political, deviant, counter-culture. This new political deviance did not just emerge, it was also constructed – through considerable interpretive, ideological, work by the chief agencies of the new 'political signification'. Radical sociology of deviance was not just studying new forms of praxis, it was monitoring new forms of labelling or signification. Both, in Hall's view, were aspects of the new form of hegemonic struggle taking shape around 1970. Hall's description of political labelling remains a classic and illustrates the value of the then emerging fields of cultural studies and semiotics for the analysis of the social construction of images of deviance:

> The work of 'classifying out' the political universe, of building up meaningful 'semantic zones' to which deviant acts can be assigned and within which they 'make sense', the process of telescoping, of ascription, of amplifying descriptions and the attribution of 'secondary status traits', the use of charged associative metaphors which summon up old meanings in the service of explaining the unfamiliar, the way discrete events are selectively composed into composite 'action-images' and 'scenarios' of political action, the use of analogies and metaphors which 'transform sentiment into significance', win plausibility and command the assent of uninformed and remote publics: these, and other processes, compose the specificity of the *praxis* of

political signification as a discrete level within the 'ensemble of social relations'.

(*ibid.*: 279)

The analysis of how interlocking meanings can work to signify political deviance or deviant marginality was then in its infancy, but Hall's paper called for the study of the ideological codes deeply entrenched within popular discourses on new forms of social action to show how deviance is socially constructed as an ideological category. Such work was also to show how attributions of deviance were important signifiers within the continuing contest for hegemony of the nation. Deviance, then, was now clearly being rendered as an important sign within political conflict. Deviants did not have to be political for deviance to be deployed as a politically potent label. Alas, Hall was one of few; too many leapt quickly from the observation that the attribution of deviant status was a highly political and conflictful process to the claim, albeit frequently tentative, that deviants themselves were usually politically conscious.

Hall's analysis gave considerable importance to the concept of ideology. Ideologies were, he said, 'one of the principal mechanisms which expand and amplify the dominance of certain class interests into a hegemonic formation' (*ibid.*: 290). Ideologies were 'maps of problematic social reality' (Geertz's phrase). These maps had to be constantly re-worked and justified, and they were constantly challenged. The maintenance of the hegemony of the directive class was an active process, not a static social function, and the ideological formations specifying deviance (in our terms, the social censures) were an important part of that process. Consent for state rule in the early 1970s had to be won, it could not be assumed as in the 1950s. This process made the mass media very important politically, but no more than other apparatuses or institutions concerned with the construction of social knowledge. Phenomenology and symbolic interactionism had been important in drawing us to the analysis of meanings, but his analysis had to be returned to the 'level of the social formation, via the critical concepts of power, ideology, and conflict' (*ibid.*: 298).

Even though it was no more than an outline of a theoretical scheme, Hall's essay, in my view, marked the beginning of a whole new, coherent, framework for the sociological analysis of the attributions of deviance. It began to bear fruit immediately in the work of his colleagues and students in the Birmingham School of Contemporary Cultural Studies. *Resistance through Rituals* (Hall and Jefferson, 1975) brought together several important essays arguing a new theory of subcultures as ideological forms of response to problems within lived social relations, but the scheme came to full fruition in *Policing the Crisis* (Hall *et al.*, 1978).[1] Quite rightly, and in a sense naturally, the concept of deviance was being returned to its home within an ideological matrix surrounding the concept of culture. It was precipitated in the late1930s in the USA amidst much concern for the meaning of culture and amidst many political attempts to construct a coherent hegemonic culture, so for it to be eventually swallowed up by the much bigger fish of sociology of culture and political theory was nothing less than poetic justice. It could be reasonably argued that it had now been fully theorized and thus had been read right back to its roots in a political theory of culture. Once a theoretical concept has been thus re-examined, so that its roots, coherence, failings and silences are obvious, it is ripe for complete supersession or overhaul. It had done its time and so had the politics which precipitated it.

However, there was still the connotation of psychiatric validity – that lingered on in the concept and as long as that remained no amount of coherent political rethinking would have shifted the concept of deviance. Political critique would have simply remained as political critique. The discrediting of psychiatric knowledge was a necessary precondition for the final discrediting of deviance as a theoretical concept.

The discrediting of psychiatry

During the mid-1930s, the language of deviance had emerged with the union of sociological psychiatry and psychiatric sociology. Since that time, psychiatry and psychoanalysis had continued to play an important part in the development of the sociology of deviance, partly in the analysis of 'faulty' socialization and partly in the analysis of 'social' movements in the collective psyche. Goffman had all but finished off psychiatry as a valid scientific practice of individual deficiency, as we saw in Chapter 10. By the time of Laing's *Politics of Experience* (1967), the seal was set on the radical critique of psychiatric knowledge and the 1930s union was to end in a late 1960s divorce.

It was a critique of considerable potency and consequence. So much has already been written on the subject (see, for example, Fanon, 1967; Foucault, 1967, 1973; Szasz, 1973; Pearson, 1975; Jacoby, 1977; Sedgwick, 1982), but we must note the key elements briefly because it effectively pulled the epistemological rug from underneath the practice of using the term deviant. Without any implicit psychiatric validity, what could be left within the concept of deviance except a moral–political judgement? Whether or not the critique of psychiatry was entirely valid, or even fully extended (for it never tackled the Freudian left of Fromm and Marcuse) is besides the point – the fact that sufficient doubt was created within sociology was enough to sustain the divorce.

Pearson's account (1975) of the late sixties critique of psychiatry was not only a good one but also an integral part of the development of the 'new' criminology. It is therefore doubly worth our consideration here, because it not only explained the divorce but also contributed to it. It focused on what became known as the anti-psychiatry movement, rather than on the writings of people such as Foucault. Pearson summarized the anti-psychiatry position as follows:

the requirements of normality, conformity and reasonableness – in a word 'mental health' – are a suffocation which stifles, blocks, and distorts the expression of a fully human consciousness. Learning to live at ease with urban-industrial society requires that men forget and repress much of their experience of a disturbing and destructive social system . . .

Set against this, people who break-down or break-up might also be engaged in a break-through to a different and more complete experience of the self: mental illness is described as one way in which men and women disengage from the taken-for-granted routines of everyday life and undergo a disturbing self-reflection . . . Psychiatrists who disturb this unwitting attempt to reconnoitre and reconstruct the self, with mind-flattening drug therapies, electroshocks, or psychotherapies which insist on conformity to outer (rather than inner) imperatives are . . . false healers. Therapies which interrupt the flow of the person through psychotic episodes simply leave him stranded at the point where he had disconnected himself from old patterns of normality without allowing the vital reconnections to occur. What is needed, then, is not a therapist, but a guide.

(Pearson, 1975: 19–20)

Anti-psychiatry thus not only saw mental illness as a creative form of deviance, just as Durkheim had seen deviance as sometimes a creative critique of social restrictions, it also condemned society and social institutions such as the family as pathological networks which created much pain, repression and unhappiness. Deviance, at least in the form of mental illness, was thus not meaningless pathology but a bold and meaningful choice in the face of destructive adversity. In making this case, the movement thus politicized socialization because it drew the connections between the more damaging routines of everyday life and the broader political structures which produced them:

The schizophrenic stands as a symbol of how society handles individual perceptions of the world which differ from those of conforming man, and how it crushes dawning perceptions of how the world might be seen differently. Because he is different the schizophrenic becomes elevated to a semi-heroic status, both victim and critic of social systems; a victim who identifies in his irrationality the irrationality of the whole, and a hero who points to another rationality which is more completely human.

(*ibid.*: 22)

Echoing a theme which was to recur constantly within the 'new' criminology, the anti-psychiatrists, notably R. D. Laing, jumped from the very justifiable vision of deviance as a meaningful response to social repression to the more ambitious claim that it was a 'semi-heroic' solution for the individual and a sign of incipient political resistance to advanced capitalism. The ideological roots of this leap of faith obviously lay within the political culture of the 1960s. Less obviously, we might note the lack of concreteness in this perspective, as revealed by the fact that Pearson, like many anti-psychiatrists, could continue using the male pronoun as a general one when the majority of mental hospital patients were women. Like Foucault, the anti-psychiatrists glossed over the rather concrete point that the censure of madness was gendered, both in its willingness to target women and in the construction of madness as part of the world of unreason (see Foucault, 1967; Sumner, 1990b).

It is not necessary, of course, to mythologize the schizophrenic to make a valid critique of psychiatric mythology. The point was that attributions of mental illness, like deviance in general, involve many moral judgements. Szasz (1973) made the point this way:

> Our adversaries are not demons, witches, fate, or mental illness. We have no enemy that we can fight, exorcise, or dispel by 'cure'. What we do have are problems in living – whether these be biologic, economic, political, or sociopsychological . . . mental illness is a myth, whose function is to disguise and thus render more palatable the bitter pill of moral conflicts in human relations.
> (Quoted in Pearson, 1975: 26)

As Pearson said, Szasz was not denying the reality of mental illness, discomfort or difficulty but stressing that 'problems of human conduct have a moral and political character which is masked by psychiatric labels, and that medical terminology is quite inappropriate in the sphere of human conduct' (*ibid.*: 26). For Szasz, the psychiatrist is a moral judge, one of the 'secular priests of the Therapeutic State', to use Pearson's phrase. In the positivism of the medical gaze, moral judgement was invisible and madness obvious. Yet, as the Vietnam War made crystal-clear, there was nothing obvious about the attribution of threat to the communist world, when it was the United States that had surrounded that world with its warships and airplanes (Laing, 1968). Who was threatening whom? Clearly, what appeared dangerous and threatening was a moral–political judgement. Moreover, it appeared that the judges were threatening the judged, and the psychiatrists their patients. As Laing said, if people who experience themselves as robots are seen as crazy, then why not people like those psychiatrists who propound theories of human beings which treat them as robots and then even behave as if it were true?

Studies such as Rosenhan's (1973) spectacularly exposed the arbitrariness of psychiatric moral judgement, and the daily use of terms such as hysterical, deranged, deluded and paranoid to describe political militancy of left and right only compounded our worst fears; not to mention the revelations from the USSR on the political use of psychiatry, or the psychiatric attribution of a new disease of 'political malignancy' to dissidents in Africa (see Clifford, 1979). Rather than confronting moral and political issues directly, it had become all too common for the psychiatric society (Castel, 1972) to sidestep them and substitute a psychiatric judgement. Psychiatry might work to justify a liberal policy in some cases, for example on abortion, and thus protect individuals from the harsher effects of the law, but the anti-psychiatrists' thesis was not contradicted by this fact. Psychiatry might shield the deviant from state violence in some instances, but only to capture that individual for its own enterprise in a state-sanctioned diversion. For Szasz and others, psychiatry was 'a slavemaster of the State in controlling and suppressing deviant minorities' (Pearson, 1975: 29).

The anti-psychiatrists frequently juxtaposed the behaviour of the state with that of individuals to illustrate the moral–political judgements involved in both personal and public politics (*ibid*.: 39). The sanity of the girl who thinks she has an atom bomb inside her was compared with the sanity of states that used atom bombs as deterrents. Moreover, the behaviour of the former was frequently posited as an expression or consequence of the behaviour of the latter. Like Reich, they often suggested that the authoritarianism of the state produced the paranoia of individuals, through the intermediate stage of producing authoritarian family relations. From these standpoints, it was a short hop to Szasz's view that psychiatry had replaced the Inquisition as the state-sanctioned vehicle for the identification, witch-hunting and purging of devils in the individual. Like Laing, he believed that psychiatry functioned to save the state from facing up to and taking full responsibility for its actions and policies. Like Durkheim, the anti-psychiatrists saw the scapegoating of the mentally ill functioning to reinforce the (in this case, insane) values and pretences of normality. Mental asylums could be seen as the 'Indian Reservations' of the poor, old, black and female populations (Chesler, 1974) – the receptacles for the judgemental violence of the paranoid state against its surplus populations. Nevertheless, Pearson is right to argue that the anti-psychiatrists did not develop a historically informed analysis of the relation between psychiatry and the modern state, and that the status of 'educative' psychiatry or private psychotherapy is left very unclear.

Pearson argues that what binds the diverse critiques of Szasz, Goffman and Laing together is their underlying commitment to humanism. This philosophical stance was to reverberate throughout the sociology of deviance until its confrontation with a more structural analysis in the early seventies. The anti-psychiatrists owed allegiance to Sartre not Foucault. But, of course, the critique of psychiatry did not just emanate from the writings of the humanistic anti-psychiatry movement. Foucault's very non-humanistic work has been at least as influential in the long run, although it was not so widely read in the English-speaking world at the time. His *Madness and Civilization* (1967) demonstrated that psychiatry is not just an arm of the modern criminal justice system working in the service of the state but also a modern form of knowledge representing the outcome of a long struggle to separate the whole range of unreason from its deep unity with the rationality which permeates state form. Moreover, drawing on

Foucault's later works (1980b, 1985), we can see that the psychiatrist–patient relation, inside or outside the criminal justice system, is an instance of a very specific historic relation to the self. Such considerations would take us well beyond the sociology of deviance and into another text, but even their mere mention makes clear the limits of a humanistic revolt against the scientism of modern psychiatry; similarly, the work of Franz Fanon.

Fanon's *Wretched of the Earth* (1967) demonstrated passionately and lucidly how colonialism was a social system which systematically imposed imperial culture in every nook and cranny of colonized territories, and especially in the minds of the colonized. When the latter resisted with vigour and anger they were healthier; and in normal times they needed many defence mechanisms to prevent their sense of identity and worth from being crushed and expunged. When the organized resistance was low, and when damaging psychological blows took individuals across the threshold of tolerance, the colonized crowded the mental hospitals expressing the pathologies of oppression (see Fanon, 1967: 201). Psychiatry's role in these circumstances was even clearer than in the metropolitan centres: to integrate systematically violated people into a culture which was constantly violating them and threatening to expunge their identity. That was partly a moral judgement in favour of colonialism, and it did work to sustain a constant trade for the psychiatrists, but, above all, it was part of the armoury of violence of the colonial state:

> it is not the soil that is occupied. It is not the ports or the aerodromes. French colonialism has settled itself in the very centre of the Algerian individual and has undertaken a sustained work of clean-up, of expulsion of self, of rationally pursued mutilation.
>
> There is not occupation of the territory on one hand, and independence of the person on the other. It is the country as a whole, its history, its daily pulsation that are contested, disfigured in the hope of a final destruction. Under these conditions, the individual's breathing is an observed, an occupied breathing. It is a combat breathing.
>
> (*ibid.*: 50)

Pearson (1975: 99) commented that 'Fanon's words could stand as a motto for the New Left's view of the political disfigurement of the human subject.' Indeed, such a perspective was the very driving force of the thesis in *The New Criminology* which we will discuss shortly. But Fanon observed the inhumanity of colonialism and made no apology for working as a psychiatrist to heal the wounds of colonialism. He made no heroes out of those who suffered from the pathologies of oppression, nor did he romanticize 'decay'. Nor did he draw upon a notion of human nature, or a universal human health, to justify his critique of colonialism as a pathogenic evil. His writings were used by humanists in radical deviancy theory as evidence for their thesis, but above all Fanon demonstrated that mental illness was a frequent and very painful consequence of oppressive social systems.

Foucault had been profoundly critical of the philosophy of humanism, rejecting any notion of a unitary human subject which could be healed easily by providing a unitary social world for it to live in. A critique of psychiatry clearly does not necessitate a humanist position, nor did the humanism of the anti-psychiatrists seem to produce more than a huge scepticism about psychiatric knowledge and a sustained outcry about some of its absurdities and inhumanities. Nevertheless, as even Foucault himself acknowledged, anti-psychiatry did play an important political role in challenging the edifice of psychiatry. In my view, it challenged the normative validity of its whole project, and exposed that project as a profoundly normative one.

In that way, and this is what really concerns us here, the concept of deviance was finally severed from its theoretical justifications in medical science. The historic unity with psychopathology was shattered. Even at a minimum, we would have to say that there was now too much doubt about the scientificity of psychiatry to enable the category of deviance to draw upon its authority. Again, another powerful precondition for the intellectual collapse of the concept of deviance had come to pass.

Pearson wittily observed, following Ernest Becker (1964), that deviance had fallen into bad company, and the name of that company was medical knowledge. The argument in the present text is that deviance was an anomic émigré adopted by a union of psychiatry and sociology and that its step-parents' divorce caused it to have a complete identity collapse; unable to regulate its own hedonism, and drawn into too many political parties by its European friends, who indeed had deviant sociological ima-ginations, deviance imploded in an excess of over-politicization. But let us give Pearson's *The Deviant Imagination* the final word:

> When medicine inserts itself into an understanding of social diso*rder*, as it does in the medical model of deviance, it expresses an ideology of social order as a *natural phenomenon*. Conformity – rather than being viewed as a *social* accomplishment – is elevated to the status of health. Nonconformity is disqualified as 'sickness'. This embodies a notion of a purified community and a purified identity because one cannot be both ill and well at the same time, although a person can both conform (in some things) and deviate (in others). A view of conformity and deviance as a social accomplishment, which is what any critique of the medical model entails, raises the uncomfortable question of how men construct and maintain social order and how they might reconstruct it. And these are political questions.
>
> (Pearson, 1975: 48)

Without the validity of key psychiatric reference points, the concept of deviance lost a vital justification for its very name. Without a sense of psychological deviation all that is left is a moral censure and a behavioural target. Moreover, with no form of legitimate science available to justify cutting censures and diagnoses of psychopathology, logically we were left with merely swapping insults: 'Psychopath! Fascist! Criminal! Pig!' With no justificatory science behind authoritative insults, abuse had been democratized – all that remained was political interchange and moral debate in a relativist sea of moral diversity. At that point, enter *The New Criminology*.

The New Criminology

The concept of deviance was now embroiled in a vibrant European scene, with several theoretical and political approaches competing for hegemony over a blossoming, insurgent, sociology. The latter was closely connected with the cultural revolutions and street demonstrations of 1968. Thus caught up in the maelstrom of 'the great refusal', the concept would never be the same again. Its roots severed in the political storm, it could only go forward to accept the lethal logic of its own contradictions. *The New Criminology* was an outspoken voice for that logic and brought the concept to the brink of collapse.

What many people in the NDC were opposed to was articulated in *The New Criminology* (Taylor *et al.*, 1973; see also their *Critical Criminology*, 1975: 6–94). Three oppositions were outlined:

1 Against orthodox criminology. This was a rejection of criminological positivism; a rejection of the methods and assumptions which posited criminality as a real biological or psychic entity, as an individual pathology and as a cancerous outcome of social disorganization. Instead, the NDC, in a variety of ways, asserted that deviant behaviour often involved a choice and a rational appraisal of social circumstances, and therefore should not typically be seen as meaningless activity (*ibid.*: 150–4; and various essays in Cohen, 1971, and Taylor and Taylor, 1973). Positivist criminology had completely neglected the fundamental social contradictions of capitalism to which deviance was so often a comprehensible response, and instead portrayed the criminal as a distinct, defective, personality type in need of psychiatric treatment.

2 Against orthodox sociology. This involved a three-pronged critique. Part was a rejection of the kind of scientistic, statistical, 'abstracted empiricism' (Mills, 1970: 60) so common in a post-war British, Fabian, sociology, which treated crime and deviance as mere, messy, effects of poor housing and bad environment (Taylor *et al.*, 1975: 9–14); part was a contempt for the mandarinism of Parsonian, functionalist, social theory, with its often fruitless abstractions and constant, self-absorbed, distance from concrete social problems (Cohen, 1971: 15); and part was an emergent critique of the tendency of much labelling analysis to portray serious deviance as an accommodation to, rather than a rejection of, society and thus again as an effect rather than a positive choice (Taylor *et al.*, 1973: 151).

3 Against orthodox Marxism. This was an ardent critique of the Engels/ Bonger style of Marxism which tended to relegate crime to the 'dangerous

classes', or the lumpenproletariat, as a falsely conscious, demoralized, response of defeated people to oppressive economic conditions (*ibid.*: 209–36). Again, the central accusation is that the creative, human, element in deviant behaviour had been neglected at the expense of economic determinism.

What clearly united the various critical strands of the NDC, and formed the theoretical substance of its members' empirical studies, was a commitment to humanism, to a sense of the creative, subjective and positive potential of the human species. This bond enabled the diverse critiques of positivism, functionalism, determinism and Stalinism to gather some coherence. It was a driving force, and it differentiated radical European analysis of deviance from the American. The latter, although it clearly had strong sympathies for humanism, was much more driven by a populist vision of a more integrated, less divided, society and by a stronger sense of social deviants as a distinct, real, social sub-group. It was reacting against conservatism. Paradoxically, because it had stronger roots in socialist politics, European deviancy theory, from the beginning, was reacting against all forms of determinism, especially the Marxist form. Its leftist variants, in particular, were strongly anti-Stalinism and anti-economism. Consequently, the concept of deviance was dragged into a complex, quite foreign, debate within European social theory – between the phenomenological and structuralist wings of a resurgent Marxism – with transformative effects. European interactionism existed, notably in the elegant and erudite contributions of Paul Rock (1973, 1979; Downes and Rock, 1979, 1982), but it was not to be conceptually transformative.

The collision of the concept of deviance with European Marxism was by no means accidental, nor a minor intellectual event. Marxism in Europe was resurgent politically and theoretically. It had acquired a new impetus – the struggle against *all* forms of inhuman social relations. It had again become a democratic, emancipatory, spirit and was no longer tied so closely to traditional communist parties or dogmas. The heart of darkness had never known such limits; its critique had to lose its chains. Its critique in Britain, for example, could not be confined to a critique of Conservatism or Labourism. Ever since the early days of the *New Left Review*, E. P. Thompson's question (posed in 1960) had been central:

> Can the new human nature which has formed beneath the orthodox snows express itself in positive rebellion? Can a new generation, East and West, break simultaneously with the pessimism of the old world and the authoritarianism of the new, and knit together human consciousness into a single socialist humanism?
>
> (Thompson, 1978: 32–3)

There was no doubt that there was a new spirit about, or that the old 'human nature' of the cynical theories of left and right had become too limited a conception of the human capacity.

Modernity changed too fast, was too fleeting and insecure, too trau-
matic, and far, far, too insubstantial for notions of human nature to survive for long; especially after the Hitler–Stalin pact and the Holocaust.
Cynicism was quickly replaced with the most optimistic humanism, and
why not, after the Holocaust and the nightmare of Stalinism? Where else
was there to go? Nevertheless, the rational case for a positive view of the
human capacity had much to do after the war, and often it completely lost
sight of reality in its attenuated dream of a diverse and cooperative social
world. Perhaps the unreality of mass liquidation demanded its opposite –
the unreality of sixties humanism. Perhaps the fantasy of total social control spawned the fantasy of total de-regulation. Certainly, a Nietzschean
cynicism was also in vogue, especially in Foucault's work, and few could
quibble with his picture of tightly drawn links between power and knowledge, domination and morality.

In any case, the existence of a human essence was hotly debated within
the socialist movement, as the works of Sartre, Garaudy and Merleau-
Ponty were contrasted with the arguments of Althusser and Foucault.
Some of Marx's texts were translated into English, and made readily
available, for the first time, and many discussed his concept of the species-
being in the *1844 Manuscripts*, as Hegel suddenly became popular again
(especially due to Hyppolite). Students avidly read the impenetrable prose
of Marcuse's *One Dimensional Man*, a critique of alienated existence in a
one-dimensional post-war world of affluence and conformity – such reading being the perfect proof of human indomitability in the face of all the
odds. And many were aware of Habermas's indictment of the military-
industrial complex and the profound irrationality of modern society, from
his book *Toward a Rational Society*.

What was at stake was the possibility and value of an independent,
creative, human *diversity*. Not just any diversity, but a diversity of soft,
gentle, poetic, people in a warm community. This was a time to reject
firmly the forms of thought and the concepts of instrumentalism, careerism,
bureaucracy, utilitarianism, exploitation and violence.

Diversity is the word that echoes through the texts of radical criminology throughout this period, and beyond. Another D word (see Chapter 2).
It stood for something right at the very heart of deviance – deviance as an
expression of individual uniqueness and the right to be different. The heart
of darkness was being made light of. Deviance as diversity was the right
to self-expression and self-determination in a culture fostering healthy
growth. It stood sharply opposed to the freedom stamped out in the Gulags
of Hitler and Stalin. But it also represented a dimension of the human
character which many saw being eroded by the moralistic, social-democratic,
welfare state and its accompanying, high-technology, mass consumerism.
The right to engage in certain kinds of minor deviance without receiving
suffocating social censure and the value of moral deviance as a stimulant
of creative diversity were at the centre of contemporary politics in 1968. It
was not just, as American sociology supposed, that deviance was political;

it was also that the principle of a healthy diversity had become pivotal to a resurgent socialist politics in Europe concerned to overthrow *both* capitalist and communist oppressions. Diversity was a critique of Stalinism as well as of the moral totalitarianism of the West, and was soon to become the principle of freedom for many East Europeans.

The concept of deviance, as a self-defined innocent simply on tour, was caught up in the demonstrations and barricades of an emancipatory European socialist movement which saw deviance, far from being politically innocent, as an important figure in the politics of democratic diversity.

As if in a bad dream, the touring American figure of pluralist integration found itself celebrated on centre stage as an icon of disintegrative diversity. Not knowing its limits, it rather voluntarily gave up its role as tourist to don the garb of the new Eurocommunists, only to discover later, much too much later, that this new role must lead to its final dissolution. For the essential truth was, and is, that the politics of democratic diversity had no room for a concept of consensus, and barely even accepted a need for a notion of order, against which deviance could be defined. Even worse, this was a time for celebrating disorder. It was a time when consensus, order, rules and regulation were seen as synonymous with the death of the human soul. The 1968 rebellions, both cultural and political, had a strongly anarchistic streak. And if one removes the twin extremes of the Durkheimian trichotomy of crime/deviance/difference, in supposing that the present social order is completely pathological, or that any kind of desire for order is pathological, then the middle must eventually fall without its supports – the concept of deviance was losing any serious meaning and becoming a parody of itself. In the immortal words of the Pet Shop Boys a little later: 'There's a thin line between love and crime . . . and collaboration.'

This anarchistic spirit was clearly expressed in *The New Criminology* and is the key to the reading of the text, and of the very spirit of the NDC. Simply at the level of form, the book was unkempt. Arguments were overdrawn, critiques were ill-developed and often unfair, and key positions were fudged. In terms of substance, we were urged to abandon all prior conceptions of crime and deviance, yet for what? In truth, a pittance; a parody of the complexity of crime and deviance. Deviance was now presented as a form of political resistance by the ever-recalcitrant human spirit against the numbing structures of alienation. All prior criminology was stereotyped and summarily, sometimes unjustly, convicted of the sin of not granting that deviant behaviour was a choice made under oppressive social conditions. In fact, deviance was now given a cruelly demeaning extension of life; *The New Criminology* was its life-support machine. Sustained by this notion of a unity to deviance in resistance, the concept had been saved from falling apart at its indulgent, pluralistic, seams, somewhat ironically by the politics of social diversity and the 'new' criminologists.

Subtitled 'For a social theory of deviance', *The New Criminology* nevertheless presented itself as a preamble to 'a full-blown Marxist theory of deviance' (*ibid*.: 220). Representing the more Hegelian versions of the resurgent neo-Marxism of the 1960s (e.g. McLellan, Lukács, Meszaros and Avineri), *The New Criminology* contended that such a 'full-blown Marxist theory' would: (a) explain how 'particular historical periods, characterized by particular sets of social relationships and means of production, give rise to attempts by the economically and politically powerful to order society in particular ways' (*ibid*.: 220); (b) locate the labelling agencies in relationship to 'the overweening structure of material production and the division of labour' (*ibid*.); (c) assume that people had 'a degree of consciousness', 'bound up' with their position in the structures of production, exchange and domination, which would 'influence' the responses they made to being labelled criminal or deviant (*ibid*.); (d) build links between symbolic interactionist analysis and Marxist theories of social structure (*ibid*.: 220–1). Building upon a dialectical understanding of the interplay between human agency and social structure, and avoiding the twin evils of determinism and relativism, such an approach

> might enable us to sustain what has until now been a polemical assertion, made (in the main) by anarchists and deviants themselves, that much deviance is in itself a political act, and that, in this sense, deviance is a property of the act rather than a spurious label applied to the amoral or the careless by agencies of political and social control.
>
> (*ibid*.: 221)

Just as Bakunin and Kropotkin argued that to commit an immoral act was to challenge the state, the 'new' criminologists contended that 'much deviancy must be viewed as a struggle, or reaction, against such "normalized repression", a breaking-through, as it were, of accepted, taken-for-granted, power-invested commonsense rules' (*ibid*.: 169). However, at the same time, 'In so far as it is legitimate to view deviance as a challenge to authority at either the instrumental or oppositional level, it must also be viewed as ultimately predetermined by structural inequalities and ideologically enforced consensus, *no matter how complex the mediatory variables*' (*ibid*.). In short, Taylor, Walton and Young found it 'useful to view deviancy as a break from the moral bind involved in ongoing "normalized" repression' (*ibid*.), a break which was 'ultimately predetermined' by inequality and powerlessness.

It has been easy for commentators to pick holes in such formulations, and indeed *The New Criminology* does not really develop its theoretical position. For example, what is the relation between the 'challenge to authority' and structural pre-determination? What concepts were to mediate between structure and action (we were given few clues)? Was challenging authority always an intelligent thing to do, or justifiable? Exactly how often was deviance from dominant morality a challenge to authority? What justified the extraordinary claim that politicality was so characteristic of deviance that the behaviour could be defined in those (political) terms?

And, crucially in practice, who exactly decided what was political and, implicitly, 'right on' and what was not political and therefore merely quiescent or disengaged, the ultimate sin of the late sixties? And how were they to decide? Such vagueness on key points was a recipe for a new Stalinism, where the arbiters were the self-appointed politically correct and the method was not subject to public scrutiny. It is necessary to record that several of my generation of socialist-feminist postgraduate students often found the NDC itself to be a Mafia-like entity of hard men, hierarchies, party lines, splits, exclusions, put-downs and other masculinist tendencies. In this way, of course, it did no more than replicate the *Lebenswelt* of other left groups of the sixties, notably the International Socialists with whom it had some overlap of affiliation. It certainly had more democracy to offer than mainstream academic conferences. Nevertheless, it had still to learn that the politics of democratic socialism could not simply be achieved by challenging the authority of the Establishment, and, in this way, the NDC mimicked its own most famous concept of deviance.

The importance of the concept of the political in the 'new' criminology begged for an extended discussion of its meaning. It never really got one. There was a brief attempt to plug the gaps in the later book by Taylor, Walton and Young, *Critical Criminology* (1975: 9–28), but it was no-where near adequate and revealed even more unanswered questions. For example, the authors assured us that 'Radical deviancy theory can now be seen, therefore, as the beginnings of a politics that might link the concerns (with diversity) of sceptical deviancy theorists and the other politicized middle-class constituencies with movements that are capable of realizing such a diversity' (Taylor *et al.*, 1975: 19). But what would the thesis of *The New Criminology* have sounded like if its authors had admitted in the first place that their own judgement of what was political or sick was that of the radical, professional, middle class, acting on behalf of largely unconsulted subordinate classes (instead of berating Bonger for advocating 'sustained and responsible pressure by the intellectual leaderships of social democratic parties with formally Marxist programmes'; *ibid.*: 235)? Is not much of the history of the sociology of deviance an account of the exercise of moral judgement by such a radical, professional, middle class? Or an account of judgements from above made from a largely unexplicated moral and political standpoint? Some of us at the NDC had hoped that it was a first step away from the practice of over-ready judgement in general and towards a new praxis of understanding. In any case, some of us at that time were not radical professionals because we had no established profession or career, and still held to the crazy idea of overthrowing professionalism altogether (in true Castroist style). Indeed, some of us had no trust whatsoever in the ability of the middle classes (non-commercial, radical, professional or whatever) to liberate anything except for their own use.

In *The New Criminology* itself, the political stance had looked less like an embryonic new professionalism and more like a broad-based anar-chism. For example:

It should be clear that a criminology which is not normatively committed to the abolition of inequalities of wealth and power, and in
particular of inequalities in property and life-chances, is inevitably
bound to fall into correctionalism. And all correctionalism is irredu-
cibly bound up with the identification of deviance with pathology. A
fully social theory of deviance must, by its nature, break entirely with
correctionalism . . . The task is to create a society in which the facts
of human diversity, whether personal, organic, or social, are not
subject to the power to criminalize.

(Taylor *et al.*, 1973: 281–2)

So much remained unargued, unclear and unjustified – despite the fact that
this allegedly 'new' view of deviance amounted to a huge regress into theories
of deviance as a 'property of the act' (and the actor), after all that the
symbolic interactionists had done to demonstrate that deviance lay in the
labelling, and the labelling interactions, not the action. The last chapter of
The New Criminology especially illustrates how loosely the structural
analysis of predetermination sits next to the interactionist analysis of choice.
However, it seems fatuous to rebuke its authors for not adequately resolv-
ing the human agency–social structure dialectic in a book about criminology, for that is a theoretical problem social theorists have long agonized
over. Moreover, it is tough on its authors to accuse them of concealing an
anarchist position underneath their commitment to Marxism, when clearly
they were trying to articulate a balance between structure and agency.
Nevertheless, despite this, their overall position emerged as an anarchistic
one, and I believe that there are specific historical reasons for this.

Despite my analytic and political problems with their stated position,
I will now attempt to outline how this came to pass and what Taylor,
Walton and Young were trying to say, drawing on my own experience of
those days. For, at the end of the day, the book should be judged not so
much as an academic discourse but as a political brick that was hurled
through the windows of various establishments that had it coming to
them; especially since its authors backtracked on so many of their positions
only two years later in *Critical Criminology*. As such, *The New Criminology*, for all its flaws, created a space for the development of a critical,
theoretical, sociology and politics of crime and deviance; a space which
could give the political element in crime, deviance and law-enforcement its
proper place. As the authors themselves said, in their conclusion, 'the
retreat from theory is over, and the politicization of crime and criminology
is imminent' (Taylor *et al.*, 1973: 281).

Quite simply, while the text frequently attributed several key insights to
its authors' colleague and friend Alvin Gouldner, the argument owes more
to Habermas (1971), Marcuse (1964) and Meszaros (1970). Why? Because
the socio-political impetus behind *The New Criminology* was the post-war
sense of a new totalitarianism forged by the bland twin terrors of mass
consumerism and welfare-state interventionism into all walks of life. Orwell's

1984 and the spectre of Big Brother loomed large, and many social commentators and political activists observed the dull blah that pervaded everyday life. The 'new' criminologists were impressed with the view being developed by Habermas that post-war welfare capitalism involved an intense overlapping and integration of economic, political and ideological formations, and that a technocratic-instrumental rationality was all-pervasive. In particular, the American functionalist's dream meant that the political economy of the military-industrial complex had suffused all other walks of life with its deathly moral ideology. Conformity, as in the military, was all until the middle sixties, and the bland led the bland. The state of war had become the state of peace, and everything was turned upside down. Anything that challenged any part of the system was a challenge to the whole political economy since the latter had invested its death wish so profoundly in everyday life. We were all just another brick in the wall, and so to remove the brick and throw it through the nearest available window was to challenge the system. This was the precise political acuity of the 'new' criminology. As Taylor and Taylor had announced in 1968, 'we're all deviants now'. From striking worker, through homosexual, to minor delinquent and radical criminologist, all moral deviations had been converted by the totalitarianism of the system into dissidence – or so the 'new' criminologists told us.

That is why the position in *The New Criminology* appears so anarchistic. It was an effect of following the view that the system had integrated its circuits. Such a view took for granted that structural-functionalism, and its Habermasian variants, was accurate as an account of the post-war welfare society. Therefore, the better critique of *The New Criminology* is not so much that it was anarchistic but that its position depended on a picture of the post-war social system which is too grim. The system was not that strong, as we soon found out in Paris and Prague in 1968, and again in Vietnam in 1975. It simply was not that unified or that integrated. There was a certain amount of *décalage*, as Althusser called it. Moreover, the relative autonomy of so many of the parts was quite sufficient to create a huge alarm by 1970, among the conservatives and all those who feared the complete disintegration of the nation state.

In the NDC'S empirical studies, football pitch invaders (I. Taylor, in Cohen, 1971), industrial saboteurs (L. Taylor and Walton, in Cohen, 1971) and racist assaulters (Pearson, 1976) were all portrayed as resisting the local circumstances of their specific alienations, and thus as engaging in deviance with a political content – but not as dissidents from the social system in general. That would have been stretching a point. At the level of general theory there was no such coyness or circumspection: deviance was seen as a generalizable challenge to generalized oppression. The empirical studies demonstrated the limited value of the position. It begged more questions than it answered. All moral actions can be portrayed as taking place within a set of power relations; indeed it is arguable that power relations are a precondition of action having any moral content at all. But, the exact sense in which the action is political, the meaning of political and the relation of political action to the whole social system are all very difficult questions in general, which certainly needed to be answered finally in each specific instance of deviance.

To generalize deviance as a kind of dissident politics, however resonant an idea that was in the late 1960s, was to argue an anarchist case against rules or authority of any kind. More importantly, it meant that the position of *The New Criminology* was extremely hard to defend and the criticisms soon flew in thick and fast. What about rape? Political possibly, in some cases, in that the rapist may be a misogynist, but political and progressive? And were bank robbers really progressive redistributors of wealth? In any case, wasn't there a difference between meaningfulness and rationality? Much deviance may be meaningful and chosen within its context, but does that make it rational action? Can't totally irrational actions be sociologically and subjectively meaningful? Besides, ultimately, were criminal laws or consensus-supported moral rules always bad? How could one have a socialist society of maximum diversity without cooperation and rules of conduct? Was humanity to change its diversity overnight and suddenly become altruistic, non-egotistical and peaceful? Surely to celebrate human diversity, realistically, should have been to recognize that some people become, for whatever reason, complete bastards? Surely the logic of humanism was a liberal logic of 'letting it all hang out' in the hope that no one would get raped, maimed, robbed or killed (and an anxious hope at that, since all those deeds would have been prematurely decriminalized)? That may have been all right for the politics of the students' junior common room, but human history has proved infinitely more nasty.

Ultimately, Engels's three types of relation between politics and crime, outlined in the *1844 Conditions of the Working Class*, have proved a more durable analytic tool. Crime can be egotistical and detrimental to the working class, e.g. much petty theft or domestic violence; it can be political but reactionary, e.g. Luddism or hayrick-burning; or it can be political and progressive (or justifiable), e.g. exercising the right to free association in public in a banned demonstration. In sum, as the seventies wore on, the relation between deviance and politics was more evidently much more complex than pictured in *The New Criminology*. In particular, victims, women, ordinary working-class folk and *los disaparicidos* of the Third World were not impressed with the allegedly revolutionary character of crime. And it was not long before such groups found their criminological spokesmen and women. Indeed, it was not long before several of the 'new' criminologists themselves recognized the impossibility of their positions and became 'new' realists (notably Jock Young, with the spectacular change of position in his 'confessional' essay of 1975 called, suitably, 'Working-class criminology' – discussed in the next chapter). The retreat of the 'new' criminologists from their own theory was part of the final dénouement of the sociology of deviance and will therefore be discussed in the next chapter; suffice it to say here that having persuaded our ailing concept to walk at the front of the march for freedom our 'new criminological' colleagues were to withdraw their support within two years, thus leaving it wide open to a lethal assault from both left and right.

Feminist analysis of deviance

Deviance had by 1973 been massively over-politicized. It was drunk with the power of its own significance within sociology. And, like many a masculinist drunk, it engaged in not a little domestic violence. Women had been completely neglected in *The New Criminology*, a text committed to propose 'a social theory of deviance'. Concepts of 'man' were to the fore, and NDC portraits of soccer hooligans, 'paki-bashers' and industrial sabo-teurs as proto-political deviants did nothing to dissipate a sense that the masculine was a privileged concern within even a radical sociology of deviance.

From the very beginning of the sociology of deviance, women had been neglected, treated as biological entities to whom sociology did not apply, reduced to appendages or confined to the home. Their absence from the field is nothing short of spectacular. It is a silence so stunning that it demands examination for what it reveals.

Even with the growing fascination with the repressed and the unconscious in the 1930s, there was little concern with women. The official statistics presented boys and men as the criminals and delinquents, and the positivist focus of early criminology on the official crime problem meant little interest in issues relating to women. This may have had practical roots but it was hardly logical. If women were more conformist then the analysis of their conformity would have surely contributed to the theory of deviance. Moreover, the early sociologists of crime showed little interest in, for example, prostitution or even the deviance of the new women smokers, nor did they see any significance in the growing sexual openness of the 1920s or the 'pop' psychology of the *True Confessions* phenomenon. At a time when women were notoriously less conformist, this was an extraordinary silence. When the differential concept of culture ruled in the 1930s (see Chapter 3), it was easy to differentiate women out – as a different breed with a different role, presumably. Thomas (1928) had seen girls only as trainee mothers and home-makers. Davis (1937) relegated their social function to the reproduction of the species, and dismissed prostitution largely as a historic social function of men's supposed surplus sexual needs. In the 1950s, A. K. Cohen (1955) excluded girls from his subcultural theory by asserting that they were primarily interested in boys, dating and marriage and that, therefore, gang delinquency was irrelevant to them when they suffered any status frustration. Their goals lay within personal relationships and the norms of educational and occupational success were assumed to be male. The value and danger of the masculinity of such norms was not questioned, nor was the exclusion of women from the male world. Gender was not a sociological category of interest, nor was the gendered character of crime and deviance rendered of any significance. One can only conclude that gender was not regarded as a substantially sociological difference but as a simple function of the sex of the individual.

Until the rise of the labelling perspective, nothing much of any value had been said about females or about gender, and masculinity was as absent a concept as either of them. Then Becker (1963: 17) observed that, generally, men made the rules for women in society; but he made nothing of it. Goffman, Lemert and Matza said little more. Matza (1969: 122) joked that very beautiful women could get away with anything and that women's intuition depended on men's propensity to feed it (*ibid*.: 152), but that was about as deep as it got. Even the incredible difference between men and women recorded in the official statistics did not produce a single study of labelling biases against men, let alone a theoretical reflection of what the statistics said about the labelling perspective itself. It would have been a little hard to explain such a large difference in recorded crime by reference to selective labelling practices. It has been rarely commented upon, but the silence of the labelling perspective on women's low official crime rate is a monumental testimony to the perspective's limited theoretical value. If it had nothing to say about the most obvious differential in labelling practices, then it was surely little more than a series of elegant footnotes on the limits of social control.

However, as I argued in Chapter 3, this incredible silence about women and gender was not just a manifestation of ignorance – or even a consequence of focusing positivistically on officially apprehended or stigmatized deviants. It was, I contend, an effect of one of the great unconscious fears which underpinned the whole history of the sociology of deviance. The fear of women was one part of the fear of unreason (see Foucault, 1967). The unleashing of deviance from the Western unconscious had revealed that clearly. It could not help but be operative in the sociology of deviance. *Les Demoiselles d'Avignon* had remained outside the comprehension of male sociology for most of the twentieth century. Women were an alien force, and the feminine was a mystery. Sociology did not even dare to try its theories on them; it somehow knew they could not be understood by reference to zones in transition, subcultures or unfair labelling practices.

Silence about gender accompanied silence about ethnicity and the exploitation of the colonies. It was a compulsive silence – how else can we see its extraordinariness? They were all compulsive silences. There was no desire to see, and a painful subliminal sense of what might be observed if vision was switched on. The condensed image of *all* these silences, the black female prostitute of Africa, and the South in general, were never the subject of even a single sociological study – until, perhaps, Oscar Lewis's *La Vida* (1968). Such an avoidance is striking to say the least, especially given the fascination with her in the nineteenth century (see pp. 9 and 80). But the core image of deviance for the Western, male, white, imagination could surely not have been studied without revealing the whole character of its gaze. The subordination of blacks and women was, after all, a fundamental precondition for Western thought itself.

Western rationality, with all its humanism and voluntarism, was, and still is, a fundamentally masculine field of vision. To charge malestream sociology of deviance with the neglect of women is to suppose one could see an elephant with a microscope. Alternatively, it is to suppose that such a sociology could see the back of its own head. To see women there had to be a fundamental change in the instruments of vision, not to mention the discovery of a desire to understand the role of gender differences in the social attribution of deviance.

Generally speaking, I suspect that males in sociology were as likely to see the significance of sex and gender differences in crime and deviance as were upper-class sociologists likely to criticize the role of the capitalist social structure in producing class differences. It required the expansion of the universities in the sixties to bring a different class of men into sociology before Marxist-style critique was reborn, and I suspect it was the greater presence of women in the universities during that same time which brought about a feminist recasting of the sociology of deviance. It was these 'new' women who started to study women and began to open up the field of gender differences in the social censure of crime and deviance. Of course, behind that level of explanation there are deeper stories. Suffice it to short-circuit a long detour into the history of women by saying that this development marked yet another exposure of the back of the head of Western rationality. Yet again its field of vision was to be exposed as a limited one, and one that was driven by certain compulsive exclusions. It should be added that the emergence of a feminist sociology of deviance did not then immediately produce studies of black female prostitutes from 'the South' – this was still white sociology. Bujra's analysis (1982) to this day remains a lone example of what might be revealed if this phenomenon was taken to be as significant as it should be for the sociology of deviance.

Before the 1970s, the sociology of crime and deviance had been a man's game and a display of the peculiar curiosity of conventional masculinity. It had been closely connected with the official interests, statistics and funding sources of the state, that most masculine of social institutions. At its most conservative it had blamed the unregulated evolution of the city for male juvenile delinquency, and at its most radical it celebrated the challenges of young men to social systems. In neither case did it deviate from the search for a general theory of deviance. Ultimately, perhaps, this was the most masculine characteristic of the sociology of deviance. Its search for a rational general theory of something which was profoundly ungeneral, specific, contextualized, historical, local and emotive was profoundly and conventionally masculine. Of course, it was also a characteristic which melded well with the needs of a masculinist state that wanted general, universally valid, logical and neutral rules to apply in policy-making.

As the sociology of deviance 'loosened up' in the 1960s, that is, became less connected to state policy, more focused on the local and the specific, more 'micro' and more culturally specific, it paved the way for the less conventionally masculine sociologists of the labelling perspective to undercut the idea of a general theory of social deviance. What began to emerge was that the only general thing about deviance was that it was something which had been socially censured. There seemed very little in common between the various behavioural forms censured as deviance. The symbolic interactionists' use of qualitative research techniques, the focus on the local, the interactional and the specific, and the reluctance to deploy general single structural explanations of labelled behaviour, all worked, inadvertently, to feminize the field and to deconstruct its conventional masculine search for a general theory of deviance. In this respect, the attempt of *The New Criminology* to develop a unified theory of deviant behaviour as a proto-political challenge to normalized repression was more than a theoretical regression – it was a political regression into a single general theory which was unreflexive of its own historicity. It emerged at a time when the sociology of deviance was moving towards the abandonment of a behavioural theory of deviance and the adoption of a mere 'perspective' on the processes of escalation involved in emotive social conflicts. Fortunately, its incoherence as a new theory soon allowed the resumption of efforts away from a general behavioural theory of deviant behaviour.

If these perceptions and arguments are valid, then they help us to explain why the sociology of deviance, up to 1970, seems to involve a general movement away from studying those who have been blamed for social contradictions to studying the processes and structures which are involved in the social practices of blaming. And, of course, the more we look at the practice of blaming the more we uncover the ideologies behind the blaming and the fact that we blame at all (rather than mediate, persuade or explain). All in all, the feminization of the sociology of deviance in the late sixties and early seventies has been a force for, and part of, the growing reflexivity of the field – a process whereby the field has looked inwards to discover and root out its own unwarranted assumptions. In the end, it too, therefore, contributed to the erosion of the theoretical validity of the sociology of deviance.

By the early seventies, women such as Chesney-Lind (1973), Klein (1973) and Smart (1976) had begun to discuss the biases against women within the criminal justice system and generally were arguing that women were being discriminated against in various ways (see also Leonard's 1982 survey of the literature). Attention was drawn to the important fact that women were often the victims of male crime. The consequences for the concept of deviance of a structural analysis of male domination, patriarchy or gender division were, however, not registered in theory or even analysed at all at this stage. The call was mainly for more criminological attention to women. As Morris later commented, the sociology of deviance remained 'male-oriented and male-defined; only male deviants were interesting' (Morris 1987: 9).

She did it all for love

Two essays in particular focused on the sociology of deviance rather than criminology (Millman, 1975; Rodmell, 1981). The perspective presented in this book lends support to the analysis in both these essays.

Millman, for example, began with what now seems a more striking point than it did at the time. She observed that sociological stereotypes of deviance closely resemble those of popular culture, and that 'American and European fiction writers' tend increasingly 'to portray their male heroes as social deviants' (Millman, 1975: 251). The new criminologists certainly followed that code. Women, she commented, are usually presented as 'dumbly law-abiding'. She argued that it is a sociological belief that only men 'take a serious stand against society and its conventions', and that when women become socially deviant 'their deviance is understood as only secondary and politically uninspired' (*ibid.*: 253).

Millman's 1968-ish celebration of deviance does not concern us much; suffice it to say that feminist sociologists clearly shared the same attitude to deviance as their male counterparts in the 'new' criminology: the philosophy of the anti-hero ruled OK. It is her remarks around this complaint which are of greater value. She summed up well how women's deviance had been treated in sociology:

> It is derivative of their acting like women: falling in love (with a deviant man), being a little too out of control of their emotions (becoming mentally ill), using their sexuality exploitatively but not that differently from other women (becoming a prostitute), or exhibiting some other neurotic weakness or impulsiveness common to women (as becoming a shoplifter).
>
> (*ibid.*: 253)

Women's deviance was never seen as creative, unlike its male counterpart. It was rather like housework, I would say – taken for granted as part of the woman's role, and seen as peripheral to the more exciting world of men's work.

Even worse, male sociology has often completely distorted the social reality of women's deviance. For example, male studies of prostitutes, Millman observed, tend to emphasize the stereotype of competitiveness between women (distrust, disloyalty and lack of group culture). They were probably unable to see the 'complex, integrated female culture among prostitutes', because 'subordinate groups are generally better practiced in knowing and studying those in power than the other way round' (*ibid.*: 261). Millman's point is strongly confirmed by the contrasting picture painted of prostitutes by Janet Bujra (1982).

Worst of all, for Millman, male sociology of deviance has involved the disappearance of the victim from the script. Too often, the suffering of the victim, and of the deviant also, are written out or glossed over in favour of humorous ironic description of the mocking of conventional standards. Indeed, the suffering of the deviant's family never seemed to get a mention. Yet, as Millman argued, these sufferers are so often women (and children). Liberal male sociology had no interest in them. The daily task of coping with deviance, whether it be that of oneself, a family member, a relative, the boss, a colleague or a stranger, seemed not to capture the imagination of the labelling perspective; even though, in such coping processes, we experience the powerful and painful interpersonal negotiations about what is or is not acceptable.

In other places, Millman seemed to be criticizing the labelling perspective for not attending to the micro-details of everyday interaction, something which was hardly its weak point. Moreover, it could legitimately claim that, far from neglecting everyday problems with deviance, it had developed the ethnographic and analytic tools to enable a sophisticated analysis of how people cope with deviance. Indeed, some of its proponents would claim that their perspective had constantly focused upon accommodations to deviance. Nevertheless, whatever the limits and weaknesses of Millman's essay, its essential points amounted to a coherent development of a feminist perspective on the sociology of deviance. The labelling perspective, like functionalist analysis, had sidelined women and glossed over the reality of the victim's suffering. Women's relation to deviance had been left out of the picture – with the effect of producing what amounted to a considerable misrepresentation.

Focusing on male sexual violence towards women, Rodmell (1981) perceived, quite rightly, that this was an illustration that not all serious crime was taken as deviant. She asserted, quite wrongly, that sociologists of deviance had taken it for granted that most crime, especially serious crime, is deviant (*ibid.*: 146). Studies of corporate crime, from Sutherland through to the 1970s, had constantly shown that many serious crimes were not at all deviant, and radical criminologists had for years been asking such questions in their classes. Indeed, the whole point of the sociology of deviance from Lemert (1951) onwards had been to show that what was socially labelled as deviant or criminal was a matter of considerable economic, political and cultural bias. Crime and deviance were, as Rodmell said, often used indistinguishably and indiscriminately in textbooks – but that, in my experience, was because there was an equal scepticism about the validity of either as marks in a hierarchy. Durkheim may have supposed that social deviance was an overlap area between the extremes of crime and difference, but by the 1970s that trichotomy and hierarchy had been demolished, as we have shown here.

Rodmell may have been correct to say that male sociologists were too quick to think of crimes of serious sexual violence against women as deviance – although I doubt it. Her examples are unpersuasive, and certainly Taylor *et al.*'s *New Criminology* showed no readiness to think of serious violence against women at all. Indeed, I would have thought that, generally speaking, male sociologists of deviance were all too quick to ignore offences like rape altogether. In the list of classical studies within the sociology of deviance, where is the study of rape? (Let alone a study of rape which draws out some significance of the phenomenon for the analysis of deviance.) In any case, the sociology of deviance had specifically focused upon crimes without victims and the grey areas of deviance, and for specific reasons: it was precisely concerned with the interfaces between (a) crime and deviance and (b) deviance and difference. Serious sexual violence, to give male sociologists some credibility, did not enter the frame at all – precisely because they had no desire to decriminalize it. Homosexuality, drug use and prostitution, and other forms of soft deviance, were so commonly studied because liberal male sociology of deviance wanted to extend the boundaries of normative acceptability. Rape would hardly enter into that political problematic. Presumably, Rodmell's desire was a very different one from that characterizing sociologists of the labelling perspective: she wanted rape to be seen as an act which was not censured heavily or often enough and she wanted sociology to study its lack of criminalization. The feminist critique of the field thus often reversed its typical political drive away from criminalization. Until the 1980s, this tendency towards demanding greater criminalization and more extensive social regulation was not much accompanied by debates about the value of entrusting the state with such a role or about the need to re-configure completely a moral calculus which trod lightly with rape and punished petty property crimes heavily.

Nevertheless, this was one more nail in the coffin of the Durkheimian trichotomy of crime, deviance and difference. The feminist critique of the soft treatment of serious sexual violence against women, especially by the judiciary, added to the general thesis that crime and deviance were by no means levels of moral judgement. Clearly, all the accumulated examples by the mid-1970s (corporate crime, male sexual violence, tax evasion, dangerous driving, offences related to war and political corruption) represented stirrings which had to have their food. Crime was clearly not necessarily deviant, and deviance was not necessarily a milder form of behaviour than crime. Difference was sometimes seen as more repulsive and reprehensible, in certain societies at certain times, than either crime or deviance.

The labelling perspective, as Rodmell said, had effectively blurred the differences between minor and major offences with its constant empathy for the deviant. It did not therefore contribute much to the study of sexual violence, and contributed virtually nothing to the study of victimization. Nor did it have anything to say about the treatment of the victim as the deviant, as sometimes happens in rape cases. These were damning criticisms of the field as a whole, in my assessment, not just the labelling perspective. The sociology of deviance had rarely concerned itself with women's relation to deviance, women's deviance or the danger of male deviance to women. It had, as Rodmell (1981: 151) put it, failed to 'specify the power structures on which sexual relationships are predicated'. Its parameters were too narrowly defined. As Rodmell concluded, it contained an 'ethnocentric view of the world of Western heterosexuality'. The consequences of all this neglect and misrepresentation were beginning to become clear, but so also were its roots: 'Male sexual violence is recognized as an institutional power structure only in "fierce" societies.' In other words, there was a blindness to the fact that 'male supremacist attitudes' permeated the whole formation of 'both industrial and non-industrial societies' (*ibid.*: 153). While this formulation is too general and too vague to be very valuable, what Rodmell rightly pointed up was that male supremacy was one of the most fundamental normative assumptions of the sociology of deviance. It was a major blind spot which limited its vision terribly.

These two early feminist contributions to the sociology of deviance had begun to expose to the light all that which had been kept in the dark by the conventional masculinity of the sociology of deviance. Obviously, these were not minor matters. The victimization of women and children, and the glossing over of male violence, were major omissions from theoretical view – theory would have looked totally different with them at the forefront. For example, it is hard to see how the violence of fathers against their children could generate much enthusiasm for a theory of crime as creative critique, a theory of crime as a function of urban ghettoes, a theory of deviance as a subcultural solution to social contradictions or a theory of the dangers of social over-reaction to deviance. The history and direction of the field would have been totally different. Theories explaining the violent character of the male, the pathologies of relationships in industrial societies, the criminogenic consequences of the disappearance of the extended family, would have been vying with each other for attention. Such an imaginary sociology sounds much more exciting, scientific and productive than the one which actually happened. Perhaps it will now replace that which happened and has clearly died. Like the dark, the sociology of deviance simply cannot exist once light is thrown on to it. It must now be replaced with something better; something which does not have blind-spots that exclude the experience and lives of the bulk of humanity; something which reflects the knowledge and experience of women, the working class, the non-white and the underdeveloped societies; something which abandons the idea that deviance, like art, is heroic.

The feminization of the sociology of deviance in the sixties and the feminist critique in the seventies may have been part of the politicization of the field but they sat uneasily next to the 'new' criminologies. They were a gentle reminder that there was nothing heroic or progressive about some social deviations, such as domestic violence, and that the very meaning of contemporary politics was shifting. In any case, a number of texts were soon to be published in Europe, around 1975, which effectively killed off the sociology of deviance as an ongoing social-scientific enterprise. They removed its last point of refuge and left it intellectually bankrupt. In such a state, a field of scholarship dies.

Note

1 The analysis of this latter text will be dealt with in my next book, on the sociology of censures, because it is not so much part of the sociology of deviance as a vehicle whereby that field was superseded (see my review of the book: Sumner, 1981). It is very much a text which openly illustrates all the marks of a transition from one theoretical field to another. It is a text of the transition – from the sociology of deviance to the sociology of social censures. Moreover, its central focus is on a deviant category (mugging) as an ideological or cultural formation within a period of hegemonic strain and, as such, the book locates the censure of deviance within cultural studies – a clear sign that it rests within a very different theoretical problematic from the sociology of deviant behaviour.

11 Deviance as ideology: the final collapse

Steal a little and they throw you in jail,
steal a lot and they make you King.

(Bob Dylan, *Infidels*)

Foucault had inadvertently signalled the end of the concept of deviance in *Madness and Civilization* (1967), but had not followed through with the argument – and no one else did either. He showed how we could plainly see that what was called deviance in twentieth-century sociology amounted to a new category for, and a new way of managing, some very old social problems. Somewhere along the line, Foucault vaguely put it around the late medieval period in Europe, a cut had been made which sharply separated madness from rationality. Economic power began to become a more economic power. Messy but humane tolerances became a state incision into the affairs of hearts.

> The laws of nations will no longer countenance the disorder of hearts ... men were confined in cities of pure morality, where the law that should reign in all of our hearts was to be applied without concession, in the rigorous forms of physical constraint. Morality permitted itself to be administered like trade and economy.
>
> (Foucault, 1967: 37)

Economies centralized and expanded, polities organized them more rigorously and ancient cultures became narrower sciences of government. Co-production in subsistence economies gave way to a male order business, capitals grew larger, and women became housewives or were condemned as witches or criminals if they practised their traditional medicines, organized political challenges or, as in Africa, simply continued brewing (see

Sumner, 1982). A new order of gender was conterminous with a new order of capital and of scientistic dirigisme in government. Those who stood in the way or threatened disorder were confined or, in one way or another, slaughtered. Terror at first, and then the discipline of economy for profit – whether in Europe or Africa or the Americas.

Madness blossomed over the years into the plurality of categories of crime and deviance we know today, ranging from some serious crimes through to apparently minor differences. It is

> undoubtedly an uncomfortable region. To explore it we must renounce the convenience of terminal truths, and never let ourselves be guided by what we know of madness. None of the concepts of psychopathology, even and especially in the implicit process of retrospections, can play an organising role. What is constitutive is the action that divides madness, and not the science elaborated once this division is made and calm restored. What is originative is the caesura that establishes the distance between reason and non-reason; reason's subjugation of non-reason, wresting from it its truth as madness, crime, or disease, derives explicitly from this point.
>
> (Foucault, 1967: ix, x)

Madness, murder, incest, prostitution, homosexuality, illicit brewing, illegal drug use, robbery, treason and theft did not pre-exist the new order in some universal and immutable form, they were categories of censure which were gradually created, developed or re-formed *in practice* in the course of establishing and mapping out the new systems and territories of domination. Life, never having been utopian, had of course always sustained offensive behaviours and their social censure, but this was something new, a growing system of political economy, not just a collection of satrapies, which gradually established a new system of moral judgements, a formation which became systematically judgemental, not just a display of force or a declaration of authoritative ethics.

The distinguished jurist Roscoe Pound once observed that, 'Since the sixteenth century, law, the adjustment of relations and ordering of conduct by the systematic application of the force of politically organised society, has increasingly become the paramount agency of social control' (quoted in Ploscowe, 1951: v). It was a system which was to liberate populations from collective obedience to ancient decrees from above, and to undermine their passionate adherence to complex, allegedly non-rational, cosmologies, at the same time as it enclosed that secular individualism in the new chains of commodity circulation and consumer idolatry. It desired people to police themselves from within, for sake of economy – self-control/moderation/productivity/profit (see Foucault, 1977a: 219) – yet systematically, over the centuries, mocked and destroyed any moral codes, outside of the state-sanctioned church, which could guide action towards character, fulfilment and connection with the spiritual order of things. The great movement from confession of sins against an established moral code towards individual self-examination and inner censure often began with bloody legislation. Blackstone, another famous jurist, described this process of moral re-formation:

> In the year 1650, when the ruling powers found it for their interest to put on the semblance of a very extraordinary strictness and purity of morals, not only incest and wilful adultery were made capital crimes, but also the repeated act of keeping a brothel, of committing fornication, were (upon a second conviction) made felony without benefit of clergy. But at the Restoration when men, from an abhorrence of the hypocrisy of the late times, fell into a contrary extreme of licentiousness, it was not thought proper to renew a law of such unfashionable rigor. And these offences have been ever since left to the feeble coercion of the spiritual court, according to the rules of common law; a law which has treated the offence of incontinence, nay, even adultery itself, with a great degree of tenderness and lenity, owing perhaps to the constrained celibacy of its first compilers.
> (Quoted in Ploscowe, 1951: 143)

A society for the individual, but no ethical principle of organization – just the fragile comfort of the new doctrines of political expediency. Individualism without inner direction, passion or connection with a wider cosmology – a vacancy filled by ideology, the worship of idols and the propaganda of the powerful.[1] Unity with the spiritual world of unreason, insight and a higher order of things was fissured and supplanted with the unidimensionality of reason, work and self-sufficient, self-controlled, selfishness. Society and court for wealth and power; a long hard slog, the occasional sport and perpetual censure for the rest.

Resistance was constant. The new regime of censure was a perpetual site of struggle. Thompson spoke of an instance of the process in *Whigs and Hunters* (1975). Talking of the eighteenth-century agrarian forest community, he observed that they tried for some decades to resist the power of the gentry, the bishops, the new rich and royalty and to preserve their way of life, but that

> Meanwhile, the very roof-beams which housed their practical economy were being eaten away, by money and by law, above their heads. During the eighteenth century one legal decision after another signalled that the lawyers had been converted to the notions of absolute property ownership, and that (wherever the least doubt could be found) the law abhorred the messy complexities of coincident use-right. And capitalist modes transmuted offices, rights and perquisites into round monetary sums, which could be bought and sold like any other property. Or, rather, the offices and rights of the great were transmuted in this way – those of the Rangers, bishops, manorial lords. The rights and claims of the poor, if enquired into at all, received more perfunctory compensation, smeared over with condescension

and poisoned with charity. Very often they were simply redefined as crimes: poaching, wood-theft, trespass.

(Thompson, 1975: 241)

Marx, of course, had also used wood-theft as an example to illustrate the process whereby the exercise of rights was converted into crime. Things were being turned into their contrary.

What constitutes deviance, we can now see, is a series of normative divides or ideological cuts, cuts made in social practice – and the dominant cuts in our society are those made by the rich, powerful and authoritative. It is their distinctions which create the divide between deviance and normality. It is their distinctions, forged in the heat of driving interest and conflictual practical enforcement, in the practice of conquest, domination and possession, which divide the world up into the positive and the negative, right and wrong, normal and deviant. Historically, these distinctions often settle into 'custom', 'law' or 'science', often receiving support from sections of the poor and other subordinate groups, when they have an interest in the matter. They were, in some cases, converted into scientific categories commanding their content to be the province of the expert, usually the doctor, the psychiatrist, the lawyer and, latterly, the social worker and the criminologist. Morality beyond the expertise of common sense and the commoner – a people divorced from its practical reflections, practical reflections divorced from the people.

Speaking of legislation in 1723 which, at one stroke and with little debate, created at least fifty capital offences, Thompson wrote:

The Black Act could only have been drawn up and enacted by men who had formed habits of mental distance and moral levity towards human life – or, more particularly, towards the lives of the 'loose and disorderly sort of people'. We must explain, not an emergency alone, but an emergency acting upon the sensibility of such men, for whom property and the privileged status of the propertied were assuming, every year, a greater weight in the scales of justice, until justice itself was seen as no more than the outworks and defences of property and its attendant status . . . The Black Act came as much out of the mind and the sensibility of Walpole and of his associates as it did out of the emergency in two counties . . . The escalation of the death penalty did perhaps emerge out of a 'subculture' which we can clearly identify: that of the Hanoverian Whigs.

(*ibid.*: 197)

Whigs and Hunters essentially demonstrated that the new order of morality enforced by the Whig oligarchy was a practical reflection of the new order of economic relations developing apace in eighteenth-century England.[2] 'Since property was a thing, it became possible to define offences as crimes against things, rather than as injuries to men. This enabled the law to assume, with its robes, the postures of impartiality' (*ibid.*: 207).

Resistance to the destruction of a lifestyle, or a whole existence, by the anonymous and inhuman logic of property became censured as crime, and its perpetrators converted, over a couple of centuries, into a new species, 'criminals'. At which point, they became the objects, the meat and drink, of criminology, that 'ethnology of the civilizations of malefactors' (Foucault, 1977a: 253).

The historical work which flowed free after the 'new' criminology's critique of the sociology of deviance and orthodox criminology demonstrated, time and again, that the roots of disapproval and censure rarely lay in altruism alone. Marx's renewed popularity was much vindicated, and Nietzsche's *Genealogy of Morals* began to look like a very good textbook in penology. Time and again, the radical sociological demand for the history behind the labelling process revealed a sordid tale of dominant class, gender and ethnic interest. God's law was revealed to be a macabre theatre whereby the powerful dramatically celebrated their norms and interests as divine whilst consigning the lives of the weak to the dustbin of history (see Hay *et al.*, 1975). Man's law was revealed to be the law of very terrestrial men. Shakespeare had contemptuously revealed in *Measure for Measure* that the men in question were far from noble, being military, industrial, scholarly, men of cold disposition and little passion:

> man, proud man,
> Drest in a little brief authority,
> Most ignorant of what he's most assur'd,
> His glassy essence – like an angry ape
>
> (*Measure for Measure*, II. ii. 116)

As Nietzsche said, the nobility named what was noble after themselves – and violently censured the rest. Their domination was indeed 'glassy' – see-through and ever fragile.

Criminology was thus exposed, without its clothes. Criminology was made possible only by the complete objectivation of, and abstraction from, the field of madness or unreason to form a set of legal categories of crime, and of the individual as a 'criminal' (Foucault, 1977a: 254). It was none other than the alienated expression of conflictful and passionate social processes within a 'scientific' rationalization of the responses and sensibilities of the powerful. From the start, it was thus a little short of moral fibre, a mere plaything of the categorizations, statistics and political needs of those whose levity towards the lives of others had elevated them to transcendental power. The new gods of civil war now had their scientific advisers, and, like the delinquent it later spent a century abusing, criminology thus started off life from a broken home, with few moral scruples, blown hither and thither by the wealth of its clients, mixing in some very bad company and in need of victims to make a living – a male prostitute with a heart of ice. Little wonder it was to have little good to say about women; little wonder its deterministic aetiological theories of crime lacked emotion. A science of psychopathy? More of a psychopathic science.

The sociology of deviance emerged in the twentieth century as a liberal version of criminology, as part of a sociology of social control. By then, the governmental approach to the sad effects of the new order, the unemployed, the sick, the criminal, the mentally ill, the troubled and the troublesome, had become social administration, the management of the social. It was a rational, liberal-minded, attempt to make the society of the powerful more economic, more predictable, more humane and less chaotic. It was and is part of a technocratic 'liberalism' whose public face is 'social democracy'. As we have seen in this book, the sociology of deviance emerged at times and in countries within the twentieth century which were predisposed to social democracy. The concept of deviance gathered together many devils, out of the remains of the three Ds and the theoretical–political problematic of psychopathological degeneracy, and organized them as the deviant Other to the new Consensus so desired by the politicians of the New Deal. It was a project(-ion) that was part of the desire for hegemony, domination through voluntary assent to power, in a world which was falling apart at the seams and revealing the ugly, unconscious, repressions of centuries. It reflected the growing expression of the dark continent of the unconscious and helped its further emancipation into popular imagination. As such, it was an attempt to put sticking plaster over the accumulated wounds, scars and violations of an epoch; once they burst through in the late sixties, social deviance became meaningless. Drawing upon the concept of culture did not help either, since the differential concept of culture contained within itself a notion of the repressed Other as deviant idiosyncrasy. Once that concept of culture fell away, little was left except mere difference. The partner of deviance, the concept of social control, specified a hope for the voluntary adherence to an unprincipled, unspecified and value-free consensus in an expanded, increasingly interconnected and commercial world riven with multicultural and political divisions. In such company, deviance was thus bound to fail.

If crime was an alienated categorization of the minimal morality and vast power of the ruling classes, an official denunciation of the disturbing, then deviance could not hope to fare any better. Crime for the professional historian, as Thompson (1975: 194) said, was a disabling, moralistic, category to work with. It concealed the moral judgements of those with the interest to portray their victims as criminals. Thompson put it this way: 'allowing a moral judgement to precede the recovery of the evidence, and indeed to infect the categories of our own examination' is to use a 'disabling' category (*ibid.*: 193–4). Simply 'to take over the definitions of those who own property, control the state, and pass the laws which "name" what shall be crimes' prevented accurate historical research and produced pre-given moral assessments. Thompson was not advocating a value-free historiography, but historical research and assessment which hesitated before it pronounced on the moral worth of people and events. In my terms, to take the politically organized categories of state domination and the categorizations of the law enforcement officials as scientific notions is to convert the sectional and historical tools of the state into universally valid behavioural concepts. It is to take the state as God of all knowledge and to assume that even popular assent to legislation automatically transforms context-bound political judgement into universal truth. As such, it is an act of blind faith in the modern political order – or the abandonment of all principles of morality and research to the gods of career, money and ascent. In either case, it is, in either an old or new sense of the word ideology, *an ideological practice.*

In the case of the concept of deviance, its general ideological character was even clearer than that of crime, for it made no pretence to restrict itself to criminalized activities and entered the woolly world of moral ambiguity. From the start, it was defined against a normative consensus of a world yet-to-be-formed. Moreover, that consensus was a mere dream in a world which was in the process of dissolution and decay. Quite explicitly, writers like Durkheim, Wirth, Merton and Parsons called for a normative consensus articulated to an integrated social organization – it was always a demand, never an empirical reality. After the Holocaust, this became even clearer, as the need for systematization of a global world order under the hegemony of American imperialism created ever greater demand for a simple set of advertising slogans for the Free World to unify against its enemy, communism. As the tentacles of Society extended ever further, the gap between reality and state needs became ever greater. Nothing but ideology, especially the glib, sound-bite version of the age of the mass media, would suffice. Converted into the terse, *1984*-ish, slogans of the Cold War, ideology lost none of its ideological character, but drove even further away from any original empirical reference point. The undisguised utopia of the 1930s became a free-floating signifier in media hyperspace. But from the beginning deviance had been lodged within a utopian ideology.

Even re-appropriated within the radical utopia of 'socialist diversity', propounded in *The New Criminology*, deviance was beyond rescue as a scientific behavioural category of any great value. The story we have told has outlined the many ways in which the ground was cut from under its feet by the growth of radical criminology and the critique of psychiatry. The bankruptcy of the concept was finally recognized during the middle seventies, and the texts of transition to another conceptualization of the field began to emerge after 1975 (notably Hall *et al.*, 1978).

Hirst began the onslaught even before *The New Criminology* had been published. In 1972, Hirst declared that there could not be a Marxist theory of deviance, because the concepts of crime and deviance were not objects specified by Marxist theory (in Hirst, 1975a: 204). Following the epistemological positions of Althusser, and also Foucault and Bachelard, Hirst believed that scientific fields specified their own conceptual objects through the application of their established concepts. Therefore he concluded, drawing a mistaken conclusion from his own standpoint, that there could be no Marxist theory of deviance within orthodox Marxism. Radical sociology of deviance was thus denied the stamp of legitimacy by the orthodox left. After this, it really had nowhere to go – it had been denied its last point of refuge, its last escape hole.

The matter was not concluded there, however, because Hirst's conclusion was wrong, even in his own terms. He could have inferred from his own positions that there could have been a 'Marxist theory of deviance' but, to achieve this, that deviance would have to be re-worked as a concept using the categories of Marxist analysis (see Sumner, 1976). Admittedly, such a re-working would have meant that the new theoretical field would have been a Marxist theory of something else, and therefore substantially different, but still the point was that Marxism could have worked through the concept in a positive way to enable it to talk about the kinds of processes and structures which deviance attempted to deal with. Hirst's argument amounted to a negative declaration from a rather self-satisfied 'orthodox Marxism'; it was a censure from the safety of dogma rather than a reconstructive, progressive, argument using Marxism as a living tradition of value to the social sciences. It was indicative of the insularity and rather ecclesiastical nature of his standpoint at that time that he never considered that one could develop a Marxism that was unorthodox. No reason for clinging to orthodoxy was given, yet the world of Stalinism offered many political reasons against such an adherence to orthodoxy. We might add that at this point, long before the collapse of the Iron Curtain and the communist bloc, 'orthodox' Marxism was, in effect, yet again putting its head firmly in the sand. An opportunity to enter the debate about morality, justice and the ethical organization of social formations was lost. When the peoples of Eastern Europe finally rose up in favour of democratization and national identity, orthodox Western Marxism had nothing to offer them in relation to questions of social control and deviance except the old shibboleths about class domination and state ideology, whose practical reality they knew all too much about.

My own analysis of deviance in 1976, and the analysis of ideology in 1979, was probably seen as neo-Marxist or Marxisant (see Greenberg and Anderson, 1981). Yet it could have been seen as derived from the central principles of Marxian analysis as a dynamic scientific tradition, and thus as offering a way for Marxism through the mire the concept of deviance had landed in. I argued that, in his reply to the criticisms of Taylor and Walton, Hirst had in fact suggested that deviance was a concept constituted by 'practico-social ideologies' (Hirst, 1975b: 239), that this amounted to a good start in describing what deviance was about and that, therefore, we should see it as a (negative) ideological formation (Sumner, 1976: 166). It was a generic term to describe a set of negative ideological categories or condensations – a set of social censures – which were rooted in everyday social practice and were tied to the processes of regulation within social practice. Deviance, then, in terms of Marxian concepts, was a negative ideological formation, or a social censure, with a specific relation to social practice; or, *ipso facto*, it was also a generic category which referred to a number of censures. Now, however, is not the time to talk about the theory of censures. Along with others, I still see this concept as the successor to the concept of deviance and will return to it in another text (for now, see Sumner, 1976, 1981, 1990a, b; Leonard, 1982; Gransee and Stammerman, 1992; Sparks, 1992; Wing Lo, 1992; Roberts, 1993). All that matters here though is the point that 'orthodox' Marxist thought had abdicated its responsibility to face one of its most politically damaging internal weaknesses, namely the lack of a developed theory of morality, democracy and justice, and had, in the process, denied the concept of social deviance any escape route to survival.

The concept of social deviance only had a temporary respite through its brief adoption by radical British criminology. That insecure home was soon deconstructed. Pearson's *The Deviant Imagination* provided a sympathetic defence of radical sociology of deviance, but even he recognized that the main victory it had achieved was the de-reification of the categories of crime, deviance and illness. That victory certainly demonstrated that deviance was a moral (or ideological-political) judgement rooted in everyday practices and conflicts. But such a conclusion is only a beginning for, as Pearson (1975: 120) said, we have to recognize that some problems are just 'terribly awkward'. Moral judgements are necessary and even desirable: the question is what judgements, when and how? For the romanticization of deviance, Pearson agreed, was really no way forward. It was, for him, merely to indulge too uncritically in 'the deviant imagination' itself. It had been valuable to emphasize the importance of subjectivity in the construction of deviant enterprises, but not at all decisive; especially without any elaborated theory of subjectivity, of the difference between the meaningful and the progressive, or of politics itself.

Pearson was kind, although his subtlety should not be equated with support. The nettle had been grasped much more brutally by the authors of *The New Criminology* themselves. Taylor, Walton and Young's second joint enterprise, *Critical Criminology* (1975), amounted to an enormous 'confessional' (the term Jock Young used to describe his paper on 'Working-class criminology' at its first NDC conference delivery). Previous positions were reversed and dumped with remarkable speed. The concept of deviance had lost its new friends and was about to be left in the cold.

Taylor *et al.* dismissed the scepticism in liberal deviancy theory as 'a *cri de coeur* on behalf of the victims not only of an inert and conservative judicial system, but also the victims of social-welfare control', and declared that such 'sceptical deviancy theory' had 'no coherent alternatives' to correctionalism other than 'an abstracted and individualistic idealism' and was thus 'exhausted except as a form of moral gesture' (Taylor *et al.*, 1975: 13–14). True, and thus they dumped the labelling perspective part of the 'new' criminology – although the remarks at the end of this chapter indicate that such moral gestures, in the form of hyper-individualistic anti-discrimination claims, were to become a whole cultural mode in the 1980s in the USA. Then, dubbing their own earlier work 'anti-utilitarian criminology', they denounced it as being obsessed with the expressive side of deviant behaviour, over-focused upon the meaning the deviants gave to their action, neglectful of the state and over-generous in attributing free will to often highly restricted individuals. Also true. Thus they dumped the other part of the 'new' criminology, the radical romanticism. Commenting that their position had been 'idealistic', they said that

> The deviant himself is seen to embody expressively an authenticity which allows him to cut through the taken-for-granted world of conventional culture . . . he was accorded an unreal ability to transcend the exigencies of everyday life . . . [It was] a crude attempt to utilize Marx's notion of alienation with a view to seeing in deviant behaviour the activity of men struggling against situations of constraint and what later we were to term 'normalized repression'.
> (*ibid.*: 17–18)

Political realism was setting in and the anti-utilitarianism of the late sixties was being abandoned. Nevertheless, they also refused to base a movement towards 'radical diversity' on 'the Labour Party–social work axis of liberalism'. Espousing a limited version of Marxism, they argued that 'rule-creation' and 'crime-creation' are ultimately bound up with 'material reality' or 'the material basis of contemporary capitalism'. They held that it was still possible 'to envisage societies free of any material necessity to criminalize deviance' (*ibid.*: 20). Such a materialism would prevent critical criminology from degenerating 'merely into moralizing' (*ibid.*: 44). Was scientific socialist analysis of 'material reality' thus to provide the correct morality for the society of radical diversity? Was moral debate not a good thing? The political correctness so oppressively inherent within the Stalinist monolith was raising its head again. Clearly, the value of deviant practices was now a question of their progressiveness. Positions were not only being changed, they were being reversed: now the value of deviants' practices was to be decided without any reference to their subjectivity at all, presumably by the arbiters of political correctness. In any case, by the mid-1970s, many were realizing that unreason contained excess and that excess could be no more unlimited than rule itself. Excess had its dangers, just like social control. It had to be regulated. But with the concept of social control discredited, a new perspective on regulation was required.

The deviants had been dumped and so was deviance. The talk was now of crime and law. Deviance was now merely moral gesture at best. Taylor *et al.* dropped the term from their discourse: apart from the first few pages, their long editorial essay in the 1975 volume simply ignored deviance. They even included in the volume the essay by Hirst, discussed earlier, which declared the impossibility of a Marxist theory of deviance. Their new concern was to develop a historical materialist analysis of legal norms:

> Much of modern criminology continues to operate in ignorance or avoidance of the essence of crime – that, above all else, it is a breaching of a legal norm – and that legal norms, like any other social

norm, can be outmoded or obsolete. The reconstruction of criminology requires a re-examination of the ways in which such legal norms are constructed, their function, and the extent to which they are appropriate and relevant 'categorical imperatives' at all levels in the social structure and at all points in culture and time.

(ibid.: 46)

Taylor *et al.* said little about the extensive work already developing in the sociology of law, but it was the case in practice, during the late seventies and the whole of the eighties in Europe, that radical criminology basically melded with the sociology of law. Apparently, once the notion of deviance as proto-political critique had been seen to be a flawed idea, there was no further role for the concept of deviance in socialist criminology.

The second essay in that volume, 'Working-class criminology' by Jock Young, can be seen not only as a 'confessional', as he called it, but also as an explanation for the abandonment of the concept of deviance. Young now described the work of the 'new' criminology of the NDC as a 'crass inversion' of utilitarianism which led to an idolization of the deviant. He rejected the relativism which he himself had espoused in *The Drugtakers*. Indeed, referring to the romanticism involved, he went so far as to describe his previous positions as an 'astonishing accomplishment – the development of a criminology that does not deal with property crime, and a criminology whose subjects live in a world not of work, but of leisure' (Young, 1975: 68). This relativistic romanticism emphasized 'expressive deviancy', crimes without victims and the interference of social control with individual liberty. As he put it, this perspective left 'too many problems . . . unresolved'. Having accused himself of left idealism, Young now charged full steam ahead in the opposite direction. Extraordinarily, he now claimed that there really was a consensus on crimes against the person and against property and it really was the case that certain 'ecological areas' were socially disorganized after all. The latter really did connect with the 'aetiology of deviant behaviour'. Some human behaviour really was irrational and there was a problem of 'psychic disturbance'. It was a spectacular retreat.[3] We could be forgiven for saying 'what next?' or 'with friends like this did the concept of deviance need critics?' Deviance was now not looking like a very revolutionary form of praxis, as Young elaborated upon the brutalization of the working class by brutal economic conditions (Engels was now rehabilitated, having been expelled in *The New Criminology* two years earlier – such are the vicissitudes of political correctness). Workers were now the main victims of crime, so they were right to support 'law and order campaigns'. Deviance was now very clearly a Bad Thing.

Even 'crude' Marxism was compared to the ideology of Nazism in its essential form (merely substituting 'bourgeoisie' for 'Jews') (*ibid.*: 81–2), as Young's repentance surged painfully on. 'Proponents of diversity', he said (apparently forgetting that he was one of the main ones, and that the previous chapter which he had part authored still sustained a concept of diversity), 'forget that this consensus throughout society corresponds to the uniformity of the mode of production dominating the social order' (*ibid.*: 82). What consensus he was referring to was never really clear. Even Conservatives at this time, 1975, a year after having been forced out of office by consistently fierce opposition from the organized working class, would have been hard-pushed to argue that one – such was 'the uniformity of the mode of production'. Indeed, the whole subsequent Thatcherite platform sustained the idea that consensus was no longer necessary, as it mounted an overt and powerful attack on the trade unions and socialist movement. Such political considerations could hardly be excluded from any assessment of the consensus on criminal law in Britain. It was thus extraordinary when Young went on to say that the social deviations 'of those without real power' were 'tolerated'.

There was even a hint that the earlier psychopathology of crime was partially justified, when Young stated that it 'is at the desperate end of the social spectrum where the overwhelming milieu precipitates men into highly determined roles wherein the tyranny of the organism is best displayed' (*ibid.*: 85). We could continue, but suffice it to say that Young had not only abandoned the concept of deviance existing within Western sociology, but had come close to turning back all the gains of the sociology of deviance hitherto. Explicitly, he called for 'a radical paradigm change in the study of deviancy'. The basis of his preferred new 'paradigm' was outlined as follows:

> It is unrealistic to suggest that the problem of crimes like mugging is merely the problem of miscategorization and concomitant moral panics . . . We have to argue, therefore, strategically, for the exercise of social control, but also to argue that such control must be exercised within the working-class community and not by external policing agencies.
>
> (*ibid.*: 89)

This was the birth of left realism, a 'realism' that supposed that the state, or even the electorate, might somehow permit or welcome the development of 'no-go' areas the size of the North of England, Scotland and half of Wales. It was a realism which believed that ideological categories like mugging were crimes, and which 'strategically', or opportunistically, supported the declining notion of social control in order not 'to leave the political arena open to conservative campaigns for law and order' (*ibid.*: 89). It was a realism which contrasted sharply with the battle-plans being drawn up on the new Thatcherite right at that time for an abandonment of the whole 'welfare state–consensus politics–social control–one nation' philosophy of conservatism which had just been despatched to the shires by the electorate and the trade unions. Supporting social control, in the political conjuncture of Britain in 1975, was indeed unrealistic since the early seventies had proved that the welfare–consensus–end of ideology model of British politics (which sustained the concept of social control) was dead. Orthodox Marxism had stuck its head in the sand; this 'realist' variant of socialism looked backwards. In either case, the concept of deviance was simply abandoned.

That extremely influential historian of the New Left E. P. Thompson added his seal of approval to the abandonment of romanticism in 1975, arguing, like Young, that because 'we can show that offenders were subject to economic and social oppression, and were defending certain rights, this does not make them instantly into good and worthy "social" criminals, hermetically sealed off from other kinds of crime' (Thompson, 1975: 193). If we choose to look, he said, directly referring to radical criminology, there is ample evidence of the 'brutalization and demoralization which often accompany the life-style of groups which live outside some social norms, whose livelihood is precarious and parasitic, and whose lives may be every day at risk' (*ibid.*).

Spitzer (1975) developed the critique further in arguing that the 'problematic quality' of deviant groups 'ultimately' resided in the threat they posed to capitalist relations of production. This threat included challenges to socialization practices and revered forms of social organization. Deviant statuses, he argued, were 'social categories'. His essay tended to class-reductionism and neglected deviance deriving from ethnic, gender or nationalist divisions, and it overlooked the fact that the status character of deviance does not mean that deviance is a status. That status, logically, derives from a prior existence of a censure of deviance. Nevertheless, his essay was a further sign of the movement away from the sociology of deviance towards a sociology of social censures.[4]

All in all, deviance was now consigned to the realms of ideology. Whether it was the ideology of the law-makers or the morality-definers, whether it was widely shared or not, and whether it was the ideology of the deviants reflecting the contradictory social relations within which they lived, deviance was now ideological – both as a category of moral censure and as a category of behaviour. *Resistance through Rituals* (Hall and Jefferson, 1975) confirmed, albeit from a different theoretical perspective from Young's, that what was stigmatized as deviance was not to be assumed to be some kind of pure critical practice. Subcultures, the authors argued, could be seen as imaginary resolutions of problems deriving from contradictory social relations. The wheel had turned full circle: both the definition and practice of deviance were now to be seen as ideological practices. Politicization had exacted its toll: transformation of the field was now in the offing. The category 'ideological' certified the intellectual death of the field. Censuring a concept as ideological does not, of course, of itself invalidate it, but in the world of the social sciences at that time it was the sign that scholars used to indicate that they now believed a concept had nothing more to offer intellectual enquiry. We all had our preferred new directions, and I am aware that to assert a preference for one's own position is no proof that others' are bankrupted. But, in this case, as we have shown at length, there are good reasons for believing that the concept of deviance died in mid-Atlantic returning home after its disastrous European tour. Its ghost lives on in American sociology courses, but that is none of our business. It is a mere appearance. Its life-force has actually expired. It is an irrelevance how many scholars continue to use it as opposed to how many do not – popularity or unpopularity should never be taken as a test for genuine conceptual vitality. In this case, the decline in the significance of the sociology of deviance is an effect of its conceptual bankruptcy. It no longer reflects the dynamics of our lived history.

Epitaph

The behavioural concept of social deviance had run its course by 1975. The texts published around that year finished it off. In terms of any kind of coherent theoretical development, it had lost its potency. Fatally damaged by waves of successive criticism and undercut by its own logical contradictions it ceased to be a living force. Its time had passed and it did not recover.

Its evident internal weaknesses were legion. To remind ourselves of a few of the important ones discussed in this book:

- The consensus against which it was to be set had never materialized. This meant that always the question was: deviant from what? And if deviance was merely a passing feature of specific situations, contexts and cultures varying in behavioural content from one to another, then it clearly was not a behavioural phenomenon.
- Even if the consensus had materialized, there was no logical reason why the deviance should be said to inhere in the behaviour and not the relation between the behaviour and the norm. Since the norm or censure specified the deviance, it made more sense to begin looking at deviance as inherent within the signifying elements of the censure.
- It was never established, or even properly investigated, that alleged social deviations were in fact breaches of the dominant moral code; that is, that they really were *socially* deviant.
- The relations between deviance, crime and difference were totally incoherent. Some crime was clearly not deviant, some was, and some minor differences clearly were deviant while other more serious ones were not. It was never clear what the relation between the three was meant to be. Moreover, if social deviance had been a concept which had been aimed at decriminalizing certain practices and at treating important threats to social order which were not crimes as subject to the same management procedures as crime, then it had itself blurred the conceptual basis for its existence. The call for flexibility and tolerance had been interpreted to mean de-regulation from the top and, of course, in a parliamentary democracy, who was at the top varied regularly, even though their vested interests remained constant. What was defined as criminal, deviant

or different was all beginning to look very arbitrary. It seemed to depend upon who was judging and when; so we appeared to have just a morass of censures.

- Foreknowledge of social norms clearly did not grant any unity to the range of behaviours censured as deviant. Breaking a social rule of itself offered no substantive core for a theory of deviant behaviour as proto-political resistance. Many forms of censured practice could be seen to be subjectively and sociologically meaningful without being politically progressive or even rational.

- The search for a general concept to encompass such widely varying practices, problems and situations was itself logically misguided. There could be no behavioural unity to a diversity of practices which were so variably censured in such a variable range of situations, cultures and contexts. The search for a general theory of deviance was a major conceptual error; such a search only made sense as a political imperative.

- It did not so much provide us with a conceptually strong way of understanding moral ambiguity as with a new way of organizing the censure and administration of groups who posed 'social problems' for the state. However, its clinical sound and implicit reference to psychiatry were betrayed by its political value in denouncing extra-parliamentary opposition to the social order, by the painfully obvious moral judgement needed to establish the existence of any deviance and by the contingency involved in the whole process of getting stigmatized.

- It was driven by a world-view which had not come to terms with its repressed unconscious – the fear of women, blacks, radicals, the working class and the colonized – and its realization in sociological research thus exhibited a series of blind spots that ultimately undercut its scientific pretensions. Corporate deviance, the relation of women to deviance, the lack of moral-political consensus, and the relation of deviance to oppression were all neglected, and their uprising eventually precipitated the collapse of the concept as a social-scientific category.

There may have been a time and a place when a concept of social deviance as behaviour appeared to make sense, but it has gone. Its roots in social democracy meant that the Thatcher–Reagan regress had no natural place for it. The eighties marked a return to an older set of moral judgements about wickedness and its fiscal cost. With the demise of welfarism and the rise of the openly capitalist, morally aggressive, right, the consequent social polarizations have made it clearer than ever that moral judgements are politically loaded and that they militate against any social-scientific theory of deviance as a behavioural form. Now, the ideological and political character of moral censures is so open to view, and the rulers' fear of their social divisiveness so minimal, that the concept of social deviance is revealed as a notion within the politics of social democracy and therefore truly a creature of the post-Depression era, of the 'end of ideology' phase. Ideology is again blatant, and the concept of social deviance stands disrobed as an ideological censure, as rudely as its forerunners, the concepts of moral degeneracy and social inadequacy. The return of a pure enterprise culture does not mean that there is a renewed need for the concept of deviance along with some old-fashioned social democracy. It is true that society could be characterized as a patient again, *à la* Frank, but we no longer see things in those terms. That time and its discourse have passed: our vision is now too politically aware to slip back into the language of psychopathology and psychiatry; deviance cannot therefore be restored, nor does anyone want to do that. Next time around, if there is one, social democracy will have to be different, and so will any accompanying concepts.

The time has passed for behavioural concepts of social deviance, degeneracy, inadequacy or even criminality. No one seriously concerned with social science can take them as valid scientific concepts. Since 1975 there has been an inadvertent coalition between left and right within criminology to abandon aetiological analysis of spurious behavioural concepts – it has become more manageable or politically realistic to focus on crime prevention, police accountability and victims. The right declares that aetiology has failed and the left fights for political legitimacy by wanting to protect the victims of crime. No one celebrates deviance any more, and the term has declined in usage, especially in Europe. The concept of social control has also been much discredited and is falling rapidly out of use. Few social scientists could present contemporary forms of repression and regulation as representative of any great consensus or any coherent policy.

We are faced with societies which often seem to be spinning out of control, blocs of societies disintegrating and local small groups fragmenting. The late modern nightmare has begun. It is a time where our societies present themselves increasingly as 'nations of victims' (Sykes, 1992). Massive atomization, combined with social polarization and the collapse of the great social-democratic ideals such as health care and education of quality for all, have produced a heightened political awareness at the same time as a stupendous political cynicism. This book was written mostly in Canada, Germany and Spain – all countries where the illusions of social democracy have been shattered. Hegemonic majorities feeling threatened by immigrants, a recurring lack of national identity, recalcitrant indigenous peoples wanting funded self-government, loss of a sense of a moral community and escalating economic problems. Such processes are clearest in the USA, although they are developing everywhere.

Armed with a sense of their rights and much angst, the citizens of the USA, as Sykes argues, are now developing a new form of social ascent – ascent or satisfaction through allegation and lawsuit. Everyone feels harassed and recurrent censure is the name of the new game: constituting society through constant slander. The caesura between reason and unreason has multiplied to the *n*th degree, so that anything that infringes the right of difference is actionable.

In the evolution of the modern American, Economic Man has been succeeded by Anxious Man; Other-Directed Man by Narcissistic Man;

but all have seemingly evolved into Annoyed Man, or rather... Annoyed Person.

The National Anthem has become The Whine.

Increasingly Americans act as if they had received a lifelong indemnification from misfortune and a contractual release from personal responsibility ...

Unfortunately, that is a formula for social gridlock: the irresistible search for someone or something to blame colliding with the unmovable willingness to accept responsibility. Now enshrined in law and jurisprudence, victimism is reshaping the fabric of society, including employment policies, criminal justice, education, urban politics, and in an increasingly Orwellian emphasis on 'sensitivity' in language. A community of interdependent citizens has been displaced by a society of resentful, competing, and self-interested individuals who have dressed their private annoyances in the garb of victimism.

(Sykes, 1992: 15)

Difference, differentiation, panic and envy dominate in a battle for increasingly scarce resources. As the concept of culture has been deconstructed so too has any distinction between deviance and difference (two items conflated in the concept of culture) – all that remains is complaint. The old moral blocs are splintered and some regroup for a new assault, but rule is now in the hands of the 'politically correct': a direction-less, politics-less, liberal middle class which is so anti-discrimination and pro-complaint that it cannot discriminate between one political policy and another, between common sense and rhetoric, or between reality and fantasy. Its subjects know that their affluent world of hyper-individualism is threatened – but their answer can not be any of the old unifying politics such as socialism, especially after the final discrediting of the fallen Stalinist bloc, it must be the politics of victimism.

One of the key forms of that politics is the strategy of conquest and ascent by censure and allegation. The man who is elected as President, for example, is the one who can best survive slander and abuse of anything but his politics; the latter have become an irrelevance and indeed a hindrance to office. The process is replicated throughout the social structure. It is the logic of postmodernity: there are few founding norms surviving, they are almost an extinct species, and the intrinsic war of all against all is now conducted with little restraint other than an injunction against discrimination of any kind. But discrimination also refers to the wisdom of being discerning, not just the practice of systematic bias. Without discrimination, we are reduced to mindlessness:

The claim that we are all victims accounts not only for what one critic calls an outbreak of 'emotional influenza' in the United States but also for the increasingly shrill and carping tone of social debate – and for the distrust and unease in our day-to-day relations. At times it seems we can no longer talk to one another. Or rather, we can talk – and shout, demand, and vilify – but we cannot reason.

We lack agreed-upon standards to which we can refer our disputes. In the absence of shared notions of justice and equity, many of the issues we confront appear increasingly to be unresolvable ...

This attitude may account not only for the paucity of serious public debate but also for growing divisiveness along lines of race, class, and gender, and for the tribalization of American society as groups define themselves not by their individual worth or shared culture but solely by their status as victims.

(*ibid*.: 15–16)

Thus the censure and complaint proliferate apace, into hitherto accepted modes of conduct and into the most private parts of life. Hyper-individualism, aggressively pursued in the context of economic recession, a moral-political vacuum and media hyperspace, abandons concepts of consensus, social control and social deviance in favour of the sacralization of a selfish endogeny. It is producing the censorious society of proto-saints – an entropic entity with no goals other than the slander and defeat of the immediate enemy today. Enemies are recycled daily in this ecologically sound form of societal self-mutilation and tomorrow is not on the agenda. As in the old Stalinism, no one is now safe from allegation: the difference is that there is no organizing party and no stated governing norm. The censure floats free of restraint and has become as anonymously unattached as money. Indeed, it has become even more attached to money than ever before.

The commoditization and privatization of discipline has produced a new industrial field whose financial profit lies in social censure – the lawyers and journalists benefit as usual, but are now joined by the human rights specialists, anti-discrimination consultants, harassment officers and human relations scientists. This is big business and easy money, for, in the politics of victimism, hard evidence, civil rights, logical claims and justice go out of the window – to be replaced by (hyper-)sensitivity, the victim as judge, unclear rules and the *ad personam* attack. Anyone can play and anyone can join in – it is a fully democratized, anti-élitist, anti-structural, anti-rational and anti-anything, totally individualist, update of Stalin's rather collectivist original model:

Americans have long prided themselves on their pluralism and their tolerance of the incredible diversity of viewpoints and ideologies represented by this country's various cultural groups. But insistence on the irreducible quality of one's victimhood threatens to turn pluralism into a series of prisons ... In a culture of sound bites and slogans substituted for rational argument, the claim that one is a victim has become one of the few universally recognized currencies of intellectual exchange ... Victimspeak insists upon moral superiority and moral absolutism and thus tends to put an abrupt end to conversation; the threat of its deployment is usually enough to keep others from even considering raising a controversial subject.

(*ibid*.: 16–17)

Things have gone so far that writers like Sykes have called for a 'moratorium on blame' (*ibid.*: 253). Others, like Paglia, call for a 'fusion of idealism and realism' (Paglia, 1992: viii), which would herald the return of the sixties generation to the forefront of progressive social change, for 'the palace has been taken over by shallow upstarts, raiding and wasting the treasury laid up by so many noble generations. It's time to clean house' (*ibid.*: 248). Indeed. Unfortunately, the politics of blaming has now become a very big business, so it is unlikely that the call will be heeded by many, until they can see which way the wind is blowing. Indeed, like many things American, it will no doubt be exported, to add to our own, already well-developed, European version.

These contemporary American concerns must be the subject of another book on political correctness, and no doubt many will be written on the subject before the blaming industry is tamed, but their relation to the sociology of deviance is obvious. We now live in a world of censure. It is a concept whose time has come, unfortunately. The Cold War between the two Superpowers has been replaced by a multiplicity of censorious mini-wars between aggressively selfish smaller units. Social deviance, in contrast, is conceptually and empirically dead. To reverse Horowitz and Liebowitz's argument of the late sixties, there is now a convergence between social deviance and political marginality towards a greedy instrumentalism which consumes both. The Thatcher–Reagan years have rendered deviance an empirical obstacle to employment and a conceptual irrelevance to thinking about the world around us. The unprincipled, pluralistic, amoral, politics of blaming have taken over and the only currency now is the censure.

American society itself in the late 1930s was in search of a self-definition, a self-image, and indeed its soul. The sociology of social deviation was part of that process of self-recognition by which modern society began to understand itself as an entity whose existence and survival was fragile and dependent upon the principled collaboration of a wider constituency of its members; and as an entity prone to self-destruction whose capacity for violence far outweighed its desire for peace. As such, it was part of a process of moral renewal and ethical reconstruction, part of a social-democratic movement which held that society itself was the patient. Its weaknesses have been much criticized by radical criminologists since the late sixties, and rightly so. But I wonder if many students of the sociology of crime and deviance appreciate its strengths, and how many realize the relevance of its history to our present age. At a time when social-democratic and socialistic movements are floundering, very much because of the neglect of their roots in a moral critique of free-market capitalism and bureaucratic dictatorship, it is more than apposite to re-examine the poorly understood history of a sociology which grew out of the late 1930s.

The sociology of deviance was a child of its time. It had its faults. But it took us away from the psychopathology of degeneracy, threw attention on to the agencies of social regulation, taught us that most social deviation is merely the clash of differences in complex societies and urged us to think twice before stigmatizing people, especially when our own interests were involved. The sociology of censure that will succeed it must take that legacy as part of its starting point. In a world with few bearings, we would do well to remember the history of the sociology of deviance as we begin any new analysis. Any movement against excessive censoriousness must develop a new social ethics: the struggle, as always, begins there.

> Modern art must be killed. This means that one has to kill oneself, if one is to continue accomplishing things.
>
> (Pablo Picasso)

Notes

1 On the definition of ideology, see Williams (1976) and Sumner (1979).
2 An interpretation of the book which E. P. Thompson himself affirmed in a seminar at the Cambridge Institute of Criminology in 1979. His final reflections on Althusserianism were never intended to alter this message.
3 It was sustained in Lea and Young (1984) and amplified in the development of left realist criminology in the 1980s.
4 Foucault later talked of 'moral problematization' in his book *The Use of Pleasure* (1985). For him, the important thing was to analyse 'not behaviours or ideas, nor societies and their "ideologies", but the *problematizations* through which being offers itself to be, necessarily, thought – and the practices on the basis of which these problematizations are formed' (Foucault, 1985: 11).

References

Adler, A. (1937) Psychiatric aspects regarding individual and social disorganiza-tion. *American Journal of Sociology*, 42(6), 773–80.

Ahire, P. T. (1991) *Imperial Policing: The Emergence and Role of the Police in Colonial Nigeria 1860–1960*. Milton Keynes: Open University Press.

Albertyn, C. and Davis, D. (1990) The censure of 'communism' and the political trial in South Africa. In C. S. Sumner (ed.), *Censure, Politics and Criminal Justice*. Milton Keynes: Open University Press.

Alexander, F. (1937) Psychoanalysis and social disorganization. *American Journal of Sociology*, 42(6), 781–813.

Allen, F. L. (1969) The revolution in manners and morals. In M. Plesur (ed.), *The 1920's: Problems and Paradoxes*. Boston: Allyn and Bacon.

Allin, B. W. (1937) Is planning compatible with democracy? *American Journal of Sociology*, 42(4), 510–20.

Allsop, K. (1968) *The Bootleggers: The Story of Chicago's Prohibition Era*. London: Hutchinson.

Altick, R. D. (1986) *Deadly Encounters: Two Victorian Sensations*. Philadelphia: University of Pennsylvania Press.

Anderson, N. (1975) *The Hobo: The Sociology of the Homeless Man*. Chicago: University of Chicago Press.

Appleyard, B. (1992) This liberal McCarthyism. *The Times*, 2 September.

Aristotle (1980) *The Nicomachean Ethics* (trans. D. Ross). Oxford: Oxford University Press.

Badger, A. J. (1989) *The New Deal: The Depression Years, 1933–40*. London: Macmillan.

Bailey, R. and Brake, M. (eds) (1975) *Radical Social Work*. London: Edward Arnold.

Bain, R. (1936) Sociology and psychoanalysis. *American Sociological Review*, 1(2), 203–16.

Bauman, Z. (1973) *Culture as Praxis*. London: Routledge and Kegan Paul.

Becker, E. (1964) *The Revolution in Psychiatry*. New York: Free Press.

Becker, H. S. (1963) *Outsiders*. New York: Free Press.

Becker, H. S. (1970) *Sociological Work: Method and Substance*. New Brunswick, NJ: Transaction Books.

Becker, H. S. (1974) Labelling theory reconsidered. In P. Rock and M. McIntosh (eds), *Deviance and Social Control*. London: Tavistock.

Beirne, P. (1987) Adolphe Quételet and the origins of positivist criminology. *American Journal of Sociology*, 92(5), 1140–69.

Beirne, P. and Messerschmidt, J. (1991) *Criminology*. San Diego: Harcourt Brace Jovanovich.

Bell, D. (1962) *The End of Ideology*. New York: Free Press.

Benedict, R. (1961) *Patterns of Culture*. London: Routledge and Kegan Paul.

Bensman, J. and Gerver, I. (1963) Crime and punishment in the factory. *American Sociological Review*, 28, 588–98.

Berger, J. (1972) *Ways of Seeing*. London: BBC and Penguin.

Berle, A. A. and Means, G. C. (1932) *The Modern Corporation and Private Property*. New York: Macmillan.

Berman, M. (1983) *All That is Solid Melts into Air*. London: Verso.

Bernstein, C. (1992) Idiot culture of the intellectual masses. *The Guardian International*, 3 June, 3.

Bittner, E. (1967) The police on skid-row: a study of peace-keeping. *American Sociological Review*, 32, 699–715.

Bloch, H. A. and Prince, M. (1967) *Social Crisis and Deviance: Theoretical Foundations*. New York: Random House.

Block, A. and Chambliss, W. J. (1981) *Organizing Crime*. New York: Elsevier.

Blum, A. (1974) *Theorizing*. London: Heinemann Educational Books.

Blumenthal, A. (1936) The nature of culture. *American Sociological Review*, 1(6), 875–93.

Blumer, H. (1937) Social disorganization and individual disorganization. *American Journal of Sociology*, 42(6), 871–7.

Bowlby, J. (1952) *Maternal Care and Mental Health*, 2nd edn. Geneva: World Health Organization.

Bowman, C. C. (1936) Imagination in social science. *American Sociological Review*, 1(4), 632–40.

Box, S. (1983) *Power, Crime, and Mystification*. London: Tavistock.

Boyle, K., Hadden, T. and Hillyard, P. (1975) *Law and State: The case of Northern Ireland*. London: Martin Robertson.

Bracher, K. D. (1970) *The German Dictatorship: The Origins, Structure, and Consequences of National Socialism* (trans. J. Steinberg). Harmondsworth: Penguin.

Braithwaite, J. (1984) *Corporate Crime in the Pharmaceutical Industry*. London: Routledge and Kegan Paul.

Bredemeier, H. C. and Stephenson, R. M. (1962) *The Analysis of Social Systems*. New York: Holt, Rinehart and Winston.

Bremner, R. H. (1985) The New Deal and social welfare. In H. Sitkoff (ed.), *Fifty Years Later: The New Deal Evaluated*. Philadelphia: Temple University Press.

Brittan, A. (1989) *Masculinity and Power*. Oxford: Basil Blackwell.

Brogan, H. (1985) *Longman History of the United States of America*. London: Guild Publishing.

Bronner, S. E. and Kellner, D. M. (eds) (1989) *Critical Theory and Society: A Reader*. New York: Routledge.

Brown, D. (1970) *Bury My Heart at Wounded Knee*. New York: Pocket Books.

Brown, J. A. C. (1964) *Freud and the Post-Freudians*. Harmondsworth: Penguin.

Brown, N. O. (1959) *Life against Death*. London: Routledge and Kegan Paul.

Bujra, J. M. (1982) Women entrepreneurs of 'early' Nairobi. In C. S. Sumner (ed.), *Crime, Justice, and Underdevelopment*. London: Heinemann.

Bulmer, M. (1984) *The Chicago School of Sociology*. Chicago: University of Chicago Press.

Burnham, J. C. (1968) The new psychology: from narcissism to social control. In J. Braeman, R. H. Bremner and D. Brody (eds), *Change and Continuity in Twentieth-Century America: The 1920s*. Columbus: Ohio State University Press.

Burrows, T. (1937) The law of the organism: a neuro-social approach to the problems of human behavior. *American Journal of Sociology*, 42(6), 814–24.

Cain, M. and Hunt, A. (eds) (1979) *Marx and Engels on Law*. London: Academic Press.

Carr, E. H. (1961) *What is History?* London: Macmillan.

Carson, W. G. (1981) *The Other Price of Britain's Oil*. Oxford: Martin Robertson and Company.

Castel, R. (1972) *The Psychiatric Society*. New York: Columbia University Press.

Cayton, H. R. and Drake, S. T. C. (1946) *Black Metropolis*. London: Routledge and Kegan Paul.

Chambliss, W. J. and Seidman, R. B. (1971) *Law, Order, and Power*. Reading, MA: Addison-Wesley.

Chapin, F. S. (1936) Social theory and social action. *American Sociological Review*, 1(1), 1–11.

Chesler, P. (1974) *Women and Madness*. London: Allen Lane.

Chesney-Lind, M. (1973) Judicial enforcement of the female sex role. *Issues in Criminology*, 8(2), 51–70.

Chesney-Lind, M. (1978) Chivalry re-examined: women and the criminal justice system. In L. H. Bowker (ed.), *Women, Crime and the Criminal Justice System*. Lexington: Lexington Books.

Chunn, D. E. and Gavigan, S. A. M. (1988) Social control: analytic tool or analytic quagmire? *Contemporary Crises*, 12, 107–24.

Cicourel, A. V. (1976) *The Social Organization of Juvenile Justice*. London: Heinemann.

Clifford, W. J. (1979) *An Introduction to African Criminology*. Nairobi: Oxford University Press.

Cloward, R. and Ohlin, L. (1960) *Delinquency and Opportunity*. New York: Free Press.

Cobban, A. (1962) *A History of Modern France*, 3rd edn. Harmondsworth: Penguin.

Cohen, A. K. (1955) *Delinquent Boys*. New York: Free Press.

Cohen, A. K. (1968) Deviant behavior. In *International Encyclopaedia of the Social Sciences*. New York: Macmillan.

Cohen, S. (ed.) (1971) *Images of Deviance*. Harmondsworth: Penguin.

Cohen, S. (1973) *Folk Devils and Moral Panics*. St Albans: Paladin.

Cohen, S. and Scull, A. (eds) (1983) *Social Control and the State*. Oxford: Blackwell.

Cohen, S. and Young, J. (eds) (1973) *The Manufacture of News. Deviance, Social Problems and the Mass Media*. London: Constable.

Cole, B. and Gealt, A. (1989) *Art of the Western World: From Ancient Greece to Post-Modernism*. New York: Summit Books.

Collings, M. (1992) Resistance heroes of art. *The Guardian International*, 20 May, 18.

Connell, R. W. (1987) *Gender and Power*. Cambridge: Polity Press.

Cooper, D. (ed.) (1968) *The Dialectics of Liberation*. Harmondsworth: Penguin.

Corrigan, P. (1979) *Schooling the Smash Street Kids*. London: Macmillan.

Crothers, C. (1987) *Robert K. Merton*. Chichester: Ellis Horwood.

Cuber, J. F. (1940) Some aspects of institutional disorganization. *American Sociological Review*, 5, 483–8.

Culler, J. (1974) *Structuralist Poetics*. London: Routledge and Kegan Paul.

Davis, K. (1937) The sociology of prostitution. *American Sociological Review*, 2(1), 744–55.

Davis, K. (1938) Mental hygiene and the class structure. *Psychiatry*, 1, 55–65.

Davis, K. (1961) Prostitution. In R. K. Merton and R. A. Nisbet (eds), *Contemporary Social Problems*. New York: Harcourt, Brace and World.

Debord, G. (1977) *Society of the Spectacle*. Detroit: Black and Red.

Debro, J. (1970) Dialogue with Howard S. Becker. *Issues in Criminology*, 5(2), 159–79.

D'Emilio, J. and Freedman, E. B. (1988) *Intimate Matters: A History of Sexuality in America*. New York: Harper & Row.

Descharnes, R. and Néret, G. (1992) *Salvador Dalí*. Köln: Benedikt Taschen.

Dollard, J. (1935) *Criteria for the Life History*. New Haven, CT: Yale University Press.

Dostoyevsky, F. (1972) *Notes from Underground/The Double* (trans. J. Coulson). Harmondsworth: Penguin.

Downes, D. (1966) *The Delinquent Solution*. London: Routledge and Kegan Paul.

Downes, D. and Rock, P. (eds) (1979) *Deviant Interpretations*. Oxford: Martin Robertson.

Downes, D. and Rock, P. (1982) *Understanding Deviance*. Oxford: Clarendon.

Durkheim, É. (1933) *The Division of Labor in Society* (trans. G. Simpson). New York: Free Press.

Durkheim, É. (1966) *The Rules of Sociological Method* (trans. S. A. Solovay and J. H. Mueller, ed. G. E. G. Catlin). New York: Free Press.

Durkheim, É. (1970) *Suicide* (trans. J. A. Spaulding and G. Simpson, ed. G. Simpson). London: Routledge and Kegan Paul.

Ekirch, J. A. A. (1969) *Ideologies and Utopias: The Impact of the New Deal on American Thought*. Chicago: Quadrangle.

Elliott, M. A. (1944) Crime and the Frontier Mores. *American Sociological Review*, 9, 185–92.

Eribon, D. (1991) *Michel Foucault* (trans. B. Wing). Cambridge, MA: Harvard University Press.

Erikson, K. T. (1966) *Wayward Puritans*. New York: John Wiley and Sons.

Ermann, M. D. and Lundman, R. J. (eds) (1978) *Corporate and Government Deviance: Problems of Organizational Behavior in Contemporary Society*. Oxford: Oxford University Press.

Fanon, F. (1967) *The Wretched of the Earth*. Harmondsworth: Penguin.

Fanon, F. (1970) *A Dying Colonialism*. Harmondsworth: Penguin.

Faris, R. E. L. (1967) *Chicago Sociology, 1920–1932*. Chicago: University of Chicago Press.

Fennell, T., Jenish, D., Lowther, W. and Corelli, R. (1991). The Silencers: a new wave of repression is sweeping through the universities. *Maclean's*, 27 May, 40–50.

Fine, B. (1977) Labelling theory: an investigation into the sociological critique of deviance. *Economy and Society*, 6(2), 166–93.

Finestone, H. (1964) Cats, kicks and color. In H. S. Becker (ed.), *The Other Side*. New York: Free Press.

Finestone, H. (1976) *Victims of Change: Juvenile Delinquents in American Society*. Westport, CT: Greenwood Press.

Fletcher, R. (1978) How CIA money took the teeth out of British socialism. In P. Agee and L. Wolf (eds), *Dirty Work: The CIA in Western Europe*. London: Zed Press.

Ford, J. (ed.) (1923) *Social Problems and Social Policy: Principles Underlying Treatment and Prevention of Poverty, Defectiveness, and Criminality*. Boston: Ginn and Company.

Ford, J. (1939) *Social Deviation*. New York: Macmillan.

Foster, H. (ed.) (1983) *The Anti-Aesthetic: Essays on Postmodern Culture*. Port Townsend, WA: Bay Press.

Foucault, M. (1967) *Madness and Civilization: A History of Insanity in the Age of Reason* (trans. R. Howard). London: Tavistock.

Foucault, M. (1973) *The Birth of the Clinic*. London: Tavistock.

Foucault, M. (1977a) *Discipline and Punish: The Birth of the Prison* (trans. A. Sheridan). London: Allen Lane.

Foucault, M. (1977b) Nietzsche, genealogy, history. In D. F. Bouchard (ed.), *Language, Counter-memory, Practice*. Ithaca, NY: Cornell University Press.

Foucault, M. (1980a) *Power/Knowledge* (trans. C. Gordon, L. Marshall, J. Mepham and K. Soper, ed. C. Gordon). New York: Pantheon Books.

Foucault, M. (1980b) *The History of Sexuality. Volume 1: An Introduction* (trans. R. Hurley). New York: Vintage.

Foucault, M. (1985) *The Use of Pleasure. (Volume 2 of The History of Sexuality)*. New York: Pantheon.

Frank, L. K. (1925) Social Problems. *American Journal of Sociology*, 30, 462–73.

Frank, L. K. (1948) *Society as the Patient: Essays on Culture and Personality*. New Brunswick, NJ: Rutgers University Press.

Fraser, S. and Gerstle, G. (eds) (1989) *The Rise and Fall of the New Deal Order, 1930–1980*. Princeton: Princeton University Press.

Freud, S. (1930) *Civilization and Its Discontents* (trans. J. Strachey). London: Hogarth.

Freud, S. (1973) *New Introductory Lectures on Psychoanalysis* (trans. J. Strachey). Harmondsworth: Penguin.

Freud, S. (1975) *The Psychopathology of Everyday Life* (trans. A. Tyson). Harmondsworth: Penguin.

Freud, S. (1977) *On Sexuality: Three Essays on the Theory of Sexuality and Other Works* (trans. J. Strachey). Harmondsworth: Penguin.

Freud, S. (1979) *On Psychopathology: Inhibitions, Symptoms and Anxiety and Other Works* (trans. J. Strachey). Harmondsworth: Penguin.

Friedlander, K. (1947) *The Psycho-Analytic Approach to Juvenile Delinquency*. London: Routledge and Kegan Paul.

Fromm, E. (1941) *Escape from Freedom*. New York: Avon Books.

Fromm, E. (1989) Psychoanalysis and sociology. In S. E. Bronner and D. M. Kellner (eds), *Critical Theory in Society*. New York: Routledge.

Fuller, R. C. (1942) Morals and the criminal law. *Journal of Criminal Law and Criminology*, 32, 624–30.

Fuller, R. C. (1943) Review of Brown's *Social Pathology*. *American Journal of Sociology*, 49 (July), 104–5.

Fuller, R. C. and Myers, R. R. (1942) Some aspects of a theory of social problems. *American Sociological Review*, 6, 24–32.

Fyvel, T. R. (1961) *The Insecure Offenders*. Harmondsworth Penguin.

Garfinkel, H. (1967) *Studies in Ethnomethodology*. Englewood Cliffs, NJ: Prentice Hall.

Garland, D. (1985) *Punishment and Welfare: A History of Penal Strategies*. Aldershot: Gower.

Garland, D. (1986) The punitive mentality: its socio-historic development and decline. *Contemporary Crises*, 10, 305–20.

Garland, D. (1990) *Punishment and Modern Society*. Oxford: Oxford University Press.

Geary, R. (1986) *Policing Industrial Disputes 1893 to 1985*. London: Methuen.

Geis, G. and Meier, R. F. (1977) *White-Collar Crime: Offenses in Business, Politics, and the Professions*. New York: The Free Press.

Gelsthorpe, L. and Morris, A. (eds) (1990) *Feminist Perspectives in Criminology*. Milton Keynes: Open University Press.

Gerth, H. and Mills, C. W. (1954) *Character and Social Structure: The Psychology of Social Institutions*. London: Routledge and Kegan Paul.

Gibbons, D. C. (1979) *The Criminological Enterprise*. Englewood Cliffs, NJ: Prentice-Hall.

Giddens, A. (1966) *A Contemporary Critique of Historical Materialism*. London: Macmillan.

Giddens, A. (1971a) *Capitalism and Modern Social Theory*. Cambridge: Cambridge University Press.

Giddens, A. (ed.) (1971b) *The Sociology of Suicide*. London: Cass.

Giddens, A. (1978) *Durkheim*. Glasgow: Fontana.

Gill, O. (1977) *Luke Street: Housing Policy, Conflict and the Creation of the Delinquent Area*. London: Macmillan.

Gillin, J. (1936) The configuration problem in culture. *American Sociological Review*, 1(3), 373–86.

Gilman, S. L. (1985) *Difference and Pathology: Stereotypes of Sexuality, Race, and Madness*. Ithaca, NY: Cornell University Press.

Glueck, S. and Glueck, E. (1950) *Unraveling Juvenile Delinquency*. New York: The Commonwealth Fund.

Goffman, E. (1962) On cooling out the mark. In A. M. Rose (ed.), *Human Behavior and Social Processes*. London: Routledge and Kegan Paul.

Goffman, E. (1968a) *Asylums*. Harmondsworth: Penguin.

Goffman, E. (1968b) *Stigma*. Harmondsworth: Penguin.

Goffman, E. (1972) *Interaction Ritual*. Harmondsworth: Penguin.

Gold, M. (1966) Undetected delinquent behavior. *Journal of Research in Crime and Delinquency*, 3, 27–46.

Gouldner, A. W. (1970) *The Coming Crisis of Western Sociology*. London: Heinemann.

Gouldner, A. W. (1975) *For Sociology*. Harmondsworth: Pelican.

Gransee, C. and Stammerman, U. (1992) *Kriminalität als Konstruktion von Wirklichkeit und die Kategorie Geschlecht: Versuch einer feministischen Perspektive*. Hamburg: Centaurus.

Green, P. (1990) *The Enemy Without: Policing and Class Consciousness in the Miners' Strike*. Milton Keynes: Open University Press.

Greenberg, D. and Anderson, N. (1981) Recent Marxisant books on law. *Contemporary Crises*, 5, 293–322.

Gusfield, J. (1955) Social structure and moral reform. *American Journal of Sociology*, 61, 221–32.

Gusfield, J. (1963) *Symbolic Crusade: Status Politics and the American Temperance Movement*. Urbana: University of Illinois Press.

Gusfield, J. (1967) Moral passage: the symbolic process in public designations of deviance. *Social Problems*, 15(2), 175–88.

Habermas, J. (1971) *Toward a Rational Society*. London: Heinemann.

Habermas, J. (1974) *Theory and Practice*. London: Heinemann.

Habermas, J. (1976) *Legitimation Crisis*. London: Heinemann.

Habermas, J. (1979) *Communication and the Evolution of Society*. London: Heinemann.

Habermas, J. (1985) Modernity – an incomplete project. In H. Foster (ed.), *Postmodern Culture*. London: Pluto.

Hall, S. M. (1974) Deviance, politics, and the media. In P. Rock and M. McIntosh (eds), *Deviance and Social Control*. London: Tavistock.

Hall, S. M., Critcher, C., Jefferson, T., Clarke, J. and Roberts, B. (1978) *Policing the Crisis: Mugging, the State, and Law and Order*. London: Macmillan.

Hall, S. M. and Jefferson, T. (eds) (1975) *Resistance through Rituals*. London: Hutchinson.

Hankins, F. H. (1937) German policies for increasing births. *American Journal of Sociology*, 42(5), 630–52.

Harris, R. and Webb, D. (1987) *Welfare, Power, and Juvenile Justice*. London: Tavistock.

Hawley, E. W. (1979) *The Great War and the Search for a Modern Order. A History of the American People and Their Institutions, 1917–1933*. New York: St Martin's Press.

Hawthorn, G. (1976) *Enlightenment and Despair: A History of Sociology*. Cambridge: Cambridge University Press.

Hay, D., Linebaugh, P., Rule, J. G., Thompson, E. P. and Winslow, C. (1975) *Albion's Fatal Tree*. London: Allen Lane.

Haynes, R. (1984) Suicide in Fiji: a preliminary study. *British Journal of Psychiatry*, 145, 433–8.

Haynes, R. (1987) Suicide and social response in Fiji: a historical survey. *British Journal of Psychiatry*, 151, 21–6.

Healey, D. (1990) *The Time of My Life*. London: Penguin.

Hebdige, D. (1979) *Subculture: The Meaning of Style*. London: Methuen.

Heidensohn, F. (1985) *Women and Crime*. London: Macmillan.

Hepworth, M. and Turner, B. S. (1982) *Confession: Studies in Deviance and Religion*. London: Routledge and Kegan Paul.

Hirst, P. Q. (1975a) Marx and Engels on law, crime and morality. In I. Taylor, P. Walton and J. Young (eds), *Critical Criminology*. London: Routledge and Kegan Paul.

Hirst, P. Q. (1975b) Radical deviancy theory: a reply to Taylor and Walton. In I. Taylor, P. Walton and J. Young (eds), *Critical Criminology*. London: Routledge and Kegan Paul.

Hoffman, F. J. (1968) Fiction of the Jazz Age. In J. Braeman, R. H. Bremner and D. Brody (eds), *Change and Continuity in Twentieth-Century America: The 1920s*. Columbus: Ohio State University Press.

Hollingshead, A. B. (1941) The concept of social control. *American Sociological Review*, 6, 217–24.

Hooton, E. A. (1939) *The American Criminal: An Anthropological Study*. Cambridge, MA: Harvard University Press.

Hopper, E. (1945) *Edward Hopper*. New York: American Artists Group.

Horney, K. (1936) Culture and neurosis. *American Sociological Review*, 1(2), 221–30.

Horowitz, I. L. and Liebowitz, M. (1968) Social deviance and political marginality. *Social Problems*, 15(3), 280–96.

Hughes, R. (1981) *The Shock of the New: Art and the Century of Change*. London: BBC Publications.

Hutton, W. (1991a) Counting the cost of 'freedom'. *The Guardian*, 11 February, 13.

Hutton, W. (1991b) A great deal has been lost. *The Guardian*, 25 February, 14.

Ignatieff, M. (1978) *A Just Measure of Pain: The Penitentiary in the Industrial Revolution 1750–1850*. London: Macmillan.

Jacoby, R. (1977) *Social Amnesia: A Critique of Conformist Psychology from Adler to Laing*. Hassocks: The Harvester Press.

James, C. L. R. (1969) *Beyond a Boundary*. London: Stanley Paul.

Janowitz, M. (1975) Sociological theory and social control. *American Journal of Sociology*, 81(1), 82–108.

Jones, G. S. (1976) *Outcast London: A Study in the Relationships between Classes in Victorian Society*. Harmondsworth: Peregrine.

Jung, C. G. (1933) *Modern Man in Search of a Soul* (trans. W. S. Dell and C. F. Baynes). London: Kegan Paul, Trench, Trubner.

Jung, C. G. (1970) *Civilization in Transition*, 2nd edn (trans. R. F. C. Hull). Princeton, NJ: Princeton University Press.

Kitsuse, J. I. and Cicourel, A. V. (1963) A note on the uses of official statistics. *Social Problems*, 11 (Fall), 50–8.

Klein, D. (1973) The etiology of female crime. *Issues in Criminology*, 8(2), 3–30.

Laing, R. D. (1967) *The Politics of Experience and the Bird of Paradise*. Harmondsworth: Penguin.

Laing, R. D. (1968) The Obvious. In D. Cooper (ed.), *The Dialectics of Liberation*. Harmondsworth: Penguin.

Landesco, J. (1968) *Organized Crime in Chicago*. Chicago: University of Chicago Press.

LaPière, R. T. (1954) *A Theory of Social Control*. New York: McGraw-Hill.

Larkin, R. W. (1979) *Suburban Youth in Cultural Crisis*. New York: Oxford University Press.

Larrain, J. (1979) *The Concept of Ideology*. London: Hutchinson.

Lasswell, H. D. (1966) Why be quantitative? In B. Berelson and M. Janowitz (eds), *Reader in Public Opinion and Communication*. New York: Free Press.

Laughlin, H. H. (1921) The socially inadequate: how shall we designate and sort them? *American Journal of Sociology*, 27(1), 54–70.

Lawson, A. (1985) The cultural legacy of the New Deal. In H. Sitkoff (ed.), *Fifty Years Later: The New Deal Evaluated*. Philadelphia: Temple University Press.

Lea, J. and Young, J. (1984) *What Is to Be Done about Law and Order?* Harmondsworth: Penguin.

Lefton, M., Skipper, J. K. Jr and McCaghy, C. H. (eds) (1968) *Approaches to*

Deviance: Theories, Concepts, and Research Findings. New York: Appleton-Century-Crofts.

Lemert, E. M. (1942) The folkways and social control. *American Sociological Review*, 7, 394–99.

Lemert, E. M. (1945) The grand jury as an agency of social control. *American Sociological Review*, 10, 751–8.

Lemert, E. M. (1948) Some aspects of a general theory of sociopathic behaviour. *Proceedings of the Pacific Sociological Society*, XVI, 23–9.

Lemert, E. M. (1951) *Social Pathology*. New York: McGraw-Hill.

Lemert, E. M. (1972) *Human Deviance, Social Problems, and Social Control*, 2nd edn. Englewood Cliffs, NJ: Prentice-Hall.

Leonard, E. (1982) *Women, Crime and Society*. New York: Longman.

Levi, P. (1961) *Survival in Auschwitz: The Nazi Assault on Humanity* (trans. S. Woolf). New York: Collier Books.

Levi, P. (1988) *The Drowned and the Saved* (trans. R. Rosenthal). London: Michael Joseph.

Lewis, O. (1968) *La Vida*. London: Panther.

Liazos, A. (1972) The poverty of the sociology of deviance: nuts, sluts and perverts. *Social Problems*, 20, 103–20.

Lindesmith, A. (1938) A sociological theory of drug addiction. *American Journal of Sociology*, 43(4), 593–613.

Lindesmith, A. and Levin, Y. (1937) The Lombrosian myth in criminology. *American Journal of Sociology*, 42(5), 653–71.

Luhmann, N. (1985) *A Sociological Theory of Law* (trans. E. King and M. Albrow). London: Routledge and Kegan Paul.

Lukács, G. (1971) *History and Class Consciousness*. London: Merlin.

Lukes, S. (1973) *Émile Durkheim*. London: Penguin.

Lukes, S. and Scull, A. (eds) (1983) *Durkheim and the Law*. Oxford: Martin Robertson.

Maddox, C. (1990) *Salvador Dalí*. Köln: Benedikt Taschen.

Malinowski, B. (1926) *Crime and Custom in Savage Society*. London: Routledge.

Mallet, G. (1992) Are you now or have you ever been politically correct? *Flare*, 78–80.

Mannheim, K. (1936) *Ideology and Utopia* (trans. L. Wirth and E. Shils). New York: Harcourt, Brace.

Marcuse, H. (1964) *One-Dimensional Man*. London: Routledge and Kegan Paul.

Marquis, A. G. (1986) *Hopes and Ashes. The Birth of Modern Times: 1929–1939*. New York: Free Press.

Marx, K. and Engels, F. (1968) *Selected Works*. London: Lawrence and Wishart.

Matusow, A. J. (1984) *The Unraveling of America*. New York: Harper.

Matza, D. (1964) *Delinquency and Drift*. New York: Wiley.

Matza, D. (1969) *Becoming Deviant*. Englewood Cliffs, NJ: Prentice-Hall.

Matza, D. and Sykes, G. M. (1961) Juvenile delinquency and subterranean values. *American Sociological Review*, 26(5), 712–19.

May, M. A. (1937) A research note on co-operative and competitive behavior. *American Journal of Sociology*, 42(6), 887–91.

Mayer, J. A. (1983) Notes towards a working definition of social control in historical analysis. In S. Cohen and A. Scull (eds), *Social Control and the State*. Oxford: Blackwell.

Mayo, E. (1937) Psychiatry and sociology in relation to social disorganization. *American Journal of Sociology*, 42(6), 825–31.

McIntosh, J. R. (1974) *Perspectives on Marginality: Understanding Deviance*. Boston: Allyn and Bacon.

McLaren, A. (1990) *Our Own Master Race: Eugenics in Canada, 1885–1945*. Toronto: McClelland and Stewart.

Mead, G. H. (1918) The psychology of punitive justice. *American Journal of Sociology*, 23(5), 577–602.

Mead, G. H. (1962) *Mind, Self, and Society* (ed. C. W. Morris). Chicago: University of Chicago Press.

Melossi, D. (1990) *The State of Social Control: A Sociological Study of Concepts of State and Social Control in the Making of Democracy*. Cambridge: Polity Press.

Meltzer, B. N., Petras, J. W. and Reynolds, L. T. (1975) *Symbolic Interactionism: Genesis, Varieties and Criticism*. London: Routledge and Kegan Paul.

Merton, R. K. (1934) Durkheim's Division of Labour in Society. *American Journal of Sociology*, 40, 319–28.

Merton, R. K. (1936) The unanticipated consequences of purposive social action. *American Sociological Review*, 1, 894–904.

Merton, R. K. (1938) Social structure and anomie. *American Sociological Review*, 3, 672–82.

Meszaros, I. (1970) *Marx's Theory of Alienation*. London: Merlin.

Miller, R. M. (1968) The Ku Klux Klan. In J. Braeman, R. H. Bremner and D. Brody (eds), *Change and Continuity in Twentieth-Century America: The 1920s*. Columbus: Ohio State University Press.

Millman, M. (1975) She did it all for love: a feminist view of the sociology of deviance. In M. Millman and R. M. Kantet (eds), *Another Voice*. New York: Anchor.

Mills, C. W. (1956) *The Power Elite*. New York: Oxford University Press.

Mills, C. W. (1967) *Power, Politics and People* (ed. I. L. Horowitz). London: Oxford University Press.

Mills, C. W. (1970) *The Sociological Imagination*. Harmondsworth: Penguin.

Monahan, T. P. (1957) Family status and the delinquent child. *Social Forces*, 35, 250–8.

Morris, A. (1987) *Women, Crime and Criminal Justice*. Oxford: Basil Blackwell.

Mushanga, T. M. (1976) *Crime and Deviance*. Kampala: East African Literature Bureau.

Myrdal, G. (1944) *An American Dilemma*. New York: Harper.

Nietzsche, F. (1967) *On the Genealogy of Morals/Ecce Homo* (trans. W. Kaufmann and R. J. Hollingdale, ed. W. Kaufmann). New York: Vintage.

Nisbet, R. (1975) *The Sociology of Émile Durkheim*. London: Heinemann.

Nye, F. I., Short, J. F. and Olsen, V. J. (1958) Socioeconomic status and delinquent behaviour. *American Journal of Sociology*, 63, 381–9.

Oberschall, A. (1972) The institutionalization of American sociology. In A. Oberschall (ed.), *The Establishment of Empirical Sociology*. New York: Harper and Row.

Ogburn, W. F. and Jaffe, A. J. (1937) Recovery and social conditions. *American Journal of Sociology*, 42(6), 878–86.

Ostrander, G. M. (1968) The revolution in morals. In J. Braeman, R. H. Bremner and D. Brody (eds), *Change and Continuity in Twentieth-Century America: The 1920s*. Columbus: Ohio State University Press.

Overby, A. (1972) Discrimination in the administration of justice. In C. E. Reasons and J. L. Kuykendall (eds), *Race, Crime and Justice*. Pacific Palisades: Goodyear.

Paglia, C. (1992) *Sex, Art, and American Culture*. New York: Vintage.

Park, R. E. (1921) Sociology and the social sciences: the social organism and the collective mind. *American Journal of Sociology*, 27(1), 1–21.

Park, R. E. (1925a) The natural history of the newspaper. In R. E. Park, E. W. Burgess and R. D. McKenzie (eds), *The City*. Chicago: University of Chicago Press.

Park, R. E. (1925b) Community organization and juvenile delinquency. In R. E. Park, E. W. Burgess and R. D. McKenzie (eds), *The City*. Chicago: University of Chicago Press.

Park, R. E. (1937) Human ecology. *American Journal of Sociology*, 42(1), 1–15.

Park, R. E. (1939a) Symbiosis and socialization: a frame of reference for the study of society. *American Journal of Sociology*, 45(1), 1–25.

Park, R. E. (1939b) News as a form of knowledge: a chapter in the sociology of knowledge. *American Journal of Sociology*, 45(5), 669–86.

Park, R. E. (1941a) News and the power of the press. *American Journal of Sociology*, 47(1), 1–11.

Park, R. E. (1941b) Morale and the news. *American Journal of Sociology*, 47(3), 360–77.

Park, R. E. (1950) *Race and Culture*. Glencoe, IL: Free Press.

Park, R. E. and Burgess, E. W. (1924) *Introduction to the Science of Sociology*, 2nd edn. Chicago: University of Chicago Press.

Parsons, T. (1937) *The Structure of Social Action*, 2nd edn. New York: McGraw-Hill.

Parsons, T. (1951) *The Social System*. London: Routledge and Kegan Paul.

Parsons, T. (1963) *Essays in Sociological Theory*. Glencoe, IL: Free Press.

Parsons, T. and Bales, R. F. (1956) *Family: Socialization and Interaction Process*. London: Routledge and Kegan Paul.

Parsons, T. and Shils, E. A. (eds) (1962) *Toward a General Theory of Action*. New York: Harper and Row.

Pashukanis, E. (1980) *Pashukanis: Selected Writings on Marxism and Law* (trans. P. B. Maggs, ed. P. Beirne and R. Sharlet). London: Academic Press.

Pearce, F. (1976) *Crimes of the Powerful: Marxism, Crime and Deviance*. London: Pluto Press.

Pearce, F. (1989) *The Radical Durkheim*. London: Unwin Hyman.

Pearson, G. (1975) *The Deviant Imagination*. London: Macmillan.

Pearson, G. (1976) 'Paki-bashing' in a North East Lancashire town. In G. Mungham and G. Pearson (eds), *Working Class Youth Culture*. London: Routledge and Kegan Paul.

Pearson, G. (1983) *Hooligan: A History of Respectable Fears*. London: Macmillan.

Pfohl, S. (1985) *Images of Deviance and Social Control*. New York: McGraw-Hill.

Pitch, T. (1980) *Teoría de la desviación social*. México: Editorial Nueva Imagen.

Piven, F. F. and Cloward, R. A. (1971) *Regulating the Poor: The Functions of Public Welfare*. New York: Vintage.

Playthell, N. (1992) Seeing is not believing. *The Guardian*, 5 May, 18.

Plesur, M. (ed.) (1969) *The 1920s: Problems and Paradoxes*. Boston: Allyn and Bacon.

Ploscowe, M. (1951) *Sex and the Law*. New York: Prentice-Hall.

Pollard, A. (1979) Negotiating deviance and 'getting done' in primary school classrooms. In L. Barton and R. Meighan (eds), *Schools, Pupils and Deviance*. Driffield: Nafferton.

Poster, M. (1984) *Foucault, Marxism and History*. Cambridge: Polity Press.

Pound, R. (1930) *Criminal Justice in America*. New York: Henry Holt.

Pound, R. (1942) *Social Control Through Law*. New Haven: Yale University Press.

Publications, Committee on (1935) *Report of the Committee on Publications of the American Sociological Society*. American Sociological Society.

Quinney, R. (1965) Is criminal behaviour deviant behaviour? *British Journal of Criminology*, 5 (April), 132–42.

Quinney, R. (1970) *The Social Reality of Crime*. Boston: Little, Brown.

Radzinowicz, L. (1945) The Waltham Black Act. *Cambridge Law Journal*, IX, 56–81.

Reich, W. (1970) *The Mass Psychology of Fascism* (trans. V. R. Carfagno). Harmondsworth: Penguin.

Reiman, J. H. (1979) *The Rich Get Richer and the Poor Get Prison: Ideology, Class, and Criminal Justice*. New York: Wiley.

Reiss, J. A. J. and Rhodes, A. L. (1961) The distribution of juvenile delinquency in the social class structure. *American Sociological Review*, 26, 720–32.

Roberts, P. (1993) Social control and the censure(s) of sex. *Crime, Law and Social Change*, 19, 171–86.

Rock, P. (1973) *Deviant Behaviour*. London: Hutchinson.

Rock, P. (1979) *The Making of Symbolic Interactionism*. London: Macmillan.

Rock, P. (1985) Deviance. In A. Kuper and J. Kuper (eds), *The Social Science Encyclopaedia*. London: Routledge and Kegan Paul.

Rock, P. (1988) The present state of criminology in Britain. In P. Rock (ed.) *A History of British Criminology*. Oxford: Clarendon.

Rodmell, R. (1981) Men, women and sexuality: a feminist critique of the sociology of deviance. *Women's Studies International Quarterly*, 4(2), 143–55.

Rosenberg, C. (1987) *1919: Britain on the Brink of Revolution*. London: Bookmarks.

Rosenhan, D. L. (1973) On being sane in insane places. *Science*, 179, 250–8.

Ross, E. A. (1937) Freedom in the modern world. *American Journal of Sociology*, 42(4), 459–62.

Ross, E. A. (1969) *Social Control: A Survey of the Foundations of Order*. Cleveland, OH: The Press of Case Western Reserve University.

Ross, H. (1937) Crime and the native-born sons of European immigrants. *Journal of Criminal Law and Criminology*, 28, 202–9.

Rubington, E. and Weinberg, M. S. (eds) (1968) *Deviance: The Interactionist Perspective*. London: Macmillan.

Ryave, A. L. and Schenkein, J. N. (1974) Notes on the art of walking. In R. Turner (ed.), *Ethnomethodology*. Harmondsworth: Penguin.

Sapir, E. (1937) The contribution of psychiatry to an understanding of behavior in society. *American Journal of Sociology*, 42(6), 862–70.

Schilder, P. (1937) The relation between social and personal disorganization. *American Journal of Sociology*, 42(6), 832–9.

Schur, E. M. (1965) *Crimes without Victims: Deviant Behavior and Public Policy*. Englewood Cliffs, NJ: Prentice-Hall.

Schur, E. M. (1971) *Labeling Deviant Behavior*. New York: Harper and Row.

Schur, E. M. (1984) *Labeling Women Deviant: Gender, Stigma, and Social Control*. New York: Random House.

Schwartz, R. D. and Skolnick, J. H. (1962) Two studies of legal stigma. *Social Problems*, 10, 133–8.

Scraton, P. (ed.) (1987) *Law, Order and the Authoritarian State*. Milton Keynes: Open University Press.

Sedgwick, P. (1982) *Psychopolitics*. London: Pluto.

Sellin, T. (1937) Letter to the editor. *American Journal of Sociology*, 42(6), 897–9.

Sellin, T. (1938) *Culture Conflict and Crime*. New York: Social Science Research Council.

Shaw, C. R. (1929) *Delinquency Areas*. Chicago: University of Chicago Press.

Shaw, C. R. (1930) *The Jack-Roller: A Delinquent Boy's Own Story*. Chicago: University of Chicago Press.

Shaw, C. R. and McKay, H. D. (1931) *Social Factors in Juvenile Delinquency, Volume 2*. Report on the Causes of Crime, U.S. Government Printing Office, National Commission on Law Observance and Enforcement, Washington, DC.

Shaw, C. R. and McKay, H. D. (1942) *Juvenile Delinquency and Urban Areas*. Chicago: University of Chicago Press.

Shaw, C. R. and Moore, M. E. (1931) *The Natural History of a Delinquent Career*. Chicago: Chicago University Press.

Sheldon, W. H. (1949) *Varieties of Delinquent Youth*. New York: Harper.

Shelley, L. (1981) *Crime and Modernization*. Carbondale: South Illinois University Press.

Short, J. F. and Nye, F. I. (1958) Extent of unrecorded juvenile delinquency. *Journal of Criminal Law, Criminology, and Police Science*, 49, 296–302.

Short, J. F. and Strodtbeck, J. L. (1965) *Group Process and Gang Delinquency*. Chicago: University of Chicago Press.

Simmons, J. L. (1965) Public stereotypes of deviants. *Social Problems*, 13, 223–32.

Simmons, J. L. (1969) *Deviants*. Santa Barbara: University of California.

Simon, D. R. and Eitzen, D. S. (1982) *Elite Deviance*. Boston: Allyn and Bacon.

Sitkoff, H. (ed.) (1985) *Fifty Years Later: The New Deal Evaluated*. Philadelphia: Temple University Press.

Skolnick, J. H. (1966) *Justice without Trial: Law Enforcement in Democratic Society*. New York: John Wiley & Sons.

Slight, D. (1937) Disorganization in the individual and in society. *American Journal of Sociology*, 42(6), 840–7.

Smart, C. (1976) *Women, Crime and Criminology: A Feminist Critique*. London: Routledge and Kegan Paul.

Smart, C. (1989) *Feminism and the Power of Law*. London: Routledge.

Smith, D. (1988) *The Chicago School: A Liberal Critique of Capitalism*. Basingstoke: Macmillan.

Snodgrass, J. (1976) Clifford R. Shaw and Henry D. McKay: Chicago criminologists. *British Journal of Criminology*, 16(1), 1–19.

Sparks, R. (1992) *Television and the Drama of Crime*. Buckingham: Open University Press.

Speer, A. (1971) *Inside the Third Reich* (trans. R. Winston and C. Winston). London: Sphere Books.

Speier, H. (1937) Freedom and social planning. *American Journal of Sociology*, 42(4), 463–83.

Spitzer, S. (1975) Toward a Marxian theory of deviance. *Social Problems*, 22(5), 638–51.

Spitzer, S. (ed.) (1983) *Research in Law, Deviance and Social Control: Volume 5*. Greenwich, CT: Jai Press.

Stockdale, E. (1977) *A History of Bedford Prison*. Chichester: Phillimore Press.

Sullivan, H. S. (1937) A note on the implications of psychiatry, the study of interpersonal relations, for investigation in the social sciences. *American Journal of Sociology*, 42(6), 848–61.

Sumner, C. S. (1976) Marxism and deviancy theory. In P. Wiles (ed.), *Sociology of Crime and Delinquency in Britain. Volume 2: The New Criminologies.* London: Martin Robertson.

Sumner, C. S. (1979) *Reading Ideologies.* London: Academic Press.

Sumner, C. S. (1981) Race, crime and hegemony. *Contemporary Crises*, 5(3), 277–91.

Sumner, C. S. (ed.) (1982) *Crime, Justice and Underdevelopment.* London: Heinemann.

Sumner, C. S. (1983) Law, legitimation, and the advanced capitalist state: the jurisprudence and social theory of Jurgen Habermas. In D. Sugarman (ed.), *Legality, Ideology and the State.* London: Academic Press.

Sumner, C. S. (ed.) (1990a) *Censure, Politics and Criminal Justice.* Milton Keynes: Open University Press.

Sumner, C. S. (1990b) Foucault, gender and the censure of deviance. In L. Gelsthorpe and A. Morris (eds), *Feminist Perspectives in Criminology.* Milton Keynes: Open University Press.

Sumner, C. S. (1991) Das Konzept der Devianz neu Überdacht: zu einer Soziologie der 'Censures'. *Kriminologisches Journal*, 4(23), 242–71.

Sumner, C. S. and Sandberg, S. (1990) The press censure of 'dissident minorities'. In C. S. Sumner (ed.), *Censure, Politics and Criminal Justice.* Milton Keynes: Open University Press.

Sumner, W. G. (1959) *Folkways.* New York: Dover.

Sutherland, E. H. (1934) *Principles of Criminology*, 2nd edn. Philadelphia: Lippincott.

Sutherland, E. H. (1939) *Principles of Criminology*, 3rd edn. Philadelphia: Lippincott.

Sutherland, E. H. (1940) White-collar criminality. *American Sociological Review*, 5, 1–12.

Sutherland, E. H. (1941) Crime and business. *The Annals*, 217, 113.

Sutherland, E. H. (1945) Is 'white-collar crime' crime? *American Sociological Review*, 10, 132–9.

Sutherland, E. H. (1947) *Principles of Criminology*, 4th edn. Philadelphia: Lippincott.

Sutherland, E. H. (1949) *White Collar Crime.* New York: Holt, Rinehart and Winston.

Sutherland, E. H. (1983) *White Collar Crime: The Uncut Version.* New York: Vail-Ballou Press.

Sykes, C. J. (1992) *A Nation of Victims: The Decay of the American Character.* New York: St Martin's Press.

Szasz, T. S. (1972) *The Myth of Mental Illness.* London: Paladin.

Szasz, T. S. (1973) *The Manufacture of Madness.* St Albans: Paladin.

Tannenbaum, F. (1938) *Crime and the Community.* New York: Columbia University Press.

Tappan, P. W. (1947) Who is the criminal? *American Sociological Review*, 12, 96–102.

Tarde, G. (1912) *Penal Philosophy* (trans. R. Howell). Boston: Little, Brown.

Taylor, I. and Taylor, L. (1968) We're all deviants now. *International Socialism*, 34, 29–32.

Taylor, I. and Taylor, L. (1973) *Politics and Deviance.* Harmondsworth: Penguin.

Taylor, I. R., Walton, P. and Young, J. (1973) *The New Criminology.* London: Routledge and Kegan Paul.

Taylor, I. R., Walton, P. and Young, J. (eds) (1975) *Critical Criminology.* London: Routledge and Kegan Paul.

Taylor, J. C. (1979) *The Fine Arts in America*. Chicago: University of Chicago Press.

Taylor, L. (1971) *Deviance and Society*. London: Nelson.

Taylor, S. (1982) *Durkheim and the Study of Suicide*. London: Macmillan.

Thio, A. (1973) Class bias in the sociology of deviance. *American Sociologist*, 8, 1–12.

Thomas, W. I. (1928) *The Unadjusted Girl*. Boston: Little, Brown.

Thomas, W. I. (1932) *The Child in America*. New York: Alfred Knopf.

Thomas, W. I. (1937) The comparative study of cultures. *American Journal of Sociology*, 42(1), 177–85.

Thomas, W. I. (1966) *On Social Organization and Social Personality* (ed. M. Janowitz). Chicago: University of Chicago Press.

Thomas, W. I. and Znaniecki, F. (1927) *The Polish Peasant in Europe and America*. New York: Knopf.

Thompson, E. P. (1975) *Whigs and Hunters: The Origin of the Black Act*. London: Allen Lane.

Thompson, E. P. (1978) *The Poverty of Theory*. London: Merlin.

Thrasher, F. M. (1927) *The Gang: A Study of 1,313 Gangs in Chicago*. Chicago: University of Chicago Press.

Thurnwald, R. C. (1936a) Civilization and culture: a contribution toward analysis of the mechanism of culture. *American Sociological Review*, 1(3), 387–95.

Thurnwald, R. C. (1936b) Progress viewed as a component in the configuration of culture: a contribution toward analysis of the mechanism of culture. *American Sociological Review*, 1(4), 604–13.

Timasheff, N. (1974) *An Introduction to the Sociology of Law*. Westport: Greenwood Press.

Trattner, W. I. (1974) *From Poor Law to Welfare State: A History of Social Welfare in America*. New York: Free Press.

Turk, A. (1969) *Criminality and Legal Order*. Chicago: Rand McNally.

Vaneigem, R. (1962) *The Totality for Kids*. London: Christopher Gray.

Vaneigem, R. (1977) *Society of the Spectacle*. Detroit: Black and Red.

Vogler, R. (1991) *Reading the Riot Act: The Magistracy, the Police and the Army in Civil Disorder*. Milton Keynes: Open University Press.

Voss, H. L. (1966) Socio-economic status and reported delinquent behaviour. *Social Problems*, 13, 314–24.

Waller, W. (1936) Social problems and the mores. *American Sociological Review*, 1(6), 922–33.

Weber, M. (1949) *The Methodology of the Social Sciences* (trans. E. Shils and H. Finch). Chicago: Free Press.

Weinstein, F. and Platt, G. M. (1973) *Psychoanalytic Sociology: An Essay on the Interpretation of Historical Data and the Phenomena of Collective Behavior*. Baltimore: Johns Hopkins University Press.

Weis, J. G. (1971) Dialogue with David Matza. *Issues in Criminology*, 6(1), 33–53.

Whyte, W. (1943) *Street Corner Society*. Chicago: The University of Chicago Press.

Williams, R. (1976) *Keywords*. Glasgow: Fontana.

Winch, P. (1963) *The Idea of a Social Science*. London: Routledge and Kegan Paul.

Wing Lo, T. (1992) *Corruption and Politics in Hong Kong and China*. Buckingham: Open University Press.

Wirth, L. (1928) *The Ghetto*. Chicago: University of Chicago Press.

Wirth, L. (1931) Clinical sociology. *American Journal of Sociology*, 37, 49–66.

Wirth, L. (1940) Ideological aspects of social disorganization. *American Sociological Review*, 5, 472–82.

Wirth, L. (1964) *On Cities and Social Life* (ed. A. J. Reiss Jr). Chicago: University of Chicago Press.

Wolfe, T. (1970) *Radical Chic and Mau-Mauing the Flak-Catchers*. New York: Farrar, Straus and Giroux.

Wood, M. (1989) *Art of the Western World*. New York: Summit Books.

Wordsworth, W. (1979) *The Prelude*. New York: London.

Worsley, P. (1967) *The Third World*. London: Weidenfeld.

Young, I. M. (1990) *Justice and the Politics of Difference*. Princeton, NJ: Princeton University Press.

Young, J. (1971) *The Drugtakers: The Social Meaning of Drug Use*. London: Paladin.

Young, J. (1973) The Hippie solution. In I. Taylor and L. Taylor (eds), *Politics and Deviance*. Harmondsworth: Penguin.

Young, J. (1975) Working-class criminology. In I. R. Taylor, P. Walton and J. Young (eds), *Critical Criminology*. London: Routledge and Kegan Paul.

Young, P. V. (1938) Defective social intelligence as a factor in crime. *American Sociological Review*, 3, 213–17.

Index